T0294398

WHAT'S NEXT?

WHAT'S NEXT?

Southern Dreams,

Jewish Deeds and

the Challenge of

Looking Back while

Moving Forward

JANICE ROTHSCHILD BLUMBERG

Bartleby Press

Washington • Baltimore

The publication of this edition would not have been possible without the support of the following:

Sydney Simons
Elizabeth Levine
Jerry and Dulcy Rosenberg
Judith and Mark Taylor
Rabbi Peter Berg and Karen Kerness
Jack and Ellen Holland
Jackie and Tony Montag
Tam Institute for Jewish Studies, Emory Universary
Southern Jewish Historical Society

Copyright © 2022 by Janice Rothschild Blumberg

ISBN 978-0935437-63-8
Library of Congress Control Number: 2021945689

Bartleby Press
JACKSON WESTGATE PUBLISHING GROUP
8926 Baltimore Street #858
Savage, MD 20763
800-953-9929
www.BartlebythePublisher.com

Printed in the United States of America

To my son, Bill
With deep devotion, gratitude and love

Contents

ONE

LIFE WITH MOTHER

My childhood was molded by my mother, Carolyn Jesse Goldberg Oettinger, a determined rebel against the culture that had nurtured her. Born in Columbus, Georgia in 1901, she began life as what was later called an Jewish American Princess and lived it as a combination of Auntie Mame and a 1960s hippie.

Mother did not intend for me to be born in Atlanta. Instead, she wanted to stay in Boston where she had met my father, Waldo Edouard Oettinger, and raise a large family where both he and his father, Adolph Joseph Oettinger, were born and raised. Grandpa Joe belonged to a mushroom picking society, collected antique pewter, owned and operated the Musician's Supply Company on Tremont Street, and had interesting friends like Boston Pops conductor Arthur Fiedler and the Italian restauranteur who taught my mother how to make authentic spaghetti sauce.

Carolyn Goldberg probably didn't notice that her mother-in-law-to-be mostly stayed home doing housework. Rose Hamburger Oettinger, whose parents came from Amsterdam, was also born and raised in Boston. Her father was a rabbi. Grandpa Joe's father was a stained-glass artist and glazer and a founder of the city's first synagogue from which he subsequently resigned.

Congregational conflict with its rabbi caused my other grandfather, also the son-in-law of a rabbi, to leave his congregation. David Simon Goldberg was a small-city Georgian who, despite being born in Oswego, New York, where his mother had been with her mother since childhood, was the only true southerner among us. His grandmother and two of her sons settled in Macon, Georgia from Bavaria in the mid-1840s. After Dave's father died, his already twice-widowed mother remarried, was soon widowed again, and then brought her five children to the middle Georgia city of Macon, south of Atlanta, for her mother, Sarah Waxelbaum, to help raise them. When Dave's two sisters married and moved south to Columbus, Georgia, a small but growing industrial city on the Chattahoochee River, he went with them to work for his brother-in-law, Max Simon. It was there he met my grandmother Lylah, the rabbi's daughter. My mother, their only child, was born in 1901.

In Columbus, Mother never saw white women ironing clothes and scrubbing bathtubs as many middle-class Boston women did. Owning a furniture store and rental properties enabled her father to hire employees, four Caucasians for his business and two African Americans for his home. Mother's knowledge of domestic skills was limited to flower arrangements and decorative needle work. She augmented her public-school education with lessons in ballet and piano, as did her friends, and, like them, attended an all-female college, in her case Smith. There, to the dismay of her unsuspecting parents, she gained awareness of the greater world in which women expressed liberal views and smoked cigarettes.

Grandfather Dave once told me that the worst mistake he ever made was "letting those women send that girl north to college." Those women were my grandmother Lylah, who was born in Peoria, Illinois, and grew up mostly in New York with her brother Jesse, two years younger; and Sophie Weil Browne, their mother, whom I called Mamama. She was a brilliant and highly educated Victorian feminist born and raised in Evansville, Indiana, who lived in several cities, including Atlanta, as wife of the maverick rabbi Edward ("Alphabet") B. M. Browne, whom I called Papapa. He was a *wunderkind* from a small Slovakian town in the

Austro-Hungarian empire and emigrated when he was twenty on one of the first steamships to take passengers after the Civil War. Papapa quickly came under the tutelage of Rabbi Isaac Mayer Wise, the Reform Judaism pioneer. In their old age, the couple lived with their daughter Lylah in Columbus. Papapa died when I was five. Mamama survived throughout my childhood and influenced me to seek whatever ladylike qualities I may have acquired.

My father went to war, not college. He met Mother through family connections when she was a sophomore at Smith and he was just back from France after the first World War. His parents invited her for their traditional New England Thanksgiving dinner, which posed a problem because in 1918 the trip from Northampton wasn't a one-day commute and Smith didn't allow students to skip classes on Thanksgiving Friday. Mother went anyway, became engaged to my father, and continued her studies at Boston University. They married the following summer.

I barely knew Dad's family in faraway Boston. To us during the Great Depression, it was as inaccessible as Europe. My father, before going to France as a *doughboy*, had clerked for his father, who was not only the poor man's Brahmin as Mother imagined but also a German-style autocrat. Dad was gentle, loving and good-looking, characteristics which Mother probably conflated with those she so admired in his father.

Grandma Rose visited us when I was four and I remember my surprise seeing her iron our laundered bed linens, which Mother thought unnecessary. When Grandma died eight years later my parents took turns at the wheel, taking more than two days to reach Boston. I slept on the back seat. They lay down to sleep only once, in Richmond, where we stayed overnight with relatives. When my son, a baby boomer, once asked me why we didn't just take the train, I had to explain that we couldn't afford the fare.

Dad would have continued to work for his father had the income been sufficient to support another family, but when Mother graduated college she was ready to have children. Grandfather Dave offered him a position in his thriving home furnishings business, a triple-front main street establishment, but Mother refused to go to Columbus. She thought her parents should move to Boston.

Possibly for the first time ever, Dave Goldberg said "no" to his strong-willed daughter. After explaining the economics that discouraged transferring his family, home, and business to Boston, he offered to set up my father in his own business if they came south. Mother reluctantly agreed, but no further south than Atlanta. To finance the move, Dave mortgaged his store with the prime property it occupied.

My father, untrained and temperamentally unsuited for business management, went into the home heating business and failed at the beginning of the Great Depression. With businesses everywhere faltering, Dave couldn't repay his mortgage and thus lost the store. Our next-door neighbor gave Dad a job selling General Electric refrigerators and Dave went to work managing the Georgia Sand and Gravel Company, while Lylah grudgingly managed their remaining rental property.

According to Mother, she planned to give birth on February 13, 1924, as a gift to her father on his fifty-seventh birthday. Legend has it that her last words as they anesthetized her for delivery in the final hours of February 12 were, "If the baby comes before midnight, don't tell me about it."

I obliged and waited, although not in Boston as she wanted. I arrived after midnight at Piedmont Hospital in Atlanta.

Always Southern, although never typically so, Atlanta in 1924 was busy but not yet a city "too busy to hate." Jim Crow reigned supreme, the Klan burned crosses on Stone Mountain, people celebrated Confederate Memorial Day instead of the national holiday, and they rose to their feet on hearing the first strains of "Dixie." Calvin Coolidge was president after the sudden death of Warren G. Harding. Nine years after the lynching of Leo Frank local Jews still cowered, fearing another anti-Semitic outbreak. In neighboring Decatur, the board of education shifted its school week to Tuesday through Saturday to discourage Jewish families from moving in, while the county unit system kept Georgia solidly Democratic, anti-urban and backward.

When I was five months old we moved into the white stucco house with red brick trim at 2243 East Lake Road, NE. It was between railroad tracks, a single one crossing our street a few houses away toward Atlanta and double tracks plus a trolley line eight houses away, just over the line into Decatur. There were woods between those tracks that ran into downtown Atlanta and our deep backyard where Mother grew roses, irises, strawberries and asparagus. She often took me, trowel and bucket in hand, across the street and through our neighbors' backyards to deeper woods bisected by a new street not yet paved and a stream where she dug ferns and pitcher plants for her shade garden. I hopped along on the flat rocks in the stream, swinging on low-hanging vines and branches of trees, anticipating our picnic of peanut butter and jelly sandwiches.

My neighborhood playmates were Charles Douglas, who lived two doors away, Ann Niebling, who lived across the street, and Dorothy Alexander, who lived next door. Dorothy taught me how to pull the centers from honeysuckle blossoms to taste the honey, how to catch lightening bugs (AKA fireflies) in a mason jar, and how to climb the hickory tree at the edge of our backyard to get whatever nuts the squirrels had missed. When I was six years old my father taught me to swim and attempted to teach me tennis, a sport he had played as a boy. Swimming succeeded; tennis did not. Running and sweating didn't appeal to me; splashing and sunning did (and still does).

I also began to play theater at a tender age when Mother took me to spend the day with Betty Lowenstein. She lived in a handsome house on "little" Ponce de Leon Avenue near Fairview, with downstairs heating units concealed beneath wide, deep windowsills. We used one of them as our stage, possibly ruining Mrs. Lowenstein's silk brocade drapery by frequent use as a theater curtain.

My parents' closest friends were Sophie and Abe Schwartz, a childless couple from New York who, like themselves, were newcomers

Janice at four

to Atlanta. They lived in a yellow brick apartment building on Ponce de Leon, and Abe worked in his own business, the Royal Cigar Store on the corner of Walton and Forsyth Streets across from the old post office. To me, they were Aunt Sophie and Uncle Abe. They treated me as if I were their own, and only now do I fully realize how much they enriched my childhood with their love.

"Blue laws" were strictly observed in the Bible Belt South, so we had no public entertainment on Sunday. Many people went driving after their midday dinner, as we did with Aunt Sophie and Uncle Abe, often to Candler Field, the airport, to watch the airplanes take off and land, or to Ft. McPherson to see the officers play polo. Mostly, however, we drove out to West Paces Ferry Road and Habersham to look at the palaces being built by some of Atlanta's Coca-Cola royalty and their friends. Two of the homes were said to be originals transported stone by stone from Italy, although one of those was the Swan House, now part of the Atlanta Historical Society and known to have been designed by Atlanta architect

Philip Shutze. The other, an ivory-colored castle on Paces Ferry at the end of a long straight driveway, caused traffic jams when drivers lined up to view it through its tall stone gates. The estate is now sectioned into lots with large homes along a winding road that cuts off the view.

On Sunday nights we usually ate supper with Aunt Soph and Uncle Abe at their apartment, then listened to Amos 'n Andy on the radio, followed by Eddie Cantor. After that the adults listened to Rudy Vallée, whose pre-Crosby crooning put me to sleep. During our three-mile drive home I stretched out on the back seat of our 1924 black Chevrolet, sleeping or guessing where we were as we jiggled along.

On Thursday nights (maids' night off, although we didn't have one) we often joined Aunt Soph and Uncle Abe for dinner at the S&W Cafeteria downtown on Peachtree, across from Davison Paxon's department store. In the center of the Cafeteria there was a blue tiled fountain with goldfish, which I was allowed to visit if I behaved properly and ate everything on my plate. The latter posed no problem because I always chose the Cafeteria's famous cream cheese and crushed pineapple aspic.

Mother considered it a waste of time to play cards or Mahjong as Aunt Sophie and most of her other Jewish friends did. They joined the Temple Sisterhood and the National Council of Jewish Women but usually weren't active. Since women had finally won the right to vote, Mother actively volunteered for the League of Women Voters and the NCJW, as did her special friends from Smith College, Rebecca (Reb) Gershon and Josephine (Jo) Heyman, and Hannah Shulhafer, who went to Barnard. Reb, who had no children of her own, became a special friend to Hannah's daughter, Helen, and to me. Bea Haas and Aline Uhry were also like-minded friends, but younger and not yet active in the community. They were our distant cousins, as was Helen Wiseberg, who was older and a much beloved mentor to Mother.

Lacking household help, Mother often took me with her to meetings and kept me entertained by giving me small tasks like folding programs or stuffing envelopes. Thanks to her fascination with time and motion studies, she taught me a technique that still enables me to astonish friends with my speed and efficiency when we work together on such projects.

Mother sparked my interest in foreign languages by singing "Frère Jacques" and "Au Clair de la Lune" while I was still in a high chair and counting "un, deux, trois, quatre..." until I finished eating everything on my plate. As a result, I learned to count in French before I could count in English. Unfortunately, those lessons tapered off. My introduction to German, which Lylah and Mamama spoke fluently in my presence when the subject was *nicht für Kinder*, stopped abruptly when Hitler came to power.

Mother gave me my first book, *A Child's Garden of Verses*, which I so loved that I memorized my favorite verses. When I could read she provided children's editions of Greek mythology and world history, which had a lasting effect.

My introduction to fine arts began when I was five. Mother enrolled me in ballet class at the Harbour-Sharp School of Dance, located on Peachtree just past the Prado, and in "elocution" classes, which included acting at the Studio Arts Building, a crumbling red brick mansion on the southeast corner of Peachtree and 14th Street. Soon after that, she commandeered a small violin from Grandpa Joe in Boston and arranged for me to take lessons on it. I showed slight promise in elocution, none in ballet or music, but the latter didn't discourage Mother. She acknowledged that I wasn't destined for a future *en pointe* but determined that she could cure my tin ear by persisting with the violin.

I started school in September 1929, when I was five and a half years old. Mother reasoned that since I was tall for my age and advanced intellectually, I should enter the first grade at Druid Hills School. Formerly operated by Emory University under a different name and primarily for faculty children, Druid Hills had just reopened as a DeKalb County elementary and high school combined on its own campus near Emory with eleven grades: seven in lower school and four in high.

Mother, rarely deterred by rules with which she disagreed, deemed it irrelevant that my birthday was in February, well past the cut-off date for grade assignment, and convinced school authorities to make an exception for me. At the end of first grade she persuaded the principal to let me skip second grade. After my first few weeks in third she disagreed with the teacher, pulled me out, and tutored me herself at home. The following year family finances were so bad that my parents couldn't afford to heat the house through the winter, so Mother sent me to live with my grandparents in Columbus. There I attended the 16th Street School and had the same teacher, Miss Jodie Johnson, who taught Mother when she attended the 4th grade there. Back at Druid Hills in the 5th grade, still tall for my age and klutzy, I felt ever more like an outsider.

I spent much of my childhood with my grandparents and great-grandmother in Columbus. We drove there so often that I could recite the names of every town on the way. We routinely stopped in Chipley to call Lylah and Mamama and assure them that we had safely crossed Pine Mountain, which hardly qualified as a mountain by altitude but was the final major elevation at the southern end of the Piedmont plateau. The roads were often washed out by heavy rains, and before farmers planted kudzu to bandage the gory gashes on either side, red clay bled down onto the pavement causing slides. Lylah and Mamama were worriers.

Our Columbus home was a three-story red brick apartment building on Second Avenue trimmed with gray granite, built by my grandparents in 1912. Named "The Carolyn" in honor of my mother, it was considered the city's first modern apartment building because of its speaker system whereby guests identified themselves and were buzzed in automatically.

Across the front of the second floor where my grandparents lived there was a gray wooden balcony draped on one end by wisteria drooping lavender blossoms in the spring. By the time I came along, the first and third floors had been divided into smaller rental units, and I was always reminded to play quietly so as not to disturb Miss Georgia Wilkins, the single lady from Warm Springs, Georgia who lived on the third-floor front. She moved in after selling her family home to New York Governor Franklin D. Roosevelt for a polio treatment center.

The Edwardian excess of my grandparents' furnishings fascinated me. I patted the gleaming brown chests of the snarling mahogany lions that flanked the fireplace mantel as well as the arms of chairs in the library, and I fantasized about the mahogany nymphs floating above green velour upholstery in the parlor. I was not allowed to go there unaccompanied. I loved having Mamama take me there because she told me interesting stories about the things I saw. The urn holding fragrant rose petals from my grandparents' 25th wedding anniversary party was actually an antique Chinese cookie jar. Inside the French curio cabinet were souvenirs from distant lands—a rope of tiny white shells that Mamama brought from Egypt, an olivewood inkwell in the form of a camel from Jerusalem, a pair of clogs made of teak with mother of pearl inlay from Turkey. Most intriguing of all was a black armband that Papapa wore when he marched as an honorary pall bearer in the funeral of President Ulysses S. Grant. That room stirred curiosity about travel and history.

Mamama presided over the kitchen with great attention to cleanliness and nutrition, especially mine. Because I'd been an anemic baby she plied me with "beef juice," de-fatted drippings from steak, which made me an enthusiastic carnivore, and calves' liver, which I hated. Farmers came by each morning in wagons shouting their wares—fruit, vegetables, and live chickens which Mamama hung from the back-porch rafters until it was time for them to be plucked and cooked. I also frequently saw her draining the whey from cooked milk curds to make cottage cheese, which was not yet available in Columbus grocery stores.

Downtown homes were set far back from the street and close to the sidewalks, with paved paths bisecting broad, largely untended sweeps of lawn. Children were permitted to mark the paths for hopscotch, which I did, as well as spend many hours blowing dandelions and making clover chains. I rarely had a playmate because most families of my parents' generation had moved to the new suburb of Wynnton. My only full-time friend was Betty Loeb, whose parents remained in their ancestral home downtown. During the Christmas holidays Dorothy Mathis from Cleveland, Ohio, joined us in Columbus to visit her grandparents, the Rothschilds, on Third Avenue, only two blocks away. I wasn't allowed to speak to any of the dirty, barefooted children who sometimes wandered over from other neighborhoods. One of the boys called me a dirty Jew once, but it didn't bother me because it was the only time anything like that had happened. I pretended not to hear it and continued looking for four-leafed clovers.

Sometimes on summer afternoons I wandered up the street to the duplex where I usually saw Lylah's friends, Ida Greentree and her sister-in-law, Leah Solomon, in rocking chairs on their front porch. They always invited me to join them, which I enjoyed doing because George, their Negro house man and driver, would soon appear with lemonade and cookies. When I saw Morgan Freeman in *Driving Miss Daisy*, I thought he was George reincarnated.

Across the back of our apartment, as in many southern homes, there was a screened porch where the family slept on stifling summer nights.

Four generations, 1936. Janice with her mother Carolyn Goldberg Oettinger, grandmother Lylah Browne Goldberg, and great-grandmother (Mamama) Sophie Weil Browne

As a young child I was sequestered there for a nap each afternoon and passed the time quietly thanks to the "rotogravure" section of the Sunday *New York Times,* which arrived by noon on Wednesday or Thursday. The pictures introduced me to imaginary friends, children of the rich and famous such as the British princesses, Margaret Rose and her older sister, Elizabeth, who was almost my age. I remember huddling close to the radio with my parents to hear their uncle renounce his throne for the woman he loved. The static was terrible.

I actually met another of my imaginary friends, one of America's royal children, "Sistie" Dall, then living in the White House with her grandparents, President Roosevelt and First Lady Eleanor. She and her brother, "Buzzie," were frequently photographed playing on the lawn with the President's dog, Fala. A half century later, at a luncheon after ground-breaking ceremonies for the FDR Memorial in Washington, while chatting with a woman standing beside me at the hors d'oeuvres table, I mentioned having written a documentary about FDR and receiving a complimentary letter from his daughter, Anna. The woman smiled appreciatively and said, "She was my mother."

When we introduced ourselves, I realized that she, Eleanor Dall Seagraves, was the "Sistie" of our childhood years. She laughed when I told her.

In those days, it was safe for children to walk alone in downtown Columbus, and Lylah often sent me to the bakery for a loaf of pumpernickel bread or gave me a dime so I could go to the movies. She had become a drudge and seldom went out—never socially anymore—but she took me for medical and dental checkups and walked me the six long blocks to the public library down by the river. I obsessed over Heidi, and later the Nancy Drew mysteries. When I was older Lylah also encouraged my writing, suggesting thought-provoking subjects for my theme assignments in high school.

As soon as I was old enough, Mother sent me to Columbus alone on the Central of Georgia train, assuring me that Dave would be at the station to meet me. In the unlikely event that he was late, she instructed,

I should "just go up to the old colored woman who is always there, tell her that you are Dave Goldberg's granddaughter, and she will take care of you until he comes." The emergency never occurred, but I always looked for the kindly custodian just in case.

Atlanta was on Central Standard time then, and in December, when the train slowed down after dark, I could see Christmas lights in houses along the way. I remember feeling a vague sadness then, not because of the trees and colored lights (which I had, as did all my Jewish friends), but for a reason I couldn't identify at the time. Now I think I probably missed the warmth that those lights implied.

In Columbus the holiday spirit became palpable for me on Christmas afternoons when we visited the Bickerstaffs', Christian friends who lived next door to my grandparents when Mother was a child. Now they lived in an antebellum mansion on part of the historic Hilton plantation. They had a Christmas tree so tall that it touched the high ceiling of their parlor and was reflected in a floor-to-ceiling mirror at the far end of the dining room opposite. In the center of the parlor a large table held small, beautifully wrapped gifts, usually sweets, one for each friend who came, lovingly prepared by Nonie Bickerstaff and her two daughters. When my children were very young I tried to emulate that for Chanukah but without lasting success.

I loved being with my grandfather Dave, loved sniffing smoke from his cigar as he settled into his deep tufted brown leather chair to read the *National Geographic* magazine, and delighted in walking with him to the post office to pick up mail. Sometimes he took me with him to his job at the Georgia Sand and Gravel Company to spend the day with Rebecca Morris, whose family owned and lived on the land where the plant was located. We had great fun climbing the mountains of gravel and playing house on the giant sand piles. The house where she lived, like those of many rural southerners, was an unpainted wooden farmhouse without running water or indoor plumbing. When we were thirsty we drew water from a well. As for going to the bathroom, after one time at the outhouse I controlled my urge. If not for those days in the mammoth sandbox, I might never have realized the comparative luxury in which I was privileged to live.

My sense of not belonging hung on as I grew older. Dual loyalty may have contributed to it because I proudly clung to my Yankee heritage while surrounded by peers taught to cherish their (often imaginary) plantation heritage. That became painfully apparent when we studied American history and were assigned to bring stories from our own families' Civil War experience (referred to as the War Between the States or the War of the Northern Aggression). Most students related how their great-grandmothers hid the family silver or shot a Yankee soldier before he could rape her. Proud to be among the few Jewish students with ancestors in America during that war, I related a story Mamama told me about her childhood in Evansville, Indiana, across the river from slave-holding Kentucky. It wasn't about hiding silver; it was about her parents hiding slaves on the Underground Railroad. I was too naive to understand why it was not well received by my teacher and classmates.

Southern society was not stratified entirely by wealth. Ancestry, not affluence, determined one's status within the Temple-going Standard Club group to which we belonged thanks to family connections. Mamama was the niece of Atlanta pioneers Herman and Wilhelmina Haas. I had *yichus*, but didn't yet know it because no one I knew spoke Yiddish.

In our southern middle-class German Jewish cocoon, little girls were programmed to marry well and preside over comfortable households of no more than three children with full-time help. College degrees were nice but not necessary for girls. Beauty was. Aunt Sophie lectured me on style and grooming, and when I misbehaved Lylah and Mamama scolded me with the maxim, "Pretty is as pretty does."

Mother opposed such dicta but didn't always practice the contrary. Beneath her bravado she submerged insecurity about me, wavering, constantly threatened by unsolicited advice from Lylah, Mamama, and Aunt Sophie. Struggling to subjugate inherited mores under progressive theses, she understood that women were as capable as men, should choose husbands based on congeniality in bed as well as elsewhere, judge others only by the content of their character, and volunteer community service unless economically forced to earn their living in the workplace.

When it became obvious that she needed to join the wage-earners, Mother applied to the school system to teach and was occasionally called to serve as a substitute, but the Great Depression and sexist hiring practices thwarted her attempts at steady employment. As a young girl she had been an accomplished pianist and wanted to teach that as well as continue studying it, but few people could afford piano lessons during the Depression. Likewise unable to afford lessons for herself, she persuaded Atlanta's master teacher, Hugh Hodgson, to accept her as his student in exchange for her service as his administrative assistant. Mr. Hugh, as his students called him, opened an exciting new world for Mother and soon became a major factor in my life as well.

With help from Mamama, Mother bought the Steinway baby grand piano that now graces my living room and enriched my childhood practicing the glorious music of Bach, Beethoven, Brahms and Chopin. The not-so-glorious side of that was her devotion to Mr. Hugh. At times, I felt that she cared more for him than for my father and me. I remember a late autumn day when I wanted to take the one flower left blooming in our garden to my teacher but Mother said "no" because she wanted it for Mr. Hugh's studio. It seems trivial now, but it wasn't trivial to me then. Nevertheless I liked Mr. Hugh and revered him as an artist, teacher, mentor, and true friend to my parents and me.

Mother, having already met some of the "Bohemian" beaux arts community, now bonded with Mr. Hugh's devotees, who belonged to Atlanta's top social set. One of them, Marjory Dobbs, became her close friend. Mrs. Dobbs lived in a Tudor mansion on Valley Road with three small children and her husband who was rarely there. My father, who had worked at Rich's department store until his health deteriorated, then went on the road selling maternity dresses for his cousin, Eddie Stern, out of Boston. As he was often away on weekends. Mrs. Dobbs sometimes invited us to keep her company, which I enjoyed immensely because her home was like nothing I'd ever seen except in the movies. She even had a pipe organ on the landing of her double staircase.

What made those weekends still more remarkable was that a young man came to play classical music on the organ during Sunday dinner. When I was a teenager he played accordion at some of our parties. He was Graham Jackson, later a chief petty officer stationed near Warm Springs, Georgia. When President Roosevelt died, the iconic picture of Jackson playing accordion with tears running down his cheeks as he watched the train carrying the President's body leave the station became known worldwide.

Natasha Davison was Mother's other socialite friend. She and her husband, Dr. Hal Davison (our family physician), remained close friends throughout their lives and became equally close to me and my

Janice and her
mother, Carolyn

husband. Natasha loved to entertain, especially on occasions with Russian significance such as when the Ballet Russe de Monte Carlo performed in Atlanta, and on Russian Easter when she served traditional Russian holiday dishes. Mother brought me to those events, which I generally enjoyed. When I became bored I went upstairs and read bedtime stories to Aloysha, their younger son, who later succeeded his father as Mother's primary care physician.

Mother became active in the Atlanta Music Club, where she was warmly welcomed as a knowledgeable volunteer. I noted as an adult in a similar situation that the thinly veiled anti-Semitism still evident in southern society didn't prevent collegial association, and in some cases, true friendship, which I attributed to the fact that neither of us showed interest in joining their social circle. Sometimes Mother brought them to our house for late supper after a concert and they went into the kitchen to help, still wearing their hats and camellia corsages. She went to after-concert parties with them, but not to luncheons or dinner parties.

I don't recall exactly when I asked Mother if we were Jewish or what prompted the question, but she said it meant that we had a different religion from our neighbors. We didn't worship Jesus as they did, but we believed in the same God. Churches and temples were basically the same since God was everywhere, so it didn't matter where we went to pray. One Sunday, when I was in the garden helping her divide and replant iris roots, she noted that it was "church day" and said, "This is where God is for me."

During my childhood Mother never attended Temple services or a Jewish holiday ritual like Passover Seder. Once she sent me to services with Reb Gershon, once to a Temple Seder with Dad, and once to a Purim Ball for children where I won the prize for best costume. I went as a dressing table, wearing my hoop skirt from the dancing school recital with a mirror hung around my neck and holding a tray with a hairbrush and comb.

Had great-grandmother Mamama not interfered, I might have been raised as an Episcopalian. Mother often helped Mr. Hugh at St. Luke's Episcopal Church where he directed the music and eventually she joined the choir, which required her to be there on Sunday mornings. When I was old enough to begin Sunday School, the Temple was still downtown on Pryor Street, and since she couldn't be in both places at the same time she planned to enroll me at St. Luke's. Mamama and Lylah were horrified. To appease them, Mother offered me a choice: I could go to St. Luke's with her, or wait until the following year when the Temple's new building on Peachtree at Spring Street was scheduled to open and she could arrange a carpool. Mamama bribed me with the offer of a weekly allowance if I chose the Temple.

Thanks to Mother's work with Mr. Hugh and her activities with the Atlanta Music Club, I met enough celebrities in those days to suppress fervor over meeting them in later years. I spent an afternoon with violin virtuoso Yehudi Menuhin when I was eight years old and he was fifteen. Mother had arranged for him and his father to audition a talented young violinist who studied with the same teacher as I did, and she took me along. All I remember is that the adults conferred and Yehudi gave me an autographed picture of himself.

Mother formed lasting friendships with many young concert artists whom she hosted when they came to Atlanta, and some of them later became quite famous. Metropolitan Opera diva Helen Jepson was one of those. When I learned that she was coming to Atlanta for a concert that also featured the screen star Nelson Eddy my tween-age excitement knew no bounds. I had seen *Naughty Marietta* nine times and was ecstatic at the thought of actually meeting him. Alas, it never happened; an untimely case of the flu confined me to bed the day of the concert. I did receive a memento, however. Mother told Mr. Eddy about my mishap as they were leaving the concert and he plucked a rose from Ms. Jepson's bouquet for her to give me. I cherished it until it crumbled.

Like most kids, I wanted to do what the others did, look like they looked, and go to the places they went. Mother explained that we couldn't afford tickets both to games *and* to concerts, and concerts were more important. That was small comfort, even realizing that I was privileged to hear the world's most celebrated musicians in person. Now I realize that what I mostly enjoyed were the intermissions, leaning over the balcony rail watching Atlanta's socialites stroll up and down the aisle in their evening gowns.

The Atlanta concert that I most appreciated was that of the great diva Marion Anderson in 1939. Never before in the south had an African American performed publicly before a racially mixed audience, and Atlantans of all ages took pride in their city for having achieved it. Planners adhered to the law against "race mixing" by dividing the auditorium down the middle, with whites on one side, people of color on the other—throughout, rather than being relegated to the top balcony as usual. It was a glorious concert, and not only because of the music.

During my high school years, Mr. Hugh acquired the Atlanta Conservatory of Music on Broad Street and Mother worked there as dean and manager. On most days, after attending school at David Hills, I walked down North Decatur Road to Emory's entrance at Oxford Road where the streetcar line ended and rode downtown to the conservatory. I took practically every course offered— harmony, theory, composition, and private lessons on piano as well as violin. None of it improved my ear. I enjoyed the learning, however, and even thought of becoming a music critic. I began by writing articles about local musical events for suburban papers.

One morning the Cable Piano Company building where the conservatory was located burned down. Thankfully, Mother had gone out shortly before it happened. Several people were killed, among them my piano teacher, Ruth Dabney Smith. The conservatory never reopened, but Mother's reputation and an improved economy enabled her to launch a successful career teaching piano. Mr. Hugh, having established the Department of Fine Arts at the University of Georgia, was spending his weekdays in Athens and no longer occupied her time as before.

When Mother finally accepted the fact that I would never be a soloist, she wisely switched me from violin to viola. In those days, violists were so rare that even those who played off-pitch like me were sought after by conductors to beef up their string sections. By listening to the player next to me I could correct my fingering quickly enough to be welcomed in orchestras. During my last year in high school I played in five, including Emory University, the University of Georgia, Druid Hills High School, the In And About Atlanta High School Orchestra, and what then served as the Atlanta Symphony.

That year the orchestras occupied so much of my time (and consequently Mother's for driving me to rehearsals) that she rebelled when the need arose to drive me to the Temple for mid-week confirmation rehearsals. Again she gave me a choice: confirmation or the orchestras, not both. When I hesitated, reluctant to drop out of Sunday School and miss being confirmed with my friends, she asked why I wanted to be confirmed. "Presents," I answered honestly.

Mother, reminding me that I was also graduating high school that year, asked, "Do you really think friends will give you two presents at the same time?"

Checkmate. I opted for the orchestras.

Much as I enjoyed that aspect of my life, it didn't fully compensate for lack of popularity with my designated Temple/Standard Club crowd. The girls formed a club, the Lucky Thirteen, into which I was among the last to be invited. Having no taste for practical jokes, I was nauseated by the initiation, being blindfolded and forced to eat small strands of oiled spaghetti identified as worms. Spending the night with friends equally appalled me. One of the girls wanted to "play sex" and another urged me to sneak into her parents' bedroom with her to observe. Neither seemed right to me. I was out of sync with my peers.

We began boy-girl togetherness with afternoon ballroom classes when we were ten years old. The real partying began a year later with evening socials called prom parties in our homes. Boys and girls paired off for short walks—promenades in the neighborhood. Our mothers served punch and cookies, and supervised an occasional parlor game like Spin the Bottle. A spreading spirea bush at the far edge of our front lawn invited more spinning without the bottle after the walking resumed.

A year or so later, we took ballroom classes on Saturday mornings at a studio across from the Fox Theater on Peachtree, and afterwards went bowling. Sometimes we paired off as dates for lunch at the Jacobs Drugstore in the corner of the Fox building, and then went to a movie. I enjoyed that, especially with Tory Jacobs, grandson of the pharmacy chain's founder and son of my parents' friend, Sinclair Jacobs. In addition to personality, good looks and flaming red hair, Tory's assets included getting special attention from the soda jerks at Jacobs pharmacies. We received extra syrup in our Cokes and an extra slice of ham on our sandwiches.

In later years when the boys could drive and a few of them had their own roadsters with open rumble seats in back, we began going to the Standard Club dances. We made late dates with another partner for midnight snacks, either at someone's home or a drive-in. Sometimes we climbed Stone Mountain, which had no surrounding development then. We girls took off our shoes and stockings, hitched our long evening dresses into our panties, and followed our dates up the back slope.

Alongside my social life I continued a passion for writing, especially after Bob Gaines, who taught humanities and directed the orchestra at Druid Hills, engaged a select few of us in a course on creative writing. While still practicing to become a journalist, I became enamored with poetry. My attempts to emulate Shakespeare's sonnets, Vachel Lindsay's onomatopoeia, and Swinburne's Gothic romanticism embarrass me when I read them now, but I'm glad I saved them.

Toward the end of that year, although I hadn't thought of acting since the elocution class when I was six years old, I tried out for the senior play. Mother suggested it, realizing that winning a part would boost my self-confidence. The night before tryouts, which consisted of reciting Edwin Markham's "The Man With A Hoe" from memory, Mother drilled me relentlessly, several times reducing me to tears and only permitting me to go to bed at four o'clock in the morning when I could no longer stay awake. Her efforts paid off, however. I won the leading role and it did wonders for my quavering ego.

Graduation gave me another lift. My long apricot-colored organdy dress competed admirably with those of my classmates, and an older student from the Emory orchestra took me to the parties afterward. Best of all was that I looked forward to spending the summer at the National Music Camp in Interlochen, Michigan.

Mother's early attempts at sending me to summer camp didn't work. When I was eight or nine years old she enrolled me at a Girl Scout camp in the North Georgia mountains, which I hated. Having disliked scouting since my initiation as a Brownie, my attitude was not improved by spending summer nights in a tent with rain pouring down and bugs seeking shelter between me and my pajamas. After one week the camp director called Mother to come and take me home.

Most of my friends went to camps in Maine, which Mamama and Lylah would not support because Maine was too far from home. A year or so later, Mother enrolled me for the second half of the season at Camp Carlisle, then a non-sectarian camp in Hendersonville, North Carolina. After my first night there I woke up at ten-thirty the next morning to find my cabin mates lounging on their bunks and foot lockers, astonished that I had slept through the commotion of the night before. Our cabin was the closest to the stables, which had burned down overnight, killing two of the horses.

Carlisle appealed to me, primarily because of the wonderful man who taught horseback riding. We rode Tennessee Walkers on exquisite mountain trails, and I learned the basics of English style.

Although I enjoyed the experience, I still felt out of sync. It never occurred to me to notice that no other camper was Jewish.

Mother finally found the camp I loved when she assisted its founder, Dr. Joseph Maddy, in establishing the In-and-About-Atlanta High School Orchestra. In appreciation for her promotional efforts (and possibly because violists were hard to find), Dr. Maddy offered me a part scholarship for the 1939 season. It included a trip to New York for the orchestra to perform at the World's Fair.

This camp I loved. I loved the people, the ambience, the seriousness with which everyone approached his or her activities, and perhaps most of all, the fact that sports were available but not required. We were expected to spend two hours a day in some form of outdoor exercise but the choice was ours. I chose swimming (although I didn't enjoy swimming in lakes) because after passing the proficiency test we had permission to use the canoes, which I needed access to in order to visit friends in the Russian colony across the lake.

Our orchestra conductors were musicians of note, including composer Howard Hanson, from whose 1st Symphony the orchestra took its signature theme for its nationally-broadcasted weekly concerts. Another of our conductors was Loren Maazel, an amazing nine-year-old boy who tinkered with toy cars as other nine-year-olds did when he wasn't working.

My teacher, Mihail Stolarevsky, was a member of the Cincinnati Symphony and taught at the Cincinnati Conservatory. In addition to viola lessons and classes in composition, I signed up for radio and drama, and appeared in a play that the instructor, Stewart Bosley, wrote and dedicated to me. One of my radio classmates was Mike Wallace, but when we met seventy years later neither of us remembered having met at camp. I told him that if I'd known he was going to grow up to be a celebrity I would have paid attention.

Attending the New York World's Fair at the end of that 1939 camp season was exciting but uncomfortable. We had to wear our camp uniforms—dark blue corduroy knickers with light blue shirts and knee-high socks—designed for summer in the Michigan woods, not for August in Manhattan and Queens. While sightseeing in the newly-erected NBC Building at Rockefeller Center, we looked so out-of-place that someone stopped us to ask if we were from the National Farm School, a facility for training immigrant Jewish boys for employment.

Mother met me at the Fair and took me to exhibits that were not included in the camp's program. I tried to keep up with her but tired quickly. The only exhibit I remember was General Motors' amazing "World of Tomorrow." It seemed like science fiction. We couldn't imagine ever having such futuristic highways and overpasses, much less using them until they needed upgrades as they do today.

We were still in New York on September 1st when the war began in Europe. The news had a chilling effect even though we had anticipated it, and for Jews, even minimally connected ones like us, it brought hopeful possibilities of saving European Jewry. The death camps did not yet exist, but we knew that Jews were endangered. When I was eight or nine years old a Jewish girl from Germany had lived with us temporarily after arriving on a *Kindertransport.* At home I never heard talk about anti-Semitism until then.

Among my happiest memories of high school and college years were Sunday evenings when Mother entertained her young friends, mostly Emory graduates who studied music with Mr. Hugh. We rarely knew who or how many would come. She offered heavy conversation and light supper, usually waffles and sausage, after which everyone gathered around the piano for sight-reading, much of it from opera. I couldn't sing but followed the melody on my violin, which I continued to use on occasion. I loved those evenings and yearned to emulate them in a home of my own.

Two men who came often but weren't musicians encouraged my writing and gave me seminal advice. Walter Paschall, who broadcast the evening news for WSB Radio, and Ralph McGill, then a sports writer for the *Atlanta Constitution*, both advised me to seek knowledge and experience in order to have something to write about. Ralph, whom Reb Gershon introduced as a friend from her high school days in Chattanooga, became known for insightful reporting of economic distress in rural Georgia. Later, as the paper's editor and publisher, he won a Pulitzer for his courageous editorials on civil rights and received the Presidential Medal of Honor. Both men remained my good friends.

My life with Mother was a mixed bag of happiness and grief, her tutelage a volume of mixed messages. Dad was a sweetheart, much too gentle to stand up to her, increasingly emasculated as much by her temper as by his inability to support us. My frequent back-of-the-hairbrush spankings for early childhood misdemeanors didn't harm me psychologically, but I still flinch when I recall her verbal abuses to him.

At times Mother repeated a supposedly clever *bon mot* to the effect that children should be caged until age twelve, after which parents should close the feeding hole. I realized it was a joke but sensed its deeper meaning as I assume she did not. In spite of the insensitivity it implied, she enjoyed entertaining my teenage friends, and they adored her. She encouraged me to bring them to our house after parties, no matter how late, preferring to be awakened rather than anguish over where I was and how much my date had been drinking. When she heard us enter she cheerfully grabbed her robe and dashed into the kitchen to whip up waffles.

My friends loved her not only for that, but for her openness. They could tell her anything and she would listen without shock or reprimand. At their curfew time the girls usually called their parents for permission to stay longer, and if refused, the boys took them home, then often returned for more talk, sitting with Mother on the living room floor in front of the gas log fire. Once, several of them stayed until daybreak.

Along with her misguided perceptions and "my way or the highway" attitude, Mother excelled in intellectual curiosity, openness to new ideas, generosity, and empathy for strangers. She was far ahead of her times regarding sex, accepting differences so readily that gay men in search of their identities turned to her as a confidant. She may have harmed more than she helped because of her certainty that homosexuality was a choice induced by a traumatic relationship with a parent of the same gender, but she gave comfort nonetheless. Her greatest success was raising me to be free of homophobia, no small achievement in the 1930s.

In those days people like Mother were called Bohemian. Many years later a gay man who had grown up in our crowd rebuffing my efforts to be friendly, presumably because he didn't want female friends, asked me if my mother was still alive and how she was doing. When I assured him that she was alive and well, he smiled wistfully and remarked, "She was a hippie before we knew what hippies were."

Yes, she was. And I sometimes wonder how much of it she instilled in me.

Two
TRAVELS ON A LEASH

The best of my college years wasn't at college. Life between Mother and marriage spanned many miles, exciting times in unlikely places, each of which broadened my perspective and advanced maturity, but none of which occurred in a classroom.

College began badly. I was fifteen years old, too young, according to parents and grandparents, to accept my Interlochen viola teacher's offer of a partial scholarship to the Cincinnati Conservatory of Music where he taught. I wanted to go there, but Mother extended her leash only as far as the University of Georgia in Athens, where Mr. Hugh and his wife, Miss Jessie, could keep an eye on me. I didn't know, nor apparently did Mother, that UGA was considered a party school.

Given the social mores of the day, teenage girls tended to focus on socializing rather than books. At UGA girls' social lives centered around sororities, which I shunned both from choice and family instruction. Lacking knowledge or desire to seek community via Jewish organizations, I became a somewhat reluctant loner. Worst of all, I was unaware that the UGA chapter of the Jewish fraternity Phi Epsilon Pi had an unwritten law precluding members from dating Jewish girls at the university, so friends from "our crowd" at home never called me. Nor did my gentile

Janice as a student
at UGA

friends from the orchestra. I hadn't previously encountered that aspect of anti-Semitism.

I tried to drown any social disappointments in educational waters—less than sparkling in most cases. Mr. Hugh's classes and projects were the exceptions. I engaged in activism only once, during my sophomore year when Governor Eugene Talmadge risked losing the school's accreditation by firing the state's Board of Regents. In October 1941 I went with friends on the students massive motorcade to the state capitol in Atlanta, which succeeded in attracting the public attention that forced the governor to back down.

Although I didn't go home for the premiere of *Gone With The Wind*, I did get to Atlanta whenever something of interest there beckoned me. Thanks to Mother's friends in the Metropolitan Opera, I obtained walk-ons as an extra in some of their performances in Atlanta. In *Carmen* I did so well as a flower vender that the stage manager sent me back to dance on a table with the Cigarette Girls. In *Lohengrin*, standing on a balcony of the castle as a page boy, I had a hard time not laughing as I looked down on the rotund *heldentenor* struggling to embrace an equally rounded Elsa as they sang their love duet.

My most valuable lessons evolved from my summer of 1940 when I returned to Interlochen as a college student with a part-time job. Supervisors soon discovered my talent and bumped me from dishwashing detail to writing program notes for the concerts. Adding to my good fortune, two nice guys vied for my attention—ironically, because at Interlochen I no longer obsessed about popularity. One of them, much older than I, taught me to drive. The other, Alex, a boy my own age still in school, sent small gifts the following winter and came to visit during spring break.

At that stage of life, I never considered him or anyone else in terms of marriage. Nor did Mother, until he came to Atlanta and Mr. Hugh terrified her with that possibility, noting that he wasn't Jewish. Since Mr. Hugh himself wasn't Jewish, I didn't understand his objection. Now I see it as a convoluted aspect of a deep-seated, unacknowledged attitude towards Jews. Mr. Hugh studied in Germany in the early 1900s when the so-called scientific theory that "race mixing" was genetically harmful prevailed, as did the belief that Jews were of a different race from other Caucasians. I believe that Mr. Hugh absorbed those misguided convictions and was genuinely concerned about my future.

The following summer Mother took me to California to keep me from going to Michigan and seeing Alex. She corresponded with his mother, arranged to meet the two of them in Chicago on our way home, and thus amicably ended our relationship.

Ostensibly to attend a national music club convention in Los Angeles, Mother rented out our house for two months to good friends in need and prevailed on her two aunts to get us a good rate at the apartment-hotel where they lived, on the corner of Wilshire and Normandy. We went by train and bus across the southern states, stopping first in New Orleans to sightsee and visit aged relatives, then viewed the Carlsbad caverns and Grand Canyon. My learning experiences picked up when we reached California where for the first time I tasted chopped liver and gefilte fish, heard talk of statehood for Hawaii and animosity toward Japan. In Georgia we worried about German U-boats off the coast near

Savannah, but we were unaware that the Japanese had occupied strategic islands in the Pacific.

Of note was the earthquake we experienced while there. (Actually it was two earthquakes, only one of which was seismographic.) They rumbled when I asked Mother for permission to change my college major from music to drama and erupted when she refused. I argued, eventually becoming hysterical, at which moment our room shook, the chandelier swayed, objects fell off shelves, and we realized that forces beyond my temper tantrum were in play. That afternoon on the way to Hollywood we saw a deep crack and rubble in the middle of Vine Street. Soon afterward, a slight crack appeared in Mother's determination to make me a musician and she permitted me to split my major between music and drama.

We noticed a sign for the Guy Bates Post School of Drama a few blocks west of our hotel and I enrolled there for the remaining weeks of our visit. The course included diction, Stanislavsky's method of acting, and basic fencing, but my most significant learning came from other students. They were already in rehearsal for George S. Kaufman's *Stage Door* so I received the only part still open, Little Mary, and the only free space at the makeup table. It wasn't the end space, but next to it. The end space was routinely reserved for the African American, whose only role had to be the servant.

Jim Crow didn't prevent collegial friendships from blossoming in L.A. Several of us often stopped off together after the show for hamburgers, and one of the guys going east on Wilshire past Normandy walked me to my door. Frequently my escort was John, who played the butler. On the last night of the play, when we wouldn't see each other again, he kissed me good-bye. I automatically included this kiss in my nightly debriefing to Mother. It elicited no comment, but she reprimanded me when I mentioned having invited Ruth, my female friend of color, to visit me if she ever came near Atlanta. I was devastated by Mother's reaction. If racially mixed hamburgers and cheek-kissing were okay—both cardinal sins according to Jim Crow—what was wrong with inviting a female friend to visit?

"Think about it," Mother said. "How will you entertain her?"

"The same as always," I replied. "We'll go downtown for lunch and movies and..."

"Where?" she asked.

I'd forgotten that Georgia law forbade "race mixing" in public places. "Well," I conceded, "We'll go to the club."

"I don't think so," she said.

As she suspected, Ruth never called.

The other profound lesson I learned from my classmates at the Post School of Drama was what it took to get ahead in show business. Most of my classmates sought opportunities in Hollywood. Had I ever considered it, I would have ceased immediately after hearing from the other girls about the "casting couch." Gloria Hallward, the best actress among us, spoke openly about her use of it as necessary for success, and ultimately proved the point. As Gloria Grahame, she co-starred with Jimmy Stewart in two films, won an Oscar for her supporting role in *The Bad and the Beautiful*, and was nominated for another.

We returned from L.A. by train, up along the coast and across the Canadian Rockies. This I especially enjoyed because at Banff and Lake Louise I did some sightseeing on horseback. Back at school in September with an improved outlook, I added California-inspired Spanish to my studies along with courses in drama and won the female lead in the upcoming production of *Pride and Prejudice*. However, my triumph was tarnished when, even before rehearsals began, I was bumped to a smaller role, presumably because the wispy blonde who supplanted me announced her real-life betrothal to the man playing Darcy.

On December 7, 1941, I was at midday-Sunday dinner visiting my roommate, Jeanne Wolff, in Savannah when someone called us from the table to hear the breaking news; Pearl Harbor had been bombed. The next day, the strong yet calm, authoritative voice of President Franklin Roosevelt told us it was "a date which will live in infamy." We were at war.

We returned to school, but it wasn't the same. Now I focused on getting out and going to work to help the war effort. Dropping out wasn't an option in my family, so I took an extra course, went to summer school, and graduated a semester ahead of schedule. Disdaining the ceremony, I went home immediately after turning in my final exam.

The government was training women to do jobs formerly reserved for men. I took a three-month course at Georgia Tech to qualify as an assistant draftsman and went to work for the Army Corps of Engineers at Ft. Benning, Georgia, near Columbus. I commandeered the front section of my grandparents' apartment as living quarters. My downstairs neighbor, the commandant's secretary, shared her car with me for rides to work and another tenant, a perky lady from Mexico, coached me in Spanish.

Work was easy, socializing likewise and surprisingly informative. First, it surprised me to learn that my co-workers from New York who looked and sounded Jewish were actually from Greek and Italian backgrounds. During our lunch breaks, I often went with them to a nearby fence and tried to speak with the Italian prisoners of war detained on the other side. My vocabulary was limited to phrases from Italian opera.

After my workday, a captain named Gordon Gray often spent time with me. He took me horseback riding, tried to teach me golf, and invited me to swim at the Officers' Club. I thought he was joking when he said he was a cousin of Lady Nancy Astor, but now I believe it was probably true. After the war he held high positions in Washington and later became president of the University of North Carolina.

I didn't anticipate meeting celebrities, certainly not in the way those meetings sometimes occurred. One day in the Officers' Club's crowded dressing room, as I stood up after crouching to step into my bathing suit, I collided with the largest pair of breasts I'd ever seen. They belonged to Jane Russell, a Hollywood star and popular pin-up girl.

One actress who actually became my friend was Emily McNair. Her actor husband, Efrem Zimbalist Jr., later became most well-known for his role in the television series *The FBI*. Emily directed the Columbus

Little Theater, cast me as a lead in her production of *The Cat and The Canary*, and inspired me to promote the theater by contributing a weekly column about it to the *Columbus Ledger-Enquirer*. I didn't get paid for my work, but I enjoyed the experience nonetheless.

Weekend socializing usually took place with my Jewish soldier friends in Atlanta, where Mother turned our house into a one-woman USO. She began her patriotic service volunteering at a hospital reception office but quit in disgust when she saw emergency patients turned away because they couldn't pay. Then she volunteered for civilian defense, tracking planes on a radar screen, and continued there as long as there was need for it. Her major contribution, however, was offering bed, breakfast, and Sunday dinner to "her boys" in uniform, regardless of whether they were Jewish. She saved her meat ration coupons during the week to serve the soldiers thick steaks for dinner on Sundays. Whoever came found a place to sleep, even in my bed when I wasn't there. One night someone arrived late, found all beds and sofas occupied, and sacked out on the front porch glider.

Some of the soldiers wrote home telling their parents about us, and some of the parents wrote to Mother thanking her and establishing ongoing friendships with us. Two of the men, Bud Weiss from Pennsylvania and Bud Mantler from Connecticut, became like brothers to me and settled in Atlanta after the war. I think Mother expected me to marry one of them.

I didn't realize how her memory of WWI impacted her reaction to this war and to the fact that I was the same age as she was then.

By the fall of 1943 many of "our boys" had been shipped overseas, and I wanted to go too. I applied for a job as assistant draftsman at Ft. Clayton, Panama Canal Zone, where the army was opening a school of malariology, a disease ravaging our troops in the Pacific. Quinine, with Japan in control of its sources, was no longer available to the Allies for treatment, so the army needed to train personnel to recognize the cause and teach prevention. Grandmother Lylah went ballistic at the thought of my going so far away, but Mother cheerfully approved, possibly recalling her own frustrations during WWI. My surrogate brother Bud Mantler said it was good for me to get away from Mother but Panama wasn't far enough.

Bud knew us better than we knew ourselves. I wrote home in detail every other day, letters which I now blush to read. Thankfully my adolescent obsession with fashion and men was occasionally relieved by surprisingly insightful comments on character, culture, and the availability of commodities within and outside of American jurisdiction.

My adventure began with the train ride to Miami. It arrived late, which caused me to miss my flight to Panama and stay overnight in a strange city with no available hotel room. The only person I knew in Miami was Rosemary Aubert, wife of a concert pianist Mother had hosted, currently serving in the army overseas. Rosemary lived on a small house boat in Biscayne Bay and worked at night pulling in seaplanes. She didn't need her bunk until morning so she offered it to me for overnight.

The next day I embarked on my first flight ever in a ten-year-old China Clipper seaplane converted for troop transport with fixed bucket seats. Bumpy skies churned my insides. Cables being unreliable, I (correctly) suspected that no one would know to meet me when we landed. That so, and with telephones equally unreliable, I took directions onto a shuttle train with instructions to get off at the Miraflores locks, about two-thirds of the way across the isthmus and directly across the road from Ft. Clayton. However, the conductor said he wouldn't stop there because he couldn't let a lady off in the wilderness with no one to attend to her luggage.

After a nervous ride during which I was nonetheless fascinated, seeing dark jungle across the canal and weird gray branches of treetops rising from Lake Gatun like arms of drowning ghosts, the train incurred a slight accident just as it reached Miraflores locks. That attracted a crowd, an MP contacted the post for me, and the colonel sent his secretary in a jeep to pick me up.

Living on an army post was different from merely working there as I did at Ft. Benning. At Ft. Clayton we five young women, the only female residents, were simultaneously highly privileged and unusually restricted because of the commandant's responsibility for our safety. I shared a comfortable three-bedroom, two-story stone house in the officers' quarters with two other girls. Its tile floors, stucco walls and jalousie windows provided livable temperatures, the cool floors so welcoming that we stepped out of our shoes at the front door. We even had the luxury of a do-all Jamaican house maid. Once, in the closet, I found a scorpion in one of my shoes, but besides that had no further encounter with the hazards of life in the tropics.

The colonel protected us as if we were his daughters, even going with us into town after hours if we needed to do so, as I did my first night there to cable home that I had arrived safely. Cables and long-distance telephoning could be dispatched only from one central station on either end of the canal. Calls needed to be scheduled in advance, and even then usually required hours of waiting to be connected. They took place in a stuffy soundproof booth with a censor listening who once cut me off when I mentioned a man's name to Mother.

We weren't allowed to walk alone on the post and needed a male escort after dark, even if we were two or more women together, but we could always call for a jeep driver to take us wherever we wanted to go on the post. A jeep awaited us at our door each morning at seven to take us to work, at four to bring us home, and both ways for lunch either at home or the officers' club.

Along with officers' privileges came another restriction which I unwittingly disobeyed before learning of it. After going to dinner with a non-commissioned officer, a brother of a friend in Atlanta, I was called in by the colonel and reprimanded for "conduct unbecoming an officer." We were not allowed to socialize with enlisted men.

At first work consisted of setting up for the school's opening, but without sufficient equipment. Four of us, including officers, had to share one typewriter. My job was to enlarge images from textbooks so they could be seen hung from the classroom wall. Officers, lacking knowledge of how to proceed, often ordered busy work such as my assignment to draw and paint a malaria-infected blood cell with intricate detail to be reproduced as the school's insignia on all motor pool vehicles. Conditions improved and real work began when the medical instructors arrived.

Food was plentiful and, in many ways, better than at home, where meat, coffee, sugar, butter, and many processed items such as chili sauce were strictly rationed. Here we could buy whatever we wanted that was available, but supplies vanished quickly, especially canned, frozen or dried fruit and vegetables. Canned milk and eggs from Argentina were readily available as well as fresh tropical fruit. Many foods rationed at home and unobtainable in the Canal Zone we obtained over the line in the Republic of Panama. There the only thing rationed was gasoline, and even *that* was readily available on the black market. One of my housemates even persuaded her boyfriend to bring us milk and processed vegetables from the British Embassy.

My twentieth birthday occurred less than three weeks after I arrived in Panama, but I did not welcome it joyously, yet another indication of my lingering adolescence. Despite being overwhelmed with male attention and thinking I was in love with two men stationed in combat zones, I was unhappy being the only one among my childhood girlfriends not yet married.

Captain Bob Myers, an Atlanta friend stationed in the jungle on the Atlantic side, threw me a birthday party with some of his friends at the Strangers' Club in Cristobal. That was the first time I had stayed overnight at a hotel with a man, which seemed daring then even though we surely did not share a room. I wrote to my parents stressing the separate rooms, and although I followed wartime security rules, a sadistic censor cut the letter into lace before forwarding it. Fortunately, my parents knew Bob and trusted both of us.

One feature of the weekend was Bob's inducting me into the Short Snorter Club, an exclusive society of persons who cross a sea or ocean in wartime service. The ceremony consists of a complicated protocol with each member showing his own Short Snorter bill, paying a penalty if he doesn't have it, and then signing a fresh dollar bill for the new member. I still have mine.

On another weekend in Cristobal, Bob took me to a formal affair at the British Embassy and we returned to the hotel in a horse-drawn carriage. Comedian Bob Hope and his sidekick Jerry Colonna were on the veranda awaiting a cab, and when I stepped down I heard Colonna say, "Let's take it."

Bob Hope, nodding toward me, replied, "And her, too."

I smiled, but didn't ask for an autograph.

The major highlights of my time in Panama happened thanks to our friend Dr. Hal Davison introducing me to his cousin, Dr. C. D. Briscoe. The Briscoes lived in the Panama City suburb of Bella Vista with their three daughters. The older two, Sally and Ann, attended Balboa Junior College and became my new best friends. When Sally's boyfriend Jerry, a cello player in the Panama National Symphony, learned that I'd played viola at National Music Camp, it opened a new dimension of my life in Panama.

Jerry asked me what my favorite symphony was and exclaimed "I knew it!" when I said Tchaikovsky's 6th because a violist in the orchestra, an American sailor who had also been at Interlochen, referred to that symphony as "The Janeece." At Jerry's insistence, the girls brought me to his next rehearsal where I reconnected with violist Leon Feldman, whom I had known at camp. Violists were still in short supply, so they introduced me to the conductor, Eduardo de Castro. The girls borrowed an instrument for me from Balboa Junior College, and I became a member of the Panama National Symphony.

A few weeks later, we played for First Lady Eleanor Roosevelt when she came to visit the troops. The concert was a special thrill for me because, contrary to popular opinion at home, I greatly admired her. After the concert, she stayed to speak with each of the U.S. servicemen in the orchestra, then left through the main entrance to the cheers and applause of a waiting crowd. I later reported to Mother, "Mrs. Roosevelt...isn't half as homely as her pictures because...she shows such charm."

The other major highlight of my life in Panama began when Don Halman, the Briscoes' tall, dark, handsome neighbor, happened to drop in. The following night he took me to the Carnival ball at the Union Club. He was a great dancer and a good conversationalist, and swaying cheek-to-cheek to soft Latin music on the moonlit terrace overlooking the Pacific was irresistibly romantic. At some point I recognized that the moment was ephemeral and that I was enchanted by the enchantment. I was living a fantasy, like a play with an obscure but certain closure.

The possibility of an extended run materialized when we each discovered that the other was Jewish, which neither of us suspected.

We were discussing strange beliefs and Don said that although he was Jewish he had gone to a Christian Science school, but he didn't buy its theology. That piqued my curiosity about his family's origins and I learned that his mother's forebears came to South America from Portugal several centuries earlier and his father's to the Virgin Islands from Denmark. They had briefly lived in New Orleans when two of his great uncles went there during the Civil War and fought for the Confederacy. Hearing his family's story triggered my fascination with American Jewish history.

Mrs. Briscoe tried to play Cupid, arranging a house party in Santa Clara where the Halmans and other Jewish families had beach houses. Donny didn't get there that weekend but just being on a secluded tropical beach, I happily romanticized anyway. Of course, he and I were both more acculturated by our surroundings than by our Jewishness, and I heeded Mother's warnings about cross-cultural marriage so as not to fantasize about a future with him. Even so, I later confessed to Mother that his charm and my overactive hormones led me to question my powers of resistance.

As Bud Mantler predicted, Panama was not far enough away for me to become totally free. I felt Mother's tug on the leash when she wrote that Bud Weiss and my friend Elaine, to whom I had introduced him, were getting married.

Since Atabrine had been discovered as an effective substitute for quinine in treating malaria, our work at the school had diminished to nearly zero. The two privates assigned to assist me were doing everything

I had been sent there to do. Seeing as I was spending most of my workdays *kibbitzing* with my boss, the major, who also had little to do, it didn't seem unpatriotic to resign and go home for the wedding. I could get another government job stateside.

An Air Force pilot made a scrapbook for me of plexiglass slabs from a downed plane as a farewell gift. I've kept it with my Short Snorter dollar as mementoes of that first adventure abroad, which I now believe gave me a great step forward toward the me I became.

Instead of seeking work after Bud and Elaine's wedding, I applied to Emory for graduate studies in journalism. Before that materialized, however, a far more enticing opportunity arose. I received an announcement from The Experiment in International Living, an organization dedicated to world peace through international friendships, offering a six-week home stay in Mexico followed by two weeks of travel. I signed up immediately. Because of the war, only one group of six girls were to go that year, but because a former Experimenter applied at the last minute, the Experiment's founder, Dr. Donald B. Watt, and his wife formed a second group, asking for four volunteers to go with them to a different city. I joined them and went to Guanajuato, a once wealthy silver-mining center high in the mountains of Mexico's central plateau.

By 1944 Guanajuato had lost its colonial splendor and no longer attracted tourists. Our host families appeared to represent a broad spectrum of society which, surprisingly to me, did not stratify according to relative affluence or social barriers. The father of my family, Señor Yerena, was a mine supervisor and worked away from home. Other host families were headed by men in politics or business. Their wives were light-skinned *mestizos* whereas Señora Yerena appeared to be pure Indian and illiterate.

The other families lived in apartments aboveground with facilities similar to those in average American homes. The Yerenas' rooms were flush with the narrow cobblestoned street. We had a wood-burning stove in the kitchen, no refrigerator, and in the bathroom no fixtures but a primitive toilet with a leaky water box that often didn't work. We washed with cold water and used strips of newspaper for tissue. Despite this appearance of poverty, the family employed a maid and spoke of having a country house with all customary conveniences. I failed to understand the rationale of living with primitive facilities when one could afford household help and modern equipment elsewhere. But adapting was part of the Experiment's *raison d'etre* and I did not find it onerous.

The Yerenas had a daughter my age, Elena, who had graduated from a trade school, knew a little English, and operated her own beauty salon next door. Señora Yerena appeared wedded to the church even more so than the other women, all of whom seemed fanatically devout, unwavering in their certainty that whatever the priest told them was literally true. Apparently, all social life connected with a religious tradition.

Señora Yerena knew we had been warned against eating raw vegetables and drinking un-boiled milk or water and went out of her way to please me. I enjoyed the food, eagerly consuming everything she served except pig's feet. That one rejection caused her such regret that the next day she made "American style" hot cakes for me—the best I ever tasted!

Our new friends immediately asked us what our religion was and apparently were deeply troubled that those who were not Catholic were ineligible for heaven. I had no problem because they knew nothing about Jews other than the revered biblical ones and the Mexicans were afraid to offend by asking questions. Two of my three colleagues, a fallen Catholic and an Episcopalian, knew enough to say "Catholic" and "almost Catholic," but the third innocently admitted to being Presbyterian and was barraged with attempts at conversion for the rest of her stay. Presumably due to their respect for my biblical ancestors they left me to my own beliefs, although much later in our visit a very special friend did tell me sadly, in Spanish, "You are so *sympatica*, it's a pity you're not Catholic." That clearly meant I wasn't eligible for a reunion in heaven.

We spent our mornings studying Spanish with Manuel Escurdia, a boy our own age who lived in a once-magnificent colonial mansion where

Emperor Maximillian visited his ancestor, el Conde de Escurdia, on the way to his execution in Queretaro in 1867. We went to our respective homes for late midday dinner and *siesta*, then frequently gathered with our host siblings and their friends at someone's home for the afternoon, playing games and singing *rancheras*. Those Mexican folk songs were my most valuable Spanish lessons. I can still recall the lyrics and frequently sing some of them inside my head even today.

We visited an active silver mine in the surrounding mountains, attended an annual festival celebrating the opening of a nearby dam, and participated in the activities of our host families, invariably commemorating some religious event. The men and boys generally showed off unwanted *machismo*, breaking their own rules and behaving badly. Unlike my reports from Panama, my letters from Mexico mention no male friends except our language instructor Manuel, who was truly a friend, not a candidate for romance. We shared deep interests and strong opinions on everything from art and music to politics and religion.

Our Mexican friends nicknamed us with Spanish equivalents of our actual names and honored us on our Saint's Day if it occurred during our visit. We found no translation for Janice so I chose Carmen, unaware that her *dia del santo* would soon occur and entitle me to receive a *mananita*, the sunrise serenade appropriate for saints' days. I also received several serenades, mostly impromptu, but one of them the kind in which the recipient is expected to come to the window and acknowledge the compliment. For that, her troubadour must get permission from her mother. Señora Yerena allowed it after carefully briefing me on the rules: no touching, no reaching out through the grilled window, and uttering only a demure *muchas gracias* when she signaled that the time was up. She and Elena stood beside me throughout. The Experiment stressed adherence to the customs and lifestyle of our hosts, however archaic they might seem.

The most exciting thing we did in Mexico was visit Parícutin, the still-flaming volcano that had erupted in the middle of a cornfield the previous year. We were about fifteen miles short of our destination when the road disappeared beneath continuing gusts of "lava dust," black sand residue from the ash, that was so deep that our bus frequently lost traction and we had to get out and push. After dark we began to see a reddish cloud in the sky, becoming wider and milkier as we drove on. Then it disappeared and we saw reddish lights, glowing as if from a distant city.

When the bus could go no further, we disembarked and found ourselves in the middle of a huge sanded lava bed, close enough to the glowing lights to see that they were boulders of burning lava tumbling toward us. After stumbling through that eerie terrain for what seemed like hours, we reached the remaining half of a village, its church steeple the only visible evidence of what lay beneath the crawling piles of burning coals. In the remaining half of the central plaza a lone Indian slept against the door of his shed, wrapped in his *serape* with his few belongings at his side. Among them was a warm can of beer he gladly sold to us and three of us gratefully shared.

We built a fire to keep warm, sat on the shed's step, and tried to sleep. Whenever I dozed off, the earth rumbled beneath me and burning rocks moved closer. Eventually they were so close that we put out our fire and, despite the very cold night air, moved further away. When dawn finally came we saw the volcano, a big black cone that spewed smoke periodically mixed with huge flaming rocks.

On our long walk back to the bus we saw the vastness of the great black dunes smothering Michoacán's lush fields and ancient forests. Here and there a pale white *chicolote* blossom, like a large primrose, peeped out from the silt as a defiant symbol of resilience. Twice while bumping and jiggling past ghostlike deserted villages our bus stalled and we got out and pushed. The third time, we walked until the bus recovered and caught up with us. The adventure was both exhausting and exhilarating, and by far my most exciting memory of the summer in Mexico.

Our stay in Guanajuato was a sojourn in what was then a third world economy with social mores reminiscent of small-town nineteenth century USA. Leaving it, we traveled in contemporary settings, Mexico

City and Acapulco, plus brief stops in Cuernavaca and Taxco en route. In Acapulco we stayed in an inn so modest that we girls risked intrusion sharing a first-floor room open to the main thoroughfare. Nevertheless, without mishap we basked blithely on the morning beach in the morning, the afternoon beach in the afternoon, and cheered the divers at La Quebrada at night.

In Mexico City I teamed up with Barbara Baer, a former Experimenter who didn't go to Guanajuato with us but still became a lifelong friend. We eagerly explored the government buildings around the Zócalo, admiring the political statements of Rivera and Orozco depicted in their murals. We met four boys at a party thrown for our group by a local family. Those boys remained our friends for many years through visits back and forth to Mexico and the States. For me, the most memorable (and surely the most emotional) event occurred the night we went to the opera. The conductor came out after intermission, but instead of playing the overture to *Cavalleria Rusticana,* he began with the rousing tones of "La Marseillaise," announcing the liberation of Paris. The audience rose as one, belting out "Allons enfants de la Patrie..." with tears of joy rolling down our cheeks. That symbolized the nearness of Allied victory, the end of the war, the longed-for return to normalcy.

On my way home, the Mexican Customs and Border Protection official stopped me to question my taking out recordings of Mexican folk songs. This didn't make sense to me because commercial recordings were not prohibited cultural heritage, but when my savvy companions suggested that I was being detained for a date rather than for contraband, I left the records and made for the train station as fast as possible. That, too, was a learning experience.

At some point thereafter I took a course in journalism at Emory, but before that I wrote two stories about my experiences abroad that were bought and published by the Sunday magazine of the *Atlanta Journal-Constitution.* Our friend Ralph McGill, then editor at the *Constitution,* introduced me to the magazine's editor and gave me a fifteen-minute lesson on writing a lead.

In December, having applied for another government job, I reported for work with the army's Signal Security Corps in Arlington, Virginia. The living quarters were dormitory rooms in downtown Arlington, our workplace the campus of Arlington Hall, a girls' finishing school in the suburbs. We coded and decoded highly classified cables, operating around the clock in three shifts that rotated every three months with a day off after seven working days and two days off every seven weeks. I avoided the rotation by volunteering for permanent assignment to the graveyard shift, 11PM until 7AM, which gave me free evenings, enough daylight for whatever required access during business hours, and worked well even on frigid nights when I had to trudge through deep snow from the bus stop.

Our indoctrination introduced me to geopolitics. While basic and cursory, it initiated my curiosity about foreign policy and hooked me on reading a daily newspaper. Charts tracked where our troops were fighting as soon as the news became declassified, which added to what we gleaned from personal correspondence giving us clues to where our men were deployed. We didn't discuss it, even among ourselves, for we knew that the warning "Loose lips sink ships" was especially applicable to us.

Since marriage was off my radar until after the war, I wasn't bothered by learning that the ratio of women to men in the Washington area was about five-to-one. I wanted to imbibe the cultural offerings there as much as possible. Nevertheless, I did get calls from Atlanta men who were stationed nearby, and at times even had to turn down dates due to prior commitments, often with female friends who enjoyed the same cultural pursuits as I did.

My frequent companions were Rosemary Aubert, who had left Miami to work for the French Mission, an adjunct of the French Embassy in Washington, and Barbara Baer, my friend from The Experiment who worked for the Office of Strategic Services, forerunner of the CIA. I tested foreign restaurants with Rosemary and worked on my linguistic skills by attending foreign films with Barbara. Both women spoke French, which encouraged me to practice it as well as Spanish. When a Mexican

friend visited, he invited me to a State Department briefing using a pass
for foreign students, but such was my language skill that he instructed me
to remain silent for fear of revealing the fraud.

On the gray afternoon of April 12, 1945, I felt strangely sad as
I passed the White House on the bus going to meet Rosemary at the
French Mission. When I reached it, I heard that President Roosevelt
had died. I learned then that our allies are not necessarily our friends.
While Rosemary and multitudes throughout the world grieved as I did,
her Gallic boss and coworkers were celebrating. Apparently, they didn't
appreciate our President's part in freeing France.

Within a month of President Roosevelt's passing, the war in
Europe ended and I went home for a visit. On the way back, as the train
approached Union Station, I saw the Capitol dome lighted for the first
time. That gave me a thrill that resonates every time I pass the Capitol at
night, even now.

Due to the war ending in Europe, my U.S. Army job had once again
diminished without being terminated; my co-workers and I completed
our night's work by 2 AM and spent the rest of our shift *kibbitzing* over
coffee and doughnuts. With final victory in sight, I accepted Rosemary's
offer to work for her at the French Mission in the newly-established
Service de Voyage (despite my antagonism towards her superiors).

French nationals were streaming through Washington, both from
Canada, where some had been sitting out the war, and from France, en
route to the United Nations conference in San Francisco. My new job
consisted of finding rooms for them and helping them navigate through
the red tape of getting U.S. government-issued coupons to buy shoes,
gasoline, and various still-rationed food supplies. I also had to find
housing for myself since I was no longer working for our government
and found a place in one of our listings. It was an elegant mansion,
formerly an embassy, at 1744 R Street, diagonally across from our office
and owned by a gracious *grande dame* named Melinda who was pleased
to derive income from her two-rooms-and-bath servants' quarters, left
vacant since the disappearance of servants. The English basement suite

reminded me of Robert Louis Stevenson's poem in *A Child's Garden of Verses* describing "... grown-up people's feet / Still going past me in the street." An attractive French co-worker took the other room.

At tea time, when most of Melinda's guests returned from work, she greeted us with punch and cookies in the drawing room. That engendered delightful discussions in an international setting, much of it with Latin Americans who spoke less English than I did Spanish, so I practiced my Spanish. I also used it with a gentleman from Brazil who spoke only Portuguese, which sounded to me as if he had a mouthful of cotton.

In addition to her afternoon socials, Melinda promoted amateur theater and tried to lure me into an amateur production that she sponsored. I also enjoyed socializing with my suitemate and her compatriots, despite their politics, which seemed as contrary to my own as did their compatriots who cheered FDR's death. I was with them the night we heard the election news from London that the Labor Party won and Winston Churchill would no longer serve as prime minister. As before, the French cheered and I grieved, but they were charming and I accepted our differences.

Not so with the Russians, who were nothing like Russians I knew in Atlanta. Natasha Davison and her Uncle Peter Porohatchikoff were lovable, so I expected at least to *like* other Russians—all the more so because they were our allies—but those I met in Washington weren't likeable. One, a coworker at the French Mission, was dour and abrasive, and a jolly troika of Russian officers with whom I went to dinner once were brash and crude. I didn't anticipate the Cold War, but that sampling should have served as a clue.

Aside from international politics, I reveled in everything that Washington offered, from celebrating Bastille Day at the French Embassy, to hearing great music from the esplanade behind the Lincoln Memorial, to horseback riding in Rock Creek Park. Fortunately, I did not ride alone; lurid news items revealed that such delights could be dangerous to adventurous young women, one of whose body parts were found scattered throughout that very same park.

Foolishly, I once risked disaster by accepting an Argentine diplomat's invitation to a Sunday picnic in the country. I'd met him at one of the USO-like parties for international visitors. I realized that he was much older than I (and probably married) but saw no harm in going with him to a picnic. It concerned me somewhat that, when he picked me up, no others were in the car. I suspected trouble as we neared the city's outskirts. I asked him to turn back, saying that I didn't feel well, and almost panicked when he continued driving to the countryside. I stayed steady enough to act quickly when he stopped to buy fruit. As he walked towards the stand, I slid behind the wheel and drove away, leaving him holding the peaches. I parked his car in front of the Argentine embassy and walked home.

Mother saved me from any further danger by coming to visit shortly before VJ Day. She immediately ordered that I lose ten pounds before coming home and signed me up for slimming sessions at Emile's on Connecticut Avenue. I went three times a week for a month, dieted, and graduated with a report card confirming success.

On VJ Day Mother and I celebrated with friends who, like other exuberant car owners, anticipated the end of gas rationing by zooming out of town—in our case headed for Thomas Jefferson's Monticello in Virginia. When we hadn't reached Charlottesville by late afternoon, we stopped to ask directions and discovered we'd been circling Washington. No regrets. Everything was wonderful that day. A new life would begin tomorrow.

Ideally, I would have gone home for a visit, then returned to Washington and found a new job. Before leaving I paced the Dupont Circle area with a friend, hoping to find rooms we could share, but there was nothing available. Jobs were plentiful; rooms were not.

I knew that I wanted to write but needed to earn a living, and I knew that I wanted to get married but didn't yet know to whom. For that decision, I had to await the return of two much-longed-for prospects, neither of whose letters reflected hope for a quick demilitarization. And living with Mother was a problem. In a letter I told her:

Every time I've come home... we've had this same discussion, and I don't expect to convince you anymore this time than I have in the past regarding our getting along together. We both know that in two or three months I'll want to move on and you'll be relieved to have me gone for a while. Let's both understand that, say no more about it, and I'll try to be as considerate as I can while we are together so that maybe it WILL work out this time. However, you know as well as I do that you drain every bit of independence out of me and that it isn't good for either of us for me to be in Atlanta...

To pull my weight as a residing adult, I offered to assume all housekeeping duties in return for uninterrupted seclusion while studying or writing. Mother agreed but, unsurprisingly, was incapable of carrying out that agreement. In less than a month I needed to leave.

Throughout the war I had visited family friends and relatives in the northeast. In Boston I stayed with Dad's cousin, Christine, and ambled through the shaded streets of Cambridge dreaming of Longfellow, rekindling my interest in writing poetry. In Manhattan I preferred hanging out in the East Nineties on the living room couch of Cousin Alma, the elegant European widow of Grandpa Joe's cousin, Fritz, with whom he retained close contact on business trips abroad. I could never get enough of New York's art museums and theaters. Mother's concert artist friend, Wilbur Evans, had the lead in a Mike Todd production that I saw, and the sister of one of "our boys" was featured in a musical starring Ethel Merman and gave me a house seat to attend. She also managed to get me a ticket to *Oklahoma!* and apologized that she'd had to pay the scalper $6.50 for it.

Dad's cousin Rosalie, an artist who lived in the Village, educated me on one aspect of life there by taking me to a party hosted by a sculptor who was having an affair with the dancer José Limón. José's life-size bronze image greeted us, nude with an erection, in the entranceway of the sculptor's apartment, while he awaited us fully-clothed just beyond.

Rosalie also fixed me up for a date with a promising young comic named Zero Mostel. The only thing I remember about the evening is that he was very nice and at one point we were in an elevator with legendary jazz singer and band leader Cab Calloway.

As I yearned to leave Atlanta, an invitation came from Aunt Sophie's best friend in New York, keen on fixing me up with her wealthy 28-year-old newly divorced nephew. On learning that our first date went well, she delicately noted, "Marry him and you'll never have to worry about where your next mink will come from."

I didn't need to think of a mink to be attracted to Larry. He enjoyed art and classical music, played piano by ear, spoke French fluently, and took me buggy riding in Central Park. By day he worked for his father, who manufactured that era's choicest brand of men's shirts. He called me regularly in Atlanta, came to visit over New Year's Eve, and obliterated all thoughts of others from my mind.

Then he vanished. He never called again and I never learned why. It crushed me momentarily, but in retrospect it shouldn't have surprised me. Our households were so different, mine so bizarre with "our boys" still dropping in and hovering over me that the sheer nuttiness of it could have turned anyone away.

I was bloodied but unbowed. Knowing that Dr. Watt needed help retooling The Experiment for post-war operation, I volunteered to work for him and went to live with the Watt family in Vermont along with Carol O'Connor, who had been with us in Guanajuato. We shared a split-level suite similar to my digs in DC but much brighter, the scenery being Vermont's green hills and maple trees rather than "grown-up people's feet..."

The Watts' home, Himmel on the Hill, was a charming Swiss chalet they had designed themselves, furnishing each room in the style of a different country. Mine was "Balkan peasant." In the Japanese living room, paneled walls concealed shelves containing curios from around the world that Dr. Watt used for an instructive game frequently played after Sunday dinner. He'd bring out several objects and ask us to identify their countries of origin. I always scored poorly, but I loved the game and learned a lot.

Mrs. Watt was a wonderful cook with skills honed internationally. Nothing pleased us more than her homemade maple ice cream, which tasted even better after riding on the wagon with the family to sap the trees. We also went with the Watts on their weekly trip to Brattleboro to buy food and other supplies, usually staying for supper and a town meeting afterward. Because melting snow made the dirt roads impassable for cars, we piled into the family's truck for those excursions. At one point the Watts gave me my first and only experience with skis. I couldn't even stand up on them.

Carol and I worked with Dr. Watt in a large sunny office, she handling the correspondence while I helped him write two books, *Education for One World* and *Estas en su Casa*; the first disclosed the theory and motivation for The Experiment, while the second acted as a handbook for practicing it. I never learned proper typing or shorthand but took dictation directly onto the typewriter as fast as a stenographer could type it. Possibly because I constantly corrected Dr. Watt's syntax as he dictated the books, he graciously added my name to them as co-author.

After three months the books were finished, post-war conditions had improved to the point where The Experiment could resume operations with paid professionals, and it was time for Carol and me to go home. I kept in touch with the Watts for many years and with The Experiment to some extent ever after. In 1964, Mother hosted students from St. Etienne, France, one of whom connected with my son Bill, who still exchanges visits with him. Mother visited her guest's family there several times as I did once with my husband driving through France on vacation. My summer in Mexico spawned unforeseen continuance.

I was ready to think of marriage, but not to anyone I expected to meet in Atlanta. Having failed when I tried out for a job as an airline attendant, I remembered my pre-war desire for a graduate degree and enrolled for summer school at Columbia University, hoping to qualify for graduate studies in the fall. Still interested in Mexico, I took a secretarial course in Spanish and a course in creative writing. I did poorly in both, probably due to a solidly satisfying social life in New York. I went out with old friends, met new friends, and was assured of getting a job there but found no place to live when I became ineligible to stay in Columbia's dorms. Again I went home, planning to stay for a month or so, then try again.

On my first day at the Club pool, stretched out on a sun board facing the tennis court, I noticed an unfamiliar face in the foursome I was watching play. I asked Nina Brail, a close friend and distant cousin sunning next to me, who he was.

"He's the new rabbi. Want to meet him?"

I did. And that's when my real education began.

Three
THE RABBI'S WIFE

Atlanta had grown quickly, as had its Jewish component, which still numbered less than 10,000. Most Jews affiliated with a particular congregation, of which there were five. The Temple was the oldest in town and the only Reform congregation, with approximately four hundred families. Its rabbi since 1895, Dr. David Marx, had just retired and Rabbi Jacob M. Rothschild from Pittsburgh was engaged to replace him.

Jack Rothschild was a 35-year-old bachelor, fresh from service as a chaplain in the U.S. Infantry, including combat on Guadalcanal. He asked me to have dinner with him on the very day in late August 1946 that Nina Brail introduced us, but I couldn't because I was performing in a play on WSB Radio. Since the station was located atop the Biltmore Hotel where he lived, he suggested that we meet downstairs in the coffee shop after the broadcast.

Succeeding dates were problematic because he was already booked for dinner most evenings by congregants with an attractive young woman to introduce. Fortunately, none had succeeded. He called me each night

Jack Rothschild as a
U.S. Army Chaplain

when he returned and we socialized on the telephone, often working on the latest *New York Times* Sunday crossword puzzle together. Friends who had horses gave him the keys to their stables. My "brother," Bud Mantler, who had given me a temporary job in his office, understood that when I asked for the afternoon off without notice it meant that Jack had called to say he was free to go riding. To avoid any gossip that could endanger our budding relationship, we seldom went places together where we were likely to be recognized, such as the Standard Club or the Ansley Hotel for dinner, dancing, and its popular floor show featuring the Merry Mutes.

After two months, I was deeply in love and perceived that he was too, but he was hesitant about marriage. However, he came to grips with commitment after I made dates for two consecutive weekends, each with a different fellow traveling here from another city. I adhered to my parents' rule against breaking a date for any reason other than an emergency or becoming engaged to marry someone else, which pushed him over the brink to engage me. He proposed by handing me a cartoon from the *Saturday Evening Post* showing a man on his knees, hands folded in supplication, appealing to a seated woman who says, "It's really very easy. Just ask."

When I told my mentor, Mr. Hugh, that Jack and I were getting married, he counseled me, "Don't get to looking dowdy like other preachers' wives." (He obviously didn't know many rabbis' wives.) I realized later that when people said I didn't look like the wife of a religious leader they meant it as a compliment, but it offended me no less. I sensed that beyond stereotyping my looks, it implied an overall judgment of demeanor, behavior, and all facets of life visible to the public—a prescription for paranoia that I determined to reject.

We were married at the Temple on the afternoon of Sunday, December 29, 1946, by Dr. Solomon B. Freehof, whom Jack had served as assistant in Pittsburgh, and the Temple's Rabbi Emeritus David Marx—an act of incredible humility on Jack's part in view of Marx's open campaign to oust him. Refusing to accept the reality of retirement, the older rabbi had been openly hostile to Jack even while expressing special warmth to me (as he had always done, possibly because of his respect for my great-grandfather, Rabbi Browne, who preceded him at the Temple in 1877). One night, when I was at the Standard Club for dinner with my parents without Jack, Marx introduced me to his guests in complimentary terms, to which I responded appreciatively using the first-person plural "we." Rather than ignore it or make a joke about my pretending regal status, he said for all to hear, "Young lady, when I say nice things about you I do not include your future husband."

By the time my father escorted me down the aisle to meet Jack my nerves were wound too tight for me to enjoy the moment. Our attendants were four bridesmaids, four groomsmen, and my seven-year-old cousin Sydney Simons as flower girl. The entire congregation was invited to the ceremony but we had no reception, only dinner at the Standard Club for the wedding party. Mother directed all aspects of the event, ignorant of Jewish mores, disdaining advice, embarrassing Jack with members of the congregation, and stressing me out beyond endurance.

We honeymooned in New York. My first encounter as a rabbi's wife occurred after Shabbat morning services at Temple Emanu-El, going to lunch with Rabbi Nathan Perlman and his wife, Betsy. She arrived late, explaining that she had been delayed at the dressmaker's, which surprised me because I thought that rabbis' wives went only to services on Saturday mornings. Walking with her down Madison Avenue to the restaurant, I told her that I had been raised in a nonobservant family and knew nothing about protocol for a rabbi's wife.

"Don't worry about it," she replied. "I'm not even Jewish."

That wouldn't have surprised me today but it did then, and in any case, it wasn't exactly true. Her family belonged to the Ethical Culture Society in lieu of a synagogue, but in all other respects remained Jewish. Ethical Culture preached that morality can be separate from theology and ritual, but its teachings still closely paralleled what my friends and I learned going to Sunday School at the Temple.

Being the rabbi's wife in my home community had many advantages but posed difficulties as well. The very worst of them for me was trying to embrace Jack's teaching of Judaism—in practice as well as theory— while surrounded by family and friends steeped irreconcilably in Classical

Marriage of Jack and Janice

Reform. In embracing the biblical prophets as sole exemplars of Judaism they ignored all else, effectively throwing away the baby with the bath water, as I often say. We retained very few traditions, in my family's case none at all. Like our counterparts in other southern cities influenced by long-tenured rabbis, we and our parents were taught to seek assimilation in everything other than religion and shun all outward signs of Jewishness as somewhat *déclassée*. I even stumbled when first introducing Jack as "Rabbi" because all the rabbis I had known were called "Doctor," which we thought was the correct, respectful form of address. The only Hebrew anyone learned from attending services was the Sh'ma and the Boruch Hu. As Jack once noted, "Marx's job as he saw it was to turn his Jews into Americans. Now my job is to turn his Americans into Jews."

I was totally unprepared to marry a rabbi, but I wanted to learn. At first I struggled through our Bible—cover to cover, in English (of course) but without guidance, therefore comprehending very little. I didn't think to ask Jack for help, nor did he think to offer. When I asked him for books on Jewish history, because I was a beginner he recommended comprehensive texts that I found boring. Years later I noticed Jacob Marcus' *Early American Jewry* on our shelves and gobbled the two volumes down, hungry for more.

Neither of us recognized the depth of my ignorance. Like a prospective convert, I had no concept of how much more there is to being Jewish than believing in Judaism. This realization came with deep embarrassment when Jack asked me to send a bar mitzvah gift to the son of his close friends in Detroit. Since I had never known anyone who had a bar mitzvah, I selected something I thought a thirteen-year-old boy would want: a pocket knife. I later learned that it was notably inappropriate for the occasion.

Another time, when our children were toddlers, I answered the doorbell to find two men with long black beards, black hats, black knickers and long black coats standing on the stoop. Frightened out of my wits, I bolted the door and ran to the kitchen to be sure that our children and help were safely inside. When I reported the incident to

Jack, he laughed and explained that the men were *shlichim*, messengers from the Holy Land, sent to the diaspora to beg support for particular, usually impoverished *yeshivot* in what is now the State of Israel.

Both of us laughed at what I did on my first Yom Kippur, trying to be considerate of others when I was eight and a half months pregnant and therefore required to eat. Not wanting to bring lunch to the Temple on that day, after the morning service I walked to the drug store, then diagonally across Peachtree at Spring Street, to get a sandwich and a drink at the soda fountain. Neither Jack nor I anticipated that I would find it filled with members of the congregation having lunch there. They appeared to be embarrassed to see me see them.

I desperately needed a mentor, but couldn't turn to my predecessor, Nell Marx, with her husband still loudly denouncing Jack publicly. Lillian Freehof tried to help but, as the childless consort of a world-famous scholar in a large northern city, her experience had little relation to mine as the rapidly pregnant wife of a struggling new rabbi in Atlanta. She told me to wear a hat and gloves at services and Sisterhood meetings, which I already knew. That was *de rigueur* in those days for southern ladies.

At the Central Conference of American Rabbis I soon learned that other young couples endured similar problems with their emeriti. Like Marx, other reluctant retirees were rebelling against the new wave of replacements emerging from chaplaincy service during the war. While our husbands attended plenaries we aggrieved *rebbetzins* played one-upmanship, commiserating about whose emeritus made his successor the most miserable. I always won.

When Jack and I first married, our most pressing problem was finding a place to live. With affordable housing no more available in Atlanta than it had been for me in New York or DC, our only choice was the one-room apartment on the back of my parents' garage. Bud Mantler and another of Mother's "boys" had been living there due to the shortage, but she moved them into what had been my bedroom in the main house so Jack and I could begin our marriage with a modicum of privacy.

Living in my parents' backyard provided little privacy from Mother. Separated from me only by her garden, she tended her plants that winter earlier and more regularly than before, reaching our doorstep each morning just after Jack departed. She and Aunt Sophie appointed themselves mentors of what I should do and wear on special occasions, the correctness of which Jack and I frequently doubted, so I had to rely on my own untested sense of propriety.

I had far more need for formalwear than my Atlanta contemporaries, but thanks to a skilled seamstress who fled Nazi Germany and needed work, I enjoyed the challenge of recycling old worthies and constructing new ones. A smart new friend, Jan Ghertner, taught me to update hats by changing ornaments.

Grandmother Lylah gave me her modest collection of family jewels, which to my knowledge did not raise congregational eyebrows. The small fur shrug that she gave me, however, did draw a hurtful comment. One night when I retrieved it after a party at the Club, the father of one of my childhood friends, standing behind me in the coat check line, said, "I didn't know that preachers' wives wore mink."

Offended and not knowing one luxury fur from another when it came to price, I made matters worse by replying truthfully, "It isn't mink, it's sable."

During our first year of marriage I tried to follow the social patterns of my friends. When asked to join the Service Guild, a socially elite group of women who served hospital patients by delivering mail, books, and gifts to them, I agreed. Peggy Strauss picked me up for my first afternoon on the job and I was happy to bring cheer to the patients on my assigned floor. Several of them asked if we were from some church group, which I realized was a way to ask if were we Jewish. It pleased me to spread good will by replying that we were not sent from a congregation but were a group of Jewish women organized for volunteer service, much as the Junior League was among Christians. When I reported this to Peggy, she said I shouldn't have identified the organization as Jewish. In some circles, there was still discomfort in identifying oneself as Jewish. That ended my association with the Service Guild; I considered fostering good will an important reason for volunteering.

Soon afterward I encountered an even more discouraging aspect of volunteer service. I knew nothing about charities, Jewish or otherwise, when someone asked me to solicit for the Jewish Federation/United Jewish Appeal. It seemed like the right thing to do, so I said yes. The Federation was initiating independent giving among women, and since few young married women had independent means in those days, we were encouraged to contribute by saving a portion of our housekeeping allowances. The three women I was assigned to solicit were lifelong friends whose husbands worked for their hugely successful fathers-in-law. Since Jack had advised me to give $50 from my housekeeping allowance of $600 per year, I expected to have no problem persuading them to raise their previous contribution from $15 to $35 for the year. I was wrong. Each of them declined, giving a lame excuse for not being able to afford more than $15. That discouraged me from direct fundraising. I learned how to help in other ways.

I never succeeded in emulating the purely social activities that appeared to be requisite for all the women of "our crowd," as it was for their mothers and grandmothers as well as the rabbi's wife. Friends invited me to join their weekly afternoons of bridge or Mahjong, although I neither played nor really wanted to learn. However, my sense of duty convinced me to try. That first summer, since I couldn't enjoy swimming at the Club after one of the older women reprimanded me for wearing a bathing suit while noticeably pregnant, I decided it was a good time to take bridge lessons.

After two weeks I gave up in despair, unable to concentrate on the cards. So many more interesting things kept popping into my mind. I fared no better after sitting in on a friend's Mahjong game. When I thanked her, explaining as politely as possible that these pursuits simply weren't for me, she looked seriously troubled on my behalf and asked, "What will you do with your time?"

It didn't take long to find answers. Having two babies within the first two years of marriage plus finding and settling into our first two homes was more than enough to fill my time.

There were, as yet, no female rabbis, and Jack clung to the theory that the congregation only hired one of us, so he never asked me to do anything at the Temple. I knew that rabbis' wives were expected to serve the congregation as volunteers and I wanted to do so, but on my own terms, although at first I didn't have the courage to refuse when the Sisterhood gave me ceremonial jobs like pouring tea. Eventually I found the courage to say no and discovered my niche with creative work such as programs and publicity, not only for the Sisterhood but also for the new Couples' Club that Jack organized. Because I met most of the many Jewish newcomers to Atlanta as soon as they joined the Temple, I readily spotted potential new leaders and recruited them as members of the Sisterhood.

Old-timers expected the rabbi's wife to serve at least one term as president of the Sisterhood as Nell Marx and even her daughter-in-law, Mary Marx, had done. By the time the ladies approached me with that honor I'd gained enough backbone to decline, pointing out that I could serve the Sisterhood better by continuing to do what I was doing. When they pressed further, I reminded them that I was already working on the same level as the president and asked, "Why would you want just one of me when you now have two?"

That worked, but its flip side surfaced when the question arose of who besides the president deserved to be sent to a national conference in New York at the Sisterhood's expense. The Sisterhood never considered me directly; they assumed I'd be going with Jack anyway, acting as a second delegate that could represent them at no additional cost to the organization. Even so, friends knew how much I wanted to go and assured me, "It wouldn't be you. They know you'll continue working just as hard anyway."

The position was opening opportunities for me that I might never have found otherwise. Had it not been for my efforts to help Jack by working with the Sisterhood and the Couples' Club, I might never have discovered I had talent for writing musical parodies and eventually more serious dramatic pieces for stage, radio and television. My first Sisterhood production, a parody on Gilbert & Sullivan entitled *Trial By Jewry*, launched me on a series of wider opportunities within the Jewish community. After seeing the show, Hildegarde Bennet, a professional dancer and choreographer, asked me to partner with her to help write a benefit production she was hired to present for B'nai B'rith. Our partnership continued for years, during which she was commissioned to produce similar shows for the National Council of Jewish Women. We did so well together that friends called us Atlanta's answer to Rodgers and Hammerstein.

During those years I was also writing serious pieces for Sisterhood programs that I produced and directed myself. That became problematic when Jack asked me to restage one of them for services on Sisterhood Sabbath. At one rehearsal, adapting the original staging to suit the larger space of the sanctuary involved my giving a direction with which some of the performers disagreed. When I stood firm, one woman sweetly suggested that we take a vote on it.

I knew from training and experience that it was unheard of for anyone to question a director's instruction during rehearsal. Flabbergasted, I tried to stay cool and asked "Would you have made a suggestion like that to Hildegarde?"

"That's different," came the reply. "She's a professional."

That was the last time this amateur directed a show at the Temple. I continued to write them on request but thereafter the Sisterhood had to pay a professional to direct and produce. I had found my voice and was determined never to suffer the same insult twice.

Being a *rebbetzin* in my hometown and in the congregation where I grew up was advantageous in that I knew all the old families and was accustomed to socializing with them. It was a disadvantage in other respects, however. Because they knew me, friends with complaints about the rabbi brought their "friendly suggestions" to me rather than to him. A primary example was when the same dear friend who suggested we take a vote on my stage directions advised me to tell Jack that it didn't look nice for him to play golf at the club on Saturday afternoon. I didn't have the nerve to ask her how that differed from her husband, president of the congregation, playing tennis there on Saturday, nor did I remind her that Reform Judaism doesn't forbid leisure activities on Shabbat. I just smiled and said, "Thanks."

My worst encounters of this kind came at Christmas. Our closest friends threw an annual Christmas Eve party that Jack enjoyed but I did not. While he pleasantly chatted over a scotch and soda, old friends pulled me aside to ask why he insisted on preaching that Jews shouldn't celebrate Christmas. I was made miserable because I was forcing myself to deny something that I still missed, whereas he could relax and enjoy socializing because it had no meaning for him personally and he spoke of it as a teacher, not an enforcer.

I always enjoyed entertaining and regretted that Jack's schedule as well as his position circumscribed our ability to do very much of the spontaneous personal variety. As soon as we had a home we began holding open house receptions for the congregation on Rosh Hashanah afternoon, the first of which we had catered. Thereafter I prepared the food, beginning during the summer and freezing much of it. At the Central Conference of American Rabbis (CCAR) one year, Rebecca Brickner, wife of Cleveland's distinguished Rabbi Barnett Brickner, offered us newly-minted *rebbetzins* a session on how to conduct these High Holyday receptions in our homes. We expected clues on minimizing expenses and perhaps even a recipe or two for those of us who couldn't regularly afford a caterer, but that didn't happen. It's still a joke among those of us who survive that Becky's primary advice was to station the butler at the door and hold our receiving line in the parlor rather than the foyer.

Having no butler, Jack and I stationed ourselves at the door and relied on our wonderful friend Jan Ghertner to ensure the platters were refilled. The reception was our only means of reciprocating for all of the elaborate dinner parties and cocktail suppers that we attended throughout the year. To our dismay, most of the friends who invited us to those very shindigs greeted us after the Rosh Hashanah morning service saying, "We won't be there this afternoon. We can see you any time."

When we first married, I was uncomfortable conversing with dignitaries. Our first official guests, just a few weeks after we married, were Rabbi Maurice Eisendrath, president of the UAHC (Union of American Hebrew Congregations, now the URJ, Union of Reform Judaism) and his wife, Rosa. They were close friends of Jack's but were much older and thus intimidating to me. When left alone with Rosa, she did her best to put me at ease and gradually succeeded. I didn't do as well during that same period when seated on the dais at a public dinner next to Dr. Philip Weltner, president of Oglethorpe University, although he was very nice. I thought of this encounter years later when seated on a dais next to his son, Congressman Charles Weltner; I was engrossed throughout the entire dinner arguing with him about the Vietnam War.

I obviously overcame the problem of conversing with dignitaries. I delighted in having guest speakers at home with us for Shabbat dinner before services. When Archbishop Paul Hallinan came, although I had never served fish because Jack didn't like it, I observed the Catholic "no meat on Friday" rule and prepared baked salmon. We used the occasion to play him the recording we had brought back from New York of political satirist Tom Lehrer performing "Vatican Rag," his somewhat sacrilegious fun-poking at Catholicism. The archbishop roared with laughter, as we knew he would. Many years later, I would learn that the current Pope also thought highly of him and intended to make him a cardinal.

Rabbi Eugene Mihaly spoke at Temple on February 23, 1962, the same evening that Isaac Stern soloed with the Atlanta Symphony Orchestra. On the way back to our house after services, Mihaly asked if we knew where the after-concert party for Stern was being held. I did, but the hosts were Temple members and I didn't want the rabbi to make trouble by spiriting Stern away to our house. Mihaly promised not to embarrass us so I dialed the number for him, handed him the receiver, and was still within hearing distance when Mihaly, with a clipped British accent, announced, "London calling for Isaac Stern."

The next thing I heard was Mihaly, in a distinctly Jewish accent, exclaiming, "Yitzhak! How are you?"

Not long after that our front doorbell rang, and upon answering it I beheld a man with a big smile on his face, a violin case under his arm, and a bewildered-looking young couple standing behind him. They were the symphony's business manager and his wife, the artist's caretakers for the evening. I had hardly served the coffee (or whatever) when I found everyone sprawled out on our living room floor telling jokes, Stern leading with the same flawless grasp of various ethnic accents as he exhibited musically on his Strad. His White Russian was as authentic as his Russian Jewish, not to mention his French, Spanish, German, and Chinese. Around midnight his escorts were getting nervous about relieving their babysitter but Mr. Stern wanted to stay. We assured them we would take good care of him and they left. It was after 2AM by the time Stern and Mihaly were ready for Jack to drive them to their hotel.

The next morning, while gathering glasses and emptying ash trays, I found a gold cigarette case inscribed "to Isaac from Vera" laying on the floor. I took it to The Biltmore, hesitant to disturb Stern after such a late night but afraid to leave the valuable item with a hotel clerk. Finally, I gathered the courage to call Stern's room, took a deep breath when he answered, and squeaked, "Good Shabbes, Mr. Stern. This is. . ."

"The rebbetzin!" he exclaimed, exuberant as ever. He said he had been answering correspondence with the help of the symphony's secretary but was ready to stop and asked me to wait a half hour before coming up to his suite with the cigarette case. I did, and found him still in his pajamas surrounded by piles of papers the secretary was trying to remove in orderly fashion.

"I've decided not to go to Washington until tomorrow," Stern announced. "It's a beautiful day. If you're not busy, I'd like to see Atlanta in your convertible with the top down."

It was indeed a beautiful day for February: bright, brisk, and very cold. Like Tu B'Shevat in Jerusalem, appropriately "the birthday of the trees" because their budding indicates that spring is coming—eventually, not this afternoon. In Atlanta, it was no day to drive with the top down unless someone of Stern's magnitude asked for it.

He turned on the TV and told me to make myself at home while he showered and dressed. During that time a call came in from Marta Casals, Pablo Casals' wife, in Puerto Rico. She opted to hold while Stern finished dressing. When he came out he took the call in the living room and planned the next Casals Festival with her in my presence.

John Glenn had just orbited the earth, the first American to do so, and thinking of it gave me a parallel to my own sensation of being in orbit as I drove the man known as the world's greatest living violinist through Atlanta's lovely residential area now known as Buckhead. Isaac Stern was a delightful companion. Eventually I could no longer resist asking him about his televised friendship with Jack Benny, who made jokes about his own prowess on the violin. "Since last night I know what a talented comedian you are," I said, and then asked, "Is Benny that good a violinist?"

Stern said yes. He considered Jack Benny an accomplished violinist.

When we tired of driving, I pulled into our turnaround and brought Stern indoors to warm up. While I was making tea, he spotted my daughter Marcia's half-finished jigsaw puzzle on the family room coffee table. She thought she was hallucinating when she walked in and saw him working it.

Jack was equally surprised when he returned. Stern wanted to take us to dinner but Jack had to conduct a wedding at dinner time, so he jokingly suggested that Stern come with him, provide the music, and *then* go to dinner. Stern had a better idea. A movie he wanted to see about a Coca-Cola executive in London was playing downtown. He suggested taking me there and then meeting Jack for dinner at Fan & Bill's, to which Jack agreed. The establishment already knew what Stern wanted to eat and brought him a rare steak with head lettuce and Roquefort dressing. That concluded an unforgettable weekend.

Raising the rabbi's children presented the greatest challenge for rabbis' wives in those days. Fathers had little free time, mothers were also frequently away, and parents rarely took their children with them socially as they do today. Jack and I took few family vacations. The biggest problem for *rabbinikinder*, however, was that they were stereotyped the same as their parents.

When our children were babies, Jack and I were blessed with a wise, loving Afro-American housekeeper, Mattie Greer, who had worked in Atlanta households, both Jewish and Christian, since she was a child herself. She knew more than I did, not only about cooking and childcare, but also about members of the congregation. One day, shortly before Bill was born, she voiced her hope that the expected baby would be female. I told her, "We already have a beautiful daughter. Now we'd like to have a son, too."

She disagreed, saying, "It don't matter whether they's white, black, Jew or Gentile, the preacher's son is always the worst child on the block. Just look at that David Marx Jr."

David was a grandfather himself by that time, but the gossip endured.

Because I was unsure as a mother, I consulted a child psychiatrist. When I said we understood the pressures put on clergy kids and before ours were born had agreed not to make them behave as examples for others, the doctor smiled and said, "There's where the problem starts. Do you think the grocer and his wife have a conversation like that when they are expecting their first child?"

We soon learned that no matter how we guided our children, we had no control over what happened away from home. When a camp counselor told me that Bill misbehaved and I, agreeing that he should be disciplined, asked what had been done at the time, the counselor replied, "I told him that the rabbi's son, of all people, should know better."

I asked the same question of Bill's fourth grade teacher, who complained that she couldn't keep him from talking during lunchtime (a pleasure forbidden because the overcrowded public school needed to clear its cafeteria for the next shift). Her hardly-reassuring reply was, "Oh yes. I told him that if he didn't behave properly he would have to eat in the kitchen with the colored people."

Having to choose between speaking up for the good of humanity or remaining silent for the immediate good of my children, I remained silent.

Another challenge, though hardly unique to the children of rabbis, was that faced by Jewish families each December. The logical defense for Jews in a sea of Christianity was to emphasize our own religious holidays, which we feared we had overdone when Marcia's kindergarten teacher called us to delightedly report our daughter's response to the question of what each child knew about Thanksgiving. Marcia replied, "We don't have Thanksgiving. We're Jewish. We have Hanukkah."

Determined that our children would never suspect how much I missed my own childhood Christmas, I sought ways to make them enjoy Hanukkah that were not yet known to us in the South. When Marcia, age four, came home from a friend's house one December day saying she wished we were Christian so she could have a sugarplum tree, I thought quickly and asked her if a sugarplum menorah would do. She said yes, so I had to figure out how to make one. Candy manufacturers hadn't yet found a Jewish market in Atlanta. I was never handy with crafts, but necessity fueled invention. I connected large gumdrops with toothpicks for the base, strung small ones onto toothpicks for candles, and topped them with corn candies for flames.

Remembering the beautiful Christmas afternoons of my childhood with the Bickerstaffs' in Columbus, I wanted our children to experience the joy of personal giving by preparing small gifts appropriate for Hanukkah. Again, I had to invent. I bought eight miniature toys (party favors, really) for each of the children's neighborhood friends and, together with Marcia and Bill, assembled them, wrapped each collection in a brightly colored kerchief, placed it in a basket, and walked the children through the neighborhood to deliver them.

My greatest challenge as mother of the rabbi's children occurred when the Temple was bombed (which I'll more fully detail in the next chapter). It was October 12, 1958, the day before Marcia's eleventh birthday. Overwhelming expressions of public support bolstered confidence throughout the Jewish community, especially among Temple families still fearful of anti-Semitism even 43 years after the lynching of Leo Frank. The bombing drew Jack prominently into the news and spotlighted our family. Both of us received threats on our lives.

I never worried about my own safety and I had become accustomed to worrying about Jack's because I knew the danger was open-ended, but now it involved our children. Marcia received unprecedented public attention after news reached the press about her birthday being the day after the bombing, and ten-year-old Bill also had the unprecedented delight of having a police officer in a squad car guarding his driveway. Both situations were so abnormal that I foresaw the possibility of emotional damage and again consulted a child psychiatrist on how to avoid it.

"I can't predict what might happen to your children physically if you dismiss the police," he said. "But I can certainly tell you what will happen to them emotionally if you don't."

I immediately followed his advice, but that afternoon Bill failed to come home from school as expected. I almost collapsed worrying about him. Close to sundown he returned, thoroughly bewildered by his mother's hysteria. He had simply forgotten to call and tell me he was going home with a friend.

Members of the congregation expressed surprise that I appeared calm throughout the ordeal and didn't temporarily leave town with our children as I was told many Temple families did after the Leo Frank lynching. Nothing could have been further from my mind then, but a few years later, when public schools were likely to be closed to avoid desegregation, I drew on my laurels to prevail in my argument with Jack about sending our children to a private school. Previously I had agreed with him on wanting them to have a public school education as we had, even when the quality of that education diminished and my grandmother begged us to send them to a private school at her expense. Now I agreed with Grandmother. Jack did not.

Private schools were already turning away applicants for the following year so I was well aware that people would resent Jack's gaining admission for his children where theirs had been refused, and that some would criticize him for sending his children to Westminster, openly billed as a Christian preparatory school. With no progressive Jewish day school yet in Atlanta, many Temple children had attended Westminster with excellent results and no Jewish problem, so we had no fear on those grounds. It was the best and I insisted. When Jack still refused, I invoked the memory of our traumatic days after the bombing and the effect on our children. "They didn't ask for the life we've given them," I reminded Jack. "They didn't ask for a father who rushed away from the dinner table most nights to go to a meeting, who had to curtail family vacations to rush home to conduct a funeral. They didn't ask for any of the abnormal situations we've put them in. The least we can do is give them a good education."

When he didn't reply, I took a deep breath and softly but firmly said, "People expected me to be hysterical when the Temple was bombed. I wasn't then, but I'm going to be hysterical now if you don't call Dr. Pressley *tomorrow!*"

I had never spoken to him like that before and never did again. He met with Westminster headmaster Dr. William Pressley the next day. Both of our children were admitted to the school, and I never regretted taking a "damn the torpedoes" stance on matters concerning our children.

Being the rabbi's wife involved me in community activities, which I enjoyed, but would probably have avoided had they not been thrust upon me. In 1969, when I was asked to head the Women's Campaign for Israel Bonds, I agreed on condition that Atlanta's other *rebbetzins* serve as co-chairs—not due to a sudden burst of humility, but because there was not yet enough interest in Israel among Temple members to support the event. The women's division for Bonds customarily featured a fashion show highlighting start-up Israeli businesses supported by proceeds from the Bonds. That year, when I assembled the co-chairs at our home for a planning session, it was the first time that *rebbetzins* of all the Atlanta synagogues had met since 1947, when the others came to call on me after Marcia was born. Our togetherness was as significant to me as the event's success, which won me an award from the Israeli government.

Another time my role as the rabbi's wife led to a unique experience was during the early 1970s, when national Jewish women's organizations took turns sponsoring annual protest demonstrations against the Soviet Union on behalf of Soviet Jewish prisoners of conscience. When the National Federation of Temple Sisterhoods (now the Women of Reform Judaism) sponsored it and Dorothy Hamburger, as Sisterhood president, oversaw the Atlanta event, she asked me, as the rabbi's wife, to co-chair it with her. We invited Betty Talmadge, wife of Georgia Senator Herman Talmadge, to be Honorary Chairwoman, and leaders of our parallel Christian women's organizations as honorary co-chairs, asking only that they solicit signatures from their constituents throughout Georgia petitioning the Soviet government to cease its persecution of Soviet Jews. The program, held in the Temple sanctuary, featured the Spelman College choir singing spirituals echoing the call for freedom and concluded with the Christian co-chairwomen carrying baskets overflowing with their signed petitions down the aisles to place them on the *bimah*. Betty took them to Washington, where I joined her the following day to deliver them to the Soviet embassy.

As a publicity visual for the program, we had presented each honorary chairperson with a protest pendant like we wore, a Jewish Star bearing the name of a Soviet Jewish prisoner of conscience. When Betty and I met as planned, on 16th Street across from the old Soviet embassy at noon with the B'nai B'rith sponsored daily protest vigil, we wore our protest pendants. Mine, on that brisk windy December day, was hidden beneath an overcoat and muffler. Betty's Jewish star, her coat open and flapping in the breeze, was clearly visible and thus pictured on the front page of Atlanta newspapers the following day.

We knew, as did the press, that our petitions would not be accepted. Senator Talmadge's office had contacted the embassy asking Ambassador

Anatoly Dobrynin to receive us and the answer was "Nyet." He then requested that Mrs. Dobrynin receive us and was told that she would see Mrs. Talmadge but not Mrs. Rothschild. Betty wouldn't accept that, so we simply stood across 16th Street with the crowd for the fifteen-minute silent vigil, then walked across the street with our petitions, sought admittance at the embassy gate, and, on being refused entry, placed them on the pavement and departed. Betty took me to the Capitol, where we warmed up in the Senate Dining Room with a bowl of its famous bean soup.

Exciting as that was for me, the incident didn't end there. The following year, 1973, when a different organization sponsored the rally in a park downtown, Betty again came from Washington to attend. She and I were then working on a projected interfaith/interracial women's tour to Israel, and planned to discuss it over lunch after the rally. When a state politician died the night before, she needed to pay a condolence call before returning to Washington. Georgia's First Lady, Rosalyn Carter, also at the rally and obligated to call, suggested that I stay with them, wait with the driver and Secret Service agent while she and Betty made a quick visit, and then proceed with our plan. The bereaved family, unprepared to receive, asked them to come back in half an hour, so Rosalyn suggested that we use the time to get lunch at the Varsity drive-in nearby, which we did, and I drove Betty to the airport on schedule, discussing our project en route.

That night, my lifelong friend Bob Lipshutz, then president of the Temple and friend of the Carters, stopped by our house to discuss something with Jack before going to the Governor's Mansion around the corner. Jack, thinking the story would interest Bob, asked me, "Where did you take your famous guest for lunch today?"

"I didn't," I said, and explained. "The state of Georgia took both of us to lunch at the Varsity."

Jack laughed. Bob smiled knowingly and announced, "Janice, you may have had lunch today with the next First Lady of our land."

Who knew? "Oh, Bob," I pooh-poohed. "Herman's too old to run and couldn't win if he did."

So much for my political savvy. But two thumbs up for unexpected benefits that evolve for the wife of a rabbi.

Rabbis' wives come in all shapes, sizes, and temperaments. Among those of my generation and older, some had wanted to become rabbis themselves but were born too soon to fulfill that dream. As a result, they shadowed (and in some cases *over*shadowed) their husbands as unpaid, largely unappreciated adjuncts. Others, like Betsy Pearlman, whom I met on my honeymoon in New York, rejected all vestiges of the role. It's surely no life for the faint-hearted or thin-skinned.

One needs a sense of humor to survive. Mine was sadly lacking, but Jack helped develop it by goading as well as by example, which saved us from many difficult situations. I've recorded the best of them in *One Voice*, my book about him. I especially appreciated his response to the repeated middle-of-the-night phone calls that kept us awake during one period of the civil rights struggle. Roy Harris, a segregationist state politician from Augusta, suggested that form of heckling. Eventually Jack found the Harris's telephone number and the next time we were awakened by an anonymous call at 3:00 AM he dialed it, cheerfully telling the man who answered, "Hi, Roy. Just wanted to let you know your boys are doing their job."

We received no more anonymous phone calls.

Another annoyance that is not unique among rabbis and their wives is having some people stop speaking to them without ever learning the reason why. When two women who, with their husbands, had initially been good friends and social buddies to Jack were no longer speaking to him, others noticed and asked him what happened. He didn't know but ventured the guess, "I suppose it's because every time they see me it reminds them that they're Jewish."

By not-so-odd coincidence, one of those women was the prototype for the social climbing daughter-in-law in Alfred Urhy's award-winning classic *Driving Miss Daisy*.

Rabbis, and sometimes rabbis' wives, occasionally receive verbal darts that are intended to be compliments and can provide a good laugh if identified as such. I received one in Pittsburgh after a talk Jack gave there some months after the Temple bombing. Most people believed our synagogue was targeted because of his outspokenness on civil rights. As we were leaving the dais, a woman approached me to recall admiringly that she had been in Atlanta visiting her son on the Yom Kippur just before the bombing and thought Jack's sermon advocating social justice "...was wonderful." Then she added, "Although my son said he should have kept his damned mouth shut."

It isn't always easy to keep a straight face on receiving such compliments, and it's even more difficult when the message is embellished with a malapropism. Once after conducting a funeral, Jack was embraced appreciatively and told, "Rabbi, that was a beautiful urology."

My best example personally came from the father of a bride as I stood with him outside the chapel watching ushers escort the handful of guests to their seats with great formality for what was to be a very small, intimate wedding. At a loss for conversation, I complimented him on maintaining the beauty of traditional formality even when not required to do so. Obviously pleased, he replied, "My wife deserves all the credit. Before the ceremony she laid out a diaphragm for every guest."

My years as a *rebbetzin* were on the cusp of women's liberation, a time when we appreciated the advice of Gloria Steinem and Betty Friedan but were not yet ready to follow it. We needed a passion for doing something outside the congregation but seldom knew where to find it. We needed to establish our own identity. (So did everyone, but clergy wives probably met more impediments than most.)

Writing rescued me. After reading Jacob Marcus' books on American Jewish history I became increasingly interested and wanted to interpret it for my contemporaries who were unlikely to seek the knowledge for themselves. In 1955, with the Temple Sisterhood as captive audience and the 300th anniversary of Jewish settlement in America to be observed, I wrote and produced a pageant about Jewish women in America from colonial times to the present. That led Jack to ask me to write our congregation's hundred-year history, due for anniversary celebration in 1967.

Unprepared though I was, I took the challenge. I began by
questioning Dr. Marcus himself one day at the old Edgewater Beach
Hotel in Chicago. As Jack and I walked with him to a session of the
CCAR's annual convention held there, I asked, "Do you have some sort
of tutorial that I could study?"

He said yes and that he would send it to me, then smiled, patted me
on the head, and told Jack, "Encourage her, my boy. It will keep her out of
trouble."

I wasn't yet liberated enough to resent it.

In 1972, Malcolm Stern invited me to give a paper on early Atlanta
Jewry at the annual conference of the American Jewish Historical
Society. I was thrilled to be asked to speak to historians, and not a little
intimidated. With only a few weeks to prepare, I was further challenged
by Malcolm's instruction to use only material not published in my book
on Temple history, which left very little of interest to include. Mother,
after reading the paper, intimidated me further by asking, "What are you
going to wear?"

It had been decades since she and Aunt Sophie tried to advise me on
clothes. When I asked why she asked me that, she said, "Because this is so
dull. I hope you look pretty."

My confidence plummeted further upon arriving in Richmond for
the conference. As I edged through the crowd already seated for Shabbat
lunch at Temple Beth Ahabah, friends greeted me asking, "Where's Jack?
We're looking forward to hearing his paper tomorrow."

His paper? In those days married women were not listed in print
with their given names. Friends hadn't noticed the "Mrs." before "Jacob
Rothschild" on the conference program.

That same year, the CCAR commissioned Dr. Theodore Lenn and
his associates to compile a report on the state of the Reform rabbinate.
The rabbis asked me to write a critique of the report's section on the
rabbi's wife for the CCAR Journal, and I did not give it a good review. In
my opinion, the failure to provide a breakdown on the age of respondents
nullified the conclusions. I wrote:

"After twenty-five years of attending CCAR hen sessions, I see an entirely new ball game in *rebbetzinville* than the one I entered. Our generation formed relationships and habits before women's lib, traffic conditions, mobile society, and the disappearance of domestic help changed almost everyone's way of life."

Friends often asked me how I tolerated the life of a rabbi's wife. Firstly, Jack was no ordinary rabbi. I doubt that I could have remained married to any other, even the one who, in our old age, became the crowning love of my life. Jack, self-assured and independent, did not need me to help him succeed. He applauded my activities outside the congregation, even when performing with Theatre Atlanta required me to be onstage rather than at services on Friday nights.

Now in the 21st century when our lives have changed so much more, it may be impossible to visualize the life of an average, well-meaning, reasonably intelligent "wife of" in those days, regardless of her husband's profession. As to my own experience, which was by no means pure joy, I must clearly state that it contained some wonderful moments and, from what I could see of others, it ranked far above average. I recognized my good fortune in being married to a man of rock-solid integrity, extraordinary courage and foresight, and I savored the privilege of being with him in the vortex of historical change.

I also realized that the unjustified assessment, "But you don't look like one" also implied "But you don't act like one," both concepts of which now (hopefully) lay buried in a dusty archive. Our daughters may be rabbis themselves as well as wives of rabbis—indeed, spouses of rabbis of *either* gender—with roles unique to their own vision and ability.

Nevertheless, generations of us walked the line trying to please everyone, frequently on a very small budget. I gained insight into the rarity, if not uniqueness, of our situation in the 1970s when I was invited, along with the wives of other prominent Atlanta men, to teach a session on the "The Life of the Wife" for Emory University's Continuing Education series. Assembled for a briefing session beforehand, the wife of a department store CEO told us how she managed on a small budget when her husband was an assistant buyer. The university president's wife had a similar story about her early years of marriage when her husband was an assistant professor. The mayor's wife recalled an equally stringent budget when her husband began his legal career. None of them reported the demands and public scrutiny the other clergy wife and I experienced when our husbands were young, poorly paid, and *not* obscure.

In 1950, *American Judaism* published a breast-beating complaint, "Heaven Help the Rabbi's Wife," anonymously signed "A. Rebbitzin." I rushed to rebuttal, refuting her inference that we cornered the market on *tsuris*, asserting that we are not the only ones who live in the proverbial fishbowl. I conceded that people expected us to be role models, and while noting that it was natural for any wife to want to promote her husband's work, I admitted that was easier done for some professions than for others. Obviously, a retailer's wife enjoys modeling designer clothes more than *rebbetzins* enjoy exemplifying ethical precepts. Now the world has changed and the "life of the wife"—even the rabbi's wife—is acknowledged as her own. As for mine, I welcomed opportunities.

Four

CIVIL RIGHTS (THE KINGS AND I)

L iving at the center of positive change was a treasured privilege. I am sometimes credited with heroism as a civil rights activist but that is a flattering misconception. My role was a minor one, mostly supportive, not proactive, and in no way heroic because I never felt a need to invoke courage.

Another often heard but mistaken belief is that the Temple bombing on October 12, 1958 was largely motivated by Jack's friendship with Martin Luther King, Jr. That was clearly impossible because the men did not know each other when the Temple was bombed. It happened more than a year before the Kings moved to Atlanta.

It was shortly after seven on a Sunday morning when the telephone call awakened us and Jack scurried to my side of the bed to answer. After a long, horrified "Oh, no!" followed by a quick "I'll be right there," he put down the receiver, turned to me and said, "The Temple's been bombed."

Robert Benton, the Temple's long-time custodian, wept as he reported the news. He discovered the damage when he opened the building to prepare for Religious School. Dynamite placed against a door on the north side of the building detonated inward, trashing everything in its path. A massive steel vault in an office on the right periphery of the blast protected the sanctuary and rabbi's study.

Jack told me as he grabbed a sport shirt left out from the night before. I sat upright in bed watching, trying to focus. As he buttoned his shirt I heard myself say, "Wear a coat and tie. There may be reporters."

It was completely out of character.

"Don't be ridiculous," he shouted from the bathroom. "This is an emergency, not a fashion show."

Nevertheless, he changed into a dress shirt and tie and reached for a jacket as he raced out the door, calling back instructions for me to stay home and field telephone calls.

I began calling friends to stop them from bringing their children to Sunday School. Our own children, awakened by the noise, came into the room indicating that they needed attention. I told them what happened and sent them off on their bicycles to inform Temple families nearby.

The news spread quickly. Atlanta Mayor William B. Hartsfield heard it on his car radio on the way to church and had his driver change course to take him to the Temple. He gave reporters the forthright response that turned the near tragedy into a mitzvah and incidentally justified my directive to Jack about being properly dressed. The next morning, the front page of a New York newspaper with heavily Jewish circulation showed a picture of Jack and the mayor, captioned "Mayor Hartsfield and the hatless rabbi."

President Dwight Eisenhower learned of it later that morning at a largely Jewish political rally and ordered the FBI to investigate. That expanded our local mitzvah into a national one because multiple incidents of violence against minority institutions and their leaders had previously been ignored by the federal government.

Our telephone rang without pause. I couldn't leave it even long enough to get a cup of coffee. A friend picked up Bill to spend the day with her son and Julie Weiss came with her seven-year-old son Mike to help me. Bud Weiss, her husband and vice president of the congregation as well as president of the Jewish Community Council, rushed to the

Temple. Still on automatic, I canceled my next day's early morning hair appointment and arranged for someone to pick up the sandwiches I'd made for Monday's opening night reception at Theatre Atlanta. Julie fielded phone calls that afternoon while I drove Marcia to her class at the JCC. Instinctively, I felt the need to continue our lives as normally as possible. So did Jack, and he made that a prime consideration for the Temple as well as for us personally.

With the phone ringing constantly, Julie heated leftovers for our supper as I continued to answer, endlessly repeating, "Thank you. We appreciate your concern..."

She had just put the warmed-over spaghetti on the table for herself and the kids and handed me a plate when a call came that was unlike all the others. A man's voice said, "I'm one of them that bombed your church, and I'm callin' to tell you there's a bomb under your house and it's lit and you've got five minutes to get out."

Benumbed, I replied "Thank you," and hung up.

Julie asked, "What was that?"

Without thinking of the children or of Julie being five months pregnant, I automatically repeated what I'd heard. The next thing I knew, they were in the woods above our garden yelling for me to get out of the house. I stood at the door dazed, wondering whether to save my violin or my fur coat. Logic told me the call was a hoax but I couldn't risk being wrong.

I called Jack from our neighbor's house. He soon arrived with Bud, the police, and FBI agents. Marcia, additionally excited because the next day would be her eleventh birthday, burst into unstoppable tears. I called my mother to help. She came expecting to take the children home with her but Marcia continued to cry and wouldn't go. After the police checked and assured us there was no bomb, I got on my knees and eye-balled Marcia, repeating that we were safe and we wanted her to go with her grandmother only because she needed to sleep undisturbed by the telephone.

"You have school tomorrow," I reminded her. "You know how

the phone has been ringing all day. It will probably continue all night. People from all over the world are concerned about what happened. Even President Eisenhower interrupted his speech to say…"

At that she stopped crying and announced, "If he'd interrupted his golf game it would have really been something."

That sent all of us into laughter and she agreed to leave, but not to spend the night at her grandmother's house. She would go no farther than our next-door neighbor's, where she could keep an eye on us.

I had already arranged for Bill to stay with his friend overnight, so we were free to go with Julie and Bud for hamburgers at the Seven Steers in Buckhead. By then it was ten o'clock and we were too tired for conversation. I looked around at the other people still there, wondering if anyone of them hated us enough to have set the bomb.

At home later we called Jack's mother in Pittsburgh to assure her we were safe and returned the calls that had come in. Jack poured a scotch for himself and a bourbon for me and we tried to relax. We were sitting in our family room sipping them when we saw on the other side of the jalousie door a strange man in mountain gear with a rifle on his shoulder. Realizing he had startled us, he explained that he was a special police agent, out of uniform because he came directly from the North Georgia mountains after being called off his vacation to guard us overnight.

Finally, we went to bed. I lay awake wondering if we would wake up the next morning, and realized that Jack must have dealt with such thoughts each night when he was in combat on Guadalcanal.

Suddenly, the telephone rang. I grabbed it, hoping it wouldn't awaken him. The caller, a reporter from New York, insisted on speaking to him. I whispered that he was asleep after a rough day and I didn't want to disturb him. The reporter persisted, as did I. Finally, Jack despaired of sleep and reached across me for the telephone.

The reporter's first words were, "Was that Mrs. Rothschild I was talking to?"

Now thoroughly awake, Jack growled, "If it *wasn't* Mrs. Rothschild, do you really think I'd tell you?"

The next day, because our housekeeper was afraid to stay alone at night with the children, Jack moved his evening meeting from the Temple to our house so that I could represent both of us at a PTA board meeting.

The following week Jack had to be out of town for two days so we agreed that a police patrol should guard our house overnight, but only from 9 p.m. to 6 a.m. so the children wouldn't be aware of it. A friend from Theatre Atlanta spent the evening with me rehearsing scenes from *Anne of the Thousand Days*, for which both of us planned to audition. Sitting close together with only one script, we were reading aloud a flirtatious dialogue between Anne Boleyn and the Duke of Northumberland when we noticed a police officer staring at us just outside our jalousie door. I tried to explain, but he looked doubtful. Lesbian relationships were frowned upon in Georgia.

Both incidents played into the hand of Reuben Garland, the attorney who successfully defended George Bright, the accused bomber, in his second trial. In the first, which ended with a hung jury, Jack and I were called as witnesses for the prosecution and were not troubled by cross-examination. In the second trial Garland grilled me unmercifully, eventually driving me to the point of tears and convincing the judge to call a recess.

Long after the trial I learned why. When the FBI first questioned me about the caller, I had replied that he sounded as if he came from middle Georgia and was poorly educated. Jack explained that acting was my hobby and I could recognize regional accents. Ten days later, the FBI asked me to listen to tapes of the five men indicted for the crime reading transcripts of calls that I and others had received that evening, hoping to get a confession if I correctly identified the man who called me. I succeeded but was not made aware of it. I also didn't know that the man confessed but later recanted, so I couldn't understand why Reuben Garland went to such lengths to discredit my testimony. He pelted me with convoluted questions loaded with false statements, misleading implications, and deprecating asides, typically so twisted that I couldn't give a concise answer. An example that stands out in my memory began,

"Now Mrs. Rothschild, when you left your mansion on Arden Road and got into your Cadillac limousine to drive to the FBI headquarters…"

I forget the core of that query but remember clearly that I replied, "Mr. Garland, I don't live in a mansion as you do, and I drive a *Ford*, not a luxury limousine. Now, what was your question?"

Eventually Garland turned from trying to smear me as a capitalist to what he apparently intended as a reflection on my moral character, peppering his questions with references to my "career" on the stage. I had a minor role in *Anne of the Thousand Days*, which was playing then. Each time Garland suggested archly that I was an "actress," I demurred and added some mitigating detail such as having majored in theater arts at the University of Georgia or that I volunteered for Theatre Atlanta because the city needed a resident theater. Finally, he blurted out angrily, "But you do consider yourself an actress, do you not?"

I certainly did at that point, but I wouldn't admit it to him. As demurely as possible, I drawled, "Why, Mr. Garland! That's not for me to say."

He didn't give up easily. Now he recalled my alleged ability to identify regional accents, grilled me about the telephone call, and asked me to imitate the accent. Presiding Judge Jeptha Tanksley said I wasn't required to comply, so I didn't.

"Why not?" asked Garland, gleefully anticipating the kill.

"Because it isn't dignified," I said.

"Oh?" he responded with feigned surprise. "You put your dignity above the life of my poor, innocent client?"

A divine hand must have been holding cue cards for me. I could never have thought of those answers on my own.

"No, Mr. Garland," I replied. "I meant the dignity of the court."

After ninety minutes Garland succeeded in driving me to the breaking point with a seemingly innocuous question that caused me to think of how the event had affected our children. I choked with emotion and the floodgates opened. Judge Tanksley excused me, directing his clerk to take me to his chambers. The afternoon paper carried the news as its front page lead, captioned "Rabbi's Wife Ties Griffin to Threat." When my mother saw it she spilled a pot of hot coffee on her arm and was painfully burned.

Since Garland kept witnesses out of the courtroom except when testifying, Jack and I came in separate cars and he departed when he was dismissed. As I was whisked down the hall to the judge's chambers, reporters told me, "The Rabbi had to go. He said you'd know where he went."

Indeed, I did know. It was Wednesday. He teed off at one o'clock. It was then two minutes to one. He had abandoned me for his golf game.

I accepted the clerk's offer to get me a Coca-Cola, hoping that the machine was far enough away for me to reach Jack before she returned. I didn't want to demean him by letting anyone else hear what I was about to say. The locker room attendant caught him as he placed his tee. I heard the clerk's heel-clicks intensify. There was time enough only to blurt out my fury and hang up.

Jack, based on his own experience and our treatment in the first trial, had no idea why I was so angry. He rushed back to the courthouse. By the time he arrived, I was gone. The reporters filled him in and he hurried home.

That night at the theater our director caught me between acts to say that Jack asked him to follow me home after the show. When I arrived, I learned that our housekeeper had called Jack home from his meeting to report an anonymous call saying, "You tell Mrs. Rothschild that she identified the wrong man, and she'll pay for it."

She had waited until the children were in bed so they wouldn't overhear. Garland had publicly identified my car during his questioning, its description was carried on the evening news, and it was a sitting duck in the theater parking lot.

The trial was still in progress on Saturday morning when I took Marcia to the theater for children's tryouts and received the summons to reappear in court immediately. The police picked me up, assuring me that I would be free to return in time for the matinee at two o'clock. I waited outside the courtroom along with most of the Southeastern law enforcement, also held on call by Garland. At ten after two, just as the curtain went up at Theatre Atlanta, Garland dismissed me without calling me to the stand. The police rushed me to the theater—in an unmarked car with no siren. The first act, the only one in which I had lines to speak, had just ended.

The following Thursday I was again summoned to court. Again, Garland fought to keep my testimony out, and again he was overruled. As I took the stand he made a decidedly unchivalrous remark to me, loud enough for the jury to hear, and Judge Tanksley reprimanded him for it. He responded in clarion tones, "I'm going to try to make this as obnoxious as I can."

Garland continually requested adjournment, which the judge continually denied. Finally, his face reddening, the attorney clutched his throat, loosened his collar and gagged several times, a performance convincing enough to raise the possibility that he might really be having a heart attack and thus gain him the recess. Recovering immediately, he declared that he didn't believe a word of my testimony and planned to keep me on the stand all the next day to disprove it.

That time Jack stayed at the courthouse, consoled me, and came back with me the following day even though he was still forbidden to hear my testimony. Garland questioned me about the call threatening our house, which he had previously asked me to write down for him. Now he claimed to have lost the paper and asked me to write it again. When I did so he pulled the original from his pocket, compared the two, and pointed to one word that differed from what I had just written. Years later, I learned that he had forged the change on the original.

He then questioned me in detail about what I did on the day of the bombing, his voice dripping with sarcasm, and asked why I hadn't bothered to go to the Temple to see what had happened. Having again been wound into an emotional knot, I broke while answering. "Because I considered it more important to keep people from bringing their children there for Sunday School than it was to satisfy my curiosity!"

Again, the afternoon paper carried the story on its front page, this time with the caption, "Tearful Rabbi's Wife Ends Testimony."

Jack predicted that the accused would go free and his attorney would go to jail, which is exactly what happened. Bright was acquitted and Garland was sentenced to forty days in jail for contempt of court, mainly for his treatment of me. He entered the facility wearing blue satin pajamas.

The man's *chutzpah* knew no bounds. While incarcerated, he ran for the office of state solicitor and called me to ask my help in the election. "I was just trying to save the life of my poor, innocent client," he cooed. "I don't have anything against Jewish people and I'd appreciate it if you'd tell your folks at the Temple so they'd vote for me."

Knowing his reputation, I realized he was being truthful. He didn't hate people; he hated *losing*.

Flabbergasted, I replied, "Mr. Garland, your lack of respect for the American system of jurisprudence is so appalling that whether or not you are anti-Semitic is totally irrelevant."

Jack said I should have told him, "I wouldn't vote for you even if you were Jewish."

It was Mother who introduced me to Martin and Coretta King. Jack met Martin shortly after he moved to Atlanta and joined the biracial "dinner group" a few ministers formed to keep conversation going when all public dialogue across Atlanta's racial divide had ceased. The group had no formal structure and no agenda; it was merely a mechanism for having dinner together every two weeks.

Mother met Martin one day when she was having lunch at Paschal's, one of the only two restaurants in town open to a racially mixed clientele. When she learned that Coretta was a musician, she invited them to dinner along with us and a few close friends. That's when I met them.

I tried to arrange a dinner at our house soon after, but both Martin and Jack had such busy schedules that it took some six months for Coretta and me to find an evening when both of the men were free. Meanwhile, in November 1960, while Jack was on a fact-finding trip to Germany, Martin was arrested with students in a peaceful demonstration at Rich's, Atlanta's iconic department store. I called Coretta to offer sympathy and we talked for almost an hour. She told me that she and Martin realized he would go to jail at some point, but had not yet prepared their children for it because they didn't expect it to happen at this demonstration.

They had two children younger than ours, but I didn't know exactly how much younger. "I'm not so concerned about Marty," Coretta told me, referring to her son Martin Luther III. "He's too young to know what's happened. But Yoki [Yolanda] heard it on the car radio coming home from school, and I need to explain it to her."

The Kings were not yet the icons that they later became, nor had attempts on Martin's life been widely publicized. Jack and I, on the other hand, had been threatened two years before. I felt like an experienced older sister whose ideas might be helpful.

Because the Kings had recently visited India and reportedly were deeply inspired by the Mahatma, I suggested, "Couldn't you tell her about Gandhi, how much her father admired him, and how Gandhi went to jail so many times to help free his people?"

Coretta listened politely, then replied, "Janice, honey, this child's only five years old. She doesn't even know she's colored yet."

That ended my advice, but not our conversation. Coretta told me some of the problems faced by African American mothers trying to raise their children with healthy self-esteem. I hadn't thought of what it meant for newspapers to publish pictures of only white brides, white models, and other beautiful white women, and for movies and television to follow the same practice. Nor did I remember how unattractive I considered myself as a teenager with Semitic features in the years before Sophia Loren and Barbra Streisand taught us that we could be beautiful without being snub-nosed, flat-chested, and skinny blond.

The New York Times was running fashion ads then for a new line of expensive designer dresses for children, each week showing a full-page image of an adorable young model over the caption, "Aren't you glad you have a little girl?" A few weeks after my conversation with Coretta the ad featured a child of color and I sent it to her for Yoki.

When Coretta and I finally set a date for dinner at our house, I invited a few others, including the president of our congregation and his wife, my mother, and several close friends. In the days leading up to it I felt an unusual excitement, thrilled and wanting to tell friends but not doing so because it would have been boastful and could possibly have caused trouble.

A few days before the dinner I discussed the menu with Bessie Jucks, our housekeeper, when we sat down for lunch. Usually when we had guests I prepared the entrée and dessert myself. This time, when I told Bessie we'd have coquilles St. Jacques for the entrée she rose to her feet, looked me in the eye, and announced, "Miz Rothschild, you may know what your fancy friends like to eat, but I know Baptist ministers. We're having barbequed chicken."

End of conversation. Obviously she was as excited as I and intended to prepare the featured dishes herself, including her apple pie for dessert instead of my sachertorte.

Jack and I always opened the front door ourselves when guests arrived, but this time Bessie got there before us to admit the Kings. I introduced her, then led them into the living room to meet the others. They apologized for being over an hour late, and although we assured them it was okay, Martin insisted on giving a full explanation. He said that in addition to being unfamiliar with our part of town, they couldn't read the house numbers because of the poor lighting on our street and finally had to drive up to one of the homes to inquire. "But I was careful not to embarrass you with your neighbors," he assured us. "I let Coretta go to the door so they wouldn't recognize me and they'd think we were just coming to serve a party."

I still choke up when I think about it. Until then I hadn't realized that people of color seen in our neighborhood after dark in those years weren't safe unless they were seen as servants.

At dinner Coretta complimented me on the coquilles St. Jacques broiled in ceramic shells served as the first course and asked for the recipe just as Bessie was clearing her place. I caught Bessie's eye victoriously.

The evening went much too quickly, with conversation varying from the sorry state of public affairs to jokes about how some of us were attracted to movie stars of the opposite race. Jack admitted his admiration for Lena Horne and I acknowledged a crush on Harry Belafonte. Martin introduced us to him a few months later when the singer came to speak on behalf of the Southern Christian Leadership Conference.

Jack and Martin's biracial dinner group, like so many others in those days, was exclusively a boys' club. Wives were invited only once, for Christmas. While chatting with me that night, Coretta mentioned that she was suffering from back pains and asked if I knew of a good specialist. I did, but something she had said made me suspect that he wasn't the specialist she needed. I asked, "Are you sure you don't want to see an OBGYN?"

"Oh, no," she assured me. "I'm definitely not pregnant."

She and Martin already had three children, and this was their fourth— Bernice, whom they called Bunny. She was the only one to follow their family tradition and become a minister.

Coretta amazed me with her ability to entertain at the drop of a hat despite having four young children and no regular household help. When she learned with only two days' notice that Xernona Clayton, a television personality from California, would be in town for a day, she invited twenty of us to an elegant luncheon in her home to meet her.

Martin equally impressed me by dropping in to visit with us ladies after driving their children's carpool for Coretta that day. In an era of gender-designated family chores that was highly unusual.

The celebrated Atlanta dinner honoring King as recipient of the 1964 Nobel Peace Prize took place in January 1965. Jack was one of the small group that approached Mayor Ivan Allen soon after the winner was announced to say that the city should honor him. Allen wholeheartedly agreed and plans proceeded, chaired by newspaper editor Ralph McGill, Archbishop Paul Hallinan, Morehouse College President Benjamin Mays, and Jack, whom they designated to emcee the event. My involvement began in December 1964 when Jack returned from a committee meeting and asked me, "What do you think we should give Martin at the dinner?"

The standard medium for awards in those days was silver, but that required maintenance and Coretta had too much work already without another piece of silver to polish. I suggested a crystal bowl from Steuben, the legendary glassmaker and engraver.

The next evening, after another committee meeting with the mayor, Jack told me, "Ivan likes your idea. He says go ahead and get it."

Who, *me*? Awesome as it was to be the friend of a Nobel laureate, being responsible for choosing the city's gift to him was beyond belief.

The Atlanta dinner, only six weeks away, was unprecedented for being racially integrated, and many Atlantans vociferously opposed the Nobel committee's decision to choose King. If they learned of the event in time to derail it they undoubtedly would do so. Fearing leakage to the press if I ordered the gift locally, I decided to call Steuben headquarters in New York.

Meanwhile, I had to wait until morning to make the call. I took a discarded envelope nearby and sketched my idea for the bowl's inscription. Because Atlanta calls itself The Dogwood City and because of a Christian legend connecting the dogwood tree to Jesus as the Prince of Peace, I thought the image of a dogwood blossom encircled by the inscription would be appropriate, and roughed it out.

I called Steuben when their offices opened the next morning and asked to speak to the president. A vice president came on the line, heard my request and, noting that Christmas was less than two weeks away, said he doubted that the order could be filled in time for the dinner on January 27. His engravers were given a vacation after working overtime to fill Christmas orders. Nevertheless, he offered to ask them if they were willing to forego their vacation to inscribe the bowl—in strictest confidence— for Dr. King. He told me to call back the next day.

I had one more question before hanging up: how much would it cost? The committee set a very tight budget to keep the price of tickets low enough for a maximum of King's followers to attend. As I feared, Steuben's price for the bowl was almost double what I was told we could spend.

I reported this to Mayor Allen.

"Whatever it costs, we're going to do this thing right," he said. "I'll pay the difference myself if need be."

Happily, that wasn't necessary. As a tribute to Dr. King, Steuben authorities voluntarily cut the price to fit our budget, and when the engravers learned for whom the bowl was destined they agreed to forego their vacation to finish it on time.

The afternoon of the dinner, Jack and I were resting when Coretta called. She wanted to know what I was planning to wear that evening. The men who were dais guests had received a dress code directive for black tie, but there was no word for the women.

I replied that I planned to wear something simple on top of my long black skirt, a staple for such dais-sitting formalities. Knowing that it was unlike her to spend time chitchatting about clothes and that as a concert artist she certainly owned a spectacular long gown, I didn't understand why she continued the conversation. She finally revealed her reason: she said she didn't want to embarrass Martin's women followers who couldn't afford a formal dress.

My Big Sister Syndrome kicked in again. "You're the most important woman there," I told her. "People expect you to look better than the rest of us. Go for it."

It took some persuasion but she did, and afterward a fashion reporter who couldn't get close enough to her to see the details asked me to describe the dress. It was a sleeveless yellow brocade with beading around the decolletage. I'm told that it is now on display at the King Center along with the Steuben bowl.

The dinner was amazing. Waiting in the holding room beforehand everyone was in the holiday mood, congratulating each other that this event was actually taking place. The excitement rose higher when Martin and Coretta arrived. Coretta looked radiant as she accepted congratulations and Martin joyously embraced everyone, giving each of us women friends an affectionate kiss.

The event exceeded anything we could have imagined. The 1,000 places that the committee hoped to fill were sold out a week in advance. At that time, since the fire code permitted only 250 more, those were pulled for the press. Top executives, previously silent, had their secretaries calling all over town begging for tickets. When the president of Rich's, a good friend, asked Jack as a special favor to get him a few more tickets,

Rabbi Rothschild presents Steuben bowl to Dr. Martin Luther King, Jr. *"Citizen of Atlanta*; Recipient of 1964 Nobel Peace Prize; With Respect and Admiration; January 27, 1965"

Martin and Coretta Scott King with Jack and Janice Rothschild

Jack called Daddy King thinking that the family might be able to help. Mama King said Daddy was out searching for more tickets himself.

The entire ballroom wall opposite the dais was covered by journalists with their cameras standing three-deep, one above the other on bleachers. Tables were set so close together that we had to walk sideways as we proceeded through to the dais. The applause was so loud that we couldn't hear the voices of friends as we passed, many of them reaching out to touch us so we would know they were there.

Jack and I sat with Martin and Coretta at the center of the head table. Our families—my mother with our two teenagers, and Dr. and Mrs. King Sr. with Martin and Coretta's children—were at the center table perpendicular to us, close enough for an occasional exchange of sentiments. Mama King caught my eye several times, each time shaking her head in disbelief, as if trying to convince herself that she wasn't dreaming. Twice she looked up at me and said, "To think this could happen in our lifetime! The grandson of a sharecropper!"

The euphoria ended three years later when Martin was assassinated in Memphis. It was on the news almost immediately. Father Noel Burtenshaw, aide to Archbishop Paul Hallinan who lay in the hospital close to death, picked up Jack around ten that evening in a driving rain to visit Coretta. I begged to go with them but Jack adamantly forbade it, fearful of violence in the streets. There was none in Atlanta, and they had no problem going through town. Jack reported finding Coretta alone, calm, and appreciative of their visit.

Coretta went to Memphis the following day, so I didn't try to visit her until the weekend. I called Billye Williams, a mutual friend, to ask if she'd like to go with me on Saturday afternoon. She wasn't sure she could but said she'd let me know. When I hung up the phone my cleaning man, having overheard the conversation, told me, "If Miz Williams can't go with you I'll drive you. Ain't safe for a white lady alone in a convertible to go through that part of town."

Fortunately that wasn't necessary, both because Atlanta remained calm and because Billye went with me. We had become friends years earlier as a result of her husband, Rev. Dr. Samuel Williams, becoming Jack's close friend. We didn't meet often but bonded nonetheless and through her, as with Coretta, I gained gutwrenching insights to some specifics of the unequal treatment to which they were subjected. I once told her that I thought southerners would integrate more quickly and peacefully than northerners after we legally banished Jim Crow. She told me that I was hopelessly naive.

When Billye and I called on Coretta after Martin's death Coretta wasn't at home, so we left and sat in the car for a long time, sharing our grief with each other. At one point I had an idea seemingly so preposterous that I hesitated to tell her. Eventually I did.

"In the twelfth century," I said, "There was a great Jewish scholar, a physician as well as rabbi, named Moses Maimonides. His impact was so great that people compared him to the prophet with the saying, 'From Moses to Moses, there was no one like Moses.' I believe that centuries from now, when Christians study history they will say, 'From Martin Luther to Martin Luther, there was no one like Martin Luther.'"

Considering a personal friend a candidate for historical immortality may have seemed ridiculous. Billye, who knew Martin far better than I, gave me a pitying look and half smile as she had done when I predicted an easier adjustment to racial equality in the south than in the north. I'm now convinced I was right on both counts.

Friends found it hard to believe that we were not invited to Martin's funeral. Sam Williams, Martin's mentor and close friend, was certain it was an oversight and called to set it right. He was wrong. He was told that we didn't make the cut because there were too many with higher priorities to be considered. The Kennedys, government officials, and Hollywood royalty all had to be accommodated in the small church and still leave space for its members. Rather than stand in the crowd outside under the broiling sun, we chose to mourn in the quiet of our home, where we could hear and see the service on television and reflect on our friend's life undistracted by discomfort.

The city was crowded. At midnight the night before we received a call from a young man who identified himself as a friend our son Bill at Yale. With all hotels filled, he and another student who had come to Atlanta for the funeral could find no place to sleep. We gave them directions to our house and put them in Bill's room. Several hours later, we were awakened by a knock on our bedroom door. It was Bill, wondering who was sleeping in his bed. He had joined some other students after class and took turns driving through the night. No cell phones yet and no time to call us in advance. The boys had one female passenger whom they dropped off at my mother's house before coming to ours.

I told Bill and his fellow travelers to take his sister's room since she was also at college, and they slept there the few remaining hours before it was time to leave again. I hustled to make an early but hearty breakfast for them so they could park and get close enough to the funeral to see something of it. Having no time to come back for dinner because they had classes the next day, they thanked me and said goodbye. I convinced them to stop on their way out of town long enough to use the bathrooms and pick up the deli sandwiches and cokes that I'd have waiting for them.

Shortly after that I wrote a story about Coretta for the *Atlanta Journal-Constitution* Sunday Magazine, describing her in the personal

terms that defined her as I knew her then. Charlotte Hale Smith, one
of the city's top writers on the staff of the paper, read it in manuscript
even before publication and commended me for it as a "sensitively drawn
portrait of an extraordinary woman of our time."

Not everyone agreed. I received an anonymous note saying, "I'm
glad I am not a Jew. My Jewish neighbors were deeply hurt after reading
your article."

Obviously it was the writer herself who was significantly offended,
but in those days it would have also been conceivable for some Jews to
have been so insecure as to have been made nervous by a rabbi's wife
writing glowingly of her friendship with the Kings.

Most importantly, I treasure the note of thanks I received from
Coretta herself.

I was never intentionally an activist. Neither Jack nor I went to the
protest marches, even to Selma. He desperately wanted to go there but
knew that by satisfying his personal feelings he would, by the publicity,
sacrifice his continuing effectiveness in serving the cause. The only time
he marched—and I marched with him—was to protest the USSR's
Berezovska Ballet's performance at Atlanta's civic auditorium while the
Soviet government was unjustly imprisoning Soviet Jews.

Because Jewish students at area universities insisted on marching
despite the urging of community leaders not to do so, the leaders decided
to join them to insure against possible violence. Rabbis, physicians,
attorneys, and professors wore their professional academic robes,
replacing the hoods with placards stating the dollar equivalent of what
it would have cost them for exit visas if they lived in the Soviet Union.

The event remained peaceful and the brisk November night remains
a happy memory for me. I only joined two other protest marches, both
decades later in Washington. One was to support Roe v. Wade, the other
gay rights.

When people ask me how the congregation responded to Jack's
outspokenness, I point out that in most cases we have no way of

knowing because those who criticized usually did it behind our backs. The one incident that came to our attention, however, underscored the congregation's official position by the Board's reaction to it. What made it remarkable was that Jack didn't do it. Our daughter Marcia and I were the culprits.

In 1960, the daughter of my longtime family friend Walter Paschall and his wife Eliza, both community activists, invited Marcia to a Friday night sleepover party, which normally included going downtown for lunch on Saturday. Knowing the family as I did, I reasoned that the guests, early teenagers, would be racially mixed, which was highly unusual because in those days few families socialized across the race barrier. I also suspected that they planned to join lunch counter sit-ins. Before permitting her to go, Jack and I questioned Marcia to be sure she understood and could handle the possible consequences. Long afterward, I learned that the girls were even more proactive than we thought.

On the Monday morning after the event a woman called our home asking to speak to Rabbi Rothschild. He wasn't in, so I identified myself and asked if I could deliver a message. She gave me her name, which I recognized as belonging to the congregation, then said, "I can't believe it, but my Christian friends told me they saw the rabbi's daughter downtown with a *Nigra*."

I waited a long moment before responding, "Yes?"

She then blurted, "Well, it couldn't be true, could it?"

I paused again to denote bewilderment before answering, "Yes, is there a problem?"

"Well," she sputtered, "I couldn't believe that Rabbi Rothschild would let his daughter be seen having lunch with a Nigra. I'm so embarrassed for my Christian friends!"

I replied, in my best honeysuckle-and-magnolia accent, "Oh, honey, I wouldn't worry about my Christian friends if I were you. If that's the way they feel about people, they couldn't be *very Christian*, could they?"

End of conversation, but not end of story. The woman's family resigned from the Temple soon after. At the board meeting when their resignation was read, followed as usual by the motion "to accept with regret," someone objected. "Leave off the 'with regret,'" he said. And they did. That was how the congregation officially responded to what was Jack's supposedly reckless behavior.

My only self-motivated contribution to civil rights was a dramatic dialogue I wrote that was performed at the Temple, the Unitarian Church, and on public radio. Listening to the Akeidah story at services one Rosh Hashanah morning, I realized how the sacrifice of Isaac related to what was currently happening in southern cities where parents risked their children's lives desegregating public schools for the sake of justice. On the nightly news we watched little girls of color, six-year-olds dressed in their finest for the first day of school, walk the path between rows of angry white women, mean-faced adults shouting epithets and even spitting on the children as they attempted to exercise their right to attend a public school. Their parents, I believed, anguished facing that test of their own faith as much as Abraham had done deciding to obey God's directive to kill his only son.

I wrote of a sacrifice being questioned by two fictional parents based on what I knew at that time about Martin and Coretta King. I didn't yet know them personally but knew that they had one very young child and equated their move from progressive Boston to segregated Montgomery, Alabama, with Abraham's and Sarai's move from sophisticated Ur of the Chaldees to the wilderness of Zin. I will never know whether or not my piece influenced anyone to empathize with Negro parents and their children, but writing and submitting it to the public gave me the satisfaction of having contributed something personal toward the achievement of racial justice.

When the Supreme Court decision outlawing segregation in public schools forced action in Georgia, the National Conference of Christians and Jews organized a day-long seminar exploring the basis of prejudice. It featured a panel of four mothers representing different races and religions discussing the subject "Rearing Children of Good Will." I was the Jewish mother, Eleanor Troutman Bockman was the Catholic, and Dorothy Wang and Coretta Scott King were the Protestants. The event fulfilled its mission by inspiring church groups, PTAs, and other organizations of white women fearfully trying to adapt to what they believed would be a dangerous situation to invite us to repeat our program. It was such a success that we sometimes needed substitutes to replace us.

Following passage of a bill in the Georgia state legislature that would have closed all public schools when ordered to desegregate, our children's school, Morris Brandon, sent a questionnaire to parents through its PTA asking:

1) Do you favor local option on integrating public schools?
2) Do you favor controlled integration rather than closing public schools?
3) Are you opposed to any form of integration in the public school?

Because I suspected that the results would be withheld if contrary to the ones that were politically correct, I volunteered to count them and thus was one of the few who learned that the majority of parents favored a racially integrated school over no school at all. Fortunately, Georgia's public schools did *not* close, but that outcome remained in doubt until the final moment.

No sooner had the school situation been resolved than the struggle began to desegregate all public facilities. Restauranteurs held back, each waiting for their most prominent competitor, the popular upscale eatery from Washington, Fan and Bill's, to make the first move. Whereas protests there had been mild, students were trashing Leb's delicatessen downtown on a daily basis to demand desegregation, action that gained national attention on the nightly news. Mayor Ivan Allen called restaurant owners to a meeting, asking Jack to address them from a religious viewpoint.

During this time, I received an invitation from the United Jewish Appeal to a fundraising luncheon at Fan and Bill's. Outraged that a Jewish organization would hold an event there under the current conditions, I first checked by calling the restaurant and asking for a reservation. This was soon after we had been there with Isaac Stern so I knew the manager would remember me, which he did. I could almost taste the syrup through the telephone as he assured me of having the best table in the house. I thanked him, then added, as if an afterthought, "And one of my guests will be a lady of color. That's all right, isn't it?"

"No. It is not!" he spat out as he slammed down the receiver.

When I reported this to the local UJA office, I was brushed off with the excuses that they didn't know, that it was too late to change the venue, and that the event was to help Israel. I replied that doing wrong to do right is still wrong, then called Charles Wittenstein, regional director of the American Jewish Committee, and told him. Thereafter, having unloaded my outrage, I let the matter rest. Whether Charles took it from there I never knew, but someone notified the New York office of the celebrity television journalist who was to be the guest speaker at the luncheon and, lest he be pictured crossing a student picket line to enter the restaurant, he canceled his appearance. People blamed me for calling the network. I never learned who did it.

Regardless, my involvement drew punishment. When Isaac Stern gave his next concert in Atlanta, we went backstage afterward to say hello and he asked us to go to the party being thrown for him later. When the hostess confirmed the invitation, we thanked her and prepared to leave, saying we would see her at her home.

"Oh, no," she corrected. "Not at my house. At Fan and Bill's."

We had to decline, of course. When we explained to Mr. Stern why we couldn't go, he declared that he wouldn't go there either, and we had to plead with him to convince him to do so. "We live here," we reminded him. "If you don't show up, your hostess will hate us forever."

He went to the party as we asked, leaving us to muse over the adage that no good deed goes unpunished.

I saw Coretta again in Waltham, Massachusetts, where she and Jack participated in the investiture of our friend Morris Abram as president of Brandeis University. Nineteen years later, after I moved to

Washington and spent six months trying to reach her to ask her to write an introduction for *One Voice*, my book about Jack's work in civil rights, she replied via Steve Klein, one of her assistants, who said she would be happy to sign an introduction if I would write it for her. I did.

After three more months, at approximately ten in the morning on July 4, 1984, Coretta called to say that she had rewritten my introduction (she made it far more complimentary than I dared to do). I thanked her and expected the conversation to end there, but it did not. We continued to chat about various matters, including politics, for the better part of an hour. Election campaigns were revving up and there was much to discuss. The press was full of conjecture as to whether she would endorse the candidacy of Jesse Jackson, one of Martin's followers in the early days. When I asked for her take on the subject she was as discreet with me as she was publicly, but did give a hint. "Jesse just isn't going to go away," she sighed, and I think I understood what she meant.

At that time more than ever Coretta was extremely careful of every word she spoke, knowing that however her words were reported would impact her campaign to get a federal holiday honoring Martin. As she was frequently in Washington then for her lobbying effort, I had no difficulty getting her to accept an invitation from my friend Edith Fierst, who, after reading *One Voice*, wanted to give a book signing party honoring me and Coretta together.

The party was memorable and so was the evening that followed. Coretta stayed overnight at my apartment. She preferred not to go to a restaurant for dinner because of the attention she regularly received from strangers, and assured me that whatever I could put together for a light supper would be fine. I scrambled some eggs.

The next morning, when I offered to take her wherever she needed to go, she said that was both unnecessary and forbidden. She was instructed not to go even downstairs in our building until the Secret Service came to escort her. When her security detail arrived, she thanked me and departed. I never saw her again.

Like many of my and my mother's generations, I had accepted

racism without recognizing it and abhorred it when I began to see it clearly. My reaction came in increments. In 1950, before becoming aware of a civil rights movement, I resisted southern mores by refusing my grandmother's offer to install a toilet in our basement for the help to use. The illogic astounded me. How could people believe that others were unclean yet rely on them to nurse their babies and prepare their food? It made no sense.

The years with Jack in the forefront of reform brought me much closer to being the person I would like to be, but I'm not there yet. I still occasionally recognize traces of racism in myself, which makes me wonder how much longer it will take to complete the cure globally.

I'm an optimist. We're in the "two steps backward" phase as I write this, but behind that I see great progress. It's like climbing Mt. Everest.

Five
SEARCHING FOR ME

As rewarding as it was to be involved in synagogue activities and civil rights activism, I eventually realized that something was missing. It took years, but creeping frustration began to assert itself.

At first, home and family challenged me. Marcia was born during our first year of marriage, in October 1947, and Bill thirteen months later in November 1948. We moved into our first house a few months before that. The combined responsibilities kept me too busy to examine my psyche.

Raised with patrician tastes during Great Depression austerity, I threw myself into do-it-yourself projects for home embellishments that we couldn't otherwise afford. I transferred designs from the bathroom wallpaper to paint trim on bathroom curtains. I sewed fluffy ruffled curtains for Marcia's bedroom. I enjoyed the required entertaining albeit without an experienced cook or caterer, and collected esoteric recipes from the *New York Times* Sunday Magazine for our Rosh Hashanah receptions. One recipe called "Egyptian bean dip" was actually hummus, but we didn't know that in 1950. Although that effort was satisfying, I missed the personal socializing that diminished almost to extinction as Jack grew busier and obligations increased.

Our small family underwent great changes during the first ten years of our marriage. On the plus side, in addition to the birth of our own two children in 1947 and 1948, Jack's sister Jean married Calvin Levinson and began their family of two boys in the mid-1950s.

Sadness shadowed us when my father died of heart failure in 1953. Jack and I, assured by the doctors that his death was not imminent, last saw him when we stopped by the hospital on our way to the airport to attend a meeting in New York. By the time we returned to Atlanta, Mother had made all arrangements without consulting us. Had she asked me, I probably would have agreed on cremation, which Dad as well as his parents favored, but when theory turned to reality it appalled me.

The memory of that misguided farewell stays with me as a symbol of lost opportunity to fully know and appreciate the good, loving man who fathered me. Only recently, I discovered and read his letters home from the front in France during the first World War. They revealed him—his early self that I didn't know—as an activist and organizer, sensitive to the arts as well as scenic beauty, and a soldier whose efficiency led to his being scheduled for promotion to lieutenant just as the war ended.

I was still dealing with Mother's dictates during those years, the pressure intensifying annually when Jack's mother, Lily Rothschild, came to visit. At first Mother Rothschild, long employed as a ladies' dress buyer for a Pittsburgh department store, detoured to see us on her way home from buying trips to New York. Those visits went well. They were necessarily brief and she occasionally brought me a new dress, which I deeply appreciated. She had excellent taste. That pattern soon ended, however, when the store's lease expired and its owners retired, closing the business and leaving her unemployed. Only in her fifties, she intended to continue working, but after one or two unpleasant experiences she gave up and retired.

In those days one did not need to reserve a return flight when booking a round-trip ticket, which we did periodically to bring Mother Rothschild to Atlanta. With no responsibilities and little social life at home, she stayed a month or more, giving us no clue as to when she planned to leave. I truly admired her for many reasons, not least of which being her strength of character and sense of humor, but she was a large woman and it was difficult having her hover over me in a small house with Jack rarely there to help. She was nearly as strong-minded and opinionated as my own mother, and no matter what I did she pointed out a better way of doing it, especially regarding the children. Nevertheless, I determined to get along with her, gave a luncheon for her to meet special women of her age whom I knew, and encouraged her to call them on subsequent visits after they had entertained her. It did no good. Her only interest was staying home and watching our children.

While I struggled to learn the rudiments of housekeeping, mothering and *rebbetzin*hood, those visits from Mother Rothschild drove me crazy. I never commented about it, but some friends obviously noticed.

On one visit we took her to an elaborate party where a full dinner buffet with desserts too good to refuse followed a lengthy cocktail hour with many of my favorite hors d'oeuvres. I pigged out on the beef tartare and martinis and awoke the next morning wondering whether to blame the booze or the raw beef. Unfamiliar with hangovers as well as intestinal disorders, I was too sick to lift the telephone receiver and ask our doctor and close friend, James Weinberg, what to do. When Jack called him the first question Jimmy asked was, "How long has your mother been there?"

Despite such grievances, we bonded and I turned to her rather than to my own mother for advice on personal matters involving Jack. No matter how upset I was with him I remained fiercely protective of his reputation, even within my family. As when I called him from the courthouse, I determined that knowledge of anything remotely derogatory be limited to his mother and me, the two of us who loved him unequivocally.

Mother Rothschild died of cancer in 1962. Jack and I visited her in Pittsburgh the day before and returned to bury her, assured that she had died in peace.

In those early years, I wanted to learn more about sports in order to enjoy them with Jack even though he didn't encourage it. He took me to baseball games which I had no trouble understanding, especially inspired by his two good friends, Bob Elliott and Elbie Fletcher, then playing with the Boston Braves. Once, when we were in New England on the Fourth of July, Bob and his wife Skippy invited us to stay with them over the holiday and attend the doubleheader. That was a great treat.

At home, baseball was less exciting. Before Jack's schedule became filled with evening meetings, we occasionally attended a minor league Atlanta Crackers game at Ponce de Leon Park. I enjoyed spending the time with him but found the games boring. He understood that I would lose interest long before I did. My epiphany came one night at the ballpark when I became so excited about a particular rhyme in a parody I was composing in my head that I grabbed Jack to tell him about it with three men on base. That's when he stopped taking me to ball games.

Whenever feasible, I lowered my stress by accompanying Jack to his out-of-town meetings, especially when they were in New York. Both of us loved theater and crammed in as many Broadway shows as possible, usually stopping afterward for a nightcap at the Elysee bar to enjoy Tom Lehrer's macabre satire. We saw the biggest hits, although I wasn't as eager as Jack to include musicals in place of classics and soon-to-be classics such as Tennessee Williams' *A Streetcar Named Desire*. We compromised, taking in one musical for each classic per trip. This proved enjoyable for both of us when we agreed on José Ferrer's performance of *Cyrano de Bergerac* and an Ethel Merman musical. A few years later, our friend Wilbur Evans played Sancho Panza to Ferrer's Don Quixote in *Man of La Mancha*. Because Ferrer's driver's license had been suspended and Wilbur was responsible for getting him home safely, Wilbur brought "Joe" along with us after the show and we had the double delight of having a midnight snack with both of them.

At first when we traveled, Jack didn't share my enthusiasm for sightseeing. Driving from Pittsburgh to Quebec for the Central Conference of American Rabbis convention in 1947, he showed me Niagara Falls by slowing down as he drove past it on the American side. Driving through Yosemite after the CCAR meeting in Colorado, he didn't even slow down. When I complained that he didn't turn at the sign for Bridal Veil Falls as directed, he told me to look at it through the back window.

Even on our first trip to Europe in 1958 to attend the World Union for Progressive Judaism with the Weisses and Sinclair Jacobs, Jack resisted some traditional sightseeing. He declared only half-jokingly that we must show him a synagogue for every cathedral we visited. He didn't balk on touring Notre Dame because we also saw the so-called Rothschild synagogue on the Rue de la Victoire. By the time we reached Rome, he went with us to St. Peter's without mentioning a quid pro quo. At museums, he usually found a bench near the entrance on which to wait while we admired the art. He made an exception at the Prado, however, and was so intrigued by the satire of Hieronymus Bosch that when we returned to Spain fourteen years later he wanted to see those paintings again.

I was happiest with Jack when we traveled because then we pursued things of genuine interest to both of us. He loved Paris as much as I did, even the sightseeing, and on every visit he went with me to bask in the exquisite serenity of the Sainte-Chapelle. Both of us enjoyed meeting people, and on our first trip there shocked our traveling companions by making a dinner date with a Swedish airline pilot and his Lebanese wife, whom we met sitting next to us at La Grenouille, a "naughty" restaurant specializing in sexual innuendoes. Both of us enjoyed *kibbitzing* with taxi drivers, especially on another trip there that took place over Bastille Day when our driver expressed the same irritation with "le bon Charlie" (de Gaulle, his president) that we felt.

Alone on subsequent vacations, Jack drove and we regularly picked up hitchhikers, which in those days was safe both in Europe and Israel. In Ireland, our first hitchhiker, a professor at the national university in Galway, gave us an introduction to Gaelic, and our second, a young American woman traveling alone, thanked us with the gift of a book on Irish history.

Jack enjoyed driving and left the itineraries to me. One summer we drove through the Loire Valley, visiting several châteaux and basing our stay in Amboise, where he stopped to pet an Irish setter sitting in an open window and I discovered a fabulous appetizer called *fond d'artichauts farcis*. At the hotel manager's suggestion we changed our route south to Cahors, where we stayed overnight in a sky-high hostelry built by an eleventh century archbishop, and made love in the afternoon.

Carcassonne seemed too hot and busy for us, so we continued on to Avignon, where I looked forward to standing *sur le pont* that I had learned about in the nursery song Mother taught me when I was two. In Carpentras we convinced a suspicious caretaker to show us the oldest synagogue in France, which wasn't yet open to tourists. Thanks to our rented Peugeot getting a cracked windshield on the outskirts of Arles, we spent an afternoon wandering through neighborhoods that inspired the vibrant rhythms of Bizet and the psychotic visions of van Gogh.

In Greece, with limited time and no language skills, we booked a bus tour to Delphi on which, in addition to relishing the history and mythology, we tasted the most delicious lamb of our lives at a pit stop on the way. We didn't need the Oracle to tell us to order shish kebab. The bite-size chunks came straight from the outdoor grill on eight-inch wooden skewers, unmarinated and unadorned, handed over the counter on squares of paper and seasoned with freshly-picked mountain thyme and sea salt. I've tried to replicate it ever since without success, even growing my own thyme.

Jack did not always share my penchant for tasting traditional local food. At breakfast in Edinburgh a few days after Neil Armstrong landed on the moon I ordered black pudding, not knowing what it was or what else would be served with it. When Jack saw the waiter approaching with a plate containing the slices of pudding piled high atop an assortment of meat, eggs, and various other breakfast staples, he slid down in his chair trying to disappear. Undaunted, I smiled at the waiter as he placed it before me, then picked up my fork and attacked it. As I swallowed my first bite, a dignified-looking elderly Scotsman in formal kilts seated with his lady on the level just above us leaned over the railing, caught my eye, and said, "I admire you, my dear. That's the spirit that got you Americans to the moon."

So much for black pudding. It was forgettably bland, quite the opposite of an equally black stew we were served for lunch by a Nigerian friend at her home in Stockholm. She proudly identified it as the signature dish of her homeland. Although I usually enjoy spicy dishes, this one was too hot for me to detect its flavor. Jack was fortunate enough to have been suffering severe pain since the night before and was awaiting a house call from our host's nationalized healthcare physician. I knew that his pain, though not yet specifically identified, had nothing whatsoever to do with his digestive system, but he nevertheless successfully used it as an excuse for not eating and grinned at me maliciously whenever our hosts urged me to eat more. That stew and *rijsttafel* at a Batavian restaurant in Amsterdam are the only dishes that ever defeated me.

In Cork we had a memorable experience due to our choice of restaurant and Jack's curiosity about an Irishman named Goldberg. Guests were seated on one floor for drinks and hors d'oeuvres, then transferred to another when their dinner was ready to be served. While waiting with drinks we noticed the maître'd seating two couples in the booth next to ours and addressing one of the men with marked deference, obviously the host, as Mr. Goldberg. That piqued Jack's curiosity. I tried to restrain him, but when he could resist no longer, he went to their table and introduced himself to Mr. Goldberg. Mr. Goldberg from Cork responded cordially to Rabbi Rothschild from Atlanta, introducing him to Mrs. Goldberg and their guests, and nodding genially when we left them to go upstairs for dinner.

Before bringing our dessert, the waiter served us brandy courtesy of Mr. Goldberg. When we stopped by Mr. Goldberg's table to thank him, he asked if we had plans for the remainder of the evening and, learning that we did not, invited us to follow him home and spend it there. Not only did that result in our enjoying an evening of interesting conversation, but also in visiting the equivalent of a museum. His home was filled with Jacques Lipschitz sculptures and rare books of Judaica, many of them first editions. Mr. Goldberg, we learned, was a leader in the Cork community, a noted barrister, and owner of the restaurant where we met him.

Traveling was wonderful but our real life, of course, was at home with Jack at work. As he aged, tennis and horseback riding became problematic for him, so he turned to golf. It was the only game he ever played that he couldn't master, which fueled his incentive to continue. His Wednesday and Saturday afternoons at the club became sacrosanct, which I understood and accepted without complaint, but when he came home and engrossed himself in a sportscast on television without even finding me in the house to say hello, I began to resent it. To me, football seemed more barbarous than bullfighting because it brutalized humans rather than animals who were destined to be slaughtered anyway.

I still adhered to the idea that on Shabbat it was inappropriate to pursue everyday activities away from home, although for several years I used Saturday afternoons to get a manicure and hairdo. I had once thought of taking up golf myself, but Jack discouraged it on the grounds that I was not athletic by nature (which was true).

The tensions of Jack's work and our lack of mutual leisure activities frayed our relationship. I grew resentful, feeling rejected and possibly even bordering on clinically depressed. I never spoke of it to anyone or considered seeing a psychiatrist, although one of my friends noticed and suggested that I do so.

On one particularly lonely weekend I intentionally tried to get drunk. Instead, I developed a terrible headache and slept it off. Even then, I wouldn't admit there was anything wrong in our marriage that time and perseverance couldn't fix.

By the time our children were in high school I had begun to value my abilities and seek evidence that others recognized them. This emancipation began modestly enough with my writing skits and worship services for the Temple Sisterhood. The National Federation of Temple Sisterhoods (now Women of Reform Judaism) considered them good enough to be made available to other congregations, some as far away as Havana, Cuba and Sydney, Australia. They paid no royalty, but my ego was needier than my purse and it was enough to know that they were well-received. The one rejection that I know of was the Sisterhood in Charleston, South Carolina. They were apparently unaware of Rabbi Mordechai Kaplan's Reconstruction movement in Judaism as they thought the word referred to post-Civil War political Reconstruction and abhorred any mention of it.

This taste of success led me to media where I was sometimes paid—not much, but any pay at all more than compensated in terms of self-respect. It qualified me as a professional, no longer merely a "wife of" filling her days with busy work and I enjoyed spending the few discretionary dollars that came from it.

I wrote some one-minute spots on Georgia history *pro bono* for radio, and likewise two television documentaries produced by WSB-TV that were broadcast nationally on the educational network. One of them, about Franklin Delano Roosevelt at Warm Springs, rewarded me with a letter of commendation from the President's daughter, Anna Roosevelt Boettiger, that I mentioned years later to her daughter Eleanor Dall Seagraves, my imagined childhood playmate.

When "Brother" Bud Mantler hired me to write a script for a business promotion, it gave me the idea of seeking employment at an advertising agency. I applied to an agency owned by a friend who liked my work. He was about to hire me when his longtime top assistant, an unmarried woman, objected on the grounds that I didn't need the position because I was married and there were single women who could do the job. That was my first brush with women in the workplace.

Remembering that the *Atlanta Journal-Constitution* Sunday Magazine had published my work during the war, I submitted stories there and the paper bought them. My next comeuppance with a woman in the workplace erupted when they published my story about a French provincial home in Atlanta, unusual because of the owner's personal touch. The day after publication, George Hatcher, the editor, called me to say that the piece caused a brouhaha in his office, so he would be unable to take any more stories from me about homes or gardens. A female staff writer considered the topic *her* turf and would not tolerate competition. She even complained to the owner of the house for showing it to me.

I soon found my niche for subjects in which apparently no one cared to compete. Initially I wrote about people—Theatre Atlanta actress Joan Anderson becoming a success in soap opera, Morris Abram becoming president of Brandeis University, Coretta King as I knew her—as well as the history of the Temple on the congregation's 100th anniversary. With the onset of the Six-Day War in June 1967, I found my best subjects writing about Israel, by which I jokingly became the magazine's uncontested "foreign correspondent." That also launched me on another interest. Mr. Hatcher noted that he couldn't send a staff photographer to Israel with me as he did to local venues, and advised me to buy a Yashica 4x4 ("the poor man's Rollei," he said) to illustrate the stories myself. Following that, photography overtook my passion for writing at times, and I eventually sold a few photographs, mostly from exhibits but also through a stock photo company.

My success with the Sunday Magazine led to acceptance in other publications, notably *Atlanta Magazine, Georgia Magazine, Hadassah Magazine*, and even as a stringer for the Jewish Telegraphic Agency. In 1972, the national editor of *Hadassah* assigned me two books to review, saying as he handed me one of them, "If you don't like this, don't bother to write the review. The author's mother is on our board."

It was *The Provincials* by Eli N. Evans, and I loved it despite the inaccuracy in what he wrote about Jack and me. It was flattering but he got his facts wrong, giving me undue credit for triggering Jack's interest in Zionism. Although I told him so when we met a year later, he repeated the error in each of his subsequent editions.

That did not preclude our becoming good friends, however. I understood that as a popular author rather than an academic one, he couldn't let factual details interfere with a good story. His indulgence is only a blip in the saga of southern Jewish history, meaningful only to me and my family. I hope to correct this blip for posterity in the course of this narrative. Popularizing the subject as he did, Eli made a groundbreaking gift to the study of Southern Jewish history.

By the mid-1960s, the Temple Sisterhood had younger enthusiasts and no longer needed its rabbi's wife to spur incentive. I became an *éminence grise*, not yet gray but still expected to be seen and not heard. I attended meetings and tried to remain silent as I had wished older members did when *I* was young. Other women's auxiliaries asked me to present programs for them, shows and slide lectures, and I enjoyed doing it, especially because it gave me insights into what those organizations were doing. Meanwhile, I reached the comfort zone that enabled me to step out of my strictly Jewish orbit into the broader scene of arts in the city at large, the milieu I had known as a child.

My interest in performing revived in the mid-50s, when stage-starved Atlantans were putting their acts together to develop locally produced professional theater. "Little theaters" abounded, amateur and unrecognized, seldom offering an evening worth paying for.

When the three leading groups combined to form Theatre Atlanta in 1957 I joined, at first writing publicity releases and background pieces for its playbill. Eventually I tried out for a major role and got it, which meant going to a dress rehearsal and performances on several Friday nights when I would otherwise have been at Temple. Jack encouraged me, as did Bill Schwartz, then president of the congregation.

That experience confirmed for me two suspicions about myself: First, I was not a gifted actress. Second, my hormones were still active enough to be triggered without my permission when an attractive man who was *not* my husband romantically embraced me. I sensed that more of the same might lead me where I didn't want to go.

I did take one small role after that, but not one involving an embrace. It was in *Anne of the Thousand Days*, a play about King Henry VIII and Anne Boleyn. I played Anne's mother, Elizabeth. I also served as dramaturg, coaching the cast in the show's historical background and finding special directors for the authentic Tudor period music and dances that were part of the play. One of the things that Jennings Hertz, Jr., who performed as the much-married king, may have learned from me was that his character had dallied with each of the women portrayed. He gallantly acknowledged this on opening night by leaving a small bouquet and naughty note signed "Henry" at each of our places at the makeup table.

Because of the play's success, its run was extended and coincided with the second trial of George Bright, alleged bomber of the Temple. When defense attorney Reuben Garland held me at the courthouse until after our two o'clock curtain on the Saturday of our matinee and the police obligingly rushed me to the theater in the first available squad car, unmarked and lacking its siren, I arrived breathless and trembling only to find that the first act had gone smoothly without me. If that didn't discourage a would-be actress, what would?

Not yet completely turned off, I joined an acting class taught by Frank Wittow, an accomplished actor and director who established the Academy Theatre, long Atlanta's showcase for cutting-edge drama. While studying favorite scenes from Tennessee Williams, I realized that method acting required inner probing akin to psychoanalysis, which I feared. I sensed a danger in that psychoanalytic probing calls for professional guidance to ensure successful resolution, and I had no desire to risk failure. That, too, could endanger my marriage and my children. It convinced me to give up acting entirely. I then tried playwriting, but that too proved unsuccessful.

Soon thereafter Theatre Atlanta became professional, employing Equity actors and dependent ever more crucially on social popularity to inspire support. For that purpose, Helen Hunt Cartledge, one of the few theater activists who belonged to Atlanta's social elite, organized a Women's Guild, which I joined. Our immediate duties consisted of taking our director, Jay Broad, to morning parlor meetings in which he tried to convince Atlanta matrons that sustaining theater with annual subscriptions, whether or not every play pleased them, was comparable to their husbands continuing to support the Georgia Bulldogs or Georgia

Tech Yellow Jackets after a losing streak. We nearly drowned him in coffee, but the strategy worked.

One spring day in 1962, Helen asked me to come to her home to work on future plans for the Guild. We began by going through her membership file, pulling cards of possible leaders. I knew very few of them, so I frequently asked her who someone was. When we came to the name of Frania Lee, Helen said, "Forget her. She just joined because she's my mother. She knows so little about theater that she thinks 'The Deputy' is a western."

The accuracy of that assessment later came back to haunt us when Frania, a practicing Catholic, learned that it was about the Pope.

Only weeks later, on June 3, Helen and her husband, along with a hundred other Atlanta arts patrons, perished in the Air France crash at Orly. To memorialize her and carry on her work, Frania became a major donor to Theatre Atlanta.

Until then I had no idea who Helen was other than a lovely person, a friend, and a talented actress with a flair for teaching. I noticed that her home in Ansley Park was finer than starter homes of other young marrieds whom I knew, but the source of wealth was not a subject I pursued so I didn't know hers—until our first Guild meeting after the crash. Frania, her mother, proposed building a theater in her name as a suitable memorial, with funds "from Texas." Helen's father, apparently, was H.L Hunt, the Texas oil tycoon then much publicized for advocating Christian family values. He lived with his wife and other children in Texas. Frania and her children by him had also lived there as his family until recently, when she married a man named Lee and moved to Atlanta.

For the next few years, whenever Theatre Atlanta needed money, Frania responded, "Don't worry. I'll call Texas," which, like most benefits that sound too good to be true, ultimately fizzled. The building went up at 1374 West Peachtree, just north of 17th, beautifully adhering to our director's specifications. Finished much later than the promised date, the season's delayed opening caused a severe operational deficit. As before,

Frania rescued the situation with a loan and voiced reassurance that it could be repaid whenever feasible.

Then politics and *The Deputy* entered in. True to Helen's description, her mother thought that the play was a western—until it was chosen for production and Lila Kennedy, a doyenne of the theater miffed at being unseated as its top authority, told her what the play was *really* about (basically a criticism of Pope Pius XII for not forcefully opposing Hitler's treatment of the Jews). Frania, a devout Catholic, found it offensive and threatened to call in her loan unless we cancelled the production. We would not cancel and she did indeed demand payment. However, the news media came to our rescue and the public responded so generously that it enabled us to meet the current payment. The final blow came a year later when Frania and Lila Kennedy, her alter ego, again tried to override a program decision of the board and director. I was serving on the board then and on the front line of battle.

It was 1968, an election year. Richard Nixon was running for President and bat-wielding segregationist Lester Maddox was governor of Georgia. The show was *Red, White and Maddox*, a musical written by director Jay Broad and journalist Bruce Galphin satirizing Lester Maddox, whose flagrant racism revealed him as a bigoted buffoon. This time when we defied her Frania pulled the plug and foreclosed, effective at the end of the run.

Then came an angel in the form of Broadway producer Edward Padula. He saw the show, liked it, and arranged to bring it to New York. The publicity drew advance ticket sales that gave us hope for earnings sufficient to relocate our theatre back home in Atlanta. We excitedly planned an opening night celebration, honoring Jay and the cast at an after party performing parodies on all of the show's songs in which we satirized our company's woes.

Although I wrote most of the parodies, I didn't plan to go to New York for the opening. It simply never occurred to me to do so. I had never contemplated going anywhere just for the fun of it without Jack.

Friends couldn't believe it. "But you're president of the Women's

Guild," they argued. "You're a member of the board! That's like being one of the producers."

It did sound tempting, but that sort of excursion on my own was off my radar. I couldn't even reach Jack to consult him about it. By then it was January 1969 and he was in Israel on a UJA mission.

My friends continued. "This is something you don't want to miss," they insisted. "How many times in your life will you have a chance to dance on the tables at Sardi's?"

That did it. All the old clichés from my acting days erupted in my head and I went to New York for the opening. I climbed onto the table at Sardi's with the others and even danced a few steps with them there as we performed for the performers. I was living out a long-forgotten dream: the nice, middle class Jewish girl from the provinces stepping out with the sophisticates of Broadway.

The best part of the evening occurred when the first reviews came in with the radio news. I was sitting with Jim Garner, who played the leading role of Maddox, and shared the moment with him when we heard the high praise that launched him on his Broadway career. He gave up being a school teacher in Atlanta, changed his name because of the well-known actor James Garner, and the next time I saw him, he was Jay Garner playing Benjamin Franklin in the Broadway production of *1776*.

It was a heady occasion for all of us at Theatre Atlanta, but for those of us who went back home, the celebration was short-lived. Just when the word began to circulate that *Red, White and Maddox* was a show worth seeing, along came a blizzard that cut the momentum and the show had to close after 41 performances, far too few to have earned enough to save Theatre Atlanta. It revived in later years, but by then I was elsewhere, both in interests and in residence.

When I became president of the Theatre Atlanta Women's Guild in 1967, schools and other public facilities had finally been opened to all by federal law, but the fight to end *de facto* segregation was by no means over. Although I didn't realize it at the time, I believe that the situation in America for people of color was parallel to what we Jews had been experiencing in parts of western Europe ever since Napoleon gave our ancestors the rights of citizenship. Being legally accepted by the nation was only the first step, and it could take a very long time, even a century or more, for the next level to be reached.

This was so regarding acceptance within Atlanta's social and cultural organizations when the Women's Guild asked me to become its next president. I was totally flabbergasted, first because no Jewish woman that I knew of had ever headed any of the cultural-but-semi-social groups in Atlanta, and I certainly had never aspired to be one of the first. I had actually *avoided* all of the Guild's social events other than opening night receptions, and I never contemplated holding any office in the organization, even a minor one. I belonged only to support the theater.

When I asked why they wanted *me* to become president I was told, privately, that it was to avoid nominating the member who wanted the honor, had worked for it, and really deserved it, but had apparently irritated the others by trying too hard to get it. What they didn't tell me (but what I surmised) was that she, while not Jewish, was of Greek origin, another ethnic group largely excluded from high society. The main difference was, apparently, that she wanted the social leverage of the position and I didn't. The ladies considered me a safe bet.

Couching their explanation as politely as possible, they confided their suspicion that she would bring "less desirable" friends into the Guild. I tried to warn them that I had no intention of crashing their parties, but I *did* believe in defeating Jim Crow. I let them know that I intended to invite *all* who cared to support Theatre Atlanta through the Women's Guild to join, regardless of race.

The NBA Hawks had just come to Atlanta, and wives of the players and staff were attractive women, some of whom I believed would welcome an opportunity to become part of the community off the court. We invited them to our gala spring luncheon meeting, held at Dr. Marvin and Rita Goldstein's home around their swimming pool. Three of the Hawks' wives who were African American accepted, and the good time had by all was dutifully reported in the next day's newspaper with pictures of these lovely ladies. I don't remember if they joined the Guild as we invited them to do, but I made my point and heard no repercussions. By then, I think, most Atlantans (at least in what is now known as Buckhead) were tired of the struggle and ready to accept the inevitable—as long as someone else took the lead.

While I was presiding over the Theatre Atlanta Women's Guild, other happenings were also impacting my life. In the spring of 1967 the Temple observed its centennial with a celebratory weekend featuring a special Shabbat service, a Sunday afternoon concert open to the public at which the congregation presented a gift to the city, and a gala banquet attended by Hollywood celebrity Bert Parks, who grew up in the congregation as Bert Jacobson. Most exciting for me personally was the publication of my first book, the Temple history *As But a Day*. I was further thrilled when the buyer for Rich's book department called saying she wanted to feature it (as the store routinely did for work by local authors), but the Temple board ruled that out, insisting that copies were gifts for members only, not for sale.

The recognition for what I could do as distinct from being a "wife of" went a long way toward boosting my ego, but not far enough to effect a solid cure. Something was still missing. I was too busy to dwell on the subject and plumb for an answer, but luck was with me and eventually I learned. It was as if the many threads of my interests merged into one strong, vibrant, unbreakable cord.

In 1967, while we in America nervously followed news of Egypt's Gamal Abdel Nasser's threats to annihilate Israel with unlimited manpower and Soviet planes, Israelis themselves launched a celebration commemorating the 50th anniversary of Habima, their national theater. As part of the celebration, Habima sent one of its leading actors, Misha Asherov, to lecture in theaters across America. As president of the Theatre Atlanta Women's Guild, I hosted him here.

Jack and I invited a few people, including the Israeli consul general Zeev Boneh and his family, to our home after the program to meet Asherov. It was May 22, and our thespian conversation disguised our anxieties anticipating Nasser's next move. Conversations came to a halt at ten o'clock as everyone gathered around the television to hear the nightly news. That night confirmed our worst nightmares: Nasser had closed the Straits of Tiran, choking off Israel's access to the Red Sea and making war inevitable.

The party ended, but a new friendship began for Jack and me. Being together with Misha as we anxiously followed the news bonded us with him forever, and eventually also with his wife, actress Dalia Friedland. As Dalia tells it, she was not pleased when Misha told her he had invited a rabbi and his wife to contact them when they came to Israel. Like most Israelis, she stereotyped rabbis and their wives even less favorably than the well-meaning Americans who told me that I didn't look like one. To most secular Israelis, there could hardly be a more distressing task than entertaining a foreign *rebbetzin*. We still laugh at the thought of what she expected me to be and how angry she was with Misha when I called from Jerusalem the following summer to say I was coming to Tel Aviv and would like to see them.

Dalia and I remain close friends to this day. She is one of many Israeli friends who helped me find myself. I was almost forty when the process began.

Six
ISRAEL AND ME

Until I met Jack I believed that Zionism, the political expression of Jewish statehood, was detrimental to Jews situated comfortably in western democracies (although I realized that the Holocaust and its aftermath created a condition wherein some form of independence for Jews was necessary). Jack strongly supported Israel but never viewed himself as a Zionist because he had no desire to live there. When we married, he was struggling to educate his largely anti-Zionist congregation about Judaism worldwide and he avoided bringing such problems home to me.

For these reasons, I was nearly a total stranger to Zionism when, a few weeks after we married, Jack called at four o'clock in the afternoon to say he was bringing a guest for dinner. This guest, a close friend of Jack's from when they were both assistants in Pittsburgh, was a Christian minister in Atlanta representing Christians for Zionism.

I was terrified. With two hours' notice and no way to get to a grocery store I was stuck with serving the chicken I planned to roast for the two of us as my first attempt at cooking a chicken. The sky darkened as threateningly as my outlook. By the time they arrived, soaking wet because of their long walk from the front driveway to our apartment behind the garage in a downpour, I anticipated the worst.

Jack appeared at the door with a tall, blond, craggy, moon-faced man holding a bouquet of drooping flowers which he handed me saying, "I'm Carl Voss. These were left over from the *shiksas'* luncheon this afternoon."

Thus began a lifelong friendship and my interest in Israel. Carl, shocked at my ignorance and lack of enthusiasm for Zionism, spent most of the evening convincing me to embrace it. His words took years to bear fruit, but that night he planted the seeds.

At first the seeds grew imperceptibly. A few years later, soon after the State of Israel gained independence in May 1948, the Women's Division of the local UJA Campaign asked me to write a promotional dialogue stressing Israel's need for tools. It went over so well that Hadassah repeated it at a convention held nearby. After the performance, Rose Klotz, a leader of Hadassah whom I knew only slightly, embraced me emotionally and said, "Don't tell me you're not a Zionist. You couldn't have written that if you weren't one."

Even then I didn't burn with enthusiasm. When, after the Temple bombing, Jack and I had our first opportunity to attend the World Union for Progressive Judaism meeting in London and remain abroad for a lengthy vacation, neither of us thought of going to Israel. It wasn't until our good friend Nelson Glueck, president of the Hebrew Union College-Jewish Institute of Religion, led his Board of Governors (which included Jack) to Israel for the dedication of its school in Jerusalem in March 1963 that Zionist began to sprout.

This trip was especially meaningful in Reform Judaism because of the many delays in construction caused by Israel's Orthodox establishment, determined to prevent any visible presence of non-orthodox Judaism from arising in the Holy Land. Glueck's school was the first to do so.

Glueck had distinguished himself both as a biblical archaeologist and war hero; before my first trip to Israel, I read his books and crammed Hebrew courses at the Jewish Community Center to progress from beginner to third level within three weeks. That didn't enable me to speak

Hebrew, but it gave me a base vocabulary that proved useful, occasionally even to Jack. His knowledge of Hebrew was Biblical, not contemporary.

That first visit evoked deep emotions, mostly positive. Not at first, however. Tel Aviv reminded me then of lower Collins Avenue in Miami Beach: no five-star waterfront hotels, Michelin-rated restaurants, or Museum of the Diaspora. Sightseeing was limited to the Glass Museum, Jaffa, and the Weizmann Institute in Rehovot.

The director of the Cincinnati Museum, a Christian who had been our seat companion on the flight over, gave Jack and me a new perspective, first noting that it would seem strange to him to be in a country where he was not of the majority religion. That became clear (and he thought it hilarious) when in Jaffa the guide explained who St. Peter was. As I wrote home, every moment brought us a new perspective.

Yesterday and today have been so thrilling that I can't begin to describe them. Our guide made 5,000 years of history come alive for us...made me for the first time in my life realize what a sense of identity really is...

My excitement began on the way to the Negev when we made a pit stop at a place on the beach designated to become a major port. We saw skeletons of a few buildings and stakes in the water indicating where piers would go. The only completed structures were a dormitory for workers and the service station where we stopped.

We saw where Jonah was supposed to have...been regurgitated... It was desert, and still is except where they've built apartments (2,026 units), supermarkets, taxi stands, and rose bushes blooming in beds in the center of streets that have just been paved. There are as yet no sidewalks and no people except the construction workers and concession keepers...but by 1964 they expect it to be their main port.

That was Ashdod, now Israel's primary industrial port on the Mediterranean with skyscrapers that, in 2016, I saw from as far away as the Palmachim Airbase.

Israel grabbed me when we reached the Negev. That stark, barren landscape with its sharp buttes and canyons materialized my visions of biblical wilderness. It touched me deeply. I felt my roots.

From the heights of Avdat, the tel of a sophisticated Nabatean city that he had excavated, Glueck pointed to vegetation far away explaining that it was an experimental farm being cultivated using only tools known to the Nabateans in order to learn how they did it. Among other techniques, they saved dew to moisten the land.

In Beersheba, where we stopped overnight at the newly opened Desert Inn, folk dancers entertained us after dinner. I foolishly accepted the performers' invitation to join them in their concluding dance and developed such sharp pains that I feared a heart attack. But a good night's sleep revived me, and by the time we reached Jerusalem I was a born-again Jew.

The road up followed the path of an ancient road, steeper and more winding than the one we use now. Our bus had to proceed so slowly that we could read the markers identifying groups of soldiers who died in the burnt-out vehicles left in place as memorials from the War of Independence. I saw markers in English of Americans who died there, of *Les Sionistes d'Alsace* who died there, of Jews from every place imaginable—not standing out like ghosts for shock value, but blending in with the trees that had reclaimed them from the wilderness.

Red poppies, yellow daisies, mustard, blue anemones...growing all over ... where our Zionist friends a few years ago like our ancestors 3,000 years ago, picked up stones, made terraces of them, and forced the most barren land you can imagine to grow...we can't imagine it without seeing it because our country is so fertile (the poor North Georgia farmers have a thousand times more to work with.... Some [water] comes from underground, but not much. Most of it is from irrigation, and their second largest river at its greatest point looks like Peachtree Creek in a drought.

As soon as we reached Jerusalem we went to the school for the opening ceremonies. Jack gave the dedicatory prayer and affixed the *mezuzah*. Later, at the convocation where David Ben-Gurion and Golda

Meir spoke, Jack marched in the procession behind them and the other dignitaries and sat with them in the front section. I sat midway back with our friend Helen Dalsheimer from Baltimore, the first woman to serve as president of a major Jewish congregation. Her husband Hugo was, like Jack, a member of the Board, so they marched together and sat in the front.

In Jerusalem, I gained new insight into the benefits of being Jewish. We bumped into our friend Esther Blumberg from Dothan, Alabama, in Tel Aviv with her brother to dedicate a new hotel of the Dan chain in which he was part owner. That included not only the Dan Tel Aviv where we were staying, but also the King David in Jerusalem. When Esther asked us if our room was comfortable, offering to get us a better one if we wished, Jack thanked her and declined because we were there for just two nights. He did, however, request a favor for our check-in at the King David in Jerusalem: he wanted a room on the back of the hotel so I could wake up with a view of the Old City.

Esther obliged and it was *glorious*. I could see the Jaffa Gate, a landmark otherwise denied Jewish tourists in those years before 1967 when Jerusalem was reunited in the Six-Day War. We didn't realize it then, but those rooms still weren't completely safe. We found bullet holes in the wall, souvenirs of a Jordanian sniper.

I harbored no such fears while romanticizing on that first visit. We slept with windows open to the delicious mountain air and awakened to the chant of the muezzin calling the faithful to prayer. Later that morning, our group was received by President and Mrs. Ben-Zvi at Beit HaNassi–the official President's residence.

... on the inside looks like a cozy ski lodge filled with art treasures... It's about half the distance from the main street as the White House is from Pennsylvania Avenue, but the walk is lined with other houses that look exactly like it except that they have no coat-of-arms over the entrance and no guards standing by.... Mrs. Ben-Zvi is like a darling little grandmother. When we were introduced she pinched my cheek and said, "With a face like that you could be a Jerusalemite."

I tried to thank her in Hebrew and must have sounded as ridiculous as I looked in the photograph that David Rubinger captured of me saying it. Rubinger later became famous with his photos covering the Six-Day War for *Life* Magazine, but in 1963 he was just beginning his career and content to work recording our mission. He told me that Rachel Ben-Zvi, the First Lady who seemed like a darling little grandmother, was a feisty, much admired Labor Zionist and educational leader since she emigrated to Palestine in 1908.

After the reception we went to Mount Zion to visit the traditional tomb of King David, the Crusader-built church over it, the room where the Last Supper was supposed to have taken place, and the location still revered as a memorial for Jewish martyrs throughout history. The commercialization appalled me. The bearded old men behind tables holding containers for tourists to deposit money into spoiled whatever feeling of reverence I had and obliterated my sense of its history.

Determined to taste the flavor of the city, I asked our guide for the name of a place where students gathered to relax, argue, and sing. He told me, "This is Jerusalem, the Holy City. Nothing like that happens here."

I didn't believe him. Where there's a university, there's a place where students go. I asked Glueck and he directed us to Savta, a basement club on King George Street. As Jack and I walked down the paved path from the street to its entrance we heard the music of "When the Saints Go Marching In." We didn't understand the Hebrew lyrics, but we knew we'd found the right place. As I described it in my letter home:

...an accordionist plays and everybody sings. For a floor show two very talented boys (couldn't be over 20) play guitars and sing folk songs from all over the world... Later they sang many of our Negro spirituals, sometimes in English... those who didn't know English joined in with the Hallelujahs. It seemed strange singing the songs about Jerusalem in Jerusalem itself...

I returned to Savta thirteen years later, when my son Bill was a student in Jerusalem performing there with a bluegrass group. It was still the place where students unwound.

With Jewish sightseeing then restricted to western Jerusalem, we had few ancient sites to visit. We did marvel at contemporary ones, though—the Chagall windows at Hadassah Medical Center, the Henry Moore sculpture on the grounds of the Israel Museum, and the Dead Sea Scrolls. Our best view of the Old City where most of our holy sites are located consisted of rooftops and domes from a lookout point on Ein Rogel Street at the base of Abu Tor. It faced the Jewish Quarter with the Kotel, also known as the Western Wall, which we could only imagine based on the pictures we'd seen. After services on Shabbat we went without a guide to Mea She'arim and the Mandelbaum Gate. Then, incongruous as it seemed on Shabbat in the Holy City, as on Christmas in America most of us had lunch at a Chinese restaurant. They served very good kreplach as wonton soup.

As we left Jerusalem there were a few sour notes. Hotel clerks, apparently confident that our Jewish hearts would forgive overcharging, delayed almost everyone's checkout disputing with us as we questioned erroneous items on our bills. Our group, comprised primarily of couples who, like me, had previously been lukewarm if not cool toward Zionism and became enthusiastic supporters on the trip, felt disappointed but not disillusioned. We were like family, offended and complaining but still connected.

Before leaving Israel, instead of continuing with the tour Jack and I joined Rabbi James and Helen Wax to travel north with a private car and driver. We stopped at a village of Indian Jews and took pictures with the children. Their school holiday for Pesach had just begun so they were all at home, helping their mothers do the traditionally mandatory thorough cleaning before celebrating the festival.

... Everything gets taken out of the house, even the bedsprings.... Also made friends with some bedouin children and took pictures with them... including their camels, tents, and their father's truck parked alongside...

At lunch by the sea at Caesarea, Jack made friends with a dog (as he frequently did). That led to acquaintance with the dog's owner, manager of the Caesarea Golf Club, who told us that the seed for their greens comes from Tifton, Georgia.

Caesarea was the most spectacular setting you can imagine... the sea so blue and the sand so bright... saw one Roman column that had a crusader cross nailed to it, then torn away by the next people who came. The last were Moslems from Bosnia... just 80 years ago.

We also visited Akko, Safed, and Tiberias, none of which enchanted me, although I found them interesting because of their history. I thought that Safed had lost the Old World flavor that Jack reported from there in 1950. Now that foreign tourists were arriving, it had more people and less charm.

[In Tiberius] Maimonides' grave was a disgrace. Wish we hadn't gone there. Exquisite country, though.

I reported ecstatically about the vegetation in the Galilee, the gray rocks, green-gray olive trees splashed with yellow mimosa, trees and bushes, splashes of blue flowers that looked like bachelor button or larkspur, dark green cypresses and cedars, red poppies and golden daisies. Also amazing to me were all the fruits that I saw growing in addition to the oranges—figs, olives, bananas, dates, peaches, plums, and breadfruit— in the Rothschild Gardens at Zichron Yaakov.

Nazareth interested me because of the new part of the city: row upon row of apartment houses hanging off the side of the mountain, all recently built for the newcomers, in addition to a factory for them to work in. Like the other shrines, I found Old Nazareth, with its references to Jesus' childhood and ministry, commercialized and cheap (though colorful) in the Arab market.

In Haifa we visited Technion, the Leo Baeck School, and a *kibbutz* with beautiful gardens on the mountainside overlooking the sea. On the way to Tel Aviv and the airport we saw a lady soldier waiting for a bus —a beautiful, petite blonde who looked as if she'd come off the set of *The Sound of Music*—and gave her a ride. She spoke no English, but we questioned her in French and learned that she came from Tunis, had been in Israel with her parents for seven years, and was studying to be a chemical engineer while doing her time in the army as an office worker.

On our way home we visited Greece, as did several other rabbinic couples from our group, one of whom arranged a memorable impromptu Seder for us at the Hotel Grande Bretagne. The organizing rabbi borrowed a Haggadah from a nearby U.S. Army post while his wife taught the hotel chef how to prepare charoset and matzoh balls.

We stayed in Paris for a couple of days, where we joined another couple from the Israel trip for a salacious experience at a restaurant specializing in Rabelaisian innuendoes and good food shaped to shock the straightlaced. At midnight, they took us to Les Halles for an early breakfast of the traditional onion soup before boarding our overseas flight to New York. Having breakfast in Paris and dinner that same day at home in Atlanta was a novelty then, when jet travel had just begun. It was a remarkable way to end the most remarkable journey of my life and begin a series of new ones, each more remarkable than the last.

The Israeli consuls based in Atlanta boosted my enthusiasm for Israel. We became lifelong friends with Nahum Astar, the first Israeli consul, and his wife, Renate, when they arrived in 1956, and likewise with their successors, Ilse and Shimon Yallon, four years later. When we told the Yallons that, unlike many American Jews, we had no known relatives in Israel, they offered themselves as surrogates. That made all the difference on subsequent visits.

Jack and I organized a tour of Israel for Temple members in early January 1968, as soon as possible after the Six-Day War. Fewer than the minimum number of people applied, but the thirteen who went returned with rave reviews. That paved the way for today's biennial Temple tours that bring hundreds of Temple members to Israel each time, the latest trip numbering more than 250 participants. We few on that first trip had the advantage of seeing the country and meeting a variety of its citizens at a unique point in their history, a time of boundless euphoria and optimism that hasn't been equaled since.

Because the Yallons were home from service overseas, Jack and I traveled a few days ahead of our group to spend time with them. On our first day there they took us to Ramallah for lunch, a Friday tradition for many Jews during the British mandate before the Jordanians occupied it. Then they took us to visit one of their friends in Beit Jallah, an Arab town on the opposite side of the mountain from Bethlehem overlooking the part of Jerusalem where they lived, and showed us trenches in his garden from which Jordanian soldiers had fired rockets at their neighborhood. It had been barely eight months since the Yallons spent days and nights huddled under the staircase of their apartment building to avoid being killed by those rockets.

The Yallons referred to their friend not as a Palestinian, but simply—and non-pejoratively—as an Arab. Jews and Arabs back then used the term "Palestinian" in reference to long-established families of whatever faith. It implied status as an elite, someone descended from generations of Jerusalem residents. The term "Palestinian" had not yet been co-opted to mean only non-Jewish residents of the area.

We learned more the next day when the Yallons took us to visit their children and grandchildren at Kibbutz Beit Alfa. As personal guests, we stayed overnight in the quarters of another *kibbutznik* who was away at the time. Children still lived in children's houses, visiting their parents when the parents finished work and having dinner with them in the large dining hall. Parents then took their children to the children's house to say goodnight. I went with Ilse to tuck in her two young grandsons.

Because it was Shabbat, it surprised me to see men digging a huge hole in the center of the *kibbutz*. When I asked why they were working on their one day off, Shimon explained that they were doing it voluntarily. They were excavating for a communal bomb shelter. That awakened me to the idealistic component of socialism, seeing it work well in a setting such as that, a homogeneous group of Zionist pioneers, but I was doubtful about its endurance when Israel achieved its goal of being more prosperous and urbanized, "a nation like any other nation." We didn't know it then, but *kibbutzim* were already changing.

When our Temple group arrived, we concentrated on sightseeing, starting with biblical sites in the Old City.

A tourist seeing it for the first time feels as if he were being shuttled up and down through civilization on a high speed elevator... We started out one morning visiting the wailing wall and the Dome of the Rock, the spot where Abraham laid Isaac to be sacrificed, and ended up in the late afternoon at a fashion show, watching mini skirted models slither down a staircase in the latest suedes and knits. It was as if someone had run off 4,000 years of newsreels in a single sitting!

The party and fashion show took place at the home of Ilse's best friend, Fanny Rosenbloom, who owned Jerusalem's finest dress shop. Two of Fanny's guests, Lebanese friends from British mandate times who weren't Jewish, drove down from Beirut for the event. Yet another lesson learned: based on our media-fed view of Mid-East conditions, it surprised me to see the camaraderie resumed after nineteen years of hostile separation.

On what was supposed to be our last night in Jerusalem we awoke to a major surprise. Normally King David Street resounds with the sound of traffic long before the average American tourist is ready for it. On that morning, nothing moved except for falling snow.

It was Jerusalem's heaviest snowstorm since 1950. 12 inches fell! All motor traffic stopped other than the few vehicles with four-wheel drive reserved for emergency use by the municipality. Even helicopters couldn't move. The police rode donkeys to get around.

I pulled a parka over my nightgown and robe, grabbed my camera, and hurried out onto the balcony to take pictures.

The hotel staff couldn't get to work and the night workers couldn't get home. Later in the day a few employees arrived on foot, but the skeletal staff was still overwhelmed trying to service 500 guests, many of them VIPs, including foreign diplomats furious at having their schedule interrupted. One chambermaid who passed me in the hall, after wishing me a cheerful "Good morning," shook her head and commented on the overworked, understaffed situation. "It's like Yom Kippur but with food," she said.

When a maid finally reached our room to make the bed and bring fresh linens, I helped. Some, on finding a guest in the room as they came to clean, just emptied the waste baskets, smoothed back the bed, and handed a dust cloth to the guest saying, "You finish. I have too many more to do."

We were supposed to leave and go to Masada so our luggage was already on the bus for an early departure, but we had our warm jackets and headgear because the only access to Masada in those days was via the Roman road. To reach it required driving across the desert from Arad in a WWII open half-track, a very cold excursion in winter. The only thing we were missing for going out into the snow was suitable footwear. We solved that by tying plastic laundry bags over our shoes, then went onto the terrace of the King David to build a snowman. Tourists, scholars, diplomats, religious pilgrims, people on professional or business missions all milled about the lobby, attempting to speak to each other despite the many tongues and trying to help each other forget that a rare and precious day of sightseeing or work was being lost.

We called friends who lived in the city to see how they were doing. The Leshems, who had followed the Yallons in Atlanta, were frantically preparing to leave for their new post at the United Nations. The storm was a frustrating interruption for them, but their two small boys were delighted. They had never seen snow and thought it would be like that every day in New York.

Shimon Yallon walked to his office and then to the hotel to visit us. He found us late in the morning, about time for a Bloody Mary, but we couldn't get into the bar because a group of Italian tourists were holding a Bible reading there.

By mid-afternoon the snow stopped, the sky cleared, and we were rewarded with a glimpse of the Dead Sea, rarely visible from Jerusalem.

The train from Tel Aviv and Haifa still came and went, but although the station was only a few blocks away, we couldn't get to it through the deep snow. The night before, when the snow began, our guide Max had called a friend who owned a broken-down truck and spent the next 24 hours repairing it sufficiently to get us to the train the morning after.

Another bus met us in Tel Aviv to continue our tour. A woman from Haifa boarding the train with us commented, "Ach! In Jerusalem, it's always something. If not the Arabs, it's the weather."

For us it was a great experience, but only one of many that we encountered on that memorable trip.

Masada was another highlight. On our way back across the desert we met a bedouin on a camel. Our guide spoke to him in his native dialect to assure him of our friendship, and he handed over his dagger to assure us of his. It was hard to believe that this was happening in the same country where, a few miles away, other men were experimenting with peaceful uses of an atomic reactor.

One day we flew over the Sinai Desert. We saw Egyptian airstrips, tank tracks, and hundreds of abandoned and burned-out Soviet-built tanks. Mostly covered over by drifting sands, they seemed like mites' specks across the barren landscape. Then we suddenly saw Mount Sinai jutting up into the sky with awesome majesty. I recalled the Gustave Doré engravings in my grandmother's large family Bible and wondered how Doré could have portrayed it so accurately in the 19th century without having seen it from an airplane.

We flew on to the Red Sea, continuing south as far as Sharm El-Sheikh and the Straits of Tiran, then turned northeast into the Gulf of Aqaba to land at the northern tip of Eilat, just a few miles east of Ezion-Geber, the ancient port city where the Queen of Sheba landed when she came to visit King Solomon. Nelson Glueck discovered that in 1939, along with evidence of King Solomon's copper mines only a short distance away. We saw the remains of the smelting furnaces and workshops, and the mounds of black slag discarded 3,000 years ago. Nearby, at Timna, the Israelis mine copper today in a modern plant that produces more and better quality copper, but they credit King Solomon—and our friend Dr. Glueck—with having shown them where to find it.

Realizing that our Temple members had little background in Biblical or Zionist history, I wanted them to see places they could relate to from popular culture and our southern Bible Belt background. Most of them had read *The Source*, a popular historical novel by James Michener, so when we went north I planned to visit Meggido (Armageddon, where many believe the world's final judgement will take place) because it's one of the inspirations for Michener's story about Hoopoe's tunnel, the secret source of water that enabled possessors to prevail over attacking forces ever since Pharaoh Thutmose III prevailed there in the 15th century BCE. I wanted to see if the well still held fresh water.

We descended slowly, wonderingly... Suddenly it was cold and dark yet not too dark to see and neither dank nor eerie... It seems a long way going down... Finally we reached the bottom and... the well... after all these years, 3,000 or more, still has water in it. Clear and... pure.

Our wonderful guide, Max Walzer, had been Michener's guide, so I expected him to be equally enthusiastic about showing us the Akko prison where Michener described the daring breakout of Jewish boys condemned to death by the British for smuggling Holocaust survivors into the Holy Land. On the contrary, Max did not want to go there and used every possible argument against it. I insisted, and we went.

While Jack and I were in the room where four of the boys had been hanged, looking at their pictures and realizing that they were about the same age as our Bill, Max came up to us quietly and stood beside us. We were overcome with emotion and so was he. Eventually he spoke. "I didn't want to come here," he said. "It's the first time I've been back since the breakout. I'm one of those who escaped."

We later learned that both he and our new friend, Zvi Avrami, manager of the King David Hotel, were among those members of the Irgun who blew up a wing of the hotel that housed British soldiers in 1946. During the Holocaust, Max and Zvi were captured parachuting into Europe for the Jewish Agency, together surviving a concentration camp from which they were rescued by Americans. Hearing their stories and others like them then structured our view of Israel as nothing at a later time could have done. Future tourists would have more to see, but the emotional impact of that moment was ephemeral and unique.

Six months later, Jack and I returned to Jerusalem for the biennial convention of the World Union for Progressive Judaism. I stayed on after he left to produce documentary vignettes for Atlanta's local morning show on WAGA-TV, an assignment I had arranged in order to test myself on being able to manage alone.

I had begun to obsess over the fact that Jack had an alpha personality, chain-smoked, and was more than a half-generation older than me. It stood to reason that I would be left without him sooner or later. He had once told me that himself years earlier, when we were much younger and had no apparent reason for thinking of it. Out of nowhere he suddenly said, "Given the difference in our ages and family longevity, it stands to reason that you'll have a large part of your life to live without me. You should go for it. Start over with someone else."

I thought that was a strange thing to say, but was too busy to dwell on it then. In the wake of Martin Luther King's assassination, the memory surfaced and I wondered how I would manage without him. I had been independent enough before we married, but now I was out of practice. I had never traveled without him, never made a major decision on my own, never even bought a small kitchen appliance without asking his approval. He didn't demand it. I simply assumed that was the thing to do.

Without my dwelling on it, the seed germinated. I decided to test my independence that summer in Israel and arranged with the Israeli government to facilitate my production of human interest pieces for Arden Zinn's morning show on WAGA-TV. The station supplied film and Israel provided the crew, even covering my extra hotel bill. I wanted to show how Israelis, despite the prevailing danger, went on with their daily lives as if conditions were normal.

After the convention, Jack and I spent a week at Caesarea where the Yallons joined us, and by chance Joan and Nathan Lipson from Atlanta were also there. When Jack left for Europe and home I checked into a

On the WAGA-TV set of *Gates: A Dream,* written by Janice Rothschild for a 1969 UJA Campaign for which it won a national prize. With producer Mike Field.

seaside hotel in Tel Aviv for the few days before I was due to begin work in Jerusalem, planning to luxuriate on the beach during the day and meet friends for dinner each night.

I did none of it. My test of independence went so badly at first that when the Lipsons called to offer me a ride to Jerusalem the next day I accepted despite knowing that my reservation at the King David didn't begin for several more days and all the hotels there were fully booked. Ilse kindly sheltered me in the interim and added interestingly to my social life by introducing me to Bernard Cherrick, the vice president of Hebrew University. He filled my spare time with special sightseeing, intellectual British-accented conversation, and an introduction to the world of the Orthodox Jewish elite by inviting me to a party he hosted for visiting Hadassah leaders. Never before had I tasted world-class kosher catering.

As always, I had a marvelous time being with the Yallons and their friends, although the pleasure was tempered by another Jerusalem weather phenomenon, this one less pleasant than snow. It was a summer *hamsin*, a hot wind from the desert that carries fine grains of burning sand into everything, including human faces. When I awoke the first morning, Ilse had already closed all windows, shutters, and drapes, and turned on the bathroom shower, sprinkling its water as far as possible into adjoining rooms. It reminded me of my grandmother closing everything like that to resist the heat during long ago summers in Columbus.

Thankfully, the King David had air conditioning. My film crew picked me up to start work at 7AM. By 9AM. it was already hot, and by 11AM. the heat was too exhausting for us to continue. When the guys dropped me off at the hotel around noon I ordered cold cuts and a Bloody Mary at the bar, then went to my room, showered, and slept in bed for an hour or more. When the crew picked me up again for work at 4 p.m. I was born again and ready for a new day. We filmed vignettes at the children's zoo where an amiable chimpanzee perched on my shoulder, in Bethlehem spotting a bride as she entered the Church of the Nativity to be married, and at the excavation on the southern steps of the Temple Mount where Professor Benjamin Mazar—now recognized as the dean of biblical archeologists—lowered me to the first-century level he'd just reached and permitted me to brush the sand off one of the steps. I later wrote a story about it for the Atlanta newspapers, focusing on the fact that it was the entrance Jesus would have used when he arrived via the Valley of the Cheesemakers to observe the festivals.

The most exciting event of that visit was going to Bethlehem with Joan and Nathan Lipson for the performance of Verdi's Requiem in Manger Square, organized and directed by Zubin Mehta, conductor of the Israel Philharmonic Orchestra.

We went to hear a concert, about 3,500 of us with tickets, an estimated 3,500 more without. They hung from over the balconies and on the rooftops of the buildings...

Intended hopefully as the kickoff for an annual music festival celebrating peace, it evoked emotions more than sufficient to override the unsatisfactory acoustics and unseasonable light rain. Those factors notwithstanding, we enjoyed the music and returned to Jerusalem ecstatic with unrealistic confidence that Mehta's peace initiative would succeed.

As soon as I returned to Atlanta I began thinking of ways to go back. The answer came in the form of an assignment, worked out with the University of Georgia television director Hill Bermont in cooperation with the Israeli government, to make a documentary for NET, the educational network. I drafted the plot—about Israeli schoolchildren questioning archaeologists' statement that there had been no habitation at Arad during the period of the Exodus. I asked for no pay other than to go on location with them. As it turned out, Hill and his crew actually needed me to help with our volunteer actors, kids from Arad on their Passover vacation. They were three 12-year-old girls, two 14-year-old boys, and a freckle-faced, undersized 11-year-old boy, Udi, whom we affectionately called Dennis the Menace... *The kind you could never forget... Israel's secret weapon... The girls... were the type destined to direct the course of history by the power of chicken soup...*

On our first day of filming we stopped in Arad to pick up the children, then continued down to the Dead Sea, the descent to 400 feet below sea level so sharp that our ears popped. The landscape was my idea of the moonscape—surrealistic cones, columns, tabled chunks of salt and shale, tortured twists of gray, white, yellow, copper, all looked as if they were giant leftovers from a science fiction set.

We went first to the oasis of Ein Gedi, where high pink cliffs towered over tangles of bamboo, acacia, eucalyptus, palm, and fern. Bananas, dates, pistachio, figs, and myriads of flowers tumbled beside waterfalls spilling dozens of feet into clear green pools.

Our guide Micha served as interpreter, with some help from one of the girls who came from Argentina and communicated with me in Spanish. In Hebrew, "no" is an equally simple one-syllable word, "lo," but the children didn't understand it in any language. Near the top of Masada, Udi spied a crane before I did and climbed into its basket. When I spotted him, he was swinging some 1,500 feet over the Negev desert.

At a bedouin encampment near the tel of ancient Arad we convinced the leader to let us film his camels, after which he invited us into his tent for coffee. We sat on crates and drank from used jelly glasses, incongruous with what I saw when our host reached out to pour our coffee. He wore a fine gold watch and emerged with the sleeve of a leather jacket peeking out under his bedouin robe. We didn't see any women because their custom required them to be sequestered out of sight of the male visitors.

One night we stayed late to film a scene on the Arad hotel grounds and were repeatedly delayed by mishaps such as a guest tripping over a cable and another guest taking a flash photo, both requiring retakes. We returned to our hotel in Beersheba well past midnight. The director, Hill, left a call for each of us for six o'clock the next morning, which made me wonder if I was not a bit superannuated for such hours and exercise.

On the last day of our shoot we were caught in a sandstorm that wobbled our truck and obscured the road. The sun's rays blotted out all scenery, changing our view from opaque yellow to opaque pink as we chugged up from the Dead Sea to return the children to their anxious parents in Arad. We returned to Jerusalem exhausted and full of sand, but pleased with our results. The documentary won a national award.

In those days the government of Israel strongly promoted Arab businesses, housing many of its guests in Arab facilities and encouraging guides to take tourists to Arab shops for purchases. When we first arrived, the government sent us to the International Hotel on the Mount of Olives. Because it was a luxury hotel with a panoramic view of Jerusalem, my colleagues were delighted to stay there. I was not. It was anathema to many Jews because the builders included stones taken from Jewish graves on the ancient cemetery there. Its East Jerusalem location was also problematic for Jews due to terrorist attacks, not yet carried out on an international scale as with the Rome to Tel Aviv plane hijacking that occurred three months later, but enough to signal us to stay away. During the two days we were there preparing for our shoot my Jerusalem friends were afraid to visit me or pick me up there for dinner. The government found space for me at the King David when we returned.

(above and opposite)Israel, 1969

I never welcomed luxury accommodations more than I did that night. After room service and a long hot bath, I fell asleep immediately. An hour later the telephone rang. It was London calling. "Wrong number," I mumbled, and went back to sleep.

Again, the telephone awakened me. Again, it was London calling. Again, I refused the call and dozed off.

When it happened the third time I'd had it with the operator and he'd clearly had it with me. In his very clipped, haughty British accent he demanded, "You *are* Mrs. Rothschild, are you not?"

"Yes," I mumbled.

"And you *do* have a son, do you not?"

"Yes."

"Well," said my antagonist, "he is in London and he would like to speak with you."

"No," I replied, now reasonably awake. "My son is in New Haven, Connecticut, and does not wish to speak with me because he is probably asleep, which I would very much like to be." I hung up.

I then called the hotel operator and asked to have my phone blocked for the rest of the night. In Israel and in Europe the name Rothschild can be a curse as well as a blessing. There, people assume you are one of *the* Rothschilds, a relative of the charming Baron Guy de Rothschild. On our first trip to Paris it proved to be a blessing, providing me with royal treatment at Elizabeth Arden's because the proprietress mistook me for a cousin of her client the Baroness.

Hill and his crew stayed in Israel a few more days to film Christian sites and I stayed to celebrate Seder in Jerusalem. That year the eve of Pesach fell on the night of Good Friday so I went to the Old City with my colleagues that morning to film the Procession of the Cross. We found a likely rooftop at the third Station of the Cross and climbed up to await the action. While waiting, I noticed David Rubinger, the photographer who memorialized my conversation with Mrs. Ben-Zvi, looking for a place from which to shoot. I signaled to him to join us, which he did, and we had a great reunion. By then he had become known for his coverage of the Six-Day War, and it gave me great pride to assist a famous photographer in finding a shooting perch in his own hometown.

Bernard Cherrick and his sister took me to their friends' home for

Seder. As it was my first time in an Orthodox home, I'd forgotten that the rule requiring separate utensils for food during Pesach precluded using the family's finest as we do, so I was initially surprised to see the table set with mismatched plates and old jelly glasses. I learned another lesson when encouraged to ask questions, which I thought referred to the probability that I wouldn't understand much of the Hebrew. Not only was the conversation and much of the service in English, but the questions to which they referred were a Seder tradition, like a game, evoking hair-splitting arguments of the Talmudic rabbis known as *pilpul*. Most surprising of all was that everyone joined freely in the ritual, enjoying and prolonging it rather than rushing through it to serve the soup. Afterward everyone stayed at the table singing until after midnight, even the family's teenage daughters and their friends.

Again, I returned home with an expanded outlook and a multitude of new experiences to build on. Each visit to Israel differed completely from the one before.

As I perceived it, Jewish fundraisers and philanthropists, in their zeal to help Israel, confused giving with investing, using the same talking points for Israel Bonds as they did for the United Jewish Appeal. I considered it a disservice to both. To address it, I began writing a column *pro bono* for our local Jewish weekly, *The Southern Israelite*, entitled "Made in Israel," using material supplied by the Israel consulate to publicize Israeli businesses recently established with help from Israel Bonds. I included such exports as international construction projects in Africa, but concentrated on commodities available locally such as Jaffa oranges, Osem soups and Naot shoes.

At about the same time, the Israel Ministry of Tourism organized volunteer committees in cities worldwide to promote tourism to Israel for reasons other than religion and politics. They asked me to head the effort in Atlanta and I accepted, naming it the VIP (Visit Israel Program) Committee. I recruited well-known men and women, interreligious and interracial, to serve on it. We offered ourselves as luncheon speakers for organizations, highlighting aspects of Israel appropriate to the organization's interest and our own expertise. While I was never an expert in gardening, I targeted garden clubs with a slide lecture about Neot Kedumim, the biblical garden where scriptural metaphors become relevant and understandable today.

In November 1969, while in Boston with Jack at a meeting of the American Jewish Federations, I received a call from the Atlanta consulate to join other tourism committee leaders in Israel two days later for a week-long tour. I flew home in a flash, unpacking and repacking so quickly that I forgot my bathing suit, a mistake I sorely regretted when we went to Sharm el-Sheikh and I couldn't go swimming in the Red Sea with the others. We traveled from the Golan Heights to Sharm el-Sheikh and back in six days. Possibly because I was the lone woman in the group of six, the ministry sent a woman, Ylana Pearlstein, as our escort. We bonded immediately and remained close friends for many years.

A few months later I went back to Israel again, this time with Jack for the Central Conference of American Rabbis. Our friends Jerry and Rita Rosenbloom also attended, and after the conference they went with us to the site of Shomron, capital of the biblical kingdom of Israel, home of the Samaritans.

Our guide pulled the car to the curb on a semi-residential street of sturdy stone houses, some with shops on the ground floor, and asked us to wait while he went inside one of them. We could see three men dressed as Arabs, with long coats hanging loose over pajama-like shirts and trousers and Turkish fezzes on their heads, seated at a table playing some sort of game. One of them, an aristocratic, dark-bearded giant of a man, came out to meet us.

"I am Jacob Cohen, son of the High Priest," he announced in startlingly good English, extending his hand to greet us. "If you will follow me, I will show you our synagogue."

We followed him up a long flight of steps to the entrance of an adjoining building. As we reached the top, one of his companions came scurrying after us with two keys. Mr. Cohen introduced him as a cousin, a member of another priestly family. There were three such families, to each of which the community entrusted a different key to the synagogue, with all three keys being required to open it.

We entered a large rectangular room. A mosaic of prayer rugs formed a smaller rectangle in the interior of the room. Stiff-backed armchairs stood rigidly against the two long walls. In the center of the wall to our left, facing Mount Gerizim, we saw the curtained ark with a portable lectern nearby. Then, with skepticism rising, we listened as the son of the high priest proclaimed, approaching the ark, "In a moment you will see the oldest book in the world. This Torah is more than 3,000 years old, personally written by the Prophet Moses himself."

Tenderly he lifted the Torah from the ark and brought it to where we stood, his cousin following with the portable lectern. We could see that the book was very old, many times repaired and patched.

As usual, I didn't have my flash equipment with me when I needed it. Noting my dilemma, Mr. Cohen scooped up his supposedly 3,000-year-old sacred scroll and carried it outside into the drizzle to give me sufficient light for my picture.

After that he took us across the street to his home where he had cabinets filled with artifacts for sale. We demurred on the apparently authentic and expensive ones, but bought two miniature cult figures for souvenirs.

In February 1971 the Ministry of Tourism invited me to Israel again, this time to join a group of women editors for a week of fact-finding. I fulfilled my obligation as a supposed editor by profiling special Israeli women we met and sending the articles to the consulate for distribution to the Jewish Telegraphic Agency. The women were Enam Zuabi, an activist for women and wife of a Moslem member of the Knesset; Zena Harmon, Nobel Peace laureate and wife of Avraham Harmon, former ambassador to the United States; Aviva Glezer, a noted pilot and instructor for the Israeli Air Force; and Ruth Dayan, who developed cottage industries for new immigrants—then divorcing her hsuband, Moshe Dayan. I was especially pleased to meet her because I knew her parents, who were friends of the Yallons.

My objective in getting to Israel just then was to cover Israeli Fashion Week for my column in *The Southern Israelite*. After the group tour ended, the government housed me at the Shalom Hotel in Tel Aviv for a few days so I could report on some of the fashions. I enjoyed that immensely, especially the Gottex collection of elegant beachwear. I also had my own special shopping mission—to buy a formal gown for the Temple's upcoming celebration of Jack's 25th anniversary as its rabbi. I found the dress at Maskit, Ruth Dayan's outlet for the typical Middle Eastern handmade items first produced by the immigrants in her cottage industry initiative.

My treasured purchase, a floor-length turquoise French silk version of a Middle East embroidered peasant dress, might have been ruined before reaching Atlanta had it not been for my actress friend Dalia Friedland. When I told her about having left it for minor alterations, she warned me against letting the store deliver it to the hotel, saying that it could be misplaced or stolen, and urged me to have it sent to her apartment, where I could pick it up on my way to the airport.

Janice and Jack with their children Marcia and Bill celebrating Rabbi Rothschild's 25 years at The Temple.

Thankfully, I took her advice. On my next-to-last evening in Israel, before dressing for dinner with a local journalist, I heard popping sounds outside. Assuming they were reports from military planes nearby, I paid no attention and continued sorting papers to mail home. When I heard voices in the street below yelling "Esh!" I dismissed them at first. Then I realized that "Esh" meant "Fire," but I still wasn't alarmed because I'd once been in a hotel fire in New York and trusted that the hotel's management would call all the guest rooms with information and instructions as the hotel in New York did. Nevertheless, I quickly dressed enough to open the door and sniff for smoke. I didn't smell anything, but I saw a hotel bellman leading a group of hysterical tourists toward the elevators, so I grabbed my purse and joined them. There was always a possibility of surprise attack. Only a few months before, the PLO had launched the attempted takeover in nearby Jordan known as Black September.

I couldn't understand what the attendant was trying to say with his very limited English, and neither could the Brazilian tourists. He kept repeating, "Go down! Go down!"

To me, remembering World War II, the bellman's words implied the likely approach of enemy aircraft, so when the door opened on the ground floor, I rushed out and looked for signs indicating a bomb shelter or basement entrance. I didn't see any. Finally, I asked someone for directions and learned that "go down" was a literal translation of the Hebrew expression for getting off a bus, train, or elevator.

Eventually I understood that there was no bomb threat but rather a disastrous fire in the Shalom department store adjoining the hotel which endangered guests in neighboring rooms due to the possibility of window breakage and debris from the fire. For that reason, the Brazilians were being evacuated and I was not.

I pushed my way through the crowd to a place where I could climb up and sit, confident that my dinner date would find me. Once he did, he took me to a seaside restaurant in Herzliya, a considerable distance from downtown Tel Aviv. Afterward he returned me to the Shalom Hotel only to learn that all guests had been sent elsewhere for the night due to possible smoke and water damage from the fire. It was late and all the downtown hotels were filled. I received a voucher for a hotel in Herzliya and we headed out again. When we arrived there, the last room had been taken. The clerk found me an accommodation in a hotel nearby that wouldn't have rated a single star, but I was grateful to have a room and free my chivalrous friend to go home to his wife—in Petach Tikva, another long drive in another direction.

Only when I settled into bed, exhausted and with no nightgown or clean clothes for the next day, did I realize that I was completely cut off from friends and family. In case of emergency no one knew where I was and I certainly wasn't going to call Ilse at that time of night to tell her. Fortunately, my only family member with an emergency was me. A few hours' sleep and a long taxi ride to the Shalom Hotel concluded my ordeal. And my beautiful new formal gown had escaped the smoke and water damage by spending the night in Dalia's apartment.

That trip concluded the first phase of my acquaintance with Israel and with myself. I returned home content with what had been and eager to get on with what was about to be, anticipating the congregation's anniversary gift to Jack of a six-month sabbatical, looking forward to it as a second honeymoon as well as an exciting new adventure, a time to renew our commitment to each other and to dream for our future.

Seven
ADVENTURE!

W e departed October 1, 1971, heading for Israel via the Pacific. We planned to spend the first half of Jack's six-month sabbatical touring the Orient en route to Israel. I studied tourist destinations, questioned friends with recent experience there (especially regarding hotels), then consulted a travel agent. He disapproved of two of my choices and when I persisted, he allegedly requested the reservation in one of them and was refused because it was filled for the dates we wanted. Four months in advance? I told him to try again.

Our trip began with a flight to Honolulu. Jack's generous send-off gift from the congregation included a note saying to use it for something he always wanted but couldn't afford. He chose first-class passage for us across the Pacific, which gave us coddling attention throughout the trip there.

We connected for Hilo on the big island, Hawaii, drove to Kīlauea, which was erupting but not dangerously so, and spent the first night of our adventure at the Volcano House. The next day we drove into the Halema'uma'u crater and around, then to Kona for a sense of Hawaii's seafaring past before continuing along the coast and back to the airport a day sooner than we'd planned. In Honolulu we stayed at the Halekulani

Hotel on Waikiki, one our travel agent discouraged as second-rate, and we loved it. Not yet all high-rise like its neighbors, it still offered cottages on the sand where the surf roared by night and rolled onto our toes when we stepped outside. It was exactly what we wanted.

After two days on the beach and some basic sightseeing, we departed for Japan. Shimon Yallon, then stationed at the Israeli Embassy there, met us as we stepped off the plane. He and Ilse had a car with a driver, so we rode with them and let our courier handle the luggage.

I wrote home that the Japanese were the most pleasant and courteous people I'd ever met—and the most difficult to communicate with. They had spent a generation rising up from the economic devastation of World War II, and left it to the next generation to become fluent in English.

Shimon instructed us. He said that using pidgin English was not discourteous but expected and necessary, and that we should never leave the hotel without a map indicating our destination and a card from the hotel showing the taxi driver where to go when we returned. Tokyo had no street addresses.

After the first day I caught on and stopped using the hotel card. I told the driver "Hoteru Paris" and he understood: the Palace Hotel.

Our adventures with the Yallons included a trip to Nikko, where I triumphed at lunch by successfully deboning my fish with chopsticks. Shimon scheduled an obligatory formal business dinner so that we could experience it and gave a dinner for us at the Jewish Center to introduce us there. Walter Citrin, the community leader, invited Jack to speak at the Center the following week.

Walter's wife, Judy, took me to a meeting of the Japan Israel Women's Organization (JIWO), a group of about 100 Japanese and 50-60 Westerners founded by the wife of a former Israeli ambassador with an imperial princess. It supported facilities for mentally challenged children and provided scholarships for Japanese students to attend the Hebrew University. Its meetings celebrated cultural parallels between the two countries, the one I attended featuring the harp and the koto, a Japanese harp that looks something like a bass fiddle lying down.

When we learned that Isaac Stern was in town, we searched in vain for information on getting tickets to his concert. One day we spotted him in our hotel's coffee shop. He invited us to join him and immediately apologized for not being able to hear Jack speak at the center because he had a concert that night.

"How do you know where Jack is performing when we can't find out where you're performing?" I asked the world's leading violinist.

Stern said he heard it from his friends the Citrins, and we couldn't get information about his concert because it was already sold out by subscription. He said he'd get us tickets, and at 5:45 on the afternoon of the 6:30 concert he called to tell us he was sending the tickets to our room.

I once again had to argue with a travel agent when we decided to spend our last night in the area in an authentic Japanese inn. We wanted to leave our scheduled tour of the Hakone National Park, stay overnight at the inn, and leave for Kyoto from the nearest station. The agent said we'd be uncomfortable and wouldn't like it. I assured him we would. Then he told us that we couldn't get eggs for breakfast. I told him that we didn't *want* eggs for breakfast. When he claimed he couldn't get the reservation because everything was booked, I said, "Try again."

Our inn was at the bottom of a canyon across the road from Myanoshita's grand hotel, on a fast-running stream between mountains. We descended in a cable car and were met at the station by the proprietor. He told us to call him Pinkie and announced triumphantly that he had secured eggs for our breakfast.

Pinkie and our courier, Moti, led us through paths and bridges too dark to see, including a suspension bridge over cascading water. Finally, within the inn's property but still outdoors, we followed them through more paths and tunnels to House #18, where we met a smiling, buck-toothed lady in a dark blue kimono named Mie. She greeted us with a deep bow and instructed us with gestures to remove our shoes and slip into a pair of slippers just inside the door.

Mie-san then took Jack into the bedroom to exchange his

traveling clothes for a *yukata*. Meanwhile, Pinkie-san and Moti showed me the rest of the suite, including the bathroom with its large bathtub.

"Very nice," I said. "But where is the public bath like in Japanese movies?"

Pinkie then showed me the public facilities, advising that we go after dinner because the Japanese go before. There were two dressing rooms, one for general use and the other for women too modest to use it. When we reached the huge glass-covered pool bordered with simulated rock to resemble a lake, Pinkie repeated his advice about going late to avoid company.

Returning to our quarters, I found Jack seated on the floor being served tea by Mie. When Pinkie left, Mie put me into the proper clothes, then she went for our dinner. While waiting, we sipped bourbon and laughed at our attempts to relax on floor seats. "Must be intended for men only," I wrote.

After our early dinner, I was too sleepy to await privacy in the public bath so we went then. Getting undressed posed no problem because we were alone, but I spotted two male heads above the water on the far side of the pool. They were partially curtained off by steam from the hot springs and cold mountain air, so I didn't turn back. I crouched at the nearest faucet for a quick wash, then slid into the water with deliberate speed. Jack followed, and we soaked comfortably in place until after the men left.

The dressing room was empty when we returned but we soon heard the approaching click of wooden clogs. Facing the lockers with our backs to the door we couldn't see, but we heard the clicks suddenly recede as if reversing course. On our way out a man seated in the lounge nodded to us cordially, then rose and entered the dressing room.

Sleeping on the floor with wooden blocks as pillows was enjoyable only as a one-time experience. I awoke shortly after dawn to find Jack in the far corner of a lower level alcove by the window, holding a short-wave radio to his ear. He was trying to hear the last game of the World Series, but the static was so bad that he gave up and suggested that we go for a walk. Mie-san then appeared with coffee, opened the shoji shutters so we could see the view, and soon returned with our breakfast.

We saw other guests in *yukata* and *happi* coats walking in the gardens, so after breakfast we did likewise, wearing the hotel garments but with our own shoes rather than the clogs so as not to fall. We looked so strange to the Japanese that *they* asked to take pictures of *us*.

Later we dressed in our own clothes, checked out and rode the cable car to the top, where Moti met us with our luggage and took us to the train station about ten miles down the mountain. He boarded with us, told the conductor where to let us off, pinned tags from the travel agency on us so the next courier could find us, and even stayed to wave us goodbye when we pulled out. I felt like a child being sent to visit grandparents.

On our first night in Kyoto we ate downstairs at the tempura bar, where the only others were two attractive young Japanese women in jogging clothes. They ordered rice in steaming wooden vats, looking as if cooked in broth, and, noticing our interest, asked for another bowl into which they ladled out some for us to taste. Although neither of them knew more than a few words of English, on thanking them we connected and made a date with one of them, a pretty girl named Mari, for lunch on her day off.

Sushi and other Japanese favorites had not yet become generally known in America. As we were examining plastic displays outside a restaurant one night a young man introduced himself as Shoji Goto, an English teacher who honed his language skills by befriending tourists. For the rest of our stay he watched over us like a chaperone.

Mari gave us our best sightseeing tour the day we took her to lunch. After watching a colorful parade celebrating Jidai Matsuri, the Festival of Ages, she drove us to a Zen shrine where we met the poet/priest/hermit in charge, had ceremonial tea with sweets similar to marzipan, and donned Japanese slippers to protect the paths as we walked in the garden.

Then we visited the Shinto shrine where Mari taught athletics and met the head priest.

That night for dinner we were guests of an American artist and his Japanese mistress, Aiko. Like Shoji, she taught high school English, but unlike him she neither spoke nor understood a word of it when spoken to. She read English, however, so well that with our host translating the conversation she participated fully, familiar with each book mentioned, current or classic.

After a nightcap at our host's Bohemian residence, Jack and I returned to our hotel after midnight to find a commotion ensuing on our behalf. Another tourist whom we'd met at the hotel was pacing back and forth in front of our room, concerned about our safety. He had run into Shoji, who was worried that we were out so late on the night of anti-war protests. Because the possibility of radicals causing violence ran high, tourists were kept away from certain areas. Shoji had gone to the police station to inquire about us.

On our last day in Japan we attended a performance of geisha dancers called the Kamogawa Odori, said goodbye to the Yallons, who stopped off on their way somewhere by train, and spent the evening as tourists signed up to visit in a Japanese home. Our hosts were the president emeritus of Tokyo University, his wife, and their daughter-in-law, all of whom spoke perfect English. When we returned to the hotel, we found Shoji there to bid us *sayonara*.

We left Japan after three weeks, hoping to return. I wrote to Mother that she would love it too.

You and I are both basically Shintoists—lots of beauty, nature... courtesy and consideration for people and things..."

Hong Kong, to me, was a dog-eat-dog seaport with two kinds of people (other than transients): the traders who came to grab all they could and the refugees washed up by the storm, mainly Chinese, but many others refugees in flight from themselves. We enjoyed it for special reasons but didn't *like* it. No more beautiful children, no more friendly, courteous strangers, no more sense of dignity.

Friends in New York introduced us to Philip Chiu, a delightful permanent resident who epitomized the opposite of my generalization. He had flowers in our room on arrival, took us to an excellent restaurant and recommended others, and gave us insights to the problems of native Chinese like himself who lived comfortably but were cut off from their families in mainland China.

Our dominant friend there was Marcia Lewison, who contacted us because of her efforts to spread liberal Judaism. When the World Union informed her that Jack would be there she invited him to speak to the Jewish community, writing in the formal style of a middle-aged European on psychedelically striped chartreuse stationery. She is still a dear friend, still unpredictable. Jack spoke as she asked, but unlike Tokyo where all seats were taken, here he had an audience of five.

Marcia assumed supervision of our stay in Hong Kong and went ballistic upon learning that Jack bought a gold watch without her help. While wandering alone we had seen what he wanted in a shop window, asked the price, and because it was less than the ones at the U.S. discount store that we didn't like, he bought it, leaving it for the band to be adjusted. Marcia, certain that we'd been cheated, insisted on going with us to pick it up.

"This missy live here! You no cheat my friend!" she yelled at the proprietor, expecting him to have charged us the customary tourist mark-up. The poor man looked bewildered, showed her the price, and sighed in relief when she relented. The price was so reasonable that we had to show our receipt to the U.S. customs official when we returned to prove we weren't cheating on our declaration.

We regretted taking the popular lunch tour aboard a Chinese junk in the harbor. As we boarded with other well-fed tourists we paraded along a pier, both sides of which were lined with small vessels no wider than rowboats, each packed with gaunt, starving Chinese staring up at us like rabbits in a cage. Realizing they suffered such sightseers every day made me too sick to eat the lunch. Jack suggested that if encountering poverty affected me so badly we shouldn't go to India, but it wasn't the poverty per se that struck me so; it was the *showcasing* of it.

A surprise awaited us in Singapore. On arrival I received a note from the Tourism Promotion director saying he'd set up a meeting for us the following morning with the head of the Tourist Board. In our room we found personalized stationery, a basket of tropical fruit, and a bouquet of orchid sprays.

The next morning an air conditioned car with a driver arrived to take us to the meeting, where we learned that my argument with our Atlanta travel agent over staying at the Raffles Hotel had led to our VIP treatment. Raffles had not yet been upgraded to its former glory popularized by Somerset Maugham. The Singapore agency, assuming I was a travel writer, scheduled our sightseeing as guests of the government.

After disabusing our hosts of the notion that we wanted to see a beach and an alligator farm, we enjoyed seeing Jurong Park's bird sanctuary, a cultural show, Malay fishing villages in the suburbs, and scenery enroute to Johor on the mainland, plus a rubber plantation on the way. Singapore's energy was manifest and its legally-enforced cleanliness impressive. Litter baskets hung decoratively at every turn and there were stiff fines for failure to use them.

On our flight from Japan we'd met a couple of American honeymooners around our children's age whom we planned to see again in Singapore. We invited them to dinner, assuming they'd want us to take them to an expensive restaurant that they couldn't afford on their own. Instead they led us to the Car Park, literally a parking lot by day, each night filled with tiny tables attended by masterful cooks, each specializing in a different dish. After stuffing the four of us, we found we had spent far less than the cost for just *one* person where we had originally planned to go.

As I anticipated, the highlight of our Singapore experience was staying at Raffles, the grand hotel of colonial times associated with

Somerset Maugham's writing and drinks known as Singapore Slings. Located far from the glitzy new tourist area, it had not yet been refurbished and looked as if it hadn't been touched since Somerset Maugham slept there in the 1930s. Its guest rooms encircled a huge high-ceilinged atrium, ours being on the opposite side from the elevator. The room was enormous. Without looking crowded it held two beds, two sofas, two easy chairs, a table, a long luggage bench with drawers, a dressing table, and two armoires. It also had an alcove that accommodated a rattan sofa, a table, two easy chairs, and a desk and chair.

Whenever we stepped off the elevator across the atrium we could see our attendant seated on the floor at our door. When we arrived he was holding it open for us, ready to grab our clothes to be laundered, all but undressing us as we crossed the threshold. I savored the attention but flinched at being addressed as "memsahib," a term often used by workers to address an upper-class white woman.

In Bangkok we stayed in a grand hotel on the river—fortunately, because air conditioning was problematic, especially in cars, and the weather (touted as exceptionally good for the season) was more like Columbus, Georgia in August. Lunching by the pool in wet bathing suits was the only way to survive sightseeing.

As prearranged, we met Roz and Jay Solomon from Cattanooga for dinner on our hotel terrace to watch the Loi Krathong festival, when Thais float *krathongs* (fancifully-fashioned hat-sized paper boats decorated with greens), flowers, and a candle downstream under a full moon. Boatloads of happy celebrants go up and down the river looking at them, singing, shooting firecrackers, often getting a bit too happy and falling overboard. Parents take their children to float their *krathongs* in safer bodies of water.

It was a great way to begin our visit. I enjoyed seeing the intricately decorated facades of special buildings, life on waterways, and elephants unclogging log jams. Generally, though, I disliked having to bargain for everything, even cab fare, and having everyone we encountered with his hand out, usually for some service we didn't want and he wasn't qualified to give.

In Bangkok, as elsewhere, the best part was the people we met there. One was an Israeli economist who had helped modernize Nepal's agricultural system before coming to do the same in Thailand. Another was the Israeli ambassador who invited us for tea, and his brother-in-law from Abidjan who was astounded when I asked if he was working on the new resort the Israelis were building on the Ivory Coast. He headed the project. I'd written about it in one of my "Made In Israel" columns for the *Southern Israelite.*

Another contact was a U.S. Army officer, originally from Atlanta, who was pinch-hitting for the Jewish chaplain at the U.S. naval base and asked Jack to speak at services. We admired his elaborately carved teak lamps, whereupon he offered to get similar standards for us on his next trip to Chengmai and ship them to us. They light my living room today.

Our most fascinating view of Bangkok came from Kiat and Mary, whose family owned Bangkok's leading department store and did business with Atlanta friends who introduced us. They took us shopping, shipped all our souvenirs home for us regardless of where we bought them, took us to dinner where we could see authentic Thai dancing, and introduced us to the life of a traditional polygamous Chinese-Thai family where all generations lived together. Frequently the men have several wives, each of whom is respected equally, although the first wife retains leadership. In Kiat's family, Wife No. 2 of No. 1's brother, a charming self-employed businesswoman, joined us one day for lunch.

Here, as in Hong Kong, we had a wonderful time but didn't like the city. I was glad we came and happy to leave.

In Rangoon, Burma (now Yangon, Myanmar) we experienced two days of military dictatorship. Stopping there on our way north to Nepal was due to another of my literary fixations. I didn't expect to see Rudyard Kipling's "old Moulmein pagoda" by the sea, but I *did* want to visit the more famous Shwedagon Pagoda in the capital city. It was a mistake.

Kipling's "girl awaitin'," however, couldn't have been prettier, sweeter, or more gracious than our guide, Peggy, who awaited us at the airport. While we were detained more than an hour in an otherwise empty room and had to sign seven different forms to buy stamps for mailing two letters, she seated us at a table on comfortable chairs, took our declarations after we signed them, and navigated all the customs and immigration nonsense on our behalf. Then we identified our bags and boarded a bus to the Inya Lake Hotel.

We chose that suburban venue because it wasn't safe to walk alone anywhere and we assumed that the countryside would be refreshing. The hotel, built by the Russians, was huge, filthy, bare of ornamentation, and largely unoccupied, with extensive grounds beautifully laid out but neglected and overgrown with weeds. There were no taxis so we had to eat in the hotel's cavernous dining room where only four other tables were occupied, three of them by grim-looking, Russian-speaking men in ill-fitting dark Mao suits. A rosy-cheeked lady seated alone at another table spoke to us, so we invited her to ours.

Our room was high-ceilinged, Spartan, with a very small closet containing a chest of drawers so nothing could be hung except coats. Our balcony overlooked the lake with the Shwedagon Pagoda in the distance, but the sliding doors were locked and the glass too dirty to photograph through. We also found bugs, but no exterminator.

Sightseeing was more curiosity than esthetics. We went in a dilapidated car to a few pagodas. I knew better than to wear sandals because we'd be required to remove our shoes upon entering, and it was well worth ruining a pair of pantyhose to avoid going barefoot over the filth. The shrines are on huge platforms like an ornamented covered shopping mall, with numerous small niches dedicated to deities.

The Israeli chargé d'affaires and his wife picked us up for a visit in the ambassador's limousine with the driver whom they were sure was a spy.

Our only good memory of Burma was of our beautiful guide, Peggy. She lived in constant fear that her husband would be deported under the new government's ethnic cleansing policy. We tried to keep in touch with

Peggy. She wrote to us once and sent a card the following Christmas with a pathetic message, but with no address.

We glimpsed the outline of Mt. Everest just before landing in Nepal. The crisp autumn air of the Kathmandu Valley reminded us of Jerusalem. We walked across the tarmac, enchanted by the sight of Himalayan peaks stretched like white rick rack braid on the horizon.

Our fantasy ended at the terminal. Finding no escort there to meet us, we taxied to the travel office and learned that our arrangements had been canceled—both in Nepal and throughout India. No one knew why. Hotels were filled for the wedding season, so they couldn't reinstate our reservation. The agency found us a room for that night only in the second-best hotel, considered unsafe for tourists.

We knew no one in Nepal, but the Yallons gave us letters of introduction to Israeli ambassadors along our route, so we called Ambassador Avshalom Caspi and he convinced the unsafe hotel to keep us for our full stay. He also advised against changing money anywhere other than the black market.

Black market moneychangers approached tourists faster than prostitutes on Montmartre. A boy just ten or eleven years old quickly found us and took us a few blocks, picking up comrades on the way, then led us to a minuscule room and up a ladder into an even smaller room with one shaded window. "Boss," fifteen years old at most, sat at a table while other boys stood around, one of them taking our passport numbers and returning with cash. Another tourist entered as we departed.

Comfort and sanitation were problematic. Our hotel—a former palace with squeaky beds, dripping toilets, erratic electricity, and room boys who slept on the hallway tables—advised guests to not only avoid drinking the tap water but also to distrust the boiling process. We brushed our teeth with Coca-Cola.

Among the friendly assortment of guests sharing our discomfort was a British economist who took us for an evening walk. He first showed us the "music temple" where eight ivory-faced old men squatted with sacred texts spread out before them, chanting holy words to their own accompaniment of cymbals, triangle and drum. Then he led us through zigzagged streets, pointing out his favorite buildings. One of them, with a high grilled window, was the shrine housing the "living goddess," a young girl chosen in infancy to be imprisoned and worshipped until puberty as a virgin deity.

At one point we heard the sound of music coming toward us, a chorus of many voices with a band of drums and finger cymbals. We smelled the incense as hundreds of people marched past us, each holding a burning joss stick. Then came the honorees, a wedding party in a festooned car illuminated by six pedestrians carrying flashlights.

Another night, while walking back to the hotel after dinner, we again heard the jingle of native instruments and encountered a procession, this time led by another elaborately decorated wagon carrying a wedding party. As they came alongside us they stopped, motioned for us to join them, and when we hesitated one of them leaned over to pull us up. They welcomed us with smiles and gestures, making us feel that we were leaving old friends when we reached our hotel and said goodbye. The enchantment continued throughout our sightseeing, passing neatly terraced countryside, watching Tibetan refugees working looms to the constant rhythm of a never-ending chant; guarding our handbags, not from the scrupulously honest people, but from the *un*scrupulous monkeys running rampant almost everywhere; cringing as our car scattered the precise patches of newly gleaned rice drying in the street, and sympathizing with the women who smiled as they swept it back into place.

At Yak and Yeti, a converted mansion on the edge of town, over delicious borscht and beef stroganoff reputed to be the best east of the Hindu Kush, we enjoyed *kibbitzing* with Ashoka, the maître d', as he recounted stories about the establishment's habitués. One was a penniless Pole whose bill remained permanently on the house, others American hippies known to be solvent, therefore receiving no credit.

The other best eatery, Aunt Jane's Place for People, was famous for lemon pie and American hippies. Having only six tables, its stair landing waiting room was constantly packed, mostly with young Westerners hungry for the pie and Aunt Jane's Real American Peanut Butter Sandwiches. Aunt Jane, wife of the deputy director of the Peace Corps, was training her cook to take over the restaurant when she returned to America. Our first time there they were out of the lemon pie, and when I asked if there would be some the following day she took me to the kitchen, introduced me to the cook, and said, "Memsahib wants lemon pie tomorrow."

In addition to lemon pie, Jane provided insights to the diverse backgrounds of her hippie clientele. We met two from America, graduates of Princeton and Oberlin, who had come to Nepal as Peace Corps volunteers, stayed an extra year, visited home, and then returned to help Nepali farmers. Among those in transit were two couples from Canada, college graduates, and their friend from London who shared a "penthouse" for twelve rupees a week (about $0.80 on the black market). One of the women, married but *not* to the man she was with, planned to return to her husband, study for a master's degree, and qualify to teach challenged children.

We also encountered a young woman sitting alone in an empty restaurant with a blank look on her face and a ring in her nose, cutting and rolling chunks of hashish. She was a dropout from Skidmore with wealthy parents in Seattle to whom she never wrote. She typified what we thought about our disenchanted youth before going to Nepal but represented few of those we saw and met there. Most were level-headed idealists seeking knowledge while still young and free.

Entering India at Benares, we rose before dawn to see the burning ghats and watch the sun rise on the Ganges. The faithful were already immersing themselves in the holy waters, the women washing and spreading their saris to dry on the esplanade down to the river. We watched the sunrise from a rowboat on the Ganges and I photographed a small craft in the distance, gliding across the wake of the ripe orange sun.

Our next stop was Khajuraho to see the temples encased in remarkable carvings that Westerners call pornographic. Like the art in

Egyptian tombs and European cathedrals, it reflects the need to appease deities and educate people. Decorative bands on the lower walls depict wars and conquests, the uppermost religious dogma, and in the middle, at the height of an average adult, lessons in procreation. For whatever reason, they were worth seeing.

A monkey commandeered my shoulder as we waited on a street corner for transportation to the airport. There I encountered female security guards who detained me inside the curtained booth for so long that Jack feared someone had dropped contraband into my hand luggage. It was my six-month supply of cosmetics that caused the delay. After patting me down, the guards wanted to test each item on themselves before returning the collection.

In Agra a bad cold limited my exploration of the Taj Mahal but not my appreciation of its beauty, its evocation of serenity. I marveled equally at the "Baby Taj," the delicate filigreed marble tomb of an earlier noble across the river. With mirror inlay on the lower exterior indistinguishable from the filigree, it looked like a paper and lace Valentine.

At the Red Fort, another Mogul masterpiece with buildings of a different genre, our guide identified one palace that displayed a six-pointed star as the home of emperor Akbar the Great's Jewish bride. I knew that Akbar married women from each of his ethnic constituencies, but also that the ancient symbol wasn't used as a strictly Jewish identification at that time. Either this 16th century example was one of the earliest or our guide had invented the shtick for his Jewish clients.

My primary impression of Delhi was the traffic. At intersections vehicles and animals lined up in phalanx as for battle, confronting each other across the entire area, which had no marked lanes or signals, for who goes first when the light changes. I also marveled at the Mogul architecture, especially one palace where the stone flooring formed designs of running water.

Alvin and Edith Rosenman, friends at the American Embassy, took us to Thanksgiving dinner at the ambassador's residence. We went with Grethe and George Tobias from the Ford Foundation to services at the

Judah Hyam synagogue where, unlike other Asian synagogues we visited, other worshippers were mostly local residents rather than transient Westerners. Again, Jack was asked to speak. Afterwards, at the Tobias' home, we met members of the community who answered my questions about their heritage in India. A high-ranking army officer from Bombay told me he didn't know how long his family had been there, but his wife's family came "only recently" in the 1700s.

Jack and I spent one day enjoying separate pursuits. Our embassy friends arranged a golf foursome for him with three of their wives. I watched them from our window as they teed off, then went to the hotel's spa to spend the day being pampered like a maharaja's concubine. I didn't count the cost, nor did Jack estimate his as escort for three ladies using four caddies and four *agawallas* (they retrieve the balls), but we had a happy surprise that night upon converting our expenses from rupees. Each of us had spent only about $12. The next day I went shopping.

Checking our winter clothes at the hotel in order to travel light through the south, we flew first to Madras (now Chennai), where St. Thomas preached Christianity. Christians and Jews were accorded high caste by the Hindus, attracting many converts. European colonizers were shocked to find Christians who had never heard of the pope, as were Jewish travelers upon finding Jews who had never heard of Hanukkah. In Madras we toured the Coromandel Coast south to Mahabalipuram, where a 7th century king established a rock carving school that produced magnificent sculptures, now fast disappearing into the sea.

Those remains were remarkable, but more intriguing for me was questioning our beautiful Brahmin guide about her caste and customs. To my discourteous query about the two blobs on her forehead and the diamonds in her nose and ears, she said one dot was for marriage, the other for wisdom and devotion. The diamonds were just ornamental.

The next morning we flew halfway across the sub-continent to Madurai, saw the Meenkashi Temple (which to me resembled a wedding cake), and met our guide and driver for the rest of our journey west. Stopping for a full day at a former royal hunting lodge on Periyar Lake, our morning boat tour was so noisy that wildlife stayed out of sight, away from the shore. The highlight of our stay was an elephant ride through the jungle. The small female could take only three passengers at a time, and since the other tourists were honeymooners, Jack and I opted to go separately so each of those couples could stay together. I mounted first, the guide placing us sidesaddle in alternate directions for balance. There was no saddle, only a pad tied around the elephant's belly with a coarse rope, too tight and too scratchy to hold onto. I felt momentarily insecure, but the gentle sway of the elephant's tush soon lulled me into nirvana.

Our mount cleared the path with her tusks as we went down into the jungle. She pulled small trees to one side and broke off large branches that got in the way. When my female companion lost her scarf and told the guide, he told the *mahout,* who informed the elephant, who then turned and went back for it, picking it up with her trunk and "handing" it to the owner.

We were out for an hour and a half. Then Jack's group went. They returned fifteen minutes later to let him off, in such pain that he could hardly walk. Not waiting for the guide to help him mount, he had proceeded alone as if mounting a horse, forgetting that horses' backs are not as wide as elephants'. Evidently, men are not suitably constructed for straddling elephants.

Jack recovered sufficiently by the next morning to continue our drive down from the mountains and through the lush, coastal countryside of Kerala. We passed tea plantations that looked like mountains of tightly pruned shrubbery, passed a large elephant carrying palm fronds, and stopped at a small plantation growing cardamom, pepper, and coffee. Closer to the coast we crossed forests of rubber trees, saw tapioca farms, "haystacks" of paddy straw wrapping coconut and mango trees to protect them from rain, and millions of thickly planted coconut palms and bananas.

As we were checking into our hotel in Cochin, Roz and Jay Solomon stopped on their way to the airport to tell us that Gladys and

Samuel (Satu) Koder, head of the Jewish community, expected us that night for Shabbat dinner. This was surprising because we had no contacts in Cochin. We wanted to see the city because of its history, the legacy of the "White Jews" who migrated from further south and built the Paradesi Synagogue in 1568.

The Koders treated us as if we were personal guests, even supplying us daily with local currency. Each night Satu asked how much we anticipated spending the next day and we found it each morning at the hotel desk when we came down for breakfast.

I was the only woman among very few men at the synagogue for Friday sundown services, and I couldn't see anything from behind the heavy drapery in the women's alcove. The Koders didn't attend but sent their car to take us to their home afterward. The house was huge, in my opinion hideous, and furnished in the style of Arab houses I'd seen in Israel. Gladys had a speech and hearing defect that made her difficult to understand, and she talked a lot, which gave the impression that she was somewhat mentally handicapped. Not so. She was very nice, had a good sense of humor, and was much younger than her husband. Her mother, a delightful 83-year-old suffering from a stroke, spoke glowingly of the old days in China with her guardian, Sir David Sassoon.

The dinner was more European than Asian, with conversation in British English and women dressed in "frocks" as they called them, not saris. The other guests were regulars for Shabbat, single relatives as well as friends who were not Jewish. It was the Koders' custom to encourage their married children to establish their own Shabbat traditions rather than join the family. The ritual was filled with song, singing many prayers as well as chanting them in Sephardi Hebrew. Afterwards, Gladys asked me to pose for a picture wearing the family's 400-year-old traditional wedding costume, a long, heavily embroidered black skirt with an embroidered white blouse and a deep red silk shawl that stretched from head to fingertips.

While sightseeing we were startled to see a sign reading "Jewtown" as we approached the Paradesi Synagogue, but we learned that the term was directional, not pejorative. We removed our shoes before entering. The custodian opened the ark, handed Jack one of the scrolls, and then showed us the 10th century copper plates on which the maharajah granted Jews autonomy and special privileges. Outside, Jack noticed that the numerals on each side of the synagogue's clock tower were in different scripts: Latin on the north toward Europe, Malayalam to the east, Tamil to the south, and Hebrew to the west, facing Israel.

Talk of war with Pakistan prevailed that night when the Koders took us to a dinner party at the home of a young scientist and his wife. Both were Muslims from princely families, she a Bengali, daughter of the Nawab of Rampur. The 50 or so guests— Jewish, Hindu, Muslim, and Christian, including several Americans and Canadians—appeared to be long-time friends, comfortable freely discussing the impending conflict over Bengali sovereignty. I had a nice but discouraging talk with a physician from Bengal, as Jack did with her husband. Both gave tragic pictures of the situation there. We departed the following day with glowing memories of the people we met and somber projections for their future.

We flew to Bombay, now Mumbai, and upon landing were surprised to see not one, but *two* couriers there to meet us. Had I given travel agents so much trouble that they thought their courier needed a back-up? One of them, a delicately built man with very dark skin, explained that we were actually his colleague's clients, but he asked to trade with him when he saw our name on the folder. Why? Because he was Jewish.

That surprised us because his name was Kelly. That's an Irish Catholic name to us, but apparently in India it's Jewish. He spelled it Kelli and told us it came from the first two syllables of a multi-syllabled unpronounceable town name in South India where his ancestors settled more than a thousand years ago. He took us to the Taj Mahal Hotel, where his friend in the public relations department checked us into a room on the VIP floor. There we found wine and roses, soon received a call from the housekeeper asking if everything was satisfactory, and learned that she was Mr. Kelli's cousin. She told us that in Bombay, Jews are to the travel industry as they are in New York to the *schmate* trade.

I reneged on some of the sightseeing due to a bad cold. Jack reported that I didn't miss much. The Elephanta Caves proved interesting because our guide, a Muslim doing graduate work in Hindu philosophy, explained the Hindu carvings from a scholar's point of view rather than a believer's. Hinduism fascinated me—the philosophy and myths, not the general practice.

The World Union arranged for Jack to speak to its congregation there, then the only Progressive (Reform) congregation in Asia outside of Israel. There we met presidents of all international Jewish women's organizations in India. They asked me to say something about Sisterhood and to pose for pictures with them. They then thanked us according to their custom, giving me a large bouquet and placing a huge wreath onto Jack's shoulders as if he were a race horse that just won the Derby.

Here, as well as in Cochin, the Jewish community was leaving, not because of discrimination but rather to seek better opportunities for their children. Dan and Naomi Reuben, who hosted us at the synagogue, were soon moving to Australia. They said their group was better off than other Jews, although no one was wealthy and 80% of Bombay Jews lived with huge joint families in one-room flats.

We flew to Rajasthan, stopping in Ahmedabad long enough to visit Gandhi's ashram. In Udaipur, we stayed at the dream-like Lake Palace Hotel, another marble version of a paper valentine, here floating on the water. Sightseeing was good because of our guide, a delightful old man nostalgic for the days before independence when he clerked in the British resident's office.

I saw many women with designs painted on the palms of their hands. He said it was a custom for festive occasions and that his wife did the painting professionally, then asked if I wanted *my* palms painted. Before I could answer, he headed us to his home for her to do it. After walking a very long way, we climbed a dark flight of stairs to equally dark rooms where his young wife, daughter, and small son greeted us (with smiles, no English). As his wife and daughter painted my palms with what looked like black mud, he informed Jack that "sahib would have to carry everything for memsahib until the mud dried," but he didn't alert me to other disabilities I would encounter. We took a horse and buggy back to the boat landing with children trailing us—fun until the horse began to gallop and I realized I couldn't hold on because of my wet paint!

Rajasthan appealed to me more than any other area that we visited. I'd love to go back, but not under the circumstances that ensued while we were there.

On our way to Jaipur we stopped to visit the gorgeous palace of Amber. It stands atop a steep hill and has marble inlay work comparable to the Taj. We approached it in a cushioned *howdah* mounted on a huge elephant with a barefoot musician trotting alongside, playing a fiddle made from a small gourd with a bamboo neck and five sticks for pegs. Inside the palace the afternoon light threw shadows so enchanting that I ignored Jack's calls for me to "stop the nonsense and come along" and crouched down with my camera to get the angle I wanted on one of the best photographs I ever took.

Everything changed in Jaipur. A blackout test the day we arrived indicated that India's war with Pakistan had begun. Jack felt ill and stayed in while I went with the guide to see the pink palace where Jackie Kennedy and her sister famously posed on an elephant. An alarm sounded as we were leaving but nobody paid attention to it. We heard no instructions as to where to go or what to do. Jaipur is on the air route between Pakistan and what was then Bengal, now Bangladesh. I knew there were probably Pakistani planes over Agra or Delhi and it was damned frustrating being out there with no one paying attention to the fact that there was a war going on above us.

None of the old men lolling on benches around the huge plaza seemed concerned that the sirens continued. When I asked my guide what they meant, he replied, "They're just telling us that enemy planes are overhead," and continued leading me toward his car at a leisurely pace.

I didn't appreciate his sangfroid. Eventually the sirens stopped and no bombs dropped, but I'd lost interest in sightseeing.

At the hotel, I found Jack feeling better but as concerned as I was about our plans for leaving the country the next day. We were ticketed to fly to New Delhi, pick up our luggage at the hotel, and connect for Tehran on Air France at midnight.

We called our friends at the American embassy for advice and they said not to come to Delhi because overseas flights were being canceled. We had no choice. Our winter clothes were there and it was snowing in Tehran.

Suspecting that our domestic flight might not stop in Jaipur to pick us up, we hired a driver to take us to Delhi. His car had no springs, the roads were clogged with refugees and their livestock, and the 200-kilometer trip took us more than ten hours. When we reached the Air France office at about 10:30 p.m. the attendant told us all flights had been canceled, all hotel rooms were filled, and to get an Indian Airline flight to Bombay where some international flights were still operating.

We booked the first flight we could get, which was three days later and unsure of departure, then went to the Oberoi Hotel for our luggage. They found us a room. The hotel had one restaurant still operating in the blackout, an Italian coffee shop in the basement. We ordered spaghetti and tea in our room and gratefully bedded down for the night.

Friends kept our spirits up. Edith Roseman visited twice. Grethe Tobias took us to see George's magnificent office at the Ford Foundation and then to their home for mid-day dinner. That night we played gin by candlelight on the white marble floor until we got hungry, then groped our way to the coffee shop for more spaghetti and tea. Hotel attendants led us down the steps into the coffee house and back because all lights had been pulled except for small ones in bathrooms and corridors. We were the last customers before they closed for the duration.

We finally boarded the flight to Bombay but still faced the greater challenge of getting from there to Tehran. That, in addition to being where we wanted to go, was the only en route stop we felt safe in making since all others were in Arab countries hostile to Israel, where we were headed, and our passports revealed we'd visited many times before. Jack saw that BOAC had a flight leaving for Tehran around midnight, so when we landed he rushed to the British Airlines counter while I waited for the luggage.

When I arrived with the bags, Jack introduced me to our new best friend, a co-religionist BOAC agent named Eddie Abraham. He stored our luggage in his office where he let us change into our winter clothes and gave us the last two seats on the flight to Tehran, due to arrive from Darwin in five hours.

We called the Reubens, our friends from the synagogue, inviting them to meet us somewhere for dinner. They said it was unsafe for us to leave the airport and they would come to us instead. We took a table by the window where we saw planes taking off in total darkness.

Later we searched the dimly lit waiting room for seats and eventually found two together. People clogged the floor, many of them stretched out asleep among the piles of luggage and household belongings. Foreign residents fled with as much as they could carry.

When Eddie Abraham went off duty he recruited his replacement to take care of us. Jack went for an update on our flight periodically, each time returning more troubled than before. Long overdue, at midnight it was posted for 1:45. At 1:00 it was posted for 3:45. The pilot, denied permission to enter India air space, continued arguing for permission to land.

At four in the morning an attendant tiptoed toward us with a finger on his lips, motioning for us to follow him through the darkened hall and across the pitch black tarmac to the plane. We boarded in silence, thankful to have boarded yet still apprehensive about take-off. Flight attendants brought milk for the children, checked our seat belts, and we rolled away.

Jack wrote: *The sweetest sensation I've ever felt was the lift-off of the plane we were in.*

We landed in Tehran at dawn. I wanted to kiss the ground. I knew how it felt to be a refugee.

We had no trouble getting our room and reinstating plans. After staying awake until an appropriate time to call home to say we were safe, we learned that calls to the U.S. weren't going through.

Finally we slept, only to awaken and discover that Jack was running a high fever. I dosed him with the antibiotics we brought, canceled the day's plans, and called our two contacts, the local Joint Distribution Committee director and the Israeli chargé d'affaires. Both greeted us cordially, the JDC man volunteering as our special guide for Jewish sites. He went with us to Isfahan and Shiraz as well as across the desert to Persepolis, which I especially appreciated in view of the Shah's recent celebration of the empire's 2500th Anniversary there. We saw cables and other paraphernalia still there.

Notwithstanding my special interest in Islamic architecture and Persia's Jewish past, I departed with less enthusiasm than when I came, and I think Jack felt the same way. I admired the mosques (although not as much as the Muslim shrines in India) and was glad to have visited Isfahan and Shiraz, both for their lovely gardens and architecture as well as for their history. But in Iran, unlike every other country we visited, we met no one we wanted to remember, no one we'd especially like to see again. Perhaps nothing inspired us because we had been traveling for two months and were tired.

We landed at Ben Gurion on December 14, 1971. This time we had no mission to accomplish, no hotel staff to serve us, and with Ilse in Japan, no social director. We had to develop new friends and new activities.

Because Ilse had introduced us to Professor Gershom Scholem—the world's greatest authority on Jewish mysticism—he trusted us with his famous library and rented his apartment to us while he and his wife, Fanya, were away. By chance he was in town when we arrived, so he took us there himself. It was the second floor of a duplex at 28 Abarbanel Street. A long hallway with bedrooms on either side led to a sunny parlor across the front. Books covered every wall of every room and drop-down shelf along the hall ceiling. "Read anything you want, but don't touch the books," he repeatedly admonished, which we assumed meant don't take them out of the apartment.

Sleeping arrangements were problematic, the only bed being a single stuffed into the corner of a cubbyhole by the kitchen. The side rooms had daybeds offering stretch-out space for one person at a time. I took one of them and occasionally visited Jack in his alcove.

I'd forgotten to ask Fanya if she kept kosher, so I was relieved to find a can of shrimp in her pantry. I didn't want to open it, but I needed assurance of not having to deal with two sets of everything to maintain *kashrut*. Her kitchen confused me enough as it was. One night I was boiling corn when the burner ran out of fuel. I'd heard a vendor hawking *nef* as he rolled down our street, but didn't ask what it was or why I'd want it.

Shopping without a car was no problem because grocery stores delivered, but I couldn't always find the cut of meat I wanted. An American-born friend noticed my confusion at the supermarket one day and offered help. I was looking for rib lamb chops.

"They're not kosher," she said. "Go to the non-kosher butcher on Aza Street."

That was an adventure. Every Israeli woman I met in Asia offered me the address of a non-kosher butcher in Jerusalem, which I ignored because I didn't plan to serve *tref* while we were there. I knew lamb was generally kosher but didn't know that Jack's favorite cut wasn't.

I followed directions to the shop on Aza Street and sniffed frying bacon a block away, where I also encountered a line of customers waiting to buy. Inside, I learned that it wasn't bacon that attracted them but a new shipment of shrimp. When I gave our address for delivery the tall, granite-faced woman behind me exclaimed, "*Ach!* Now I know who you are. You are Ilse's friend from Aht-lan-tah living at the Scholems'."

Jerusalem, then, was still a small town.

We missed the Yallons but saw some of their friends and other Israelis as well as part-time residents from America. On December 29 we celebrated our 25th wedding anniversary with a party, inviting everyone we knew. A snowfall that day made it dangerous to drive from Tel Aviv, but it didn't deter our friends. Everyone came, friends originally from eight different countries, but those we saw most that winter came from Pittsburgh.

I met Ellen Hirsch on our first day at the *ulpan*, which we attended three mornings a week. Jack had confirmed her at Pittsburgh's Congregation Rodef Shalom and was her husband Wally's counselor at summer camp. He knew her mother, philanthropist Kitty Falk, who had moved to Jerusalem years before. They and their friends Kitty and Harold Ruttenberg, also from Pittsburgh, became our closest friends.

We took numerous excursions that became mini adventures. On a drive to Haifa with the Ruttenbergs, Harold showed us industrial sites he had selected for the government soon after independence. One night, they took us to meet a planeload of Jews fleeing the Soviet Union. Unannounced and requiring special permits to witness, it landed at four o'clock in the morning. We saw one elderly passenger spread his handkerchief on the ground and kiss it.

A youth group lining the steps to the processing area welcomed the newcomers with songs and flowers. We greeted them in the waiting room, Jack in Hebrew with bits of German, I with my camera, both of us mostly with smiles and gestures. One young woman who spoke English told me she was a dentist, it was her birthday, and that reaching Israel was the best gift she ever received.

Nahum Astar, who had been Atlanta's first Israeli consul, awakened us with a phone call one Shabbat morning announcing, "It's a gorgeous day! We should go to Jericho. I'll pick you up in an hour."

He and his wife, Renate, took us to Hisham's Palace, the fallen walls (not those felled by Joshua), and his favorite antiquities dealer, where he added to his collection and gave us a glass vial from the Roman period. We stopped to buy fresh fruits and vegetables, then drove toward the Dead Sea for the Astars to show us where they worked as farmers when they first came to Palestine during the British mandate.

We joined HUC students on an excursion in the Jordan Valley, stopping at the King Abdullah Bridge to watch the first crossing of a public bus from Amman since the Six-Day War. One of the journalists there to report it saw me take a picture and tried to grab my camera. I resisted and Jack pulled him away but had difficulty convincing him that I wasn't a professional planning to scoop his story.

In January, Atlanta friends came on a Federation tour. We entertained them at the apartment and joined them on a one-day flight to Eilat, then an outpost with its landing strip in the middle of town. Later we returned to Eilat for a drive to Sharm el-Sheikh and back in a Rolls Royce limousine fitted with Baccarat crystal and a fully stocked bar. It was a gimmick that I intended to write about, operated by a creative emigre from New York. We stopped at the Abu Nuweiba oasis to swim and rest while he prepared a gourmet lunch featuring Wienerschnitzel and spread linens on the beach to serve it. We had dinner at Sharm el-Sheikh in a huge tent colorfully painted in psychedelic swirls, served by local bedouin newly graduated from Israel's national school for service industry workers in Netanya.

We took a one-day tour to Mount Sinai, flying to the base of the mountain, then driving up to Saint Catherine's Monastery to see the 3rd-century icons. Flying low in a very small plane, I spotted biblical sites and pointed them out for the other passengers.

On Purim we went to a party in Caesarea. Israeli adults as well as children wear costumes on the holiday and consider it *de rigueur* for parties. When Jack refused to comply, I improvised for him by connecting gem clips to hang on his back as a Jacob's ladder. I wore the blue silk Mogul-style gown I bought in India with lots of jewelry and went as Jacob's dream. Late, after all the other guests had arrived, two couples dressed as Arabs walked in speaking Arabic and fumbling with prayer beads while they meandered through the crowd greeting everyone with "Shalom aleichem." Eventually someone realized that the portly silhouette inside one of the robes was Abba Eban.

I enjoyed a different but equally intriguing Purim celebration at Yad LaKashish, or Lifeline for the Old, the workshop where children from the public schools celebrate holidays with poor and handicapped seniors.

I photographed them dancing together with bright-eyed happiness on their wrinkled faces.

Another project I pursued was reporting on a kindergarten for immigrant children from Third World countries supported by the National Council of Jewish Women. One little girl told me she had eighteen siblings and their father stayed sick in bed all day.

On the bright side, Joan and Nathan Lipson, who were building their house in Jerusalem, came twice during our stay, involving us in a hilarious yet reckless gambit against our better judgement. One morning, Nate called to say that Shlomo, their longtime guide and friend, wanted Jack to marry him to his longtime fiancée. Jack reminded Nate that Israel didn't recognize marriages conducted by Reform rabbis. Nate said it didn't matter because the prospective bride only needed to assure her mother that she was married by a rabbi. When we arrived at the King David the party was in full swing, with one of the guests wheeling Shlomo through the lobby in a luggage cart. Eventually Nate herded us into taxis, directed them to the Old City, and told us to meet at the Hurva Synagogue. It had just been restored after its trashing by the Jordanians and hadn't yet been rededicated or opened to the public. Furthermore, it was a space hallowed by the Orthodox establishment, presumably very much off limits for Reform ritual. No matter, said Nate. One of the guests, an engineer working on the Lipsons' new house who had also worked on the Synagogue's renovation, had a key. Reluctantly, we followed him into the Hurva and Jack married the happy couple, unrecognized by Israeli law but fully Jewish by tradition and gratefully appreciated by the newlyweds. When Shlomo and his wife came to Atlanta the following year, Jack remarried them legally according to Georgia law.

The sole sour note during our stay in Israel was that Jack began to suffer severe headaches. That should have alerted us something was wrong. He hadn't felt up to par since his fever in Jaipur and Tehran. One night our physician friends, Anna and Henry Schiffman, noticed that he didn't look well and his face was flushed. They sent us to a specialist at Hadassah Medical Center who treated him for high blood pressure.

The months passed too quickly for me. I was actually in tears when it came time to leave. Jack didn't understand why and I didn't want to explain. Although I missed our children, I would have preferred bringing them to Israel.

Jack had twice visited West Germany as a guest of its government and, wanting me to see it, had arranged with the German consul in Atlanta for us to stop there on our return from Israel. This time *I* was the government's guest, qualifying as a working journalist.

We landed in Frankfurt, stopped briefly in Bonn to see Beethoven's home, then went to Munich where we toured Dachau (cleaned up thoroughly and thereby devoid of impact) and I caught a cold with a fever that kept me in bed for two days. We missed places I wanted to see, picking up our itinerary in Berlin, which was still divided, with the great museums and other places of interest in the Soviet sector. It being a weekend, we were free of appointments but had little to see. Our charming escort, after making us promise not to tell her boss, suggested an elegant new nude spa in a skyscraper penthouse overlooking the city. Clothing was required throughout other than in the bath area. We enjoyed the visit. On Sunday we shivered in a beer garden watching the world go by, then procceeded to Hamburg, where we saw the harbor with acres of containers before finally boarding our flight home. In each city, I met women politicians and dutifully took notes that I never used.

My cold hung on and made me miserable during the flight. By the time we reached Atlanta I was so sick that I thought I was hallucinating, imagining I heard Israeli folk songs as we walked the jetway.

Jack heard them, too. It was our welcoming committee, Marcia and Rabbi Alvin Sugarman, Jack's assistant, with the Temple Youth Group. They had a limousine waiting to take us home. The driver provided our most needed gift by taking our bags all the way through our house to the bedroom. We were too tired to open them.

Our adventure was wonderful. Whether or not it rebooted our marriage was debatable.

Eight
JOURNEY'S END

We returned shortly before Pesach. Our children seemed to be doing well. Marcia was teaching young children with special needs and Bill was in law school. Jack, noticeably more attentive for a while, even brought me flowers on Shabbat, an Israeli custom I admired.

At home we reactivated as before, but Jack never regained enthusiasm for his work. Instead he looked forward to retirement, only four years away, and planned to begin it the moment he turned 65. He never spoke of a second career as his rabbinic classmates did. They told us their plans to teach at colleges, to write, to pursue scholarship, to turn hobbies into second professions. When they asked Jack what he wanted to do he quipped, "Play golf three times a week instead of two."

That thought terrified me. It projected a life defined by the club. That would further separate us at a time when we most needed to be together, to support each other as we transitioned into old age. I cornered him once to discuss it seriously. He cut me off saying, "Maybe I won't live that long."

I never mentioned it again.

Nor did I anticipate becoming a travel agent. That began when I gave a slideshow of our trip and, thinking it funny, described my confrontations with the travel industry. Afterward, Sid Grossman, a retired furrier who had just taken over a travel agency, asked if I'd like to work for him and treat clients as I would have liked agents to treat me. I could work from home on commission with no need to be in the office except for writing tickets (no personal computers yet) and would qualify for perks that included discounts and upgrades on airlines and hotel rooms as well as familiarization (FAM) trips abroad. I couldn't resist the challenge.

I plunged into the work vigorously and soon had several clients. My first order came from Jan Ghertner, then teaching in a fashion school and planning to take her students to Paris. Soon after, Elliot and Harriet Goldstein, going to a conference in Japan, took a chance on my adventurous advice and let me book them into the not-for-Westerners Japanese inn that we enjoyed at Miyanoshita.

Considering that in addition to my new job planning travel I was writing for more publications than before and had more requests than ever for slide lectures, including some from other cities, I expected to be content with so much to do, yet I wasn't. Despite the uplift of busyness, I sensed an onset of depression. Increasingly my thoughts dwelt on Jack's position—certainly not his tenure, for that was secure, but for his own view of his accomplishments and how that might affect his future. The issues that he so courageously championed no longer needed him. A new crop of civil rights activists, fueled by "Black Power," rejected him as they did most other Caucasians who were formerly their comrades. Within the congregation I could see no increase of interest in Judaism, either in learning or worship. I asked myself if such a remarkable man, one capable of selling social justice to a reluctant community, had wasted his years offering other aspects of Judaism to an uninterested congregation.

Half realizing that this was a distorted view skewered partially by my own demons, I knew no one in whom to confide and persisted in trying to cure myself. Always fiercely protective of Jack's reputation, I avoided giving any hint of negativism about him to anyone.

At one point Jack's chain-smoking when we were in the car began to nauseate me and I asked Jimmy Weinberg, our friend and primary care physician, what to do about it. Should I consult an allergist, a psychiatrist, or a lawyer? Jimmy just laughed, still blinded to the damage of nicotine.

On May 19, 1973, seated at one end of a long dais enduring an after-dinner speech, I became queasy and told Jack, expecting him to snuff out his cigarette. Instead he sympathized, apologized, and turned so the smoke would go in the other direction. As he went to bed he noted, "Now I'm nauseated, too. It must have been something we ate."

A moment later he had a severe headache and asked me to call Jimmy, who sent us to the hospital immediately with orders for me to drive. The fact that Jack let me do it spoke volumes. When he told me to run the red light at Northside Drive and West Wesley, I knew it was serious.

We believed our doctors when they told us he suffered a mild coronary. The next morning Jimmy finally acknowledged what most physicians still refused to believe, telling him, "You've just smoked your last cigarette."

Jack didn't argue. He followed directions precisely, without objection. Orders for no visitors other than family didn't make life boring for him because all of our doctor friends stopped in to socialize each morning after making their rounds, and thanks to the Senate's televised hearings on the Watergate break-in we enjoyed our afternoons together, fascinated by the procedure.

After leaving the hospital Jack continued to follow instructions meticulously, even foregoing attendance at his beloved CCAR's much anticipated annual convention being held in Atlanta. Some of the rabbis came to visit him at home, which cheered him momentarily, but they brought news that hurt. His colleagues had planned to elect him next president of the CCAR until news of his heart attack made it unlikely that he could serve. That was the only honor he had ever really wanted.

Doctors permitted us to go to Hilton Head for a week at the end of August as long as I did the driving. That lasted until we stopped for gas just outside of town. Jack grabbed the wheel, saying it was less stressful than watching me drive.

When we returned, he went back to work with orders to "take it easy," clearly impossible for a rabbi to do during the High Holy days and unthinkable on Yom Kippur 1973. The Israeli consul sat with me during most of the morning service but had to leave early for a briefing from Jerusalem. When the service was over, instead of resting as usual, Jack set out to walk across the parking lots to the back door of WSB-TV for the latest news, and I went with him. Being a Saturday, the door was locked. We stood waiting until a reporter arrived to let us go in with him. As I read the teletype reports, someone noticing the look on my face asked sympathetically, "Do you have anyone there?"

"Yes," I mumbled, "Everyone."

At home after services, Jack went to bed and I went to my typewriter. I wrote an article entitled, "Israel, a State or a State of Mind?" I took it to the *Atlanta Journal* the next morning and they published it in the main section.

By this time Jack appeared to be functioning as usual, so I had no qualms about resuming my life without needing to always be nearby. When NORAD invited me to fly with wives of other Atlanta VIPs to Omaha for a day's visit to its underground emergency installation, I unhesitatingly accepted. It was an interesting experience, but I didn't absorb enough of they were telling us to write a story about it.

I also went to Jamaica on a travel agents' FAM trip. We had no time to enjoy the beach but the experience was educational in ways I didn't suspect. Halfway through the week I had to ask for a change of roommates because mine was prone to locking me out for an hour or so each evening. Apparently, playing musical beds was a major activity on FAM trips.

Jack's doctors, pleased with his recovery from what they still termed a mild attack, endorsed our taking a vacation abroad, but only to a place that wasn't stressful, not to Israel. We chose Spain, flying into Madrid, then driving to the Costa del Sol, all of which was relaxing and beautiful. We returned to New York in time for the UAHC convention, which should have been equally pleasant but turned drastically otherwise when our friend Maurice Eisendrath, on the eve of his retirement as its president, dropped dead from a sudden heart attack.

Back home in Atlanta, the Temple board had insisted that Jack engage a second assistant rabbi to relieve him further in his work, but having to train someone new and, as it turned out, rather inept only added to the stress. In mid-December Jack had to conduct three funerals within three days, two of them for very dear friends. One of them was Eloise Shurgin, the Temple's executive director who had been its sole manager as well as Jack's secretarial assistant for twenty years. For us, as for many others, losing her was a personal bereavement. For the Temple, it was an operational disaster.

Members pitched in to help in the office but the chaos was overwhelming. Into that emergency arose another, an extremely sensitive issue involving a respected member of the Temple staff and money. In order to resolve it quickly and quietly so as to avoid gossip and spare the perpetrator's innocent family insofar as possible, Jack met with the congregation's president and one other trustee, both lawyers, in the former's downtown office secretly at night. Without disclosing the details to others, even to members of the board, they arranged a dignified departure for the man.

Jack developed severe angina a few days before Christmas. The cardiologist said it wasn't life threatening, subscribed nitro pills, and assured him the pain would subside in a few days given sufficient rest. At that point the Temple emergencies no longer required Jack's presence and Jewish organizational life, as always, had shut down for the week, so he really *did* rest, but the pain continued. I canceled the date we'd made with Liz and Jay Levine to celebrate our mutual wedding anniversary that Saturday night and settled in for a quiet week at home.

On Monday morning, New Year's Eve, I awoke from a frightening dream in which I saw myself at the bottom of a staircase looking up at a blinding yellow light and calling Jack's name. Awakening, I reached for him in bed but he wasn't there. I hadn't yet heard of near-death experiences, but I panicked. Then I saw him standing at the window looking out through the trees at a strange, yellow sunrise. It was years before I told that to anyone.

Jack always preferred to be left alone when he was ill, so that morning, despite my misgivings, I went downtown to the office to finalize a job, planning to come home immediately after writing the ticket. I had just entered the office when Jack called for me to take him to the doctor. The cardiologist examined him, then came out to tell me he was admitting Jack to the hospital, but only to make him rest. If the pain hadn't subsided by Friday, he would do an angiogram to determine the source of the problem and angioplasty if indicated. But I shouldn't worry, he assured me. Angina wasn't fatal.

He repeated those words of intended comfort when he told me that he assigned Jack a room next to the ICU simply to facilitate monitoring and get immediate attention if needed. I was not reassured. Common sense told me that severe pain over a long period of time would affect the heart.

It was New Year's Eve and raining. Soon after dark Jack urged me to go home, reminding me that he always listened to football games on New Year's Eve, even on our honeymoon. He didn't need company and he wanted me to leave.

"I'll be more stressed if you stay," he insisted. "It's no night for you to be driving alone on Peachtree. Go home and go to the New Year's Eve party as we planned."

I certainly wasn't going to any party, but I agreed to leave. I kissed him, told him I loved him, and went home. I had just gone to bed when they called from the hospital to come back.

Our great adventure was over.

The morning paper announced Jack's death in a lead editorial alongside a cartoon depicting the skyline of Atlanta behind a large open book. On it was a dripping pen with Rabbi Rothschild written across both pages. Friends brought us the original, signed by Baldy, the exceptionally intuitive cartoonist.

The public's reaction astounded me. Television cameras abounded and traffic clogged Peachtree for two blocks an hour before the funeral was scheduled to begin. More than a thousand people attended. I was told that the entire executive corps of Coca-Cola was there. So were Governor Jimmy Carter and his wife, Rosalynn, the incoming mayor Maynard Jackson, and the whole King family. Coretta came late because she waited at the airport to bring Andy Young, who flew in from Washington to attend. Jack would not have believed it. I kept wanting to tell him.

After all these years, things still happen that I want to tell him. How our children progressed. His namesake grandson. How his legacy took root and grew. How much we need voices like his in the twenty-first century.

Nine
REBOOTING

Eventually I remembered what Jack told me many years before, soon after we married: "Given the difference in our ages and your family's history of longevity, chances are that you'll live the greater part of your life without me. Don't hold back. Find someone else and go for it."

He said it without context. No conversation led up to it and little followed. I didn't want to think about it. Now I realize it was probably the finest gift that anyone could give to a loving spouse.

When Jack died, such thoughts were far from my mind. I *did* think of strange occurrences such as my dream the night before he died, and the two occasions ten years earlier when palm readers refused to finish reading mine. The first occurred at a party in Atlanta where a friend offered to read palms and began reading mine. After studying my hand for a few moments and making some comments, she suddenly closed it, dismissed me, and refused to say why. Later that summer, Jack and I were visiting friends in France when I learned that our host read palms. I asked him to read mine, hoping to learn why my Atlanta friend ended her reading so abruptly. He stopped exactly where she did and likewise refused to explain. I'm not superstitious, but when Jack died suddenly at age 62, I wondered how the lines on my hand could have predicted an early widowhood.

I didn't dwell on it. At the time, I just kept putting one foot in front of the other, determined to move forward.

During the week of *shiva*, the initial mourning period for Jews, Jan Ghertner came over every night after work and served dinner. When on Thursday she asked if she could bring her husband for dinner the following night so he wouldn't be alone on Shabbat, I suddenly realized that she herself had never joined us at the table. When I told her that I expected both of them to have Shabbat dinner with us, she gave me my first lesson on Jewish mourning traditions: she said it was customary for friends to serve the bereaved family during *shiva* but not to join them at the table. All Jack had told me when my father died was to expect visitors for a week and not go to parties or other forms of entertainment for a month.

The experience taught me much more. Notably, it made me marvel at the savvy of our ancient forebears, establishing practices that serve as prescriptions for mental health today. One week is fine for being coddled (more might encourage inertia). One month is sufficient for the shock to wear off and enable a person to face reality so they can begin reinventing themself. Even so, my first time out was shaky. Accepting condolences from casual acquaintances seeing me for the first time since Jack died made me uncomfortable, but only for a moment and only on my first day out.

Marcia checked appointments for me, canceled whatever I had scheduled for the first four weeks after Jack's death, and took me to the airport for my first commitment, which was in Tampa. It was a slide lecture on Israel for the Temple sisterhood, a presentation I'd done many times before so it required no preparation. In Atlanta, my new career in travel drew me back into action.

When as a child I pouted or cried, Mother would snap, "Stop feeling sorry for yourself!" Those words echoed in my head as I struggled to adapt to a life without Jack. Whenever I felt depressed I heard her scolding me, but soon a softer voice would tell me, "Count your blessings. Be thankful for your extraordinary 27 years with an extraordinary man. Be thankful for your children. Be thankful that the congregation relieved you of financial stress..."

That indeed was meaningful. The board had just drafted papers confirming financial guarantees for Jack's retirement and gave them to him for his approval. Had they been signed, it would have been his very first contract. He never wanted one because he believed that the relationship between congregation and rabbi, like a marriage, truly ends whenever either party wants out, regardless of legal documents. On New Year's Eve, when word spread at the Standard Club that Jack had died, the Temple's top executives came directly to our house in their formal clothes, conferred there ad hoc into the early hours of 1974, and informed Bill of their decision so he could assure me when I awoke in the morning that our family would remain economically sound. I was deeply grateful for that.

Having both children in Atlanta during that time helped enormously. Marcia was between jobs so she could spend time with me, and Bill, home for the holidays in his last year at Harvard Law, got permission to stay and study for the bar exam in Atlanta. Their presence preserved my sense of family and delayed my awareness of being alone.

I did wrestle with one "widowhood" offense that I suppose was not unlike that experienced by business executives and others in privileged positions when they retire. The night of Alvin Sugarman's installation as senior rabbi, after having dinner with him and his extended family, I drove some of his guests to the Temple, let them off, and found no space for my car in the parking lot. I was finally able to park on a dark street behind the Temple, walked back alone, arriving late for the service, and had difficulty finding a seat. Although I knew when Jack died that I would no longer have a reserved space for my car, on this occasion I was miffed at not having been given some special consideration.

Always wary of harboring resentment, I waited a week before calling Alvin for a heart-to-heart. He understood my hurt, agreed that consideration should have been shown to a recently widowed senior *rebbetzin*, and apologized for the oversight. I never asked for a permanently reserved space, nor did I ever again need one.

The incident reminded me of other privileges at the Temple enjoyed by the rabbi's wife, which I no longer was. Foreseeing a possible problem with new personnel who didn't know me, I suspected I'd have a difficult time getting Jack's papers when I began working on the book I intended to write about him. Remembering that documents I accumulated for researching the Temple history had been neglected for years after I deposited them there for safekeeping, I feared that Jack's correspondence would deteriorate due to a similar fate and asked where they were. Upon learning that they were in the Temple's damp basement in old cardboard boxes, I took them home. Some members of the board complained, but not directly to me. I preserved them through five moves until I finished the book and then gave the collection to Emory University's Woodruff Library, where they are carefully maintained and widely used.

That March, Kitty Ruttenberg smoothed my next stage of transition as well as Marcia's by inviting us to visit her in her Jerusalem apartment. The CCAR meeting that Jack and I had planned to attend was held there that month, so we went to the memorial session where we saw his friends. Two of them challenged me with invitations, Malcolm Stern to join the board of the American Jewish Historical Society and Joe Glaser, CCAR's newly appointed executive director, to serve on a panel of wives and widows at a conference about rabbis' retirements scheduled for the following December. It was ultimately canceled, but I benefitted from preparing for it because it inspired me to read *Widow* by Lynn Caine. I no longer needed it for therapy, but I found it interesting and relevant.

After Marcia and I returned from Israel, I buckled down to my job as travel consultant and opted for whatever trips came my way. The first wasn't a Familiarization trip but instead a week's session on promoting foreign tours at Trans World Airlines in Kansas City. Shortly after that, I went to Mexico on a FAM trip focusing on Taxco and Acapulco, which was pleasant in itself but saddened for me when I learned that "Mama" King—Mrs. Martin Luther King, Sr.—had been murdered during a Sunday morning service in her church. I mourned alone.

After six months, evenings became depressing and I wanted company. Having just turned 50, I had few women friends who were single. Those few went to dinner, shows, and concerts as a group, which didn't appeal to me. Carlyn Fisher, my one childhood friend who followed her own drumbeat, was newly divorced but rarely in town. We went out to dinner several times and that summer, after I moved to an apartment at the Paces, where she then lived, we socialized more often.

Going out with men presented different challenges. Dating customs had changed considerably since my single days. Even the word itself meant something different which made me careful to avoid using it in regards to myself.

Men seemed to feel as awkward with me as I did with them. A recently widowed friend, formerly president of the Temple, admitted the problem one night after taking me to a party. When we reached my home, he remained behind the wheel talking for a long time before reaching for the door. Then he turned to me and said, "I don't know the proper protocol, so I have to ask. Should I kiss you goodnight?"

I welcomed his candor and turned for a warm (but brief) embrace.

Another friend, after giving me a ride home from a party where each of us had arrived alone, came in for a cup of coffee and stayed for hours, bemoaning the way his ex-wife had treated him. She, too, was my friend, so I was enraged. Eventually I asked him to leave.

One acquaintance, a married rabbi from a distant city, called to proposition me. I was too shocked to respond. When another of our clergy friends, a Christian scholar *also* married and in another city, declared a more than brotherly feeling for me (albeit in far more gentlemanly terms), I admired him too much to cut him off abruptly. He was a genuinely good person and I wanted to keep his friendship. When I firmly but gently turned him down, he understood and we remained good friends ever after.

Notwithstanding these few exceptions, I was not a merry widow inundated with invitations. The only man who interested me enough for me to want to see again was David Blumberg, who was also married. He was from Knoxville, Tennessee, an insurance executive and currently international president of B'nai B'rith. Jack knew him through their work for Jewish and social justice causes, but I met him only when Jack and I were at Camp Blue Star for Roger Popkin's wedding. At the dinner following the ceremony Jack felt ill and needed to leave but wanted me to stay throughout the evening and asked David, who was alone, to bring me back to town later.

David mentioned then that he wanted to consult with me about my Visit Israel Program in Atlanta because his rabbi had asked him to develop a similar one in Knoxville. Since we had missed having coffee at dinner we went looking for a place to get it and talk, but after driving over what seemed like half of North Carolina and finding nothing open we returned to Hendersonville and said goodnight. The drive gave us time to talk, and that was all we did. Although we never touched or flirted, I didn't sleep well that night due to continually dreaming about him. Each time, I awoke wondering why. I had much else to think about then, with Jack's sabbatical only a few months away. I was busy planning a second honeymoon with my husband.

David's insurance business and B'nai B'rith kept him in the air much of the time, with frequent stop-overs between connections in Atlanta when he often had dinner with the Popkins. We saw him on several such occasions that summer when Naomi Popkin invited us to her home for dinner with him. She told us that his wife never went anywhere with him. Jack thought he wasn't married, but I knew otherwise because he told me so during our long drive in the North Carolina mountains.

Almost immediately after Jack died, David began to arrange more frequent and longer stop-overs in Atlanta. When he had too little time to come into town for dinner, I met him at the airport. My friends, perceiving that there was a man in my life and that he wasn't from Atlanta, plied me with questions. "At least tell us where he lives," they pleaded.

"Mostly in the air," I truthfully replied.

My children and Mother knew and applauded. Marcia, especially pleased, had met him at Blue Star long before I did and was actually the one who introduced us. He soon won Bill over by way of their mutual interest in sports and David's sincere interest in him. Mother was so captivated by his southern chivalry that she could hardly contain her hopes for a merger.

David and I hoped, too, but he wasn't free to make it happen. He had lived for decades in a moribund marriage, staying at first because of Jim, their only child, who was still young at the time. Not wanting to disrupt his life, they agreed to divorce after he was older whenever either of them asked for it. Now Jim was married with two children of his own, but when David asked for the divorce, his wife refused. When he persisted, she made outrageous demands. At one point his attorney learned that she hired a detective to spy on him and advised him not to be seen with me in public.

We had good company sharing our woes. Carlyn Fisher was in a like situation, awaiting marriage with Morris Abram, a former Atlanta attorney currently based in New York whose marital status as well as his involvement in public life mirrored David's. He, too, had been advised against appearing in public with his beloved. While David chaired B'nai B'rith International, Morris chaired the National Conference for Soviet Jewry. That kept him equally airborne and connecting in Atlanta. On weekends when both men were in town Carlyn and I, as next-door neighbors, arranged "double-dating" dinners in each other's apartments.

I had a recurring dream that I couldn't understand during those months. I don't believe that dreams foretell the future, but I do believe they may indicate subliminal thoughts. I saw myself living in a high-rise apartment overlooking a river. It made no sense because I had just moved into a beautiful second-story two-bedroom at the Paces, a complex with no high-rises and no river within miles. Malcolm Stern and other rabbi friends were suggesting that I move to New York, where I might have lived overlooking a river, but I had no desire to do so. Much as I loved visiting there, I knew that I wasn't prepared to live there. I wanted to live with David if that ever became possible and he lived in Knoxville, where there *is* a river, but not yet any high-rise apartments on it. I couldn't foresee how that dream could ever come true.

In November, with David's divorce still pending, I couldn't go with him to B'nai B'rith International's 1974 biennial convention in Israel so I gratefully grasped a FAM trip opportunity to visit Africa. I rejoiced at the prospect of photographing animals in the wilds of Kenya and satisfying a fascination with South Africa that had begun as a child when my parents gave me a board game about geography.

Having heard little about *apartheid* yet, I approached South Africa with no special agenda. At Johannesburg's posh Carlton Hotel we were given special keys for our closets, a colonial precaution I found more offensive than quaint, and found a shop selling witch doctors' supplies just a few doors away. I thought the city interesting but not inspiring.

I fell in love with Cape Town immediately, much as I had with Jerusalem after first stopping in Tel Aviv. The weather added delight by clearing what South Africans call the "table cloth" (a persistent white cloud) off Table Mountain so we could marvel at the views both from below and above. It likewise cooperated for our day's excursion to Cape Point, which featured equally magnificent scenery. Looking down on the swirling waters where the Atlantic meets the Indian Ocean, I thought of the mythical Flying Dutchman and could almost hear Wagner's Leitmotif introducing him. Returning to the city afterward, we stopped for dinner at one of the many mom-and-pop boarding houses dotting the road, where I learned to my surprise that they were mostly Jewish. This was South Africa's Borscht Belt.

On another evening in Cape Town I had dinner with Rabbi David Sherman and his wife, Bertha, at their home snuggled against the base of Table Mountain, surrounded by roses in full bloom. Another guest, the wife of Cape Town's Israeli *shaliach*, gave us an enthusiastic account of her day in the countryside teaching Afrikaner farmers about Israel.

Our next stop was then known as Salisbury, capital of Rhodesia (now Harare, capital of Zimbabwe), where I had two very different contacts, each of which shed light on a very different aspect of conditions there. One, a wealthy elderly Jewish couple introduced by their former rabbi, Atlanta's Rabbi Robert Ishay, took me to dinner and showed me their synagogue. They had emigrated from Rhodes when the Ottoman Empire collapsed after World War I and had no family other than a brother in Seattle. When I asked why they had chosen Rhodesia, they said they found it on a map and thought it had some connection with Rhodes.

My other contact was an American who lived with his partner on an estate about an hour's drive from downtown. They invited me for dinner and sent their Black driver to shuttle me from my hotel and back. By then I'd awakened to concerns about human rights in southern Africa, and on the drive back to town I questioned him. He considered himself fortunate because his American employers treated him much better than his friends were treated by their native white employers. I had noticed that they spoke to him with respect, even with a touch of camaraderie, but his duties included driving guests like me to town after midnight, then returning the car before traveling two more hours by public transportation to get home, only to return the next morning in time to cook and serve breakfast. Yet he considered himself fortunate.

While in that area, we flew to Victoria Falls for a photo op where Stanley greeted Livingstone and then took a brief cruise on the Zambezi River. I had a great time photographing the river banks lined by jungle casting shadows on the water and fantasized about being there on the African Queen with Katharine Hepburn and Humphrey Bogart as they struggled to survive alligators, leeches, and worse.

By then my fellow travelers were teasing me about having invitations for dinner at every stop and I assured them I'd dine with them thereafter because I had no more contacts in Africa. However, I'd forgotten about the Indian couple from Kenya that Jack and I met in the blackout in Jaipur and escaped with on the last flight from Bombay. I'd sent them a card mentioning that I'd be in Nairobi and found an invitation from them awaiting me when we checked into the hotel. I appreciated it and enjoyed seeing them, but my mind was elsewhere. David had said he'd call that night from Israel and I was in a hurry to get back to my room.

Nairobi didn't enchant me, but I loved the rest of what we saw in that part of Africa. We lunched alfresco on a beautiful farm with its British owners and watched native dances by Maasai and Samburu tribesmen. One of them became so curious about the two cameras hanging from my neck that I let him try one. With the other, I photographed him photographing me.

Leaving the city, we drove north across the equator which, thanks to the altitude, wasn't hot but more like Atlanta in springtime. We saw lush farmland and busy villagers and arrived for overnight at Treetops Hotel, where Princess Elizabeth first heard that her father had died and she became Queen. Before climbing the ladder to our rooms, we were warned against leaving anything loose for the monkeys to steal when they came in through our open windows. They and the visiting birds fascinated us so much that we forgot to nap before dinner so as to stay awake all night to watch animals come to drink at the watering hole below. I was told that I didn't miss much by snoozing off. Only a few wildebeest showed up that night.

In the morning when it was safe to go down we proceeded south, viewing Mt. Kilimanjaro from afar and reaching actor Bill Holden's luxurious Mount Kenya Club in time for lunch. While at the gate awaiting permission to enter, we attracted a beautiful oryx. He seemed quite friendly, just curious, but we kept our windows closed anyway. Our stopover that night was less elegant, but it was pleasant until we discovered a mob of sinister-looking black bugs in our toilet. The management eradicated them while we were at dinner and we slept so soundly that we missed the morning turmoil when someone found a lion in the swimming pool. By the time we awoke he'd been persuaded to leave.

That day we entered Tanzania to see the amazing herds and flocks of birds in the Ngorongoro Crater only to be detained halfway down because the king of Lesotho was also visiting and demanded privacy. Fortunately, he left in time for us to have a good look before sundown. It was a photographer's paradise.

Our last stop in Africa was Addis Ababa, which didn't impress me as a city, but the country of Ethiopia fascinated me. Many of the people were exceptionally beautiful, especially the women in their gauzy white garments reminiscent of those worn by the women of ancient Greece. Tradition traces a Jewish connection to the Queen of Sheba's visit to King Solomon. Although Emperor Haile Selassie still ruled, upheaval was in the air. On a Sunday excursion in the countryside I saw people gathered under the trees listening to speakers and thought of town hall meetings in America, which gave me the impression that democracy and peace would prevail. A few days after we departed a military coup proved me wrong.

In Athens, the very last stop of our trip, I went shopping. Having bought only tourist souvenirs in Africa, I indulged in bargains for shoes, a purse, and a hand-woven skirt that matched the junk necklace I bought in Kenya. Great fun!

Touring did divert me for the most part, but looking down as we flew over the Red Sea on our way out of Africa, I fantasized about parachuting into Israel to be with David. I had plenty of time to think. Waiting for his divorce gave both of us time to analyze our feelings and scrutinize expectations. When people remarry in mid-life they have no excuse to remain blindfolded. They should know that being in love is not enough.

I knew I loved David, but I also knew that as his wife I'd be far more restricted than I'd been with Jack. I'd have many benefits, not least of which would be the demonstrative love and attention that I craved, but that warmth and chivalry came in the same package as old-fashioned views of propriety. David would never have been as comfortable with the thought of me being alone with another man as Jack was when I told him about my and David's evening in North Carolina. David wasn't prone to jealousy, but he was unsophisticated in ways that would cause him grief if I tested the limits.

I laughed remembering the one time I thought I could get Jack to exhibit jealousy. An old boyfriend who lived in New York, upon visiting Atlanta, learned that I was going to New York for the UAHC biennial as a Sisterhood delegate and that I needed to be there a day before Jack arrived. He asked Jack's permission to take me to dinner and changed his ticket to take the ridiculously early economy flight that I had booked. When we arrived and I was unable to get my room until afternoon, he took me to his apartment, handed me a fresh robe, and offered me his bedroom with assurance that he would not try to join me there. Both of us caught up on our sleep—he, I assume, on the living room sofa. Soon after checking into my hotel room I received an orchid corsage, something that hadn't happened to me since my college days. After dinner, we went to a party. He was a perfect gentleman, never even *hinting* at impropriety.

The following morning when I went to my meeting I left the orchid in a conspicuous place in front of the mirror so Jack would notice it when he arrived. He never mentioned it. When he asked me if I had a nice time the night before I recounted every detail of the entire day, including the nap in a gentleman's bedroom, but he made no comment other than, "I'm glad you had a good time." Finally, I asked him if he noticed the orchid, and he answered, "Nice. I presume your date sent it."

I fully appreciated the blessing of having unwavering trust in each other, but a little jealousy now and then would have been nice. With David, I wouldn't need it. I'd be a middle-aged Jewish American Princess, but because I wanted to please him I'd have to behave like Mother Teresa. I asked myself if that would be a problem.

My answer was no. With David, I'd be fulfilled living within the parameters he approved and wouldn't need to prove myself to anyone because his love fully sustained my self-confidence.

I also needed to consider if I was prepared for losing him. David was one month older than Jack, and although he didn't smoke he was a borderline diabetic with no concept of a balanced diet, no longer exercising, and much more of a workaholic than Jack had been. I was barely 50. Remembering Jack's prediction that I'd be left without him for much of my life, I knew that would also apply to life with David. Was I prepared for another widowhood, one likely to be permanent?

After gritting my teeth, like Tevye I made a deal with God. I promised that if we could have five good years together, I wouldn't complain.

I fully realized that David's commitment to B'nai B'rith would be somewhat the equivalent of having a mistress for the remaining three and a half years of his presidency. It dominated his life, often prevailing over family and business. Now I worried that his health would be affected by the additional concern for me while we awaited his divorce. The proceedings were not moving forward.

David's friends at B'nai B'rith knew and sympathized, offering cover for me to join him at special events that he wanted to share with me. One was a dinner in New York at which he was making a presentation to Mayor Abraham Beame. David's friend and BBI vice president Jack Spitzer, whose wife Charlotte didn't care to come from their home in Seattle, suggested bringing me as his date. New York attorney Larry Perez, David's closest friend, reserved places for us with him and his wife, Hilda.

The evening began well. I was seated between longtime aide to Franklin Roosevelt, former Postmaster General James Farley, who generated a pleasant conversation, and a well-known Jewish philanthropist who entertained Spitzer and the Perezes by trying to make a date with me.

After the presentations David disappeared while greeting people at the front tables on his way to join us. Soon someone came to take me to him in a back room, where I found him nursing a wound on his forehead. As they were clearing the stage for dancing, one of the workers had dropped the lectern, which tumbled down onto David and knocked him out. By the time I reached him he'd regained consciousness and wanted to leave, but hotel officials tried to keep him there until a doctor arrived to check him out and cover themselves in case he sued.

Assuming I was his wife, they plied me privately with questions that, not being his wife, I didn't know how to answer. He rescued me, insisted that the bloody mark on his forehead was only a bruise, and departed for his room, promising to see a doctor in the morning. By then the wound no longer looked threatening, so David went back to work and I returned to Atlanta, still shaken but thankful.

It was mid-December and we still had no encouragement about David's divorce. Hilda and Larry Perez pleaded with him to join them and bring me along for their customary last-week-of-the-year-rest at Dorado Beach in Puerto Rico. His lawyer consented I could come. David also brought Marcia to share a room with me.

Marcia and I had a wonderful time. David spent most of each day in his room working and fighting a bad cold. He joined us for dinner each night, then stopped at the casino, where he taught Marcia to play blackjack and set her up for it before joining the men at their game. Hilda didn't like gambling any more than I did, so we retired early. The men stayed very late each night because David was winning. By the time we left he'd won enough money to pay his entire hotel bill for the three of us. That was the only time. At a casino, I never saw him win. As for losing, he explained to me that he approached gambling as entertainment, spending as much as I would for a night at the theater, and leaving the table when his chips were gone. He was well-disciplined, so his system worked.

In March the divorce *finally* came through and we could share our joy with everyone. When I told one dear friend who had been widowed and recently remarried, she hugged me and whispered, "It isn't true what they say about young love. Old is much better. The young don't even know how to do it."

We set our wedding for May 13, the first day on David's calendar with three successive days free of appointments. He immediately took me to meet his family, first to Little Rock to see his son Jim, daughter-in-law Suzanne, and two adorable grandsons. Jeffrey was almost six and Lee had just turned one. From there we went to St. Louis to visit sister Genevieve (Jean) Jaffe and her husband Irv, along with their two older daughters, Barbara and Geri, and their families. Ellen, their youngest, was away at college.

I embraced them all and they appeared to embrace me. In each household, however, I sensed something not quite *kumbaya*. Jim and Suzanne divorced a few months later. In St. Louis, Jean displayed undisguised partiality for her older daughter, Barbara, and spoke of her displeasure with Geri for not being appropriately attentive. Geri had four young children, including a baby, and a husband who, as lieutenant governor of Missouri, depended on her to run his political campaigns. I bonded with her instantly. Barbara, with two school-aged children and her husband employed in the family business, had more time for their parents. I tried to stay silent when Jean commented on family and politics but almost exploded when she vilified the Equal Rights Amendment.

The following week David took me to a meeting of Mass Mutual general agents in Boca Raton. The company president greeted me warmly and arranged for us to have premium accommodations. Remembering how I felt when Jack was called home from trips to conduct funerals, I was thinking how nice it would be to no longer fear that would happen when David received a call from New Orleans saying that his friend Label Katz, a former president of B'nai B'rith, had died. The family wanted David to give a eulogy. He left me for two days with total strangers, but I didn't suffer; they took good care of me.

We wanted to keep our wedding small and simple, having the ceremony at my apartment with only immediate family and closest friends attending. We didn't realize how many closest friends David had from New York, Washington, Knoxville, and Houston until they notified us that they were coming for the ceremony, invited or not. I was thrilled that Jean and Cal Levinson, Jack's sister and brother-in-law, planned to come. They had to leave a business convention in New Orleans for the day to do so. Alex Schindler, president of the UAHC (now URJ), offered to officiate.

Pleased as I was that so many cared, I panicked knowing all of them couldn't possibly fit into my apartment at the Paces. I wasn't comfortable with the idea of remarrying at the Temple, and I totally rejected alternatives such as the Club or other secular spaces.

Joan Lipson, wonderful friend that she was, said I should get married at her house. Her solarium could accommodate a crowd, and the weather seemed promising for a seated luncheon by the pool. Although having a *chuppah* was not yet popular within Reform, the symbolism appealed to me and was symbolically manifested by an original Monet hanging above the spot where the ceremony would take place. When Joan asked me what flowers I'd like for that room, I told her I didn't think Monet's Lilies needed gilding. I ordered a single rose for myself, another for Mother, and a bouquet of *kalaniot* (anemones, our favorite flower in Israel) for Marcia, my maid of honor. Jim stood up with his father, and Bill took care of Rabbi Schindler.

Our wedding day dawned as beautiful as could be, but I did not. I awoke with a splitting headache and the threat of nausea, neither of which abated until hours after our ceremony. It was five in the afternoon and we were strapped into our seats headed for Gulfport, Mississippi, before I returned to normal.

We took off on what was, for me, a completely new trajectory. I could never have imagined the places I'd go or the adventures I'd meet. On that day, as never before, I knew for certain that I was greatly blessed.

Ten
THE FIRST 26,000 MILES

I learned on my first full day as David's wife that there were three of us in the marriage. B'nai B'rith was a demanding mistress. Fortunately, we rivals had a good relationship from the start due to my love for David and long history of respect for B'nai B'rith. It was the social service organization to which all Jewish men that I knew had belonged, at least since my great-grandfather's generation. Jack chaired the Gate City Lodge, Atlanta's oldest, in 1950. I thought I knew B'nai B'rith very well, but being married to it shed new light.

Our seven month, 26,000-mile honeymoon began with a flight to Gulfport, Mississippi, a destination selected because David had to be in New Orleans—a mere 80 miles away—on the weekend and I wanted one full day at the beach. I soon learned that his definition of a day off meant a day with no *appointments*. After lunch he had calls and other work that would take several hours, so I basked in the sun alone. The next day he met with an attorney in Biloxi regarding a bequest to B'nai B'rith, then we continued driving to New Orleans, where he gave two television interviews, a press briefing about conditions in Israel, and renamed a local Lodge in memory of Label Katz. On Sunday we flew back to Atlanta, where he was scheduled to speak at a dinner honoring Nathan Lipson.

I developed a black eye on that day in Gulfport. At first we didn't know how it happened. The doctor we consulted in Biloxi assured us it was only a bruise and advised us to invent a good story about how it occurred on the first day of our honeymoon. David was ultimately responsible, though surely not from hitting me. While sunbathing I'd fallen asleep with my face on my right hand where I wore the roughed gold and diamond engagement ring he'd given me. That's what did it.

The complexity of B'nai B'rith and the many facets of its services throughout the world soon became apparent. The following week David had meetings in Washington with the International Council and Administrative Committee, so we moved into the Mayflower Hotel for several days. The staff and local BBI Lodges honored us with a reception where I met dozens professing to be David's devotees.

The big question then was whether BBI should endorse the Panama Canal Treaty, which would transfer the Canal to Panama, as many Catholic and Protestant organizations had already done. Delegates from Panama pushed for it. I saw the other side of that debate through Adelaide and Richard Eisenman, my long-time friends from Panama whose nephew owned and published *La Prensa*, the nation's only free newspaper. According to them, Panamanians wanted a treaty but only after the current dictator, Omar Torrijos, could be deposed and a democratic government restored.

The next week took us to New York for David to chair the National Leadership Conference. Sponsored by the Conference of Presidents of American Jewish Organizations, it focused on a response to Arab propaganda. I went with him to hear the keynote speaker, Israeli ambassador Joseph Tekoah, and to a luncheon at the UN where David presented a gift to John Scali, the outgoing American ambassador to the UN. On our way upstairs we met the tall, good-looking incoming ambassador with whom David stopped to chat. He was our future president, George H.W. Bush.

That weekend David met with BBI district leaders in Memphis and

I enjoyed a day at the hotel pool with his soon-to-be-former daughter-in-law and two adorable grandsons. Then we went back to Washington for him to meet with the executive committee of ADL, host the Romanian ambassador for breakfast in our suite to discuss David's refusal to endorse the communist dictatorship for Most Favored Nation status in his testimony to Congress, take me to an ADL luncheon featuring a brilliant address by Federal Reserve Chairman Arthur Burns, and shuttle to New York for David to present an award at a dinner of the B'nai B'rith Youth Services. Then we made it to St. Louis for a family event on the weekend.

Our two homes away from home during this period were a comfortable suite at the Mayflower in Washington with Paul Young's restaurant across the street and Duke Ziebert's around the corner as our favorite dining facilities, and a two-bathroom suite at the Waldorf in New York with Oscar of the Waldorf downstairs to feed us. Yes, it was extremely posh, and I was well aware of the need to remember that it would end in three years when David finished his term in office. "Don't get used to it, Toots," he frequently reminded me.

I soon realized that at the pace we were going, we might not live that long. The posh treatment was justified, if not actually necessary for survival.

We'd been married only three weeks when I had my first two experiences going it alone with VIPs, both on the same day. David wanted me to represent him at an ADL women's division luncheon in New York, at which First Lady Betty Ford was being honored. Since ADL was then still a part of B'nai B'rith, as its first lady I was seated on the dais a few places away from the real First Lady and alongside other celebrities, some of whom were America's most prominent Jewish socialites. David reserved a hotel room for me in which to rest and refresh after my 6 AM flight from Atlanta, but I still felt uncomfortable alone in a milieu where I knew no one and sensed that I was out of my element.

The designer-clad woman seated on my left, I later learned, was one of the Revsons of Revlon cosmetics fame. We may have been introduced, but she didn't encourage conversation. I anticipated better results with my partner to the right, legendary choreographer George Balanchine, whom I greatly admired and had actually met years earlier when he came to Atlanta for Virginia Rich and Bobby Barnet's wedding. Mentioning it to him didn't spark the ignition, though. He gave me the impression of being there under duress, probably coerced by a major donor.

Betty Ford didn't appear to socialize with anyone. Looking like a well-coiffed smiling robot, she moved and spoke as if by remote control. It was likely due to her opioid addiction, which we of the public didn't yet know about. I forget whether or not I was introduced to her, but it wouldn't have mattered.

After the luncheon I took a mid-afternoon shuttle to Washington, rested briefly, and changed into a long dinner dress to attend yet another VIP affair without David. It was a dinner cruise aboard the presidential yacht Sequoia, hosted by Nancy Kissinger in honor of Leah Rabin while their husbands had a working dinner with President Gerald Ford at the White House. David and Bernie Simon, BBI's public relations director, drove me to the dock at Alexandria in heavy rain. Again alone and

David and Janice Blumberg present a gift to President Ford on behalf of B'nai B'rith

knowing no one, I walked onto the deck feeling as if I were walking the proverbial gangplank—into the water.

I brought special regards from Joan and Nate Lipson, who frequently socialized with the Rabins in Jerusalem. In the receiving line, after a gracious welcome and introduction by Nancy Kissinger, I relayed my greetings from the Lipsons to the guest of honor and was asked, "Who?"

It was as if she had never heard of them. That was my first, but sadly not my last, unpleasant encounter with Leah Rabin.

Determined to enjoy the evening despite the odds, I pursued pleasantries with other guests, most of whom were wives of Washington Jewish insiders well acquainted with each other. Eventually I met Selma "Pete" Tannenwald, the wife of Theodore Tannenwald, a U.S. Tax Court judge, who recalled that her husband knew Jack through their mutual service on some board or committee. I especially appreciated her friendliness after my day in New York and introduction to Leah Rabin.

In late June we went to Geneva for meetings of the Claims Conference, the international organization seeking reparations for survivors of Jewish Holocaust victims. David was vice president, and soon to become treasurer, of the Holocaust Memorial Foundation. He was also an observer of the World Jewish Congress because BBI was considering joining it. We thought of that trip as a honeymoon.

At the opening reception, David's friends crowded around to meet me. I already knew Alex and Rhea Schindler and others representing Reform Judaism, including Rabbi Dave Wice and his wife Sophie, longtime friends of Jack's whom I met on my first honeymoon. I spent my days mostly with Rhea, who had been to school in the area. She had a car and took me sightseeing. On David's first free evening we had dinner with my wartime friend Rosemary Aubert and her husband Roger, the pianist and conductor, at their hilltop home on the French side with a view of Mont Blanc.

One evening Phil and Ethel Klutznick hosted a dinner party at a chateau overlooking Lac Léman. They seated me next to Nahum

Goldmann, a Zionist leader and founder and president of the World Jewish Congress. I'd heard about him, not only from news sources and gossip, but personally from Ilse Yallon in Israel, who readily referred to him as a former lover. He was silver-haired and good-looking, with a wide, toothy smile that he directed at me immediately, saying, "I understand you are from Atlanta. I had a dear friend who was the Israeli consul general there." He paused, his toothy smile broadening. "His wife was an even dearer friend."

"Oh?" I replied demurely, trying to keep an inquiring look on my face. He then began a wistful reminiscence about Ilse, delicately avoiding an overt admission of their relationship but revealing enough to suggest that he assumed I could fill in the blanks. Ilse and I had a great laugh when I told her about it.

David's meetings spread over parts of two weeks, giving us free time to celebrate his 64th birthday that fell on the weekend between. That's when I learned my next lesson about him. I suggested we spend the day at Valloire, a lovely resort at the far end of Lake Annecy in France, where we could celebrate over lunch at one of the country's five-star restaurants. There I learned the truth about his enthusiasm for food. He loved to eat, but for him McDonald's was as good as anything recommended by Zabar or Michelin. While he never balked at high prices, he insisted that high ratings merely indicated high prices, not the quality of food and service. While I obsessed over the magnificent scenery and the gourmet menu at Valloire, he remained glued to a radio eager for the latest news about Pelé, the Brazilian soccer star. David's wrap-up assessment of the day was that he enjoyed it very much because I did.

Another lesson I learned, while hugely positive regarding David and his generosity, was decidedly negative regarding the purportedly devoted BBI staffer involved, the foreign policy expert who, with his wife, accompanied us to Geneva. It surprised me when we landed that they took off immediately without asking David if he needed any help or wanted to share a cab into town. We didn't need help, but I was surprised by such absence of concern by a member of the staff. Notwithstanding,

David invited them to go with us for his birthday jaunt to Valloire, which they did.

On our way from Switzerland to Israel we stopped in Athens for David to meet with its B'nai B'rith Lodge. He had an afternoon free for sightseeing and asked me where I would like to go since we had a car and driver. I opted for the Temple of Poseidon at Sounion, which I had missed on other trips, and it was there that I learned about David's take on antiquities. He insisted that he enjoyed the jaunt because I did, but he couldn't conceal the fact that the Temple left him unimpressed. He only saw, in his words, "the ruins of an old building at the edge of a windy cliff." I was enchanted, having grown up with a copy of *A Child's Book of Mythology*.

As we stepped off the plane in Israel, Avigdor Warsha met us with a private car, drove us across the tarmac into the terminal, and led us through immigration without ever having to wait in line. I'd met Avigdor in Washington, but this was my first view of him in action. A lawyer and politician by profession, he was the longtime mayor of Kiryat Ono, his hometown near Tel Aviv, and de facto lay leader of B'nai B'rith in Israel, where it had provided social and cultural support since the 1880s. Any obstacle confronting David in Israel, from restaurant reservations to an appointment with the prime minister, he resolved immediately, turning red tape into red carpet at the flip of a telephone. I called him Mr. Can-Do. Avigdor was more than efficient, however. He was a really good friend. His first item for our agenda, before taking us to Jerusalem, was to visit an artist in Jaffa who gave us a print expressing ways to portray the word "love."

We stayed at the King David. While the men were at meetings, I spent time with Israeli friends or hung out at the pool with Rhea Schindler. I was thrilled to introduce David to my friends, and he was equally eager for me to meet his. That meant taking me with him to his appointments with Prime Minister Yitzhak Rabin, Shimon Peres, then the Defense Minister, and American Ambassador Malcolm Toon.

On a free afternoon, with a car and driver awaiting us, David again asked me where I wanted to go. I chose Herodion, one of Herod's fortresses/palaces which, like Sounion, I hadn't seen before because it was away from the city and not on the main tour routes. I thought David might connect with it more than with Sounion because Herod, unlike Poseidon, figured in Jewish history. Enriching the day for both of us, we found Hershel Shanks, publisher of *Biblical Archaeology Review,* researching a story there and he filled us in on the history.

On our way home from Israel we stopped in Paris, where David was supposed to meet Baron Alain de Rothschild, president of the Israelite Central Consistory of France and *Conseil Représentatif des Institutions juives de France* (Representative Council of French Jewish Institutions), also known as CRIF. They were to discuss a forthcoming conference they were scheduled to co-chair over tea in our suite. When I saw the hotel where Zelda Bloom, head of B'nai B'rith's travel department, had booked us, I was glad to learn that the baron was out of town and couldn't meet us. It was located well beyond the Arc de Triomphe in a fairly upscale business section but far from my idea of where to be in Paris. Its huge lobby bustled with large tour groups, airline personnel, and businessmen who looked as if they traveled on a limited expense account. I voiced my preference the next time we saw Zelda and the next time we traveled to Paris, when the baron *did* come for tea, we received him in a classic hotel on the Place Vendôme.

A great delight for me on landing in Paris was meeting Georges Bloch, president of B'nai B'rith France, who came from his home in Strasbourg to shepherd us through the rest of that day with members of the Paris Lodge. I found him to be especially congenial, and his wife, Claude, became my customary companion at international meetings.

I shocked members of the Paris Lodge when they greeted me with a secret B'nai B'rith handshake that I didn't recognize or know how to return because I'd never heard of it. In America, it may have been protocol in Great-Grandfather Browne's generation. I don't remember having spoken of it with David. I probably mentioned it as a curiosity and assume that David dismissed it as a holdover from the past, which was a general tendency among the European Lodges.

The baron's absence left us with unexpected free time, which enabled me to show David some of what I most loved about Paris. Despite all of his previous trips there, he had never seen anything but hotels and meeting rooms. Since I only had one evening to correct that, and having learned that even the best restaurant in town would leave him unimpressed, I led him to Montmartre. We had a lovely romantic tête-à-tête at an outdoor café by the Sacré-Cœur overlooking the city. We watched street entertainers, bought souvenirs for the grandchildren, and departed Paris with David cherishing the memory as much as I did.

On our return, I went home to Atlanta and found Mother in the hospital with bad news. On her 74th birthday, June 24, just before we left for Europe, she didn't seem as vigorous as usual but she shrugged off our concerns, saying she was temporarily disoriented awaiting new eyeglasses after cataract operations. Her diminished energy concerned her doctor, Alexis (Aloysha) Davison, who had taken over his father's practice. He found her at his mother Natascha's home one night too tired to come to the dinner table and ordered her to be in his office at eight o'clock the next morning. From there, he immediately hospitalized her for a cancer biopsy.

Once, decades before, I'd asked Dr. Hal to curb her chain smoking because of her incessant cough. He answered that since she enjoyed smoking more than she disliked coughing, he wouldn't try to stop her smoking.

I rushed to the hospital in the morning hoping to be there when Aloysha brought the biopsy report, but he had already seen her. He met me at the elevator with tears streaming down his face. She had cancer in both lungs, with only 5% of one lung still working.

When I reached her room, she was on the telephone telling her friends.

Mother opted for maximum treatment despite the next to zero chance that it would help, and she wouldn't hear of my staying home to be with her. She knew that David looked forward to introducing me to the BBI's board of governors at their meeting in Houston that weekend, and she ordered me to go. "Your children are here if I need anyone," she said.

I went, but with a heavy heart, in no mood for daytime socializing with the ladies. I co-hosted a reception with David for Senator Lloyd Bentsen, the keynote speaker, a politician I'd long admired, and then returned to Atlanta.

For the next seven weeks I shuttled back and forth between home and wherever David was. I was with him in Washington for the dedication of the addition to the BBI headquarters building on Rhode Island Avenue. One weekend I went with him to the B'nai B'rith camp at Starlight, Pennsylvania, for a ceremony renaming it in honor of Anita Perlman, founder of B'nai B'rith Girls and a major donor to the camp. Because she and her husband, Louis, were David's close friends, I also joined him in Chicago for their 50th wedding anniversary party, which they held at the recently refurbished Palmer House. They housed us there as their guests in the Royal Suite, which was itself a memorable experience. Upon checking in, each of us followed a separate bellman to separate bedrooms and howled with amazement when we saw them. Mine was a flossy pink contemporary with a heart-shaped bed, his an overdone Louis XV with a mirrored ceiling. Both looked as if they came from the set of a Mae West movie. We opted for his bedroom with the mirrored ceiling but were so tired after the party that we forgot to look.

Around the beginning of September, I had to stay in Atlanta. As always, Mother planned to do things her way, which meant dying at home, but hospice care didn't exist as it is today. After numerous emergencies with unreliable nurses—on one occasion her beloved gardener Travis stayed with her overnight and didn't even tell me about it until morning— we had to hospitalize her in order to keep her comfortable. She died in her sleep on September 25th at age 74.

Continuing to order things her way and knowing that I opposed cremation, Mother had appointed Bill as her executor. He dutifully carried out her instructions. For the simple memorial ceremony in the Temple chapel she had chosen the music, which included Bach's "Jesu, Joy of Man's Desiring" and possibly something from Wagner's *Götterdämmerung* (I was beyond listening); we were given an urn with ashes to bury beside my father's, filling our three-generation plot at Crest Lawn. A few people visited me afterward, but with no formal *shiva*, a ritual that wasn't yet generally practiced among our friends. I awakened to my loss in bits and pieces, deepening in time.

David, seeing that I was okay, returned to Knoxville, where I expected to join him in a few days. That night he called to say that he was giving a luncheon the following day for Moshe Dayan, who was coming to lecture at the university. He was meeting Dayan's flight from Atlanta, and, in the event that I wanted to join them, he had booked me a ticket on the same flight. I thought of what Mother would have told me and said yes.

The next morning, as I was closing my suitcase, my neighbor across the hall came to pay her condolences, bringing me a large cake. I thanked her but said I couldn't accept it and explained the circumstance. Hearing it, she insisted that I take the cake to Knoxville. "You can serve it after the lecture," she urged. "I'd be so thrilled to know that Moshe Dayan ate a piece of my cake!"

Obviously, I had to take it. I thanked her again, double-wrapped it, and put it in my suitcase. Marcia drove me to the airport. When boarding the plane I stopped to introduce myself to the Dayans, who were seated in first class, but their two burly security men sitting behind them sent me to my own seat in economy without time to speak.

We waited and we waited. Then the skies opened and it poured. The captain announced that the flight was cancelled due to weather throughout the region. We could take another flight leaving soon for Chattanooga or wait for a late afternoon flight to Knoxville. *Now* the Israeli security men came to *me*. The general wanted to know what we should do. We'd already missed the luncheon and he wanted to make sure he didn't miss his lecture.

I told them that the best way was to drive, but I didn't have my car available. "No problem," they said. They'd rent a car and drive it if I showed them the way.

We disembarked and found seats in the waiting room where Rachel, Dayan's second wife, and I sat while the men made phone calls, retrieved baggage, and rented the car. When she asked me what we should do for lunch I mentioned the cake in my suitcase and we laughed, but we realized it wouldn't satisfy the men.

I thought of the Snack&Shop at Paces Ferry and North Side Drive alongside I-75, asked her what she wanted, and called in the order. "Corned beef sandwiches to be picked up in half an hour for General Moshe Dayan and his party. Please have them ready to go because we would be in a hurry."

We arrived at Snack&Shop in a teeming rain. The security men went inside to telephone our whereabouts to their authorities while Rachel followed me into the store and went to select the drinks. When the owner said hello to me I knew he'd be interested in who his other customer was and whispered, "See that blonde lady over there? That's Mrs. Moshe Dayan."

He frowned, then looked at her, then looked back at me as if to say "Yeah, yeah," and asked, "So where's her husband?"

"He's in the car," I said. "Go look."

He walked to the door, peered out, and his expression changed. I could almost see the wheels turning in his head. Then I realized that when I called in the order I'd identified myself as Janice Blumberg, not Rothschild, the name by which most Atlantans still identify me as now despite my name being Blumberg for almost half a century. He didn't recognize the name and probably thought the caller was some crazy woman, drunk or on drugs.

The Dayans and I sat in the back of the car, Rachel in the middle. When we passed Dalton, Georgia, she spread the food on our laps for a picnic. My neighbor's cake made a great dessert.

After lunch and a brief snooze, Dayan pulled out a pencil and paper and began drawing scarabs. He told me they were designs for a set of jewelry he was making for Rachel using artifacts from some of his archaeological digs in Egypt.

I assumed the Dayans wanted to rest so I didn't initiate conversation other than to congratulate them on their recent marriage and tell them that David and I were also newlyweds. With typical Israeli candor, Dayan responded by explaining that although their wedding was recent, they had been together for many years. As I had done when Nahum Goldmann told me about his affair with Ilse, which wasn't news to me *or* to Jerusalem's elite, I smiled and pretended I didn't know.

In mid-afternoon Dayan wanted to stop for ice cream, and I suggested that we pull off the road to a shopping area in Athens, Tennessee. After that we proceeded to Knoxville and their hotel, where David met us and took me to our apartment for a brief rest before going to dinner and the lecture. Rachel sat with us for the event, but we didn't party afterward. They had to be up and away early the next day and so did we.

I never saw them again in person except for a glimpse of Rachel from afar some time afterward at a concert in Tel Aviv. A few weeks later, however, I ran into the security men on Madison Avenue in New York. "Have you seen him?" one of them asked me frantically.

"No," I replied. "Have you lost him?"

Indeed they had, and they understood the danger involved if the wrong people found him.

In October we embarked for South America with a delegation from the ADL that included Hilda and Larry Perez. David had two BBI conventions to attend in South America, one in Brasília, the other in Montevideo, Uruguay, and he had also planned stops to meet with BBI leaders in Peru and Argentina. A delegation met us at the Lima airport, the men fluent in English and eager to discuss Lodge business with David. Their wives, less linguistically blessed, swooped me away, assuming they could communicate with me in Yiddish. They seemed utterly amazed when I replied, "*No, pero hablo español.*"

I liked Lima, although our visit was too short to see much of it beyond the cathedral and the llamas in the plaza. Vendors there sold elaborately embroidered alpaca ponchos that Hilda and the other women bought for their daughters-in-law who probably never wore them. I found a perfectly plain one with no embroidery and have used it consistently ever since. The fiber, like that used by Bedouin for their tents, swells up to absorb the moisture and protect against rain.

While David worked for two days I went with Hilda and the other women to Cusco and Machu Picchu. I expected it to be the highlight of the entire trip and it was, with Cusco fascinating me as much as the Inca capitol itself. Our day for Machu Picchu began in the early morning on a train that seemed unstable. It rattled along a tortuous track, stopping at villages where local passengers boarded, many carrying produce and live hens. A small bus met us at our station to take us on an even more tortuous ride around hairpin turns up the mountain. While trying to photograph everything, I envisioned Pizarro and his armor-clad Spaniards chasing us as we climbed. Much as I missed David, I knew he wouldn't have enjoyed the adventure nearly as much as dealing with B'nai B'rith problems in Lima.

Brasília was both interesting and disappointing. Its magnificent ultra-modern structures widely separated, lined avenues broader than our multi-lane interstates at the entrances to large cities, yet I saw few moving vehicles on those highways and scant indication of people inside the buildings. I couldn't even find a salesperson who spoke Spanish, much less English, at the shopping arcade of our hotel, the city's largest, the one catering especially to international conventions. At a garden party that evening the Israeli ambassador summarized foreigners' general view of the new capitol when he replied to my mention of this being his second posting in Brazil, the previous one having been when the capitol was still in Rio. He replied, "This time it's not a post; it's a punishment."

This was 1975. I presume that Madame de La Fayette had similar thoughts about Washington when the Marquis took her there on a visit in 1824. Beautiful layout, beautiful buildings, but not yet a city. The most inspiring thing I saw in Brasília was the excitement generated by Rabbi Henry Sobel of São Paolo among the Jewish youth groups at the convention. My greatest surprise was the number of cities they came from. Some were from places I couldn't even find on a map. I scolded myself for having the same thoughtless reaction that I hear from New Yorkers when they learn there are synagogues in Fitzgerald, Georgia and Hattiesburg, Mississippi.

In Buenos Aires, I first noticed the bargains (which were unbelievable), and then the two tough-looking Israeli bodyguards stationed outside our

Janice and David greet Israeli Prime Minister Yitzhak Rabin

hotel room door (presumably deployed by the Israeli Embassy). Such was
Argentina's state of inflation that the Jewish leaders insisted on providing
David daily with whatever number of pesos we anticipated using for the
next 24 hours. The exchange was so favorable that he asked me to buy
leather purses for all the women in his family as well as for myself and
Marcia.

We were not in Argentina on official business, but as tourists filling
the time between the two conventions. Nevertheless, we received the
royal treatment, not only from the local Jewish community that honored
us with a luncheon at the DAIA, their central headquarters, but from
our own United States ambassador Robert Hill, who gave an elegant
reception for us. I still tingle with pride (plus a measure of disbelief) to
recall our arrival at the historic embassy mansion. As David and I led our
group up the broad spiral staircase to the ballroom, the orchestra changed
abruptly from dance music to salute us with "The Star-Spangled Banner."
I felt like 19th century royalty arriving at a ball, only better because we
represented the U.S.A.

Whereas the women I met in Buenos Aires spoke English, in Montevideo I had another opportunity to use Spanish. David's speech had to be translated, which necessarily diluted its impact and much of his personality. Anticipating that deficit, he asked me to precede him at the microphone, greeting the assembly in Spanish on his behalf. I loved doing it and sensed that it brought an aura of informality that broke the ice for him.

I left Montevideo with warm feelings for the city and for the people I met there. It seemed more European than other cities we visited, except for Buenos Aires, which appeared more like a European capitol, whereas Montevideo was like a smaller resort city on the Mediterranean.

From there we flew home. The flight originated in Buenos Aires, where apparently someone boarded whom Uruguayan security considered suspicious. After settling comfortably in our seats with our shoes off for the overnight journey, we were ordered off the plane along with all of our belongings. We stood on a cold, windy tarmac until each piece of checked luggage was out for us to identify before having it returned to the bay. When we finally took off, we slept most of the way to New York.

Very soon after that, on November 10, 1975, the U.N. passed its infamous "Zionism is racism" resolution. World Jewry united and mounted a series of protests to refute it. We had just returned home to Knoxville from a convention in Miami when David was called to speak the next day at a rally in New York's Garment District. With no time to prepare, he asked his BBI office to hand him a fact sheet when we changed planes in Washington so he could work out his talk during the one-hour flight to New York. Instead they drafted the speech for him, which was of no use because it was not what he wanted to say.

I was already near the nail-biting stage on his behalf when we landed and taxied into Manhattan on the unseasonably warm November day. A crowd of more than 100,000 people filled the intersection of 40th Street and Seventh Avenue, stretching north as far as Times Square. The line-up of speakers included Senator Jacob Javits, civil rights leader Bayard

Rustin, feminist Betty Friedan, and Israel's Leah Rabin, among many others. David's name appeared at the very end of an excruciatingly long list. Standing in the blazing sun, I shivered at the thought of him winging it after so many carefully planned speeches.

May I be forgiven for underestimating the wisdom of my beloved! David threw away whatever notes he had and grabbed his audience instantly with three simple words. Inspired by the African Americans' slogan "Black is Beautiful," he shouted, "Zionism is beautiful!"

The multitude roared approval. He said very little more, which was rewarded not only by hearty expressions of "*yasher koach*" from his friends, but also a banner headline across the entire front page of the next day's *New York Times*, declaring "Zionism is Beautiful" over a picture of the crowd.

Two and a half weeks later we traveled to Israel for the Solidarity Conference called by Prime Minister Yitzhak Rabin, flying with most of the other delegates from America in the nose of an El Al 747. (The flight deck was on the floor above us.) The entire first class cabin became, in effect, a private clubroom where everyone stayed up all night talking, drinking and smoking. In those days I could put on blinders and earplugs and sleep my way across the Atlantic, but on that trip, before airlines restricted smoking, I coughed my way to Israel.

The Solidarity Conference opened in the Chagall State Hall in the Knesset, filled with international Jewish leaders, most of whom I knew only from having read about them or seen them on television. Again, David was one of the speakers, but this time I had no fear that he would be ill-received.

I was comfortably seated in the front row, watching him and the others on the dais against the glowing backdrop of Chagall's tapestry. It was one of the times that I pinched myself to be sure I wasn't dreaming.

Because it was Hanukkah, the ceremony began with blessings and candle lighting, led by Golda Meir. Then she asked all of us to line up and follow her in signing the manifesto of solidarity. Normally an unremarkable exercise, this time for me and many others signing was a transformative experience. The thought of my name being on a document along with Golda's was beyond belief even as I signed.

According to the facsimile of the declaration that each of us received, the event took place on Erev Shabbat, the 1st of Tevet, 5736, but my own calendar sets it a day earlier. We spent that Erev Shabbat (Friday, December 5, 1975) at the home of my friends Drs. Anna and Henry Schiffman along with a notable group of other guests, including Lord Barnett (Barney) Janner from London and his son, Greville, who later succeeded him in the House of Lords. Lord Barney offered to take me to a session of Parliament the next time we came to London, and I didn't let him forget.

David and I began the next week with a trip to Beersheba, where we met a fascinating engineer named Batz who told us how he planned to pipe water from the Mediterranean, desalinate it, and irrigate the Negev. Then we went to the Galilee and onto the Golan Heights, where we visited an army outpost and saw a *hanukiah* made of spent shells sunken into the ground on a clifftop. It was high enough, said the soldiers stationed there, for the Syrians to see its lights in Damascus. That memorable trip concluded with a dinner party hosted by Ylana and Oved Ben-Ami at their historic home in Netanya, which he built during the British mandate so Jews would have a place nice enough to entertain visiting royalty.

Awaiting us when we came home was an invitation from Ambassador Simcha Dinitz and his wife, Vivian, to a formal dinner at the Embassy of Israel in Washington—my first. What augured like a Cinderella's ball began as a near-catastrophe on that frigid night as we exited the cab and David fell on the ice. Thankfully, he wasn't hurt. The highlight of the evening for me was when he introduced me to Barbara Walters, who interacted with him as though she had been flirting with him for years. That enabled me to tease her about being a formidable rival, and from what I've read about her since then, there's evidence that she probably *did* have a flirtation with him during the years that he'd been going to such parties alone.

By then it was mid-December when Jewish organizational life folded for the holidays, and we had a miraculous two weeks without any travel other than between our homes in Knoxville and Atlanta. I had time to reflect and try to digest all that had happened during these first seven months of our marriage.

I thought of the people I'd met, most (but not all) of whom were longtime friends of David's. Among them were Washington insiders, like attorney Al Arent and his wife, Fran. At a dinner party they hosted, I was seated next to the multi-talented David Lloyd Kreeger, who founded GEICO. He and his wife, Carmen, also amassed an art collection that they gave to the city (along with the home they built in which to house it). Among their treasures were two Stradivari violins on which he performed well enough to play chamber music with Isaac Stern. All I knew about him at the time was that when asked to entertain us at the piano after dinner, he played Broadway favorites like a professional.

At a public dinner, an annual B'nai B'rith benefit, I was seated next to Charlie Smith, who bested me in newlywed one-upmanship by saying that he and Mickie had just returned from their honeymoon that morning. I knew he was an old friend of David's but didn't yet know he was the real estate developer and philanthropist who built Crystal City and whose generosity was manifest in the Charles E. Smith Hebrew Home, Jewish School, and numerous other institutions bearing his name. We spent several evenings with him and Mickie while they were still together.

The truly close and lasting relationship that began for me at that B'nai B'rith dinner was with Aaron Goldman, the honoree, and his wife Cecile. Aaron gave an acceptance speech like no other I had ever heard. It was entertaining, without a shred of the thank-everyone routine. I later learned to appreciate him, not only as a creative philanthropist, but also as a producer, historian, and even as a playwright.

Another couple whom I met very early in that period who became close lifelong friends were Ruth and Robert St. John. I had admired Robert from afar ever since listening to his newscasts from London during the Blitz. In the '60s he came to Atlanta and interviewed Jack for a book he was working on that became *Jews, Justice and Judaism*, but Jack didn't tell me about it until afterward.

Shortly after David and I married, when I wasn't yet secure about solo appearances on his behalf, David asked me to pinch-hit for him with greetings at the opening of an exhibit at the B'nai B'rith Museum. I was terrified to mount the podium but soon became greatly comforted by the warm smiles of a dignified-looking couple in the front row. They were Ruth and Robert, to whom I was introduced immediately afterward, and was quickly drawn into the fortunate circle of their closest friends. I still think of them often and miss them greatly.

Not all of my thoughts about people I met were *kumbaya*. I picked up bad vibes about the BBI comptroller when he called David in Jerusalem to say he was handling a legal case in a way contrary to what David had directed. The call had come just as we were leaving for an outdoor evening event at Hebrew University, so I was looking at my watch as I stood waiting at the open door holding our coats. Overseas calls were quite expensive in those days and my budgetary genes went ballistic as I heard David say, "No, Joe. I want you to do it the way I told you" over and over again for twenty minutes. I'd been with David long enough to know how hard he and other volunteers worked to raise the money this staffer was spending. Unlike many whose paychecks derived from it, we felt responsible for the use of Other People's Money.

Another disappointment involved the wife of a volunteer who was one of David's old friends from Memphis. They were jewelers who catered to Elvis Presley. Late one night, while our husbands were still at a meeting, she knocked on our door to show me an elaborate diamond pin, suggesting that I ask David to buy it for me. Shocked and horrified, I tried to be polite and not say what I thought. I was tempted to sing "Take Back Your Mink" from *Guys and Dolls*, the song in which the girlfriend laments, "What made you think that I was one of those girls?"

She persisted but I stood firm, remaining at the door without inviting her in. I had great difficulty getting rid of her. Eventually her husband sold David a few modest pieces for me, but never again did either of them make the mistake of pitching the sale to me.

In time I discovered other so-called "friends" whose apparent values I deplored, but mostly I avoided them. My practice as a *rebbetzin* stood me well in that department. I knew how to smile politely and silently without telegraphing my true thoughts.

David used our end-of-the-year respite to catch up on his insurance business and list his expenditures for income tax preparation. In doing so that year he discovered that we had traveled 26,000 miles since May 13, our wedding day. He also noted that we had visited eight different countries, stopped twice in Israel, and spent more nights each at Washington's Mayflower and New York's Waldorf than in both of our homes combined. I could hardly believe we had done all of that in only seven months.

At a party in Atlanta on New Year's Eve I overheard someone in the next room say, "Guess who's here. Janice Rothschild and her husband."

That did it. David had many friends in Atlanta, but few among those I knew well, and he had been too busy for us to have a wedding reception in order to meet them. He had a superbly controlled ego, but I didn't want to test it by asking him to live in a city where I would always be known by another man's name.

With Mother gone and my children very much on their own, there was no need for me to maintain a home in Atlanta. Bill was about to leave to study for the rabbinate and might never return to live there, and Marcia, when people advised her that she'd be happier moving away from her parents, always said, "Let *them* move. I like it here."

Now new challenges confronted me and it was time to go. On the way home from the airport through downtown Atlanta I noticed a large sign on one of the buildings proclaiming, "If you lived here you'd be home now." I got the message in reverse.

David agreed. He had to keep his legal residence in Knoxville because of his business, but he realized that I was becoming disenchanted with small city life and would not be happy settling there permanently. We gave some thought to New York, but only briefly. During our trips to Washington, I remembered how much I loved living there during the war. If it was good for me then when I was alone and had fewer resources, it was surely promising now with David at my side.

Eleven
TRAVELING THE FAST TRACK

The next three years were exciting and exhausting. We frequently traveled to Israel and Europe, twice to Mexico, once each to Morocco and South Africa, and constantly crisscrossed America. I was too busy packing and unpacking luggage to study the backgrounds of the countries we were going to visit, something I had always done in the past.

My first priority in the States was finding a place for David and me to live in D.C. "I want an apartment just like yours and Eddy's, except with a balcony and a swimming pool," I told Al Elkes, a staffer, and he took me to Prospect House in Rosslyn, Virginia. I saw a two-bedroom unit with a two-storied living room, one wall of which was glass that opened onto a 14-foot balcony overlooking the Potomac, the Iwo Jima Memorial, the Theodore Roosevelt Bridge, and the entire National Mall. An upstairs dining balcony and kitchen also opened onto the view, with bedrooms and baths behind. We planned to move in April.

New Year 1976 began with an invitation to dinner at the White House honoring Yitzhak Rabin—nothing new to David, but for me a thrill beyond belief. Then I saw the date. I had to be in Knoxville as luncheon speaker for the combined Sisterhoods of both synagogues that day.

"No problem," said David. "You'll take the mid-afternoon flight to D.C. I have to be there by noon for Kissinger's luncheon at the State Department and I'll take your clothes with me so you won't have luggage to check. Put them with mine to be packed."

I did so, leaving my formal gown and wrap in a bag to carry over my arm. Late that afternoon at our hotel in Washington I undressed for a brief rest and couldn't find my bathrobe. Or my shoes (I was wearing gaucho boots from Argentina), or my evening bag, or—David forgot to pack them! I panicked.

It was five o'clock and beginning to get dark. The stores were closing and a cold rain began to fall. I rushed out of the hotel, praying that the nearby shop on Connecticut Avenue selling pantyhose stayed open after normal business hours. It did, and it carried all other necessary items except evening bags. I saw lights on in a nearby jewelry store with beaded bags on a top shelf, banged on the door until someone answered, and bought one without even asking the price.

Back at the Mayflower, I found David on the telephone arguing with Bernie Simon, who called to say that snow was in the forecast so we should use the limo service that BBI provided for us. David never used it because he disapproved of the extravagance, but I sided with Bernie and prevailed.

Upon entering the south lobby of the White House and checking our coats, we were greeted by a Marine guard in formal uniform who offered me his arm and escorted us upstairs to the main hallway into the gold and white East Room. There we socialized until we were instructed to form a line for greetings by President and First Lady Ford and their honorees who stood just inside the room's entrance. A Marine guard announced each of us as we approached, after which we exchanged a few words with the President, First Lady, and special guests before another Marine escorted us down the main hallway to our places in the State Dining Room. Married couples other than the hosts and honorees were not seated together.

Two administration insiders hosted each table, mine being Happy Rockefeller, wife of the vice president, and Brent Scowcroft, the National Security Advisor. I was seated between him and Jeff Wald, then the husband of singer Helen Reddy, who performed in the East Room after dinner. I forget who else joined us other than the young couple who were last to arrive. Mrs. Rockefeller was so excited at the prospect of meeting them that she asked Scowcroft for his place card so she could get autographs for each of her two boys.

What magnitude of celebrity causes such excitement in a room filled with luminaries? When they finally arrived I still didn't know. I recognized the young woman as figure skating star JoJo Starbuck, but it wasn't *her* autograph that Mrs. Rockefeller wanted. It was her escort's. After dinner David rushed to bring me to meet the non-government personality at his table, Dallas Cowboys' coach Tom Landry. I asked him who was at my table and learned it was Terry Bradshaw, the quarterback the Pittsburgh Steelers credited with defeating Landry's Cowboys in the recent Super Bowl.

We didn't stay for the dancing after Helen Reddy's performance. It was snowing and many guests were leaving, some awaiting cabs that didn't show. Hadassah's president, Rose Matzkin, was one of the stranded. David appreciated our limo service all the more for enabling us to give her a lift.

In February we flew to Belgium for the Brussels II conference on freeing Soviet Jewish prisoners of conscience. The day before it started, Marcia and Bob Lewison, my friends from Hong Kong who now lived in Belgium, took us to Waterloo, the battlefield of Napoleon's final defeat. With them was Anna Rosnovsky, a Russian violinist from the Israel Philharmonic who came to enlist David's help freeing her mother from a Soviet prison. It surprised me that anyone thought David important enough to do that.

The next morning as the conference opened, David learned that he was to introduce Golda Meir that afternoon. With no time to prepare, he gathered his thoughts over lunch squeezed into a booth with Hilda and Larry Perez, former Miss America Bess Myerson, and me.

Leaving snow-covered Belgium behind, we flew to a Mass Mutual general agents' meeting in Palm Springs, California. I developed a bad cold during the flight—somewhat relieved by the joy of photographing the shadow of our plane encircled by a rainbow as we repeatedly circled Chicago, trying to land in a snowstorm. We made the connection without our luggage, rented a car, and by the time we checked into our hotel I was almost a basket case from a stuffed head and sore nose. The next morning a Japanese masseur at the hotel spa walked on my back and revived me.

We returned to Los Angeles, where I witnessed an even more surprising miscalculation of David's importance than the one in Brussels. When Guilford and Dianne Glazer picked us up for dinner, they said we'd be making a brief stop on the way at the home of a friend who wanted to meet David and pulled up to a substantial but unpretentious house in Westwood. It belonged to Armand Hammer, the world-famous industrialist, art collector and philanthropist.

We had no time to see his art. His butler ushered us directly into the library where Dr. and Mrs. Hammer greeted us cordially, offered vodka and caviar they'd flown in with them overnight from Moscow, and, with the projector already set up, showed us a promotional film on the merits of shale oil production.

I found it interesting but didn't yet know that the use of fossil fuels was a hot topic in Congress, and I certainly didn't understand why someone as prominent as Armand Hammer would think David's influence was great enough to augment his own.

Other priceless opportunities that I undervalued at the time included a weekend retreat at Princeton with historian Salo Baron and economist William Haber and one-on-one time with Elie Wiesel in Knoxville while driving him to the airport. I was too awestruck to initiate meaningful conversation but happy to hear Wiesel extol the beautiful mountain scenery of East Tennessee. One weekend spent with intellectual giants when I did relax comfortably was in Cincinnati for the 100th anniversary celebration of the Hebrew Union College. Bill had been accepted into the next class of rabbinical candidates there so we took him with us and I enjoyed it all the more.

When the time came for our move from Atlanta to D.C., David learned that he had to be in Paris the preceding week. Nothing short of catastrophe could have kept me from going with him, so I scheduled the packers for the day before departure and the movers for the day after our return. On April 22nd, I flew on Eastern Airlines to connect with David at JFK for an Air France flight to Paris.

While landing at JFK my flight entered a deluge, plunged in the downdraft, and veered off the runway. We were ordered to evacuate immediately in case of an explosion. I reached the emergency door before other passengers but the attendant couldn't open it. A large man behind me succeeded and slid down the chute ahead of me. I landed in a puddle, then ran as fast as I could away from the plane, bracing myself with the thought, "I'm not going to die now. God wouldn't do that to David."

The plane didn't explode, no one was seriously injured, and cars soon arrived to take us to the terminal where BBI tourism director Zelda Bloom met me and rushed me to David at the Air France terminal. We didn't yet have mobile phones so Zelda had no way to tell him why the entire airport had been shut down for two hours. He waited frantically, suspecting the reason and terrified by the possibility that I'd been injured.

Air France attendants led me to their lounge, removed my soggy blue knit pantsuit to dry it, and gave me a glass of wine. With my first sip, I heard our flight called. With only pantyhose and bra in place, I slid into my full-skirted faux leather raincoat, belted it tightly, grabbed my huge travel purse the French called a "*baise-en-ville*" bag (roughly translated as "assignation in town"), and boarded the plane looking like a French prostitute. Air France provided a robe, brought us drinks and then dinner of foie gras and champagne, and I slept soundly until I was awakened for breakfast over the English Channel. My clothes followed me abroad and dried over the Atlantic.

Landing in France, I forgot bruises and stiffening joints. The local B'nai B'rith leader and his wife who met us knew we had nothing scheduled until the next morning and invited us to go with them for an overnight at their beach house near Honfleur. I not only enjoyed that quick trip for the famous food and sightseeing, but also for the added pleasure of being required to speak French without fear of ridicule because our hostess didn't speak English. In Paris we stayed at the Ritz rather than a busy tour group hotel. As planned for our trip to the city before, Baron Alain de Rothschild conferred with David over tea in our suite, and I told him about my difficulties in Jerusalem when my name was Rothschild.

Only after leaving Paris did I feel the results of the emergency landing at JFK. We never heard from Eastern Airlines. Larry Perez proposed (only half-jokingly) that David sue for impairment of conjugal rights.

David's meetings kept him in New York so I continued home alone for the move to D.C. As the van pulled out of the drive, I turned in my key and flew to meet him in Washington. Neither of us realized how stressful the move had been for me. When our furniture arrived, David was bogged down at the office and my nerves gave way. He understood that I needed him then more than B'nai B'rith needed him and came home to help. That was the only time I prevailed over his "mistress."

Two weeks later, after cross-country hopscotching to Boston, Philadelphia, New Orleans, and twice to Knoxville, we again pulled out our passports, this time for Mexico and Curaçao.

We stopped first in Acapulco for a Mass Mutual meeting and were surprised to be met at the airport by a government official giving us VIP treatment. At the hotel, she checked us into the suite previously held by Howard Hughes. That proved somewhat embarrassing, being more luxurious than the suite occupied by Mass Mutual's president.

The royal treatment continued in Mexico City where David convened the BBI executive committee and leaders of B'nai B'rith Mexico, one of whom hosted a fabulous afternoon dinner party at his walled-in suburban villa. Mariachi bands accompanied our initial intake of tequila with folk songs still popular from my 1944 summer in Guanajuato. When they played "¡Ay, Jalisco, no te rajes!" I couldn't resist shouting along with them, nor could I resist singing along to "La Feria de las Flores" and "Las Mañanitas." Soon I was up on the dance floor with some of the local guests doing the Mexican hat dance. If I embarrassed David, he was too dear to admit it.

While in Mexico I had a great reunion with my Experiment friend, Barbara Baer de Gomez, who had married and settled there. Another day, I joined David on his visit with former president Miguel Alemán, who had been one of my heroes in the 1940s. His home was fascinating, literally filled with Dresden porcelain—not only the iconic figurines but also lamps, tables, chandeliers, and even a fireplace mantel made of Dresden. When I described it to Barbara she shrugged and said, "I'm not surprised. He stole half the national treasury to buy it."

Our most extraordinary visit was with the president of Mexico, Luis Echeverría. I didn't join in his conversation with David, but he noticed that I followed it without waiting for the interpreter to translate and asked me how I knew Spanish. When I told him I'd studied in Guanajuato he stood up, motioned for us to follow him across the vast rotunda of the Los Pinos, and stopped at a door on the opposite side where he told us to wait. As he entered, we saw a long conference table with men seated around it. He spoke to one of them near the far end and led him out to meet us.

"*Aquí es su gobernador,*" President Echeverría told me, introducing the governor of Guanajuato. Astounded, I managed a brief conversation with him in Spanish and sent warm regards to any of my old *amigos* who might still be there.

In parting, the President gave us an Aztec-designed silver and enamel box and an enormous pictorial publication by his wife recounting his achievements. He also invited us to the upcoming celebration of his administration on the national holiday, September 16, which we unfortunately had to decline. Eventually we learned that our royal treatment was due to Mexico's tourist industry having plummeted since the country's U.N. vote equating Zionism with racism the previous November. Presumably making nice with B'nai B'rith would bring back Jewish travelers.

From there we went to Curaçao, where Shabbat at Mikvé Israel-Emanuel Synagogue brought me a bittersweet *déjà vu* when David spoke at services as Jack did when I had been there with him. David attended the Caribbean District Convention where, representing Curaçao's Jewish community (the oldest surviving Jewish community in the Western Hemisphere) as the country was gaining its independence, B'nai B'rith honored the Netherlands' royal House of Orange for its consistent friendship to its Jewish subjects. We were to deliver the award on our way home from Israel the following month.

That was the only time I ever *didn't* want to go to Israel. We'd be away on the Fourth of July 1976, America's Bicentennial Independence Day, unable to celebrate in our new home at Prospect House, the most coveted spot in the area of the nation's capital for watching the fireworks. We invited Adelaide and Richard Eisenman to use our apartment for their party and flew to Israel on June 29th.

That was the day the members of the Popular Front for the Liberation of Palestine and the German Red Army Faction made their demands after hijacking an Air France flight to Paris and landing it in Entebbe, Uganda. Over several days, the hijackers freed all their hostages except for 94 passengers they recognized as Jewish and the 12-member crew. On July 4, Israeli commandos freed the remaining hostages, and at five o'clock in the morning we were awakened by Larry Perez calling from New York asking why we weren't in the lobby celebrating.

Had we stayed at the King David as we did during our previous trips, we would have been downstairs with the other guests, but at Phil Klutznick's suggestion we had switched our reservation to the new Hilton overlooking the Hebrew University. As one of the owners, he ensured us preferential treatment.

That morning we celebrated American Independence Day with David rededicating a huge sculpture, Scroll of Fire, given by B'nai B'rith.

I then represented him at another Independence Day event while he was busy elsewhere and joined him late that afternoon for the American ambassador's reception in Herzliya. There we watched our national July 4th fireworks over the Mediterranean. Back in our room that night, we heard crackling outside our window and saw fireworks from the campus of Hebrew University. Perhaps we couldn't watch fireworks from our Washington apartment, but we certainly didn't lack explosive celebration on that Fourth of July.

Two other incidents that week bear notice. At Ilse Yallon's Shabbat gathering, conversation centered around a movement known as *Breira* (alternative), which questioned Israel's actions vis-à-vis the PLO. Because American students belonging to Hillel, then part of B'nai B'rith, participated in the movement, David was sometimes blamed for permitting it, which he did because he believed the students had a right to speak freely. One of the other American guests at the gathering verbally attacked him for it. When he politely defended his position, she arose and summoned her husband to leave. Embarrassing as it was, Ilse resumed the festivities without blinking.

A pleasant but no less misguided incident occurred when the Ruttenbergs took us to visit friends from Belgium who were conducting an excavation beneath their home in the Old City overlooking the *Kotel,* the Western Wall. The couple showed us several layers of history and artifacts suggesting that further digging might reveal objects from the Temple destroyed in 70 CE, but for permission to proceed they needed more evidence. The only way to get it *without* digging was with underground X-ray equipment controlled by the U.S. government, which they thought David could obtain. We enjoyed our visit and were fascinated by their project, but as with Dr. Hammer, we had to disappoint them about how far David's influence actually reached.

With so much happening in Israel, anything short of visiting the Queen would have made stopping in Amsterdam anticlimactic. We were joined there by Charlie Zelenka, president of BBI's Caribbean district, his wife Lottie, and my son Bill, in Europe on his way to Israel for rabbinic studies. Lottie and I had been informed of protocol for us to wear white gloves, which she didn't use in Panama, so we began by shopping instead of sightseeing. The next day in The Hague we were told we didn't need gloves.

The palace was suitably imposing but architecturally forgettable. An equerry seated us in a room where we waited a long time. After a while I went to the window to look around and saw in the graveled driveway a nondescript-looking woman in a flowery print dress inspecting the shrubbery. When we were finally ushered through the palace and down onto the rear lawn we met her. She was Queen Juliana.

Her Majesty, plain and homey as my view of her from the window suggested, greeted us cordially. We had a pleasant conversation during which a butler brought coffee and cookies. As she spoke, the queen apparently didn't notice that she was tilting her saucer. We held our breaths. When the coffee spilled, Bill thrust forward his handkerchief, which she took, first dabbing at her skirt and then pulling it up to dab her petticoat, saying she wouldn't have time to change before her next appointment. I noted with pleasure that the royal lingerie was plain, like mine.

When we rose to leave, Bill dashed up the hill into the palace ahead of us. We found him giving the equerry his forthcoming address in Jerusalem so Her Majesty could return his handkerchief. He didn't need it back, but was aware of the sensation to result from receiving a package from the royal House of Orange. It never came.

In August we had a free week after visiting the B'nai B'rith camp in Texas, so when our flight home stopped in Memphis, we picked up David's seven-year-old grandson, Jeffrey, to spend it with us. He boarded with the "W" volume of the *Encyclopædia Britannica* under his arm and absorbed himself in it until we landed.

The next day I overheard David on the telephone agreeing to meet someone for lunch at the White House, and signaled "no, no," pointing to Jeffrey to remind him that the boy expected Grandpa to take him sightseeing. David nodded "okay" and told his caller, who then invited me and Jeffrey to join them for lunch at the White House. On the appointed morning we awoke to find Jeffrey fully dressed in his best, including a coat and tie.

Our host first gave us a tour, then took us downstairs to the club-like staff dining room and began his discussion with David. It focused on the Republican Convention, where Ronald Reagan was threatening Ford's nomination. Our host, noticing that Jeffrey seemed bored, asked, "Who would you vote for, Jeffrey?"

"Jimmy Carter," he instantly replied, his voice probably not carrying as far as we feared. David looked appalled. Our host laughed and continued, asking Jeffrey, "Why would you do that?"

Without missing a beat, the boy replied, "Because President Ford gave *animission* to Israel's enemies."

David had to smile at that.

After several more weeks of shuttling between Washington and Knoxville with side trips to Nashville, Pittsburgh, Chicago, St. Louis, Hot Springs, and Memphis, we settled into Washington for BBI's biennial convention, which I anticipated with great pleasure. I didn't move into the hotel with David for pre-convention committee meetings, however, so when his son Jim arrived a few days early, he stayed with me in the apartment. The time alone together enabled us to bond as friends, relieving the quasi parent-child relationship that existed when his father was present.

I can't deny that I enjoyed being front and center at every convention event. It was exciting to chat informally with my political heroes like Father Robert Drinan, Daniel Patrick Moynihan, and Hubert Humphrey, and it was especially thrilling to hand President Ford his award from B'nai B'rith. That privilege also became daunting when the President displayed his uncanny ability to keep a conversation going while posing throughout an excruciatingly long photo-op.

When presidential nominee Jimmy Carter arrived, he made his way along the dais being introduced to each guest, shaking hands until he came

Janice and David with Jimmy Carter

to me. Without waiting for an introduction (which he didn't need because he knew me from my life in Atlanta), he leaned down and kissed me as an old friend. It made the nightly news, giving my Atlanta friends much material for teasing in light of his recently broadcast admission of occasionally lusting (but only in his heart) for someone other than Rosalynn.

Notwithstanding those joys, my aftertaste of the convention was sour. The Washington Hilton on Connecticut Avenue, newly opened, wasn't yet prepared for so many guests. Telephone operators routinely failed to post messages, key cards were new and frequently didn't work, and relaxing in a Presidential Suite was a joke because we had no time to relax. I appreciated the experience but was thankful when it ended.

In November, hardly a month after the convention, I left on the first leg of a journey that developed like an international spy thriller. David had to stay home for briefings on our forthcoming visit to Romania, so I went to Israel alone to meet Rabbi Alvin Sugarman with a group from the Temple and my Rothschild family for dedicating a forest in Jack's memory. Bill joined us for the ceremony. Afterward, while the group toured, I took Marcia to a dude ranch in the Galilee for sightseeing on horseback, returning to Jerusalem the day before I was to meet David in Vienna en route to Bucharest.

Awaiting me in Jerusalem was a frantic message from Avigdor Warsha telling me to get to the airport immediately. Having learned that airport workers planned to strike that night, he had already changed my next-day reservation to Vienna to one that afternoon, notifying the hotel there that I'd arrive a day early. With Marcia's help, I made it to the flight on time.

David arrived the next morning. While he met with local B'nai B'rith leaders one of their wives gave me a brief tour, driving past the Schönbrunn Palace, down the Ringstrasse, and along the not-blue Danube before joining the men at Freud's house. That night we attended the opera for *Die Fledermaus* and afterward enjoyed Viennese coffee and sachertorte at Sacher's. On Sunday we watched the Lipizzaner horses, thereupon fulfilling my priorities for a first visit to Vienna.

In Bucharest we were whisked directly to a reception in our honor hosted by Chief Rabbi Moses Rosen to introduce members of Romania's cultural elite, especially those who were Jewish. In his welcoming speech Rabbi Rosen addressed our concern over exit visas denied to Jews, specifying only three conditions for which that occurred. David had accepted Dictator Nicolae Ceausescu's invitation to visit in hopes of ameliorating the problem and brought documents from several *refuseniks* attesting it. After the speeches, Mrs. Rosen led me into the crowd to meet people, beginning with a man whom she introduced as one of Romania's leading playwrights. As we moved on, the young woman at his side grabbed my arm and whispered, "Don't believe what the rabbi said. It's not true. You must help me leave!"

I told her my husband would do whatever he could and that she should send us the details. She replied, "I already have."

When we departed an attendant ushered me into the left side of the town car assigned to us, then returned to the curb to open the door for David. In that instant someone opened the front passenger door, tossed an envelope back onto my lap, and disappeared. David, seeing me stuff it into my purse, asked what it was. I put my finger to my lips and he questioned me no more until we were in our hotel room alone. After making the "shush" sign again I went into the bathroom and turned on the water full force, then gave him the note and told him about the woman at the reception.

The note wasn't from her. It was from someone else seeking help. David placed it in his briefcase with the others and prepared for bed. There were twin beds, very narrow and uncomfortable, with a single thin pillow on each. David asked me if I had seen a second pillow, which I hadn't, but I said I would ask for another in the morning. I forgot to ask, but we found two pillows on each bed when we returned that afternoon.

That evening at a party thrown by Harry Barnes, the American ambassador to Romania, I spent most of the cocktail hour chatting with an attaché who had once been stationed in Kathmandu. When we were called to dinner he escorted me across the high-ceilinged atrium, continuing our conversation against the reverberation of others and the clack of high heels on the marble floor. In the midst of it he thrust a note into my hand. When David and I opened it in our hotel room afterward we saw yet another plea from another *refusenik*, not the one I met at the reception.

The next day during a formal luncheon in a downtown hotel, a messenger told me that a woman in the lobby needed to see me. The foreign minister was speaking so I couldn't leave. I told him to say I'd see her when the luncheon was over. By then, she was gone.

Our schedule included two days of touring the countryside. The next morning we were packed and ready to go, but we couldn't leave until President Ceausescu received us, which we were told to expect with only twenty minutes' notice. While waiting I received a call from the young woman, admitting it was she at the hotel and insisting on meeting us. I explained why that was impossible and promised to do everything we could to help her. When she persisted, obviously desperate, I tried to conclude hopefully and said, without any expectation of it happening, "I look forward to meeting you in Israel."

Finally, President Ceausescu received us. His office was a vast salon, at the far end of which he sat behind a large, elaborate desk adorned with an array of silver appointments. After greeting us he ushered us to a seating arrangement where, through an interpreter, he lectured us on the needs of his country. He also congratulated us on our presidential election, the results of which had just been announced (I'd gone to our embassy at dawn to hear them as they came in), and asked about our new president-elect Jimmy Carter. When David mentioned that I knew Carter personally, Ceausescu asked me what he was like. Among other encouraging points, I told him I thought Carter would be sensitive to Romania's problems because he had grown up as a poor boy on a peanut farm in rural Georgia during the Great Depression. With a slight sneer, the dictator replied, "In America, you don't know what poor is."

I was relieved when the interview ended. We enjoyed our remaining day and a half in Romania with a pleasant escort driving us to Brasov, a resort town in the Transylvania mountains where Count Dracula once lived. After a heavy dinner of deliciously spicy local specialties, we were entertained by folk dancers who concluded their performance by bringing me onto the floor to join them. I barely made it back to our room before passing out. By mid-morning, sleep and the brisk mountain air rejuvenated me sufficiently to appreciate the sights and history as we returned to the Bucharest airport.

On the way home we stopped in London, where David took me to Westminster for his appointment with former Prime Minister Harold Wilson, who gave us his new book and was charming. I was too tired to remember more.

Our next big adventure was President Jimmy Carter's inauguration. Invitations came for preceding events, to David for Henry Kissinger's luncheon at the State Department and to me from his wife Nancy for an afternoon reception there. Other guests included Shirley Temple Black, the outgoing Chief of Protocol who had been my favorite movie star when both of us were children, and Shirley MacLaine, whom I greatly admired as much for her free spirit as for her performances. Julie and Bud Weiss visited us for the festivities, arriving in time for dinner on the eve of Inauguration Day. Thanks to our two-story glass window wall, we watched the fireworks from our dining room while enjoying our dessert and coffee.

January 20th, 1977 dawned bright and clear but bitter cold. We layered our warmest clothes and brought thermoses of hot drinks, but after walking from the distant parking and waiting for the ceremony to begin we were nearly numb when it ended. Too cold to stand on Pennsylvania Avenue for the parade, we went home and cuddled up on our sofas to see it on television.

That night, before the inaugural balls, we co-hosted a cocktail supper with Adelaide and Richard at our apartment. I'd been reluctant to do it because I knew few Washingtonians and thought it would characterize me as a social climber trying to associate with their prominent friends like journalists Madeleine and Marvin Kalb. I couldn't bring in my Atlanta pals like Bob and Betty Lipshutz because, as Carter appointees, they were going to the high-level celebrations. When the time came, we did have two sets of unexpected visitors: Gene and Saralyn Oberdorfer from Atlanta and Ylana and Oved Ben-Ami from Israel. Our party was such a success that some guests didn't want to leave for the inaugural balls. Even so, the Eisenmans and I were determined to go. David welcomed the excuse to stay home, so the party continued without us.

Not all inaugural balls are what we imagine them to be. After navigating the traffic in a freezing rain, we arrived at the Armory for the Georgia ball and found it so dense that we couldn't *move,* much less check our coats. After my gown took a direct hit from someone's drink, we squeezed our way around for a few minutes and came back home. We never saw the Carters.

The next day David caught an early morning flight out so he wasn't with us when the Weisses took me to lunch at Georgetown's most popular restaurant and Henry Kissinger stopped to say hello. I'd only met him once, but he obviously identified me because he asked about David. That was sufficient flattery to override my disappointment about inaugural balls.

In February we went to Israel for the World Zionist Congress, but for us the trip held much more meaning. Bill had become engaged to marry an Israeli, Hava Tirosh, and we were eager to meet her. She charmed us with her intelligence and warmth as well as her ease with strangers such as ourselves.

I went with David to meet newly-arrived Russian immigrants, walked on the Old City walls, and visited a dig with archaeologist Magen Broshi, but beyond meeting Hava, my chief excitement occurred when Avigdor took us to the Lebanese border north of Rosh Hanikra to see the field hospital that Israelis built to treat Lebanese soldiers wounded in that country's ongoing civil war. They called it the Good Fence.

We arrived to find the mayor and other townspeople awaiting the birth of a baby. The mother-to-be, while in labor, had walked from five miles inside Lebanon to give birth in Israel at the Good Fence. With no medic there who had ever delivered a baby, the Israel Defense Force doctor, the officer in charge, had to oblige. We braved the damp wind and fading daylight with the others to know the result, and applauded when the doctor finally emerged to display the bundled newborn.

Before returning to Jerusalem we made a pit stop at the hotel in Rosh Hanikra, where it surprised me to see the International Press Corps lounging with drinks around an open fire. Because it seemed to me to be especially good news that a joyful event occurred at a place normally associated with bad news, I told them they'd passed up a great story. They rolled their eyes, reminding me that for professional journalists, good news is no news.

On our way home from Israel I had different surprises. We again stopped in London, and this time I reminded Lord Janner of his offer to take me to a session of Parliament. It surprised me that the House of Lords occupied such a small room and that members could be so contentious while adhering to the rules of British decorum.

On Wednesday, March 9th, David called me shortly before noon, beginning by saying, "Don't worry, honey. I'm okay."

"Is there any reason why you shouldn't be?" I asked.

We'd returned to town the night before and gone immediately to a black-tie dinner for the Rabins at the Israeli ambassador's residence. I was still dreaming about it. Elizabeth Taylor came with her new husband, Senator John Warner, and I was seated at the table with noted archaeologist Yigal Allon, then Israel's Minister of Foreign Affairs. I'd slept late and missed the news.

The B'nai B'rith building had been captured by terrorists. Everyone there was being held face down on the bare concrete of the unfinished top floor with machetes brandished over them. David and Executive Director Dan Thursz stopped in after a breakfast meeting with the Romanian ambassador to pick up papers for a working brunch with Rabin at the Shoreham. As they pulled up to the hotel, they were met by Secret Service agents who told them what happened in the ten minutes since they left. A group of aggrieved African Americans calling themselves Hanafi Muslims had besieged B'nai B'rith, the Islamic Center on Massachusetts Avenue, and the District Building downtown. It wasn't yet clear what they wanted.

David and Dan found makeshift operations already set up at the small hotel next door to B'nai B'rith on Rhode Island Avenue. When I asked if I should come down, David said no and that I should stay home and field phone calls—exactly what Jack said when the Temple was bombed!

This time I had to make only one call. David wanted me to assure the grandchildren in Memphis that he was safe before they heard the news. I spoke to their nanny, Mattie Coleman, who had been watching on television and saw the terrorists shoot a councilman as he entered the District Building. That man was her son and Washington's future mayor, Marion Barry.

That afternoon David asked me to bring him necessities for overnight and agreed when I asked to stay with him. On my way, I stopped at the

Presbyterian Church on 16th Street to encourage the hostages' families who were gathered there. By evening negotiations were underway with Washington's three most prominent Muslim ambassadors—Ashraf Ghorbal of Egypt, Yaqub Khan of Pakistan, and Ardeshir Zahedi of Iran—using their knowledge of the Quran to negotiate with the terrorists. As they continued past midnight, we took a room and tried to sleep.

Around 3AM the police awakened us with the good news that the hostages would be released. They would exit through the service door into the alley in order to avoid the press. No one, not even their families, would be notified until they were safely away. David and I alone were permitted to greet them as they walked out.

That weekend the police authorized a press tour of the building prior to clean-up and permitted me to join as "house photographer." I recorded trashed hallways and blocked stairwells but concentrated on personal images like children's pictures, shoes and brown bags beneath hastily abandoned desks, and flower pots in sunny windows.

No one ever asked to see my photographs. They remain filed with my shot of the Israeli medic at the Good Fence.

After B'nai B'rith honored the three ambassadors, David and I received gifts from two of them. Yaqub Khan gave us a copy of the Quran; Ardeshir Zahedi sent a Jeroboam of champagne bearing the Shah's label and a magnificent coffee table book of Iranian art compiled by Queen Farah. He later invited us to a formal dinner honoring Henry Kissinger. Knowing that cooking was his hobby, I asked him if he had prepared the cucumber soup, the most delicious dish on the exceptionally fine menu. He had not, but promised to invite us again to a smaller party that he could prepare himself because his recipe was better.

That never happened, but the following year, when David's term of office was ending, Zahedi sent him an imperial crested silver cigarette box as a parting gift. Soon after that, the ayatollahs prevailed and his own term of office ended.

Coincidentally, another political upheaval began in Washington while Yitzhak Rabin was there. His wife, Leah, went to the Chase

Bank to withdraw funds that she had deposited there for use during his tenure as ambassador and left intact afterward, contrary to Israeli law against holding bank accounts overseas. A reporter followed her and filed the story, which led to Rabin's resignation as prime minister, the fall of the Labor Party, and the ascension of the Likud Party's Menachem Begin.

On our next trip to Israel, David had appointments with key figures whom I especially wanted to meet. I'd greatly admired General Ariel Sharon since the Yom Kippur War, so when he came to speak with David at our hotel in Tel Aviv I made sure to be there. My hero worship soured as I sat next to him that day. He kept his heavy brown leather jacket closed and his ever-present half-smile formed a slight curve of his lips. Watching his face as he spoke in a friendly voice, I saw his eyes as those of a cobra ready to strike.

I had the opposite reaction to Minister of Defense Ezer Weizman, an even more daring military hero, one of the four fliers who saved Tel Aviv in Israel's War of Independence. As David and I sat across from him at his office desk I was charmed by his demeanor and his warmth. Even when David asked what he would do if Jordan deployed its recently received warplanes against Israel, his strong response sounded friendly. With a twinkle in his eye, he said, "We'd shoot them out of the sky."

My visit with Menachem Begin reversed my opinion of him, an admittedly prejudiced one due to his actions as leader of the Irgun during the British Mandate. He hadn't yet become prime minister, but as leader of the Likud Party he was an important member of the Knesset whom I wanted to meet, so when David had a date for lunch with him there I went along.

At the outset, I asked Begin for permission to photograph him while he spoke with David and he agreed. His aide, who joined us later, went ballistic when I lifted my camera.

"Mr. Begin gave me permission," I told him.

"What does he know!" gasped the hysterical young man, glancing around to see if anyone noticed.

"It's forbidden," he whispered. "The guards will confiscate your camera. How did you get into the building with it?"

It was hanging on my neck when we walked in and no one questioned me.

He shook his head despairingly and rolled his eyes. "Put it away," he ordered. "Don't let them see you with it."

That ended my photography for the day, but the one shot I took is unique. People who knew Begin well told me it's the only one they ever saw of him smiling.

In June 1977 we were again invited to a state dinner at the White House, our first during the Carter administration. When we went through the receiving line, instead of shaking my hand President Carter again pulled me close and kissed me, then admonished David to take good care of me. The Marine guard then led me past all the tables in the state dining room to the center one at the far end by the white marble fireplace, the President's table.

My already-seated companions were Texas Congressman Jim Wright, somewhat inebriated and very sociable, and the handsome young Hispanic mayor of Miami, Maurice Ferré. Because the event honored President Carlos Pérez of Venezuela and Senora Pérez, the Venezuelan ambassador and his wife as well as our ambassador to Caracas and his wife were there. The Carters, having studied Spanish, conversed with their guests in that language, using interpreters only for the formal speech.

I rarely remember the food at parties unless it's exceptionally good or bad and this was neither, but I did take note of the flowers because I'd heard that Rosalyn wanted to use Georgia products whenever possible. They were white crepe myrtle.

After dinner, we went onto the South Lawn where a stage was erected and principals from the Washington Ballet performed the pas de deux from *Swan Lake*. While awaiting them on that balmy summer evening, we saw the lighted monuments on the Mall, the Lincoln Memorial to our far right, the Jefferson on our far left, and the Custis-Lee Mansion above Arlington Cemetery in the center, a sight unrivaled in evoking history.

As an odd postscript, Hannah Sinauer, David's beloved BBI secretarial assistant, called me the next morning to ask what I'd worn to the dinner. A fashion reporter had inquired. I wore my white tucked cotton and lace Mexican "wedding dress."

That summer we stayed in Israel longer than usual and had three thrilling experiences, most meaningful of which was Bill's wedding. Because Israeli religious law forbade marriages during the weeks before Tisha B'Av (late July that year) and David co-chaired a meeting there in late June, he took a brief vacation rather than flying home for a week between.

Our first thrill occurred when we went to Jaffa for the opening of a B'nai B'rith youth center. As our car pulled up to it a broadly smiling young woman ran to me saying, "You told me we would meet in Israel, and here I am. Because of you."

She was the woman from Bucharest! Six months earlier, the Romanian ambassador to Washington told us that three *refuseniks* from our list had been permitted to leave, but only one had gone.

Her name was Lumi. She was a writer whose work had been banned, and she had asked her father's friend, the playwright, to take her to the rabbi's reception so she could seek help from "the most important Jew in America."

She meant David, and I quickly put her straight. "He really isn't," I corrected. "Whatever made you think so?"

Because the official newspapers announced our visit, she said. When other Jewish leaders came, it was reported only by the Jewish press.

Lumi also told us that she was in the Immigrant Absorption Program in Netanya and had an American boyfriend there who made *aliyah* in order to sing with the Israel Opera. I invited them to Jerusalem for Shabbat and gave them their first tour of the city, never expecting that we'd meet again soon in America.

Six months later, in Washington, I received a call from a woman identifying herself as the mother of Richard Shapp, Lumi's operatic boyfriend. He was coming to Philadelphia to sing in *Amahl and the Night Visitors* and bringing Lumi along. She wanted to come to Washington for a day while he was rehearsing.

Pleased as I was, I couldn't be sure of my schedule for the entire day, which I explained to Mrs. Shapp. "No problem," she replied. "Just call my husband's office if you need help."

Her husband's office? She hadn't mentioned it, so I asked.

It was the Commonwealth of Pennsylvania. He was the governor.

I enjoyed Lumi's visit and so did David. A few weeks later, Mrs. Shapp called again to say that her son and Lumi were getting married in Philadelphia two days before Pesach and that I should save the date. They wanted me to sign their *ketubah*. I did, and rejoiced to witness their marriage as the conclusion to her harrowing experience and my diplomatic episode in Romania.

David and I went with Bill and Hava to meet her parents, Yosef and Dora Tirosh, at Kibbutz Afikim, just south of Lake Kinneret. They spoke no English or any Romance language and we knew no Slavic ones, but we bonded with them immediately. Dora showed me her amazing mammoth mixing machine in the kibbutz kitchen where she worked and Yosef, semi-retired and an avid fisherman, prepared his morning's catch from the kibbutz fish farm for our lunch in their mini kitchen at home.

Then we drove to Haifa for opening ceremonies of the Maccabiah Games, a moving and colorful spectacle, although less so than the Olympics. Bill and Hava returned to Jerusalem while we checked into the Semadar at Caesarea. Our few days of vacation were highlighted by a performance of *Fidelio* in the ancient Roman theater. Its original walls formed the proscenium and the sea served as backdrop. With Zubin Mehta conducting, clad in his native Indian garb, gauzy white and fluttering in the breeze, we were more fascinated watching him than viewing the action onstage.

We returned to Jerusalem two days before the wedding. That morning we joined Bill, Hava, and her immediate family at an office building downtown for the "religious" ceremony required by Israeli law. Our friends, Reform rabbis Dick Hirsch and Hank Sobel, would perform the Reform rites that evening. The morning ritual consisted of the bride's father and the groom signing papers with two grubby-looking old men questioning them, then the couple standing under a *chupah* with the rest of us holding candles while the old men chanted, presumably in Hebrew but too fast, perfunctory, and singsong for me to be sure. To me it was far from religious.

David had a terrible cold, so after the ceremony we left the others and returned to the hotel. I took his temperature, which was high, so he went to bed and I called our physician friends, Anna and Henry Schiffman. They came, medicated him, and took me to the wedding.

I was pleased that Bill and Hava chose to be married at HUC in the chapel that Jack dedicated in 1963, and invited all of my Israeli friends. Joan and Nate Lipson, who were temporarily living in London, came for the wedding and opened their home to give Bill and Hava a private party following their reception. The Schiffmans and I looked in on David before going there and found him resting well.

The next day David insisted that he was well enough to speak at a scheduled luncheon and drive us to Tel Aviv for our flight home, briefly stopping in Ramat HaSharon to visit Golda Meir at her home. He'd made a date with her because he wanted me to know her on a personal level as he did. Avigdor Warsha offered to drive us there but David foolishly refused, not wanting to trouble him. However, David was unfamiliar with the suburbs and I didn't really speak Hebrew, knowing just enough to ask directions but couldn't understand the answers. We arrived at Golda's house embarrassingly late, and I was so upset that I forgot my camera.

Golda was gracious and understanding. When she offered us drinks I jumped up to help her, shocked at the thought of *her* serving *us*. Opening two bottles of Coca-Cola and taking them to the next room hardly required two people, but I had to do something.

David excitedly told Golda, "We got us a *sabra* daughter-in-law last night."

He sat back, expecting to hear a "mazel tov." In her inimitable baritone, Golda growled, "Where are they gonna live?"

Anticipating that the answer wouldn't rate a "mazel tov" unless it was "Israel," I explained that Bill was a rabbinical student at HUC and had to finish his training in Cincinnati. She then changed the subject and discussed world problems with David while I just listened, content to be like a fly on Golda's wall.

In August, when David checked into Nashville's St. Thomas Hospital for his biennial checkup, the doctors found a tumor. The biopsy identified it as early-stage prostate cancer and caused a case of hiccups that kept him in the hospital for two weeks. With a good chance of recovery whether treated by medication, radiation, or surgery, he first chose medication, which I fully endorsed despite the warning that its side effect was a temporarily diminished libido.

David began taking his medication while in Knoxville for the High Holy Days and initially recognized no side effects. When the busy season resumed and the workaholic began to act like a zombie, we realized that medication diminishing one's sex drive also diminishes other drives. He stopped taking it and sought the best urological surgeon east of the Mississippi. Dr. Patrick Walsh at Johns Hopkins Hospital in Baltimore removed the cancer and David suffered no ill effects other than another two weeks of hiccups.

We were back in the skies again before the end of the year. I felt the pressure of life in the fast lane but still loved its benefits. In Israel we visited Yamit, a seaside settlement in northern Sinai destined to be evacuated as part of the 1979 Egypt-Israel peace treaty.

A woman from Miami who met us for lunch at the little eatery she owned and operated on the beach told us that the government encouraged her to open it there and aided her financially even though the territory was in dispute. We saw children playing on a merry-go-round in the town square and strawberries peeping out from pipes in a greenhouse like buds in a forest of aluminum trees. On our next visit there we saw an empty plaza, bare metal pipes in the greenhouse, and shrubbery balled for transport. The woman from Miami and her neighbors were offered homes in the Negev.

I was thrilled when David told me we were going to South Africa in the spring of 1978. He was scheduled for a week of events in three cities there, then fly to Israel for the opening of Beit Hatfutsot, the Museum of the Jewish Diaspora. At a dinner in New York the night before departure I sat next to U.N. Ambassador Andrew Young, a friend from the civil rights days in Atlanta. He had just returned from South Africa so I asked him for points I should notice. He thought for a moment, then said, "You'll find a lot of good people there."

When I told him that as functionaries for B'nai B'rith we were unlikely to meet anyone of color, he replied, "Keep your eyes open. You'll see a lot that reminds you of our times in Atlanta."

I would quickly be reminded of those times, especially when friends attempted to show us what they considered the good side of their relationships with Blacks and "Coloreds"—the South African term for Indians, Malays and others who were not native African but too dark to be legally "White." In Johannesburg a Jewish industrialist who escaped Nazi Germany took me to see the Black township of Soweto. Boasting of having a good relationship with his Black employees there, he backed his statement by telling me that they didn't object to him calling them *kaffirs*.

I bit my tongue. That's Africa's "n" word.

At the park where police had recently massacred protesting students he said the media exaggerated and protesters staged provocative scenes for the press. I knew that had happened when the University of Georgia integrated, but there the protestors were preventing justice and the police didn't shoot.

In Durban two Jewish leaders, brothers who had fled the Holocaust, greeted us on the tarmac, then led us into the airport lounge where reporters waited to interview David. When he mentioned Andrew Young the brothers became apoplectic and whisked us away, thereafter keeping David at a distance from reporters.

So many people sought a private word with David on the trip that some, in frustration, turned to me. One young man took me sightseeing to discuss his problem as he drove. He and his wife wanted to join her brother in Atlanta but couldn't get visas.

In Cape Town I *finally* met people who fulfilled Andy Young's prediction. Women there proudly recounted their daughters' experiences, risking jail to bring warm clothing and blankets to Coloreds whose homes the government had recently destroyed in the middle of a winter night. I met nice people everywhere, but only here did I hear anyone hint of resisting apartheid.

On Sunday, when we were scheduled to fly to Israel for the Monday opening of Beit Hatfutsot, we learned we'd been booked on a flight that didn't exist. The next flight to Tel Aviv wasn't until Thursday. Our best option was to fly to Athens with a 24-hour stopover that landed us in Israel on Tuesday, after the ceremonies ended. David still had meetings to attend.

In Athens the weather was too cold and wet to go browsing. David always had work to catch up on in spare time, and I had no inclination for shopping. I left the room determined to do *something* and, by uncanny good luck, bumped into Pat Williams, my pal from Theatre Atlanta, as I stepped off the elevator. She was leading a tour but the rain canceled their schedule. We spent a delightful day together playing catch-up.

The weather was equally drab in Israel, doubly disappointing to me because David's meetings were in Herzliya and we were staying at a good hotel on the beach. That was the only time I ever *didn't* enjoy being in Israel.

Upon landing at JFK, Zelda Bloom greeted us with the news that the king of Morocco invited us to visit his country with a delegation to promote tourism. "We leave a week from today," she informed me.

I always wanted to see Morocco, but *next week*?!

A week later we were back at JFK, trudging to the end of what seemed like the longest tarmac in Queens on the hottest day of the year. The Royal Air Maroc plane had six pairs of seats in first class, the right bulkhead assigned to David and me. He didn't want to take them because our delegation was in economy, but Zelda convinced him he needed the comfort of first class in order to rest. When we sat down, the seats collapsed. We stood on the tarmac while the crew repaired them.

Rabat was hot and dusty. Our bus wasn't air conditioned and neither was the hotel. When David showed signs of exhaustion I complained to Sarfati, our escort. He was understanding but helpless. Tomorrow in Tangier will be better, he promised. He owned that hotel.

We had the royal suite. A wraparound window wall in the parlor gave a panoramic view of the harbor. Translucent silk curtains billowed from arches set inside, simulating the interior of a royal tent. The bedroom was equally beautiful, but there we had a problem. The bed was an old-fashioned double, the likes of which Jack and I had shared comfortably for 27 years, but David had never shared one and was convinced he couldn't. He said he'd sleep on the living room sofa, which I of course vetoed. I'd do it if necessary, but I insisted it wouldn't be necessary because I promised to stay on my side of the bed so as not to disturb him. I stayed awake half the night clinging to the mattress.

Exhaustion didn't impair our pleasure in Tangier. Sarfati arranged a traditional feast complete with a belly dancer who concluded her performance perched on David's knee. The next night Sarfati and his wife hosted us for dinner in their home.

In Medina Sarfati showed us his ancestral home and synagogue, currently a shoe factory. His father's family came from France in the fifteenth century. His mother's were Berber Jews who migrated from central Africa in antiquity.

Next, we toured Meknes, also rife with Jewish history, and ended in Casablanca, where most of Morocco's Jews lived. For Shabbat, at the luncheon given for us there, I was with a group speaking French and English when I noticed that the aged rabbi sitting with us wasn't following the conversation. Realizing that he probably spoke only Arabic and Hebrew, I brought Hadassah Thursz, who spoke fluent Hebrew, to socialize with him. After a brief exchange, she went to get her husband, Dan, who approached looking dumbstruck. The rabbi, on being introduced to Hadassah and noticing her height, recalled he married a very tall couple named Thursz and had last seen them just before they boarded the last ship to America as the Nazis entered Casablanca. They were Dan's parents.

That was my final trip abroad on the fast track. David had a meeting in London during the summer, but only for the weekend, so I didn't go. I did have one final adventure worth reporting, however. The weekend David was away the White House correspondent for Jewish news, who continually pestered us, invited me to the President's press corps picnic. I tried to refuse, saying I couldn't get home in time to dress for the Israel Bonds Ambassador's Ball that evening. She replied that I could use the White House press facility and give her a ride to the ball.

While socializing on the South Lawn we heard music coming from a natural amphitheater downhill and she led me there. The Carters were already seated opposite us and when the President saw me he signaled hello.

My hostess gasped. "The President knows you?"

"From Atlanta," I whispered. "When he was governor."

The moment the music ended she grabbed me and raced up the hill ahead of the crowd for a place on the path the Carters would take when they left. They spoke to each person as they passed, and the President greeted me with a kiss as usual. When my hostess saw that, she looked up at the leader of the free world and said, "You kissed her but you didn't kiss me."

A true Southern gentleman, the President then kissed her and continued into the White House.

In September, Marcia joined us in New Orleans for David's final BBI convention as president. Delegates again rejected his plea to update the organization's structure, contenders for his seat campaigned with hoopla like national political conventioneers, and he received traditional accolades that he richly deserved. I rejoiced when it ended. I'd had my fill of the fast track. After seven years of it David needed rest, and after three and a half I needed fresh air. I was glad to go home.

Twelve

NORMAL LIFE

N ot surprisingly, David's return to normalcy in September 1978 included attending another convention before returning home. We flew directly from New Orleans to Boston for a Mass Mutual meeting. When we finally reached home in DC I threw a party celebrating our newfound freedom. I looked forward to spending more time with family and friends and sharing mutual interests, including travel for the sheer fun of it.

David had many friends in Washington through B'nai B'rith and his presidency of the National Association of Life Underwriters in the early 1960s. More importantly for both of us, his younger brother Ralph lived there with his wife Gerry and their two children. I had met them, both government employees, on my initial trips to Washington with David, and bonded with them immediately. Having been civil rights advocates in Louisiana, they were closer to me than other members of the Blumberg family, both in age and in interests. For the first time in my life I would have close family nearby for holiday dinners and other occasions.

Our future remained uncertain, however. After almost a decade of ignoring his business while making larger-than-affordable charitable contributions, David had debts to pay off. Needing some additional income, he proposed using his connections to sell B'nai B'rith legacy policies for its endowment fund, taking no pay from B'nai B'rith because the commissions would meet his needs. While he was in office, both candidates to succeed him, Jack Spitzer and Murray Shusterman, as well as executive director Dan Thursz told him they agreed and would implement it at the first executive meeting of the new administration.

Meanwhile David shuttled to and from his Knoxville office, usually without me because we expected to remain permanently in Washington and I was busily engaging there. As B'nai B'rith's First Lady I'd used whatever influence the position gave me to help grow its museum, established in 1975 when Joseph and Olyn Horwitz of Cleveland gave B'nai B'rith the majority of their collection, remarkable 18th- and 19th-century Judaica rescued from the Holocaust. The long-time archivist retired, to be replaced by a brilliant young museum curator/director, Anna Cohn. The BBI staff and executive board had no idea of what they had taken on with a museum and were unequipped to deal with it. I assisted, first via pillow talk with David.

Anna desperately needed volunteers. I couldn't be there regularly while still traveling with David but I persuaded two special friends, Marjory (Marge) Goldman, who had affluent connections in the Jewish community, and Adelaide Eisenman, who knew congressional wives, to organize a committee. Adelaide attracted attention to Anna's next exhibit, Judaica from the Smithsonian, by involving Joan Mondale, wife of Vice President Walter Mondale. Now that David and I were no longer trekking across the world for B'nai B'rith, I could be there to work with them.

We also had time to extend business travel with vacations. Only three months after David left office we went to a BBI committee meeting in Guadalajara, Mexico, and followed it with three days at Puerto Vallarta, where we stayed at what I believe was then the only hotel on the beach. We appreciated its lack of activity and paid our respects to the John Huston film *The Night of the Iguana* by having dinner one evening on the romantic heights where it was filmed.

While still struggling with uncertainty about our future, on January 20, 1979, we enjoyed the greatest possible *mitzvah* with the birth of a Rothschild grandchild—a boy, to be named after his grandfather.

The *brit milah* was in Cincinnati where Bill was studying for the rabbinate and Hava was teaching. Marcia met us there, as did our close friends from Atlanta, Cecil and Hermi Alexander. Cecil would serve as godfather, *sandak* in Hebrew, and receive the honor of holding the baby during the circumcision. Everyone arrived just before a blizzard set in. But the cold and risk of falling failed to dampen our spirits or discourage 82-year-old Dr. Jacob Rader Marcus, our beloved teacher—first Jack's, now Bill's—from attending as long as someone could bring him there. I held my breath watching David climb the many steps to Jake's door and then come down again with the aged professor, arm in arm. Thankfully, they made it without incident.

In September 1978, Menachem Begin and Anwar Sadat signed the Camp David Accords with Jimmy Carter at Camp David. The following March, we were driving back to DC from Knoxville when we heard the news that in a few days Israel's and Egypt's leaders would sign the first-ever peace treaty between an Arab state and Israel. I had a momentary regret that we were no longer on the fast track and therefore no longer among the Jewish VIPs to be invited to the White House for the ceremony.

I was wrong. We received invitations, both to the signing of the peace treaty on the front lawn of the White House in the afternoon of March 26, 1979 and to the dinner that evening with an estimated 1,600 others in a heated tent on the back lawn. During the very long, cold wait for the afternoon ceremony to begin, I reflected on our incredibly good fortune to be there witnessing a turning point in history. I also enjoyed taking a close-up picture of Ted Kennedy, who sat just in front of us. Guests arriving for the dinner that night queued up at the East Wing entrance, inching at a glacial pace down the long passage to the center door and out into the huge tent on the lawn. We were seated too far from the action to see or hear very much but we were enormously pleased and honored to be there.

Shortly afterward Jack Spitzer, as new president of BBI, organized a mission to visit the capitals of both countries, including a charter flight with Austrian Airlines from Tel Aviv to Cairo, via Athens. The peace treaty had called for direct air service between the two countries, but negotiations to accomplish that were both delicate and top secret because of the Arab world's condemnation of Egypt for making peace with Israel. We joined the BBI mission, and then learned that these talks had been jeopardized because word leaked that a Jewish delegation would fly into Egypt from Israel, even though it was via a third country. Israel requested that B'nai B'rith cancel its Cairo excursion, but Israel's diplomatic and security concerns were no match for Spitzer's ego and he refused.

David deplored Spitzer's decision but could not stop the flight. He could only refuse to board it himself. We remained in Israel.

Here I must admit to one of my baser instincts. The group had dressed in its grubbiest for the likely uncomfortable flight to Cairo. This made sense under normal conditions, but before the departure we were being received by President Yitzhak Navon and his wife, Ofira, at Beit HaNassi, the Israeli presidential residence. I appreciate feeling at home in Israel, but I do *not* believe it gives us license to show disrespect. Had I been going onto the flight with them after visiting the President, I would have brought my grubbies along in a carry-on and changed at the airport. Certainly these travelers would not have dressed so casually to meet any other head of state. When we heard that their luggage didn't make the connection in Athens and arrived in Cairo only as they departed for home, I considered it divine retribution.

After BBI's next two executive committee meetings ended with no announced response to David's proposal about selling legacy policies for B'nai B'rith, it seemed apparent to us that the delay was intentional and permanent. When David pushed for an answer, he learned that Spitzer, Thursz, and Murray Shusterman, Spitzer's opponent for president, had all secretly promised that they would never advocate putting a past president on staff, paid or not. Ironically, their reason was that when David's predecessor, Bill Wexler, remarried and moved to Israel, he needed a supplemental income which David endorsed, convincing the board to employ him as a president's representative in Israel. Wexler accepted the role but did nothing substantial for the new administration. That experience convinced B'nai B'rith executives not to hire former BBI presidents, but did not address David's offer that specified he would work without salary.

David's ability to absorb deception amazed me. This was the third time I'd seen him accept such treatment without rancor, without any discernable resentment, and without appearing depressed. The first began some years earlier when Alex Schindler, president of the UAHC (since renamed the Union for Reform Judaism), sought to become president of the Conference of Presidents of Major Jewish Organizations. The Orthodox members liked David despite his not being one of them and nominated him for the position. David declined in order to support Alex; he believed it was high time the Conference recognized the Reform movement by appointing Alex. David certainly *wanted* the position, but he was willing to wait for the next two-year term. Alex agreed to back him for it then in return for his current support, and even offered to conduct our wedding.

Alex's attitude began to change as soon as he took office. When David first mentioned it to me I thought he was being overly sensitive, but eventually I too noticed the difference. Not only was Alex pushing David aside, he had no intention of stepping down at the end of his two-year term. Alex remained in office long after his initial two years. To his credit, he provided strong leadership through difficult times, but that did not alter his deception in breaking his word to David.

David's second harsh blow occurred in summer 1978, just before his retirement as president of B'nai B'rith. An executive staffer for Israel Bonds, whom David befriended earlier when he worked for B'nai B'rith, approached him with the possibility of heading its American branch. We were in St. Louis for a family celebration when the staffer called to say that the Bonds' leadership planned to name a new president at its current meeting in the Catskills, that they favored David, and that he needed to be there prepared to speak.

We drove like crazy to reach the Concord by the next night. I should have suspected all was not well when we arrived late and discovered that no place had been reserved for us at the banquet. We'd been told that the first session the next morning would roll into another, at which David would be named president. Tired as he was from the drive, he worked through most of the night to prepare his speech. The next morning, as the second session began, his supposed friend took the microphone to announce someone else as the new president-elect. He didn't even have the courtesy to give David advanced notice.

My fury knew no bounds. Although I hadn't favored David taking the position, such treatment was inexcusable and I spared no expletives in saying so. As usual, David said nothing. Cold silence expressed his ultimate fury. We checked out and drove home. The intake of fresh air and lovely views along the Hudson replaced my anger with gratitude for being free from the Jewish philanthropic mafia.

I was deeply offended by David's treatment, but in neither case did I deplore its result. I feared that neither his health nor his finances could survive another two years of unpaid public service, and after seeing how the New York Jewish organizational establishment operated, I doubted that his gentlemanly approach could succeed in such an environment. Even B'nai B'rith's own traditional brotherhood and *rachmones* seemed to be slipping.

Driving home from Florida shortly after Jimmy Carter left office, we detoured to Plains, Georgia, for a brief visit with him. David thought the Jewish leaders had been wrong in turning against him and wanted to pay his respects as one who appreciated his efforts and good intentions. When the former president told us he was really happy to be back in Plains but that Amy and Rosalynn were saddened by having to leave Washington, David smiled knowingly and winked at me, well aware that I shared their regrets.

David did not live to see Carter's anti-Israel stance in later years, which appalled me as it did many others. I can't forgive the harm he did to Jews everywhere by using the term *apartheid* in the title of his book, but as a southerner familiar with the attitudes instilled by his faith, I understand his reasoning and his frustration when rebuffed by the reality that Israelis are not latter-day saints and biblical prophets, and that Jews striving to rebuild a homeland in the ashes of the Holocaust may exercise independent thought.

Meanwhile, our lives were on hold. David commuted to his office in Knoxville each week and returned to be with me on weekends. I was enjoying the life of a kept woman, indulged by a generous lover who visited on weekends, but I couldn't let that continue, nor could I in good conscience urge him to accept the invitations of his Mass Mutual colleagues in Washington to join their offices. It would have put too much pressure on him to start afresh in a new location while he still had debts to repay. He knew, however, that Washington provided the ambience that nourished me and the challenges I craved. He would never have asked me to return to Knoxville. I knew I had to propose it.

When I was a child and refused to do something that Mother told me to do, she'd say, "You'll do it and you'll like it." I then did it, grumbling to myself, "You can make me do it, but you can't make me like it."

Now I channeled Mother's demand as a mantra. I knew I had to make myself like Knoxville and I knew the rules for doing so: get comfortably settled, volunteer for community service, develop personal talent and interests, spend time with family, and travel. I did them all.

First, I needed a condo I could call home. Knoxville apartments, including the supposedly top-scale rental we currently occupied, looked to me like the starters with cheap construction and plastic bathtubs where Marcia and her contemporaries lived. The one solid-looking building I saw had small rooms, an "old people" look to it, and was in the same neighborhood as David's former home where he didn't want to be. I found an interesting California-style unit on a pond and golf course, still jerry-built with plastic bathtubs but otherwise pleasing. David didn't mind that it was 23 miles from downtown. That was okay with me because I hadn't met any in-town ladies so congenial that I'd miss living near them. David's friends welcomed me warmly, but I'd met only one whom I thought might become a future soulmate and she, ironically, was moving to Washington.

Moving day was traumatic, my misery made worse by the movers' delay in arriving on a Tuesday as scheduled. We had to wait until Friday for the freight elevator. Living for three days in limbo with everything packed in huge boxes blocking our living room increased the gloom. I did have one delightful relief, however. The weather provided fabulous photo ops from our balcony late one afternoon. Bright sunlight alternated with clouds like a giant spotlight moving over the National Mall, continually changing focus on the monuments. I shot a full roll of film.

When the movers finally came, it was again late and they didn't finish until after ten that night. By the time we started on the road we were in drenching rain and my mood matched the weather. Having lost all ability to shield David from my true feelings, I wept almost all the way to Tennessee.

Once there I plunged into getting settled and pursuing all paths to happiness in our new home. I planted bright, multicolored impatiens in the raised flowerbed bordering our narrow stone path from the driveway to the courtyard, planted herbs in the back along with tulips that Adelaide and Richard salvaged for me from discards on the National Mall, and placed a pot of African violets on our sunny kitchen table.

When everything was in order we held an open house because so many people had asked to see it, with an inventory providing provenance on the antiques for those who asked. For friends who kept kosher I spread the dining table solely with *milchik* (dairy products), plus fruit and veggies, and I served my favorite meat hors d'oeuvres fresh from an ongoing grill outdoors. I even grew my own thyme which Marcia, who came up for the party, painstakingly frisked so that shish kabobs could be rolled in them with sea salt as I remembered doing at Delphi.

All of our children and grandchildren came to Knoxville for our first Thanksgiving in our new home. Bill blessed it with a Chanukat HaBayit ceremony, affixing the *mezuzah* to our front door.

Once settled, I set about to serve the community. I declined an invitation for lunch with the board of the art museum because I couldn't find another Jewish person involved in it. I accepted the invitation to join the board of the Bijou Theater, an art deco gem being restored as a venue for live performances, because I knew the chairman and his wife and there was already at least one Jewish board member. In the Jewish community I organized a promotion for Yad LaKashish (Lifeline for the Old) in Jerusalem, produced an event celebrating Israel Independence Day at the community center, organized and led a busload of women to Atlanta on behalf of the United Jewish Appeal, and served on the Temple board. That was especially interesting because of the sharp contrast to my former role as *rebbetzin,* and even more meaningful after being appointed to the search committee for a new rabbi.

Together David and I chaired an Israel Bonds promotion for which we brought our friend Robert St. John to speak. We chaired a musical evening at the Temple featuring a cantor and his wife, recently arrived from the USSR. When asked to produce a Jewish interest series for radio, we made a pilot of taped interviews with special people whom we met on our travels, calling the series Travels with the Blumbergs. The project died in utero because the station's signal was too weak to reach its potential audience.

Throughout these years I continued writing and studying American Jewish history, remaining on the board of AJHS and connecting with the Southern Jewish Historical Society, which was just getting started. I also pursued photography. I'd become aware of having some talent for it when Anna Cohn asked me to write a narrative background for her first exhibit at the B'nai B'rith Museum, "Jerusalem: Roots of Stone," and I mentioned having slides that could help illustrate it. When she saw them she encouraged me, and when David finished his presidency I gave the museum a collection of photographs from Israel that could be used for the shop to take orders and sell. I was elated when Secretary of Agriculture Robert Bergland ordered the picture of a *moriah* (salvia) plant that resembles a menorah.

While living in Washington I took a few lessons with a leading instructor, had some opportunities to exhibit, sold a few pictures through a stock agency, and had a solo exhibit at a gallery in Knoxville where I sold several decorative pieces. Now in Knoxville, I decided to take a course at the University of Tennessee in developing black-and-white prints and turned our upstairs bathroom into a dark room.

That didn't last long. I didn't enjoy it and my Washington instructor had advised me to concentrate on what I did best, taking the images, and leave the chemistry to professionals.

David and I finally had time to use his subscriptions to the symphony and sports events. I loved the music, of course, and enjoyed the university basketball games, but I couldn't warm up to football even with VIP parking and seats on the 50-yard line. After nearly asphyxiating while walking from the car to the stadium between rows of buses with their motors running, then becoming nauseated by the stench of alcohol at our seats, I was in no condition to join the cheering. I never really learned the game and disliked the violence.

We enjoyed going out for dinner with friends, although their favorite restaurant offered French cuisine with too much flour in the cream sauce and too much garlic on the escargots. No one apparently threw parties at home, and the only one I recall being invited to elsewhere was an elaborate bash by our senator, Howard Baker, and his wife, Joy, celebrating their 30th wedding anniversary. It was like Washington in Tennessee that night. Many of their guests flew in for the evening on their private jets.

For David's 70th birthday in 1981 I organized a progressive surprise party that extended over the weekend. Marcia, Jimmy, and his boys came for Shabbat dinner on July 3. Bill and his family and more of our extended family and friends from Washington, Atlanta, and St. Louis arrived unannounced throughout Saturday for Fourth of July fireworks and traditional picnic fare at home that evening. On Sunday the 5th,

David's actual birthday, the main party took place with all his Knoxville friends invited for dinner at his favorite eatery, Buddy's Barbecue. That was the best of all.

Although our life had settled into a comparatively sedentary one by Blumberg standards, we still traveled to Washington every few weeks for David's meetings at BBI, occasionally going elsewhere on its behalf. We also traveled to insurance conferences at resorts, to St. Louis for events in David's sister Jean's family, to Atlanta, to Cincinnati prior to Bill's rabbinic ordination in 1980, and then to New Rochelle, NY, where Bill served as assistant rabbi.

One visit to Cincinnati was especially memorable for me because of being left alone with Jacob for a short time. He was about four months old. When he started to cry I frantically offered everything I thought he might want or need, but to no avail. After all else failed, because his parents were speaking Hebrew to him so he would be bilingual, I asked *"Atah rotzeh* Mozart?" and took him to the piano where Hava placed him when she played. As soon as I turned on the stereo he stopped crying. I thought of how much that would have pleased my mother.

We were also in Cincinnati to hear Bill's senior sermon and again for his ordination. As I proudly watched him march down the aisle of the historic Plum Street Temple in the procession, I thought of his father and wondered what his reaction would have been. Neither of us ever thought he would choose the rabbinate. We expected he'd go into law. His becoming a rabbi pleased me for the education it gave him as well as acknowledging appreciation of his father's legacy, but I wasn't surprised when he returned to law after just two years as a pulpit rabbi.

Visiting Bill and his family in New Rochelle was a sheer delight. David was challenged by two flights of stairs to reach the guest quarters on the top floor, but both of us loved listening to raindrops on the tin roof as we fell asleep. And nothing compared to the joy of playing with Jacob, especially taking care of him when his parents needed help.

I often went to Atlanta alone, not only to see Marcia (who actually

preferred to visit *us*), but also to attend various events like the annual Jacob
M. Rothschild Memorial Lecture at the Temple. On one trip, however, I
was lucky to return unscathed. I'd taken David's new Oldsmobile because
he didn't want me on the road alone in my convertible. At about one
o'clock, while having lunch with Reb Gershon at Colony Square before
returning to Knoxville, I got a call from Marcia saying a snowstorm was
on the way, predicted to reach Atlanta in an hour.

I hit the road immediately and gassed up in Smyrna just as the first
snowflakes fell. Before I reached Dalton, it was a blizzard. Pulling over
to stop wasn't an option because I was in the mountains and couldn't
tell where the road ended and the shoulder began. Crawling along with
everyone else, I somehow made it to the suburbs of Knoxville. Then I
faced the more daunting question of how to get off the downhill exit
safely. Rush hour had begun, so it would be courting disaster to slide onto
the crossroad without stopping to look.

Knowing not to brake, I said a quick *Sh'ma* and slid down, bearing
to the right (which was the direction I wanted), then cutting to the right
over the curb to make it onto the curvy uphill road leading to our home.
After going a short distance, the man in front of me got stuck on a hill,
and I couldn't get enough traction to proceed when he did. It was getting
dark. I saw lights on in the nearest farmhouse, its driveway just behind
me. I rolled down, backed in, and knocked on the door to ask to use the
telephone. David didn't answer. I panicked. He had recently been put on
insulin for diabetes, needing to eat regularly and keep candy on hand
to offset a low blood sugar reaction, none of which he did. I knew he
had an appointment that afternoon on the opposite side of Knoxville, a
40-minute drive home in the *best* of conditions, and I was terrified that
he might be stuck in the snow without safety snacks.

I left a message for him on our phone, thanked the owners of the
house, and returned to the car. My fur coat, high boots, and fur hat were
in the trunk, so I put them on and started on the long trek home on
foot across the stark white terrain. Trudging past the broad blanketed

fields, cold and frightened about what might have happened to David, I envisioned *Doctor Zhivago*'s Lara doggedly crossing the steppes of Russia.

To my great relief David reached home just before I arrived, well and intact despite having been on the road all afternoon. After a mutually ecstatic hug, we set out for the farmhouse to retrieve his car.

In the winter of 1982, a few years after the BBI trip to Egypt that we abandoned on principle, we went on our own en route to David's meeting of the World Jewish Congress in Jerusalem. I prepared by reading historical fiction about the ancient pharaohs as well as Anwar Sadat's autobiography, so it was unsurprising that the Nile cruise to Luxor and beyond proved far more fascinating to me than Cairo, notwithstanding Giza and the pyramids. Watching the *fellahin* as we passed the villages and the lush bordering countryside impressed me even more than the antiquities. In one place, we actually saw men rolling wheelbarrows filled with straw to make bricks.

We left the ship at Aswan and flew to Abu Simbel. I tried to dissuade David from going there with me because I knew he'd be uncomfortable in the heat and the history didn't interest him but he insisted, not wanting me to go alone even though we'd bonded with others on the trip. As I suspected, he suffered and saw very little while I took advantage of the phenomenal light and shadows to take pictures.

After Egypt we went back to Israel. We visited Hava's family at Afikim, where even our language barrier did not prevent Dorca from understanding my rave reports on our mutual grandson. She replied largely with a smile and gestured, "For you he is Number One. For me, he is Number Seven."

Later that week our adorable grandson came to Israel with his parents, staying with us one night at the Jerusalem Hilton. Not knowing exactly when they would arrive, I'd asked the desk clerk to admit them to our suite if we weren't there. When we returned to the hotel, I was surprised to find them with all their luggage in the middle of the lobby.

When I asked the clerk why he hadn't admitted them, he responded in disbelief, "That was your son? I thought you said your son was a rabbi."

Israelis were not yet accustomed to seeing beardless rabbis in jeans and sneakers.

As we approached spring that year, excitement ramped up for the opening of the Knoxville World's Fair. David had been an early supporter so we were invited to much of the hoopla, including the opening gala that was so over-amplified that we couldn't endure it for more than a few minutes. The sound followed us all the way to the parking lot. With that foretaste we stayed away from much that followed, but we enjoyed our privileges as an incentive for friends and family to visit us and see the Fair. We had permanent entrance passes, which encouraged me to go with them and hold their places in the long lines while they viewed other exhibits.

With Knoxville expecting many visitors for the Fair, churches on Kingston Pike, the main boulevard, prepared to welcome them, each in its own way. Our congregation, Temple Beth El, chose to exhibit Jewish art in its social hall and asked me to take charge, beginning with my own photographs of Israel. I selected images that illustrated energy, the theme of the Fair, specifying "Energy of Israel," displaying them for a month before bringing in works of others in different media for each following month. My exhibit at the Temple led to an invitation from a major downtown bank to mount an exhibit featuring scenes and people from around the world.

After the Fair closed, the board of the Bijou Theater invited me to exhibit in the long narrow hall of the theater where people gathered during intermissions and receptions. I filled the small wall at the far end with a large print of a man and woman walking through the colonnade of Hatshepsut's temple in Egypt. The chairman of the theater board, an architect, and his wife, an art agent, bought the print and ordered another, an abstract of buildings in downtown Knoxville, enlarged to decorate elevator lobbies in an office building they were converting into residential condos. My new career seemed to be flying.

Despite these encouragements, I realized when the Fair closed that with all the excitement it engendered and the accolades I received for my work, I disliked Knoxville more than ever. All the things I'd done to make myself content with living there had proven useless. I felt that I was wasting the most productive years of my life being on top of the heap with no role models to inspire me. I couldn't grow. Being a big fish in a small pond wasn't for me. I wanted to swim in the ocean, even if it meant being ignored.

Although unchallenged and unfulfilled intellectually, I appreciated that I could endure Knoxville as long as David and I were well and traveling. But I didn't want to spend my golden years there, especially not without him, and because of our age difference, he would likely predecease me.

David's grandsons, Jeffrey and Lee, were growing up. They visited us in Knoxville, stayed with us overnight at the hotel when we were in Memphis, and joined us at Jim's in Nashville as well as at our many gatherings in St. Louis for their cousins' bar and bat mitzvahs and graduations.

We took Jeffrey to Israel as his bar mitzvah gift along with his best friend, whose parents also gifted him the trip for *his* bar mitzvah. Because I wanted to give them an "Experiment" experience, we rented the home of a friend, Shoshana Cohen, who spent the month we were there with mutual friends nearby. With David as driver and me as tour guide, we showed the boys the country on *tiulim*, brief excursions, to main points of interest north and south.

Housekeeping with two teenage boys wasn't as easy as it had been for me with Jack ten years earlier. Fast food franchises hadn't yet come to the Holy City so finding suitable eateries for kids was problematic. Neighborhood bistros were all *milchik* and specialized in onion soup prepared with vegetable broth, so it didn't taste like onion soup to us.

When we traveled and returned on the weekend, we couldn't pick up fresh bread on the way home for the next morning's breakfast because stores were closed on Shabbat. From where we lived in the German colony, it was easier to take the five-mile, fifteen-minute drive to Bethlehem for bread than to go to an Arab shop in the Old City, which gave special meaning to Bethlehem's Hebrew name, Bet Lehem, "House of Bread."

David and I had one very exciting (and potentially dangerous) adventure on that trip. Because of the 1982 Lebanon War and with the Lebanese Civil War still raging, the Israeli Defense Force controlled West Beirut. Avigdor Warsha arranged for presidents of international Jewish organizations who were in Israel to go to Beirut for a day under army protection. Although spouses and other family members were not allowed to accompany them and in no case would we have taken the boys, Avigdor got permission for me to go as an official photographer (again, no one asked for the photographs!). Since we wouldn't be away overnight, we felt safe leaving the boys on their own with Shoshana keeping watch over them.

Beirut was jammed with Christian Lebanese returning to their homes that they'd fled during the fighting in the south. Among the cars clogging the main road, most of them piled high with mattresses and other household goods, we saw one brightly painted sedan announcing Chabad, the Orthodox Hasidic organization whose outreach now extends across the globe. Most amazing to me was the apparent normalcy of life on either side of that busy thoroughfare. Looking toward the beach, I noticed a Ferris wheel in motion with passengers aboard, and in the upper city I saw nicely dressed women strolling leisurely along the boulevard or trying on shoes offered by street vendors while rockets burst overhead.

On our way back to Israel, as darkness approached we stopped at Tyre, leaving the main road to go to the center of town. We did the same at Sidon, where heavy shelling ensued soon after we left.

Our boys, meanwhile, enjoyed grilling hamburgers outdoors

with Shosh and her friends, then watched a Monty Python film. They considered it a great adventure, and so did we.

From time to time, the current president of B'nai B'rith would ask David to represent the organization on his behalf. On one of those occasions he presented an award to the governor of Arkansas for supporting the Leo N. Levi Hospital in Hot Springs, founded by B'nai B'rith and once headed by David. I went with him to the dinner in Little Rock and was seated next to the governor's wife, an attractive young attorney who spoke glowingly about her two-year-old daughter Chelsea. Our dinner conversation was almost exclusively with each other, as David's was with the governor. We walked out to the parking lot with them afterward. The first thing David said to me when we parted and were out of their earshot was, "You watch that young man. He's going to be our president someday."

David received two inscribed photographs with Bill Clinton, one of which included Hillary. Years later, I sent it to the White House for an updated inscription.

Another time, we represented B'nai B'rith on a trip to Costa Rica with presidents of other national Jewish organizations as a gesture of thanks to its president for moving the country's Israel embassy to Jerusalem. We stayed near San José and especially enjoyed meeting members of the Costa Rican Jewish community, which included the country's First Lady, Doris Yankelewitz Berger de Monge, and her family. As descendants of Jewish emigres from Poland, they excitedly anticipated the forthcoming visit of John Paul II, the Polish Pope, who met with his fellow countrymen wherever he traveled. We were fascinated when told that in this Catholic country, the only Poles he was likely to meet were Jewish.

Since we were so close to Panama, David and I extended our trip to visit Adelaide and Richard Eisenman at their winter home on the beach. They took us into the city for a day to see the amazing transformation that had taken place since my wartime posting there. Adelaide invited Don Halman and his wife to join us for dinner but they declined. I would have liked to see him again, to meet his wife and introduce David. I'm still interested in knowing what happened to everyone whose life connected closely with mine.

One of our most harrowing adventures occurred on a Caribbean cruise that we took only because it was a take-it-or-leave-it gift from Mass Mutual. Since we were free to book it ourselves I gave the business to my former employer, the travel agency in Atlanta.

At St. Thomas, having done the sightseeing before, we had no incentive for shopping and only went ashore to see the underwater aquarium. It was disappointing and overcrowded with passengers from all the cruise ships simultaneously docked there, so we returned to ours and spent the rest of the day on deck chatting with a couple who turned out to be neighbors living across the pond from us in Knoxville.

That night, in the Bermuda Triangle, the ship's motor failed. The absence of its humming awakened us even before we noticed the lack of air conditioning. For the next three days, David and I took turns lining up for cold food on deck while one of us held the lounge chairs we'd been lucky (and quick) enough to grab on the ship's shady side.

When power was restored, we picked up one day by not stopping at an island owned by the cruise line for lounging on the beach. Our new acquaintances, the neighbors from *literally* across the pond, returned home to find it ransacked and many valuables stolen despite having arranged for friends to check on the house daily. The thieves were apparently alerted to their absence by a story in the newspaper by an enterprising reporter who checked all local travel agencies for names of Knoxville residents aboard the cruise. Our names weren't listed because I booked the trip through my former colleagues.

I had never fully separated from my life in Washington. Traveling there every few weeks, I ached at having to miss special events connected with the museum and loathed being quartered at the third-rate hotel across from the B'nai B'rith building since BBI could no longer afford to house its board at the Mayflower. Plastic tumblers in place of water glasses and lidless toilet seats were okay for an overnight on the road, but not for a longer stay in the Dupont Circle area of Washington. While spending as much of my time as possible with friends, I began to envision my furniture in Marge Goldman's living room.

As David's business was picking up, I surmised that his financial pressure would soon be gone. In two years he'd be free of debt, free to relax, and 72 years old. I'd be 60, and I told him in advance that I wanted a condo in Washington for my birthday.

"And for you to live in it with me," I quickly added.

He agreed.

In the meantime, both of us had work to do. I realized that if I were ever to document Jack Rothschild's role in history, I had to do it without further delay. I'd begun working on it shortly after he died, which David encouraged me to continue, but at first there was no time. I also knew it would be foolish to embark on such a project when we were newlyweds. Now our marriage was firm and we were settled into a much calmer life. It was time for me to write the book.

Two years later, as we prepared to move, I had to decide on a repository for Jack's papers. Jake Marcus advised me to take time making the decision, to keep them together, and to select the location where they were most likely to get maximum use. When I learned that Emory University's Woodruff Library was interested in them for its Special Collections, which already housed those of Ralph McGill, Dr. Hal Davison, and others whom we knew, I consulted with Marcia and Bill and offered Emory the papers. At the acceptance ceremony I noted that, if indeed there *is* an afterlife, we want Jack to be with his friends.

We weren't yet fully prepared to move when Marge and Nathan Goldman told us that two corner units on their floor at The Towers at Cathedral and New Mexico Avenues, recently converted from rental to condominium, were being remodeled for initial sale. On our next trip to DC I asked their agent to show me other condos for comparison, and nothing, not even the more expensive ones she included in her tour, compared to The Towers. Its ceilings were higher, its rooms larger, and its swimming pool Olympic-length with country club amenities. That became my happy home for the next 25 years.

Thirteen
WASHINGTON

We drove up to The Towers in northwest Washington, D.C. on a Sunday afternoon, our car crammed with large ferns and other house plants waving from the back windows. We didn't see any rules and knowing no other entrance, we disembarked under the marquee and asked for assistance. With so much to unload, an unseemly array of our belongings remained outside the front entrance until all could be transported to #1105 West—not the most favorable way to meet our neighbors. But thanks to Marge and gatherings at the swimming pool, we soon made friends in the huge double building.

Marge also introduced me to nearby shops for food and other necessities as well as the best routes for reaching them (i.e., how to avoid Wisconsin Avenue traffic) and involved me in a project even before I arrived. Knowing of my interest in Neot Kedumim Park, the Biblical Landscape Reserve in Israel, she committed me to join her in promoting it in Washington. This included David and me hosting a progressive cocktail party with her and Nathan, moving from drinks and hors d'oeuvres at their place down the hall into ours for the sit-down promo.

It was fun but fruitless because we weren't sufficiently prepared and had no handouts with which to support our presentation.

Marge and Adelaide, both active in the Women's National Democratic Club, also volunteered me to lead the Israel portion of a WNDC mission to Athens and Jerusalem aimed at energizing Democrats abroad prior to the upcoming elections. I'd belonged to the club since our part-time residence in Washington and was willing to set up social events in Israel, but I had no desire to go on the trip. It would be at my own expense and meant leaving David for two weeks to visit a place from which we had just returned.

I proceeded with making arrangements in Israel while maintaining my refusal to go. Finally Mary Monroe, the club president and also a travel agent, offered to absorb my expenses but couldn't get me another room. I would need to share one with someone already signed up. I asked Lorraine Williams, a professor at Howard University. She hesitated, but after some persuasion consented and eventually told me why she'd wavered. She anticipated some criticism from other African Americans for rooming with a white woman. "I hope none of the sisters ever find out about this," she told me. It was the first of many insights into the life of an African American intellectual that I gained from rooming with her. Candid conversation across racial lines was rare, even among those of us who were friends with civil rights activists, and I'm appreciative of the brief time I was able to spend with Lorraine.

We first went to Greece, where I had an exciting encounter with Margaret Papandreou, the wife of the prime minister. My mother had been in contact with her when the Papandreous were exiled and living in America. She had saved their correspondence, which I kept along with other documents that she considered important. Anna Lee, a native of Greece and former WNDC president who had arranged the group's activities there, threw a party and invited Mrs. Papandreou. On the chance that I'd meet her, I brought along one of her letters to Mother. When I showed it to her, she asked if I wanted the letters that

Mother wrote to her and said that if I requested it in writing, she would have her staff find the correspondence and send it to me.

They found only one of Mother's letters, but it was undoubtedly the best. Written while she was visiting a friend in Athens, it described her experience in the huge crowd attending the November 1, 1968 funeral procession of Papandreou's father, a statesman and public hero taken down by a junta the year before. Mother's view of the intensity of the nation's mourning differed sharply from the government's downgraded reports seen worldwide. It documentated a signal event in Greek history.

While the others took a quick cruise in the islands, I went ahead to Israel to check on preparations for their visit there. I was lucky to have arrived safely. Although terrorists were hijacking flights between Europe and Israel, sometimes resulting in mid-air explosions, I saw no evidence of security in the Athens airport.

On this leg of the journey I had another more memorable surprise. Descending the Golan Heights, deeply moved by the story of Israeli soldiers' bravery in taking out the gun emplacements aimed at farms in the Galilee, Mary Monroe's husband Bill, a retired journalist best known as a WWII correspondent, commented, "The bravest man I ever knew was a Jewish pilot from Columbus, Georgia. Morris Hecht."

I jumped to attention. Morris was my friend, and I knew that his parents had never been told exactly how he died, only that his plane had been lost in combat. Monroe, an eyewitness, described it to me. Morris had gone down saving his squadron. The moment we returned home, I called Morris's brother Larry and connected him with Bill Monroe.

Soon after, a few weeks before we were scheduled to take a B'nai B'rith study cruise in the northern Mediterranean, David realized he had a conflicting commitment in San Francisco and insisted that I sail without him. He suggested I ask a friend to share my cabin. Rabbi Sidney Berkowitz had just died and I knew that his wife, Pauline, would be good company. A native Brit who retained her accent (and hauteur when appropriate), Pauline taught French at Kent State and, like me, was not the typical *rebbetzin*. She accepted my invitation.

At the last minute, Pauline asked if I'd object to her gentleman friend, the family's long-time physician, joining us. He booked a penthouse suite, took us ashore to elegant eateries where we wouldn't have gone on our own, and administered medical care when seasickness felled many passengers, including Pauline. Thanks partly to his administration of a behind-the-ears patch, it bypassed me.

The cruise's itinerary featured sites of ancient Jewish communities, the study of which brought Professor Norman Stillman aboard as lecturer. His wife and sister came with him and the three of them quickly bonded with Pauline and me. They were flamenco enthusiasts like us, and when Pauline's generous but aging gentleman friend opted to remain aboard during our evening in Barcelona, the Stillmans escorted us into every flamenco bar on the Ramla. When the cruise ended, Norman gave each of us a copy of his book, *Jews in Arab Lands.* I appreciated the gesture but I wouldn't read it for more than a decade, until it was assigned as a text for a course I took about Jewish life in Islamic lands. It remains a treasure in my library.

Still in the process of getting settled after returning from the cruise, I wasn't yet ready to connect with D.C. organizations. That involvement was like oxygen for David, however. He still volunteered for B'nai B'rith and the National Association of Life Underwriters (NALU), which he headed in the 1960s, but he also found time for other organizations. He became active in the Jewish Community Center, where he immediately found himself on the board, and the Million Dollar Round Table, which was headquartered near Chicago but met in various cities across the country. In addition to serving on MDRT's committees, he was for the third time a featured speaker at its annual meeting, which I was told was an unprecedented honor. He also retained his office in Knoxville, visited there every few weeks, and remained active in the Tennessee Association of Life Underwriters, attending its annual meetings to present its David Blumberg Award.

David also became president of Mass Mutual's association of retired general agents. We attended their meetings, held simultaneously with

Mass Mutual's annual G.A., and nearby but not at the posh resort facility because the Mass no longer paid for it. Since I had as little in common with the wives who went fishing as I did with the golfers, I didn't enjoy those vacations.

My own primary organizational commitment was, as always, the B'nai B'rith Klutznick National Jewish Museum, but I opted for more. Life in D.C. presented opportunities for connecting with interesting women from everywhere, including Israel, which led me to choose the Women's International Zionist Organization (WIZO) over its American counterpart, Hadassah, and to join the America-Israel Cultural Foundation (AICF). I refrained from notifying organizations in which I was a life member, but the National Council of Jewish Women (NCJW) found me. I went to one or two events but let them know they shouldn't count on me as a worker, although I did volunteer once to help prepare a mass mailing because the session was held in Shirley Koteen's home. She was an authority on American folk art and assisted Joan Mondale in furnishing the Vice President's residence, so I was curious to see the treasures she'd acquired for herself.

Celebrity homes were frequently used to attract people for political and philanthropic causes. We attended one at Ted Kennedy's ranch house in Virginia, which impressed me with its casual, laid-back informality. Another event, at the former estate of the Auchincloss family where Jacqueline Kennedy grew up, was the opposite. Its current owners preferred the spectacularly opulent, with formality that made it seem uncomfortable.

Living full-time in Washington enabled me to do more for the B'nai B'rith museum than ever before, but circumstances had changed, and not for the better. Anna Cohn, the original director, despairing of improvement at B'nai B'rith, had taken a job as head of SITES, the Smithsonian International Traveling Exhibits. Linda Altshuler, Anna's assistant who succeeded her as museum director, occasionally asked me to help, which I gladly did, but I missed the camaraderie I'd shared with Anna. When Linda's husband moved to a high-profile position in New

York and it was apparent that she would go with him, she held off notifying B'nai B'rith of her resignation until the last minute, all but forcing them to replace her without properly engaging in a search process.

BBI did appoint a search committee that included me, but they informed us of our appointments along with the date of the first meeting in a letter mailed out on the eve of Thanksgiving, and only ten days before the meeting. Some of us were out of town. Not seeing my mail until afterward, I missed the meeting and wondered if it had been called merely as a cover-up for BBI having promised the position to the woman already there temporarily as guest curator for a sales exhibit. I'd met her when she was working in Jerusalem and had reason to believe that she was either unstable or dishonest.

When I reported these misgivings to museum committee chairman Murray Shusterman, a BBI board member who did not live in Washington, he assured me that no commitment had been made and told me to pass on this information to BBI's top professional, the acting executive director. He, too, assured me that the woman in question had not been offered the job. True or not at that moment, she became the director and the museum quickly declined. BBI's top professional soon departed to become executive director of yet another national Jewish philanthropic organization, which made me question the integrity required for positions managing our *tzedakah*.

I soon became involved with local Jewish history when Hadassah Thursz, then the director of Jewish Historical Society of Greater Washington (JHSGW), asked me to speak at a session on writing congregational histories. That led to me being asked to work on a history of Washington Hebrew Congregation (WHC), which we had already joined, as it prepared for its 150th anniversary celebration in 2002. I agreed to work with others already engaged in the research, but not to lead. At the helm were the congregation's president, who vowed to devote more time to it when he left office, and Mary Lynn Kotz, who at the time was Reform's poster girl for "Jews by Choice." Both of them soon became involved elsewhere. I stayed on for research assisting Lois England and Florence Brody, who slaved over the archives, but the leaderless project floundered. Eventually the congregation employed a professional historian to write it.

When Aaron Goldman asked me to speak at a dinner for JHSGW donors, I subsequently joined and found myself on its board. I enjoyed the contacts but contributed little, if anything, since I had neither the hereditary connections in Washington nor the financial abundance to serve its needs. Nevertheless, I remained on the board for many years, attending meetings, speaking up whenever I had something to say, and doing whatever I was asked to do.

The one area in which I felt comfortable—not knowledgeable but deeply interested—was that of publishing the five-volume history of the American Jewish experience in preparation for the American Jewish Historical Society's (AJHS) centennial in 1992. Also, my involvement with the Southern Jewish Historical Society (SJHS) made me see the need to distinguish between the two societies, and possibly develop a joint membership in order to strengthen both. I argued on both boards for such a plan, but without success. In 1986, at the SJHS conference in Richmond, I became the society's president-elect and spent the next twelve months trying to learn the job. Louis Schmier, a professor at Valdosta State University and a prime mover in the society's early development, tutored me.

The most memorable characteristic of the Richmond conference was the rundown hotel in which it was held, which led me to question how many of our much-needed affluent members would return for the next conference. Since the struggling new organization couldn't survive without them, better accommodations were essential for 1985. Thanks to David's friendship with the Belz family, we obtained affordable rates at The Peabody in Memphis and held the next convention, my first as president, there.

I wanted to meet in Memphis because of its large, historic Jewish community, but only one member of it belonged to SJHS and he, my friend Jimmy Wax, the rabbi emeritus, was too ill for me to ask him for help. I appealed to his successor, Rabbi Harry Danziger, who responded enthusiastically and recruited two women for the hands-on work. Judy Peiser handled the program and Harriet Stern did the arrangements. Harriet was wonderful to work with and became a dear friend, and the meeting was so successful that it partially defeated my purpose in having it in Memphis. I'd hoped it would inspire people there to join SJHS and create an affiliate group for Tennessee. Some did join and they formed a society, but it remained local and did not become an affiliate. The lasting benefit to SJHS came years later, when the Memphis society matured and some of its members also filled leadership positions in SJHS.

My next conference was in Ft. Lauderdale, where the Society was invited by community leaders who wanted to establish a Jewish Museum of Florida, the embodiment of which now stands in Miami Beach. I included Caribbean Jewish communities based on their plantation history and other connections with the mainland South, arranging for us to be bussed into Miami for our Shabbat morning service with the Cuban congregation there. Also, with help from Adelaide and Richard Eisenman, I invited their Panamanian cousin Woodrow de Castro to come and share his research by lecturing on Jews of the Caribbean.

In emphasizing its broader parameters, I sought to increase potential for interest in the Society, gaining recognition by which to increase its membership and strengthen its organizational structure to project a vision of what southern Jewish history actually was. There were no other regional Jewish historical societies, and universities did not yet offer studies in American Jewish history. People had to be convinced that their family papers, even trivial scraps relating to undistinguished parents and grandparents, were the raw materials necessary for historians to piece together the mosaic of Jewish experience. I emphasized this in an article for Reform Judaism and in talks wherever I was invited, including Columbus (GA), Orlando, and New Orleans.

During this period I had a call from Mark Talisman who, as head of Project Judaica, sponsored "The Precious Legacy," the highly acclaimed Smithsonian exhibit on the Jews of Danzig. He wanted support for mounting an equally prestigious traveling exhibit on Jews of the South. It seemed like a natural alliance by which SJHS could raise its profile, but it required fundraising and my peers on the SJHS board wisely declared that our greater need was to fund ourselves. Had it not been for the pleasure of working on a structure for the exhibit with historian Ken Libo, I would have considered my involvement a huge waste of time and energy.

Another attempt to promote SJHS that sidetracked me was the Conference of American Jewish Educators (CAJE). I attended its conferences at the University of Maryland and at a suburban college near Atlanta to provide a presence for SJHS but accomplished very little there.

Notwithstanding our activism in various organizations, David and I spent more time than ever with our family. Living in Washington enabled us to be with David's brother Ralph and his family, going with them to Baltimore for his daughter Susan's graduating concert at Peabody and getting together for impromptu Sunday night suppers. Ralph raised delicious tomatoes that he'd bring me in late summer for gazpacho.

Sister Jean's abnormal hold on David and dominance as family matriarch demanded constant trips to St. Louis. I hid my feelings, smiling endlessly over breakfast bagels with her as she expressed her ultra-conservative views, complaining about her daughter Geri not being sufficiently attentive, airing grievances about David's former wife, and denouncing anything vaguely progressive that appeared in the daily news. This should have given me a hint about her true feelings for me, but it didn't. I mistook her confidences as indication of acceptance, freeing me to respond frankly with my own opinion on personal matters.

Occasions that I enjoyed in St. Louis were with David's friends, especially one free-spirited couple where the wife was an artist and their house pet was a cobra. Best of all were the days spent with niece Geri and her four children. On my very first visit, her three-year-old hugged my legs and said she loved me. We became even closer when she was in school and showed interest in writing. The family later moved into a humongous stone castle with lovely grounds where Geri entertained after bar/bat mitzvahs and graduations and we watched our Blumberg grandsons cavort with their cousins. In 1980, when Geri's husband Ken Rothman, then the lieutenant governor of Missouri, ran for governor, we joined the family at campaign headquarters on Election Eve and marched in their traditional candlelight parade. Ken lost in the Reagan landslide, but that brought beneficial change for the family, first hailed by us when he brought them to visit us in Washington. Soon after that he and Geri divorced and she remarried for a much happier life ever after.

We connected with my distant family in Macon when Gus and Marion Waxelbaum Kaufman hosted a multitude of our mutual relatives, even tangentially connected ones that they never met. Our progenitor in America was my great-great-grandmother (Marion's single great), buried in Macon's pre-Civil War cemetery. Among the cousins I knew existed but never met until then was Carole Goldberg Hendricks, whose father was my grandfather Dave's younger brother. He died when Carole was a child and her mother remarried, moving to western Maryland and losing touch with our family. As an adult, Carole lived in California as a successful travel agent and we immediately became close, having great times together in future years.

When Marcia moved into a home of her own, we went to Atlanta to celebrate with her. She had a party, at which Bill affixed a *mezuzah* to her door and recited prayers of dedication, the ceremony of *chanukat habayit*. It was a memorable celebration.

Bill, after two years in the rabbinate, had returned to practicing law but stayed in New York because Hava had just become an assistant professor at Columbia. When my grandson reached first grade they left their blue-collar neighborhood in New Rochelle and moved to an upscale enclave in Scarsdale. We loved it and were thrilled that our children could afford such a comfortable home, but it was not an entirely happy time for them. This was becoming increasingly apparent to David and me, made all the more distressing because we ourselves were like newlyweds, still blissfully in love.

I enjoyed spending time with Hava, especially for activities that Bill, like his father and David, did not enjoy. One afternoon we went into the city to see a classic Greek drama and talked about it all the way back to Scarsdale. I reasoned that Hava and I had a lot in common (though I lacked her scholarship) and perhaps Bill had fallen in love with her in part due to a subconscious desire to please his mother. Although he and I were mostly at odds with each other in those days, I frequently recognized an effort on her part to reconcile us.

In addition to Bill's apparent unhappiness at home, I became equally concerned about his comfort in his workplace. One Saturday when he had to work I stopped by the office briefly to meet his boss. He greeted me cordially enough, including compliments about my brilliant son, but he frightened me nonetheless. My reaction to him was the same as I'd had watching the beady-eyed general Arik Sharon close-up in conversation with David. Something inside me said that in six months Bill would either be out of that job or no longer the son I loved and thought I knew.

I didn't mention it, of course, but was not surprised when, within a few months, Bill reported that he had moved to another equally prestigious New York firm. As before, he frequently worked Saturdays and well past midnight and soon left the firm. I was thrilled when he came to Washington to be interviewed by a prominent firm there, but that too wasn't for him. He finally found his niche in Atlanta, back home where he probably wanted to be all along. Hava and Jacob stayed in New York the first year while he commuted on weekends to be with them, then they moved to Atlanta and *Hava* commuted to *her* job for a year before joining the faculty at Emory.

I kept close ties to Atlanta, always considering it home regardless of where I lived. I was usually there for the scholar-in-residence weekend in Jack's memory, and similarly for all historical commemorations. When asked to prepare an updated edition of my book *As But a Day* for the Temple's 120th anniversary in 1987, I went there several times to work on it with Beryl Weiner, the board member in charge of the celebration.

On a Sunday morning during the 250th commemoration of Georgia's founding in 1733, I spoke at the Temple and was introduced by (and to) a young professor from "up North," Mark Bauman, who has since become my mentor, editor, and close friend. Another noteworthy event during that celebration was the opening of the exhibit on Georgia Jewry at Emory's Schatten Gallery. Visitors were greeted at the entrance by a life-size cut-out of Great-Grandfather (Papapa) E.B.M. Browne, the Temple's rabbi in 1877, gesturing as if climaxing an oration. Among the photographs was an enlargement of the original that I have of Mother, age one, in her elaborate wicker baby carriage. By mistake someone else's name appeared beneath the picture, yet friends who knew her only as an adult recognized the mistake and told me, "That's your mother."

Before finishing my book and leaving Knoxville, I'd given a paper based on the third chapter at the Southern Jewish Historical Society conference in Savannah. The editor of Mercer University Press approached me after my talk to say that if the rest of the book was as good as that chapter was, he wanted to publish it. Now, two years later, the next phase produced a long period of waiting interspersed by questions from the publisher, the first being to choose another title. I do well with chapter headings but poorly with main titles. Marcia saved the day by suggesting *One Voice.*

Next came the editor's request for an introduction. I forget whose idea it was to ask Coretta King but I felt it wouldn't hurt to try. It took me six months to reach her, coming desperately close to the editor's deadline, but she agreed. When the publication finally occurred I received invitations to speak, first for Friday night services at the Temple in Atlanta and Temple Sinai in Washington, and then at Temple Sinai in Pittsburgh, where Rabbi Ed Cohn purchased a copy of the book for each rabbinic graduate ordained that year at HUC/JIR. I also spoke to the seniors at Washington Hebrew (WHC) and at the Jewish Book Fair in Nashville.

When I spoke at Pittsburgh's Rodef Shalom, to its Sisterhood at a luncheon meeting, greeters told me on arrival that Dr. Solomon Freehof was to introduce me and immediately whisked me upstairs to his study as he had requested. Knowing that I still had Rothschild family and friends living in Pittsburgh, he asked if I was staying for a visit. When I said no because I was on my way to meet Bill and David for a family reunion in Macon, Georgia, he wanted to know where the family originated. I told him that the Waxelbaums came from Fürth, Germany, near Nuremberg, whereupon he described Jewish life there in the early 19th century when the Waxelbaums were still residents. They had a rabbi so famous that Jews from all over the world addressed Halachic questions to him (as they now did to Freehof) and came there to study Talmud. In his introduction at the luncheon, the rabbi hardly mentioned me at all, but that was okay. He reminisced about Jack and I enjoyed every word of it.

During those years, thanks to the current BBI President's reluctance to travel, David represented him at a celebrity dinner in New York honoring publishing and media magnate Walter Annenberg with the Presidential Gold Medallion Award for Humanitarianism. Barbara Walters emceed, Frank Sinatra added homage, and Michael Feinstein entertained. During the cocktail hour, while David posed for photographs with notables, I enjoyed being a voyeur, glancing over my martini to observe fashions of the rich and famous. Never having owned a couturier original and assuming their astronomical price tags certified they were one-of-a-kind, it surprised me to see Barbara Walters and Barbara Sinatra wearing identical gowns, as did Annenberg's wife and daughter, as well as socialite Brooke Astor with someone I didn't recognize. Feinstein highlighted the evening with a parody of "You're the Top" listing Annenberg's attributes, concluding with the man's talent for collecting French Impressionist paintings, his punch line being "and lots of Monet."

At Washington dinner parties, certain formalities persisted even among otherwise casual close friends. Ruth St. John taught me the importance of place cards as a hostess's means of ensuring congeniality and stimulating conversation. She checked on Robert's seat partners in advance wherever they went, both to protect him from boredom and because people frequently took advantage of him to promote themselves. On one occasion, when we invited the two of them and a few other

Jewishly involved friends to meet a new executive director of B'nai B'rith, I was dismayed to see that as we adjourned to the dining room, the new director's wife sat next to Robert. I had placed her elsewhere. Ruth later told me she saw the woman slip into the dining room and change the place cards. In Washington that's a sin sufficient to strike the perpetrator from future guest lists.

Ruth and Robert gave the most enjoyable dinner parties that we or any others on their list ever attended. With gourmet dishes prepared by Ruth and impeccably served from the buffet by Robert, then in his eighties, the fare was delicious and delightful, but the main attraction was the company. I met at least half of my close friends in Washington at their parties.

Among close friends introduced at the St. Johns' were former South Africans Zelda and Izzy Heller. One day, when I stopped in at their antique silver and fine jewelry shop to have something repaired, Zelda asked if I knew a good ghostwriter. I didn't, but curiosity led me to inquire why she wanted one. She said that she and Izzy had developed a plot for an anti-apartheid novel based on actual events in South Africa, but their business kept them too busy to write it themselves. I didn't know of anyone to recommend, but the project intrigued me. My two trips there had given me a love for the country and the civil rights struggle here had given me some understanding of its problems.

I told Zelda that David and I were planning to be in Israel for the next four weeks, but if they hadn't found a ghostwriter by the time we returned I'd be interested in working with them, but as a partner, not a ghostwriter. She said the arrangement would be okay, but she wasn't sure I'd be comfortable with the content. "We're doing it as a novel so it will sell, and that requires a torrid sex scene," she explained. "Do you think you could handle that?"

"Try me," I replied, and she did. Our method was to powwow each episode for an evening, then I'd write a draft and deliver it to them for changes. We'd confer by telephone over disagreements, then I'd rewrite. For episodes such as one inside the prison, which I had never seen, Izzy would write a rough first draft to set the scene for me. We had no problem until we reached the "torrid sex scene." On that, he and I disagreed fundamentally. He sent back my draft edited with graphic detail which I rejected, not on prudish grounds, but because I believe that suggestion is sexier than graphics.

I'm admittedly prudish, however, when it comes to arguing such matters with someone else's husband. I called Zelda and told her, "He's *your* husband. *You* explain it to him."

She did, and we prevailed. When our mutual dear friend Robert St. John read that scene, he called me demanding to know which of us wrote it. "Do you really think I'd tell you?" I responded.

He said, "No, but whoever wrote it could make a good living writing cheap novels."

Robert also complimented our description of the scene by noting that reading it caused him to have the same reaction as that of our fictional hero. By then he was in his eighties.

Our 1987 trip to Israel was to take grandson Lee there for his bar mitzvah gift as we had done with Jeffrey. Geri and her children joined us, so Lee had four cousins aged six to nineteen as companions. As tour leader, I prepared overnight flight packages for everyone with footsies and eye shades I'd saved from our first-class flights on the fast track and engaged Micha Ashkenazi, who had been so wonderful as our driver and guide with the Israeli children on location for the documentary film. This time I didn't try to emulate the Experiment. I reserved rooms at a hotel with a swimming pool in the same neighborhood as the King David, but not as elegant or expensive. That may not have been the best decision, however—its swimming pool was out of order and its Shabbat food practice left us hungry.

Nevertheless, we had a wonderful time. On our first day, Micha gave us a general tour of Jerusalem by car, beginning with a brief stop at the Kotel to give the kids a sense of it as an introduction to everything else. By this time the Orthodox had instituted gender separation there so Geri, her two girls and I had no idea why the boys hadn't returned to the car after a reasonable amount of time. When they finally arrived, Lee and Geri's 19-year-old, David, announced that they wanted to have a bar mitzvah ceremony at the Wall. I reminded them that there would be no gifts as before, no party, and no friends to hear how well they read the Hebrew. They still wanted the second bar mitzvah.

"We'll discuss it with your grandfather," I said, assuming they'd forget about it after seeing so many other inspiring sites.

When we returned to the hotel that afternoon, Lee's first words to his grandfather were to request the second bar mitzvah. Geri agreed for her son to do it if Lee did, and, seeing how serious the boys were, David okayed it for Lee. I spoke up to insist that we have nothing to do with the bearded old men befriending young boys at the wall. We must ask one of our Reform rabbi friends to officiate.

Henry (Hank) Skirball, who had officiated Bill's wedding, agreed to do it and made an appointment to give the boys their assignments. Arrangements hit a snag when he started to schedule their study sessions. Micha was taking us to the Galilee and Negev the following week, and the week after that we'd be going home. Still undeterred, the boys promised to learn their *parsha* while traveling. They'd get Micha to coach them on the Hebrew.

On our first day out I was resting in my room before dinner, thinking that everyone else had gone swimming, when the boys arrived asking to chant their blessings for me. What a thrill! Seeing them so serious about enhancing their commitment to Judaism was an unexpected and enormous bonus to our pleasure in taking them to Israel.

We spent two days in the Galilee where Micha showed us Crusader castles, then drove south to Eilat through the Negev and back to Jerusalem via the Arava and the Dead Sea, finding caves for the kids to climb into. Geri and I went with them into a salt cave near the Dead Sea and crept through Hezekiah's tunnel with them in Jerusalem.

David didn't tour with us but gladly participated in the *b'nai mitzvah*. Restricted as females, Geri, her girls and I had to remain so far from the wall that we couldn't get a clear view of David and the boys. Also unable to hear them due to the shrill keening of the Sephardic women from Islamic lands who were there celebrating their sons' bar mitzvahs, we couldn't truthfully enjoy the occasion. Even so, we were happy on behalf of our boys, proud of them for the effort they made, and greatly pleased by their devotion to Judaism. On the flight home, I asked each of the kids what impressed him or her the most on the trip, and both of the older boys immediately replied, "Our bar mitzvah at the Wall."

David showed signs of decline on that trip. He was tense, nervous as people often are at airports when they are unaccustomed to foreign travel, which surely didn't apply to him. He even showed slight impatience with the children.

Back home David began to have trouble sleeping, which was also unusual for him. He submitted to an overnight sleep lab test that concluded he suffered from geriatric depression. He then agreed for me to go with him to doctors' appointments and I immediately realized that the 30-something-year-old psychiatrist at the sleep lab had no business treating senior citizens. David reached the same conclusion, so we saw a series of other professionals recommended by our primary care internist, Harold Sadin.

We first visited a psychiatric counselor whom we liked and believed capable, but after many visits that brought no results we sought help elsewhere. I continued recommending talk therapy as I had from the beginning, but to no avail. Finally, we saw a psycho-pharmacologist who combined the therapies and David began to show progress. This brought us great relief—until we recognized that the medication was draining David of his energy. His signature zest and initiative disappeared. I applauded his following doctor's orders by coming home each afternoon for a nap, but the joy vanished when we went to St. Louis for a family celebration and he asked Jimmy to give the customary toast in his stead. Then all of us knew that something was very, very wrong. We suspected the medication and sought other options.

Meanwhile, I managed my own health with therapy from body

massages, swimming laps in our Olympic length pool (when weather permitted), and becoming deeply immersed in finishing the book about apartheid in South Africa. During early summer 1989, when Zelda and I were polishing a final draft, she worked with me in the afternoons at our apartment to add descriptive details. By then David's strength had so diminished that he'd frequently spend the whole day in bed. Zelda would go back to visit him, and during one of her visits she told him about a devastating experience with similar symptoms that afflicted her when she was only in her forties. It was diagnosed as a type of depression and cured by a brilliant psychiatrist, Jim Lieberman. She and I both begged David to see him.

Finally David agreed, and Dr. Lieberman helped immensely with his talk therapy. Our lives began to regain normalcy, but not for long. David's coronary problems flared up again. Our cardiologist ordered angioplasty, which seemingly restored him to his old self. He felt well enough to drive to Knoxville—with me along, of course— to finally clear out his office and move his files to Washington.

Three weeks later the angioplasty collapsed. David's arteries were too weak. His options were spending the rest of his life as an unmotivated invalid or submitting to open-heart surgery with little chance of survival.

We agreed that any chance, however small, was better than life as a zombie. As I walked alongside the gurney taking him to the operating room, I understood, as I believe he did, that those were probably our last moments together. I wasn't allowed to see him until the next day. He was barely conscious, still with a tube in his throat, unable to speak. He squeezed my hand to say goodbye.

The next day, David was gone.

Before we married, I'd prayed for us to have at least five good years together. We were blessed with almost fifteen, for which I will always be deeply grateful.

Fourteen

TRANSITIONING AGAIN

"**Y**ou really need to start falling for younger men," Bill quipped as we left the hospital that awful morning in 1989.

Like his father, he is very good at diverting tears to laughter. At David's funeral, after mentioning David's many engaging attributes, knowing his Atlanta audience Bill added, "But what my sister and I most appreciate is that he played football at the University of Tennessee in the same backfield as Bobby Dodd [who later became the legendary coach and AD at Georgia Tech]."

It did get a laugh, even from me.

I went to Knoxville for memorial services at the Temple there and to another service held by B'nai B'rith at its headquarters in Washington. They announced their intention to publish a collection of books in David's memory, one each year for a number of years, and did actually produce one of them, *The Magen David: How the Six-Pointed Star Became an Emblem for the Jewish People*, by Rabbi Gunther Plaut. He was Jack's schoolmate and our long-time family friend, which made it more meaningful for me than the donors knew.

Our children provided great comfort and support, each according to his or her special talent. Marcia brought software for listing condolences, reminding me that I would not have Sisterhood women organized to help respond as I did when her father died. Bill renovated our bedroom closets at half the price professional companies would charge, even after adding his airfare. I was so eager to see him that I didn't question his ability. I sent him the closet measurements, and we discussed the design. He brought all the materials, including six-foot lengths of shelving from the Home Depot, which had just opened in Atlanta, and checked them as luggage on Eastern. We hadn't yet heard of the now-commonplace home improvement store in Washington. Years later, when I met co-founder Bernie Marcus, I told him about it and how much I wished I'd bought stock then as Marge Goldman did when she saw the cost of Bill's purchases. I was always afraid to risk what little I had to invest by playing the market.

Bill's visit began with the challenge of getting the six-foot strips of shelving home from the airport on a freezing January night. He fit them through the windows from front passenger's side diagonally across and through the back window behind the driver. By Saturday afternoon he'd completed the job, thoroughly professional, and went with me to Aviva and Matt Penn's home for an Israeli-style Shabbat visit. They concluded with a *havdalah* service, the first I ever experienced in a private setting and a perfect ending to a wonderful weekend.

David's son, Jim, took me shopping for my expensive needs: a new computer, a printer, and a car. He favored outlets in suburban Virginia, which worked for the electronics. I also found the Honda I wanted but postponed buying it until I could get to the dealership in Bethesda, close enough to home to give me shuttle service for check-ups and repairs.

Because Jimmy was active on the board of B'nai B'rith, he often came to visit and I greatly enjoyed his company. He introduced me to sushi, reserving one night on each trip for us to sit at the bar at Matuba and watch them make our next roll as we consumed each previous one. He was fun to be with and a loving son, but troubling to me as he had been to David regarding his own welfare. Jim had been fiscally out of control for years and there was no way I could curb it.

David's brother Ralph and his wife Gerry gave me caring support, as they had for David during his final illness. Ralph was the brother I always wanted. He and Gerry remained close, even after they retired and moved back home to St. Louis.

There was the sad spot. David's sister Jean and her husband Erv immediately turned against me, ostensibly because we buried David in Atlanta rather than St. Louis (where he only resided while at law school) and because I asked her middle child, Geri, rather than her eldest, Barbara, to speak at the funeral. I asked Geri because she was closest to me, and I'd settled on burial in Atlanta with David himself years before. He wanted me to be buried beside him, which I okayed because I knew that Jack wouldn't have cared and I didn't yet know that Jewish women were supposed to be buried next to the father of their children. I chose Atlanta because it was home and I'm a fifth-generation Georgian with a sense of history. Our children voiced no objection and it never occurred to us that anyone else should be consulted.

Jean thought otherwise. She was offended and chose the morning of David's funeral to ream me out about it. Erv joined her. I was alone and too benumbed to react.

Their younger daughters, Geri and Ellen, did what they could to dilute the poison. Ellen, whom I hardly knew because she had only recently returned home, wrote a long, loving letter apologizing for her parents' behavior. Geri also defied their orders not to contact me and brought her young son, Daniel, to Washington to keep me company during my first New Year's Eve alone. Unfortunately, Daniel got sick and the three of us spent New Year's Day at the children's hospital, after which they went home to their doctor in St. Louis. Disappointing though it was, Geri's thoughtfulness greatly brightened my outlook for that solitary New Year.

In facing widowhood, I made two rules for myself. Firstly, I determined not to fall into the morass of well-to-do widows who worried about finances, penny-pinching when they had no need to do so. I'd always lived within my means, assessing extravagant temptation and indulging it only if the numbers permitted. I wanted eyelid surgery but never mentioned it to Jack because we couldn't afford it and when I asked

David, he said "Do it if you want to, but you're beautiful as you are." With such flattery and love I didn't need the surgery, but now I did. I gave it to myself for my 66th birthday.

My other new rule was about long-distance driving, another area where I'd noticed widows crawling into their shells. Car travel was an element of freedom that I didn't want to lose. David chose it whenever possible and taught me to drive on the road, frequently giving me the wheel so he could sleep. With my experience in the snow strengthening my confidence, I continued zipping back and forth to Atlanta as well as anywhere else in the eastern USA, alone and with no need to consult my budget to see if I could afford it.

Remembering the benefit of having work after Jack died, I agreed to put my name on the slate for election to my condo board. I lost, but found my niche for service by editing the in-house newsletter. After convincing several residents to serve as reporters I enjoyed the process, but we had no control over publication and the copy never came out on time regardless of when we submitted it, so it was largely irrelevant. After a year I resigned and left the problem to the office staff and board.

I also signed up for Rabbi Joseph Weinberg's mid-week classes at Washington Hebrew, which led to ongoing benefits. Often inspired to walk there by beautiful brisk weather, I became friendly with Roz Chayes, a woman much older than I who also walked and passed my apartment on her way. Feisty, sharp, and into a myriad of activities, she was one of the most delightful people I ever knew. When she invited me to join one of her activities, a small interfaith group studying the roots of Judaism, Christianity, and Islam, I eagerly accepted. Rabbi Harold White at Georgetown University led it, occasionally joined by a priest or an imam. I delighted in the learning and the discourse, and its' meeting on Fridays at noon reminded me that the Sabbath would soon begin, arousing a sense of preparation for Shabbat such as I'd known only in Israel.

Another spin-off from attending Rabbi Weinberg's class at WHC was his inviting me to give one of the twenty-minute Layman's Hour lectures the following Yom Kippur. He asked me to talk about my life as wife of two men distinguished in public service, but I knew I wouldn't yet be ready to speak publicly about David just before hearing his name read at the memorial service. I agreed to discuss life with Jack during the civil rights era. Late that summer, when I started to prepare my talk, the morning news gave me a perfect lead with the announcement that Atlanta was chosen for the 1996 Summer Olympics. I believed that couldn't have happened without the city's forthright response to the Temple bombing, the desegregation of public schools, and honoring Martin Luther King for receiving the Nobel Prize, all of which involved us personally.

In the months before David died I'd worked with Fred Schiller, a neighbor at the Towers, as professional ghostwriter for his autobiography. I charged a flat fee that pleased me at the time, but later, when David was no longer there and Freddy found excuses to stay into dinner time, I regretted not having asked for an hourly rate. He was a nice, cultured European gentleman, appearing daily at the pool in the summer immaculately dressed for the Riviera with a cravat tucked into his buttoned-down beach jacket. Nonetheless, after several hours of work I wasn't interested in having him stay for dinner.

Freddy's story of growing up in Zagreb and surviving the Holocaust by doing the opposite of what conventional wisdom advised, mostly on a bucolic island in the Adriatic, was so lighthearted that I doubted its acceptance as Holocaust testimonial. I called it *Dancing Through the Minefields* and considered its possibilities as beach reading. We disagreed on the need to edit his account of his first teenage love affair, which was too detailed to fit smoothly into the narrative.

When we finished Freddy still refused to be edited, saying he didn't care whether or not the story was published and that his best friend, who also survived, was a successful Hollywood producer who might want it. If not, it could go to the Holocaust Museum. The friend read it and couldn't use it, and the Holocaust Museum didn't want it. Eventually Freddy moved to the Jewish Home in Rockville and I never heard from him again. He died having no surviving family and no known heirs, so according to my contract designating me co-owner of the book, it can now be edited. That may be next on my agenda.

I was still on the board of the American Jewish Historical Society in 1992 when it held its centennial conference in Washington and I chaired its program. I enjoyed working with JHSGW president Michael Goldstein and with Florence Brody, who chaired arrangements, and having long-time Washington insider Sheldon Cohen as my go-to friend ensured my success. Sheldon had been Internal Revenue Commissioner under President Lyndon Johnson, the youngest to hold that position, and he knew everyone. He advised me on VIPs and contacted them for me, thus obtaining their agreement to appear on the program.

I did little for SJHS other than attend annual meetings and do whatever small task I was given, usually introducing a speaker, giving a blessing, or serving on a committee. My one big assist was getting Alfred Uhry to speak at the conference in Alexandria, Virginia, accepting an award for advancing public interest in southern Jewish history with *Driving Miss Daisy*, his prize-winning play and film based on his grandmother. He hadn't yet grown accustomed to such requests so he initially demurred, saying he was no speaker. I convinced him that he didn't need to *speak*. He could just *talk*. He came, brought his mother Aline, and occasionally referred to her as well as to me in the course of his remarks. His informality and sense of humor delighted everyone.

David and I had planned a trip to California to see grandson Jeffrey, then in his senior year at Stanford, and that remained a priority for me now. Not only was I thrilled to see him, but also to meet his lovely girlfriend, Jennifer Paget, a student at Scripps College whom he had already decided to marry. After leaving Palo Alto I visited my newly found cousin Carole in Los Angeles. She took me sightseeing as far south as a suburb of San Diego and invited me to join her and another of her cousins, Daphne Castel, two months later on a travel agents' tour in China. I jumped at the opportunity.

We landed in Shanghai, shopped at the government store where only foreigners could buy, and visited a farm family's home as well as a school where the children charmed us. Because children are naturally charming—and we found them unusually so throughout China— meeting them did little to conceal the staged quality of the encounter. We then boarded an aircraft that seemed none too sturdy and flew to Wuhan. There we saw a recently discovered ancient sculpture of a prehistoric bird, a miniature of which I bought as a souvenir. We were supposed to fly from there to Chongqing but the flight was canceled so we went by train, an experience that could end one's desire to travel.

Our so-called luxury accommodations consisted of a compartment for four, which we shared with another passenger. I volunteered for an upper bunk because I suspected that neither Daphne nor Carole could climb into it. The train was unheated, so we retired under our thin coverings fully dressed, including hats and gloves, and prevented our noses from breaking off as icicles by burrowing into the flimsy pads that passed as pillows. Some passengers in the crowded car used the tiny bathroom facilities to launder their clothes, which threatened leaking bladders for the rest of us.

When morning came, we disembarked in the city where the great dam was being built, viewed it, and then boarded a ship that took us through the three gorges of the Yangtze, which highlighted the trip for me. I most enjoyed the day we went through a narrow gorge in small open motor boats tethered together for protection through rapids. Looking up high on the cliffs, we could see holes drilled by Kublai Khan's engineers to support roads for his cavalry and heavy artillery. At the headwater we stopped for lunch prepared by farm women of the area and saw splashes of bright yellow in the surrounding fields, the only color enlivening the gray March landscape. It inspired a surprised cry of "Rape! Rape!" from British tourists, briefly shocking those of us unfamiliar with that name for broccoli rapini.

We also visited Nanjing and Xi'an, where I was overwhelmed by the spectacular field of clay warriors and the variation of their features, identifying their remarkably broad diversity. Those details, however, could not be seen there as they were in small exhibits from the collection that I had viewed at close range in the Baltimore Museum and the Knoxville World's Fair.

I disliked Beijing but enjoyed the side trips from there, especially walking on the Great Wall. I had a memorable shopping experience at the tourist trap outside the dowager empress's palace. Exiting more quickly than others because little about the building grabbed my interest, I looked for an embroidered quilted silk jacket the likes of which I'd seen diplomats' wives wear over evening clothes in Washington. Determined not to pay more than $50, I saw one I liked, but the asking price was several hundred dollars. Since I don't enjoy bargaining, I forgot about it. The vendor and his colleagues then hounded me, offering jackets that I wouldn't have taken for free, occasionally exhibiting a good one at a lower price though never less than three times what I was willing to pay. As our bus was about to depart, the vendor came to the door with the first jacket, the one I recognized as authentic and liked, saying, "Fifty." I took it but have only worn it twice in all these years, which justifies my parsimonious resolve about buying it.

At another tourist stop I bought something that I really wanted, again at an appreciable bargain without actually bargaining. I chose three primitive paintings by an unnamed, untrained "farmer artist," one each for Marcia, Bill, and me. The check-out line was so long that we were called to the bus before I reached the cashier, who was too busy to tell me the price. I flashed a fifty-dollar traveler's check hoping he would take it, and he did. I've never had the art evaluated, but mine still hangs over my bed and I value it highly.

We returned to Beijing via a long drive through the mountains, much of which was alongside a railroad track. As a train whizzed past, recalling for me romantic novels about the China Express and the Silk Road, I dreamed of taking it one day. Otherwise, with my thoughts of Beijing still influenced by the memory of the Tiananmen Square protests, I had little incentive ever to return to China. That vast, ugly plaza exemplified the repressive government action that took place there only three years before. Our guide experienced it personally. He was imprisoned for bringing Coca-Colas to his college comrades who were peacefully protesting there.

Carole and I had further adventures together in our own country. She visited me in Washington and drove with me to Atlanta when we dedicated David's gravestone. Another time, when she was on a cruise from California through the Panama Canal, I met her in New York where she left the ship temporarily for us to drive upstate and check on our Goldberg ancestors' origins (her father's and my grandfather's) in Oswego, New York, a small city on Lake Ontario. In the center of town we saw "Goldberg Furniture" emblazoned across the facade of a corner building and, although we knew it couldn't be our family, we went inside, hoping that Mr. Goldberg could help us in our search. He told us that the synagogue had been closed for many years since his family and others moved to Syracuse, but directed us to it for a look. He also suggested that we visit the local historical society, where we found some clues.

We then went to Rochester, where our family had relocated. Carole wanted to see her grandfather's grave. We never found it, but we did find the city's historical society, where we saw fascinating correspondence. One of Oswego's Jewish businessmen described watching the fireworks over Lake Ontario celebrating the end of the Civil War. I would have loved to stay longer, but Carole had to get back to her ship while it was docked in Montreal. After driving her there, I returned to Washington with a recorded book for company and became so engrossed in it that I missed an exit and got lost in New Jersey.

On one of my trips to Atlanta, I appeared on a program of the American Jewish Committee in which a WAGA-TV news anchor questioned a panel of four Atlanta Jewish women. The other three were distinguished in their own right—Josephine Heyman, a community leader, Nanette Wenger, a world-renowned cardiologist, and Phyllis Kravitz, a judge on the United States Eleventh Circuit Court of Appeals.

It was my ill fortune to be called on last. After Dr. Wenger recounted highlights of her remarkable career, Judge Kravitz described her fruitless efforts to be accepted as a student at Harvard Law School and her experience, decades later, judging a moot court there, and Jo Heyman recalled her day hosting Eleanor Roosevelt, I was left with my only claim to fame being "wife of." I reminded the audience that, like most middle class Jewish girls in the 1930s, I was programmed to "marry well," which in my family prioritized accomplishment over wealth. By that standard, as adjunct to two men of achievement, I had succeeded twice.

During those years, I became active with a group organized by Edith Fierst to support filming Holocaust survivors as they recounted their experiences to students. Outlets, including the U.S. Holocaust Museum, did not yet exist, but those stories and their audiences' reactions deserved preservation.

I also joined two marches, both for causes upholding lifelong beliefs. During the first Bush administration, Marge Goldman corralled me to join her and several others supporting the *Roe v. Wade* decision legalizing abortion nationwide. What I remember most about that protest, in addition to the overwhelming heat, was a group near the grandstand recognizing the First Lady's progressiveness with the chant, "Free Barbara Bush."

My second march was for gay rights, a liberal cause that had also become personal. A few years earlier, Marcia had come out. She came to Washington for the march with her good friends Marianna Kaufman and Diane Aleman, stayed with me, and asked me to join them. I was busy and because I had no problem with the issue, I saw no need to address it beyond sending a membership contribution to Parents and Friends of Lesbians and Gays in honor of my daughter. Privately, Marianna convinced me that Marcia would not admit how much she wanted me to march with her, so I went and am deeply grateful to Marianna for having pushed me to do so. It was an eye-opening experience that I cherish. Contrary to official reports of few onlookers, the sidewalks were packed with cheering crowds. When our PFLAG group approached, the crowd cheered louder than ever. I heard someone call out, "Bravo! I wish my mom were there." Several times Marianna nudged me, reminding me to wave by saying, "They're cheering *you*."

Family happenings multiplied in the ensuing years. Bill and Hava divorced soon after David died and Jacob stayed with Bill, which drew me to Atlanta more than before. The following year, Hava joined the faculty at Indiana University and moved to Bloomington, where Jacob visited her on holidays and weekends. In December 1990 she thrilled me by asking if the two of them could visit me in Washington during the school holidays and invited me to go with them on a side trip to New York and Philadelphia. I had a marvelous time and was especially pleased that she permitted Jacob to attend the sophisticated theater offerings such as Noel Coward comedies that she and I most enjoyed. I underestimated his pre-teen level of maturity just as I had with Bill and Marcia when they were his age. To my great delight, he so appreciated the political satire of the troupe Capitol Steps that their show became a regular item on our agenda whenever he came to visit.

Taking Jacob places became my greatest pleasure. We went twice to the beach in Maryland and once to Callaway Gardens in Georgia, where we competed with each other photographing the butterflies. Another time, Marcia went with us to Disney World. Those precious occasions meant all the more to me because I had not done the likes of them with my own children.

Jacob's bar mitzvah in December 1991 was a joy for everyone except himself. He had a fever the night before and was miserable throughout the weekend, but that didn't prevent him from performing flawlessly. Bill conducted the ceremony, calling on those of us closest to Jacob for the *aliyot*, having given me a transliteration of my portion a year in advance so I could learn the Hebrew.

Our next family celebration was Jeffrey's and Jennifer's wedding in 1993, a sumptuous occasion in Chicago. I delighted in seeing Jeffrey embraced by a close-knit family that had treated him as one of their own since long before he was engaged to their daughter. When Jeff's attendants, a multiracial foursome of fraternity brothers from Stanford, knelt in front of Jen to sing their fraternity sweetheart song and then raised the newlyweds on chairs for the *hora* and "Hava Nagila," I noted with pleasure the absence of social bias ubiquitous in my own college days.

Several years later, grandson Lee married Lorrie Levin, his college sweetheart, in Rock Island, Illinois. It was a beautiful ceremony in her synagogue, and I was again both pleased and comforted to see a Blumberg grandson welcomed into a warm, close-knit Jewish family.

Bill, too, soon found the woman who would be his lifelong mate. Brenda Wise Ives and her two daughters became family for him and Jacob two years later. As my father had walked me down the aisle of the Temple sanctuary to marry Jack, so did I have the indescribable joy of walking Bill to the *bima* for his marriage to Brenda. Alvin Sugarman conducted the ceremony—along with every rabbi friend whom they'd invited to attend, and then en masse decided to participate as well!

The ceremony included one aspect that I have not seen before or since. Brenda's father would have the honor of bringing his daughter to the *chuppah*, but his legs could no longer climb the steps up to the *bima*. To accommodate his abilities, the *chuppah* was placed at the beginning of the steps and Brenda's father left her there. She then walked up the steps to the *bima* accompanied by the four *chuppah* holders and the *chuppah* itself!

The signing of the *ketubah*, the Jewish marriage certificate, was held in the rabbi's study before the public ceremony. I didn't understand why two bearded strangers were there and asked Alvin about it afterward. One was the rabbi of Brenda's traditional congregation, he said, the other required as a second man to sign the *ketubah*. Horrified that Alvin had suffered the indignity of being considered insufficiently Jewish to serve as a witness in his own synagogue, I exploded, "How could you!"

True to his incomparably all-embracing spirit, he replied, "*Shalom bayit*," peace in the home.

I was so happy to witness Bill's happiness that I swallowed my outrage.

My primary volunteer interest remained the B'nai B'rith Museum. I was discouraged about the museum's management but continued believing in its potential as a national Jewish museum. I befriended the new director, who shall remain nameless. She soon began traveling a lot, then stayed away much longer than expected, saying that she was suffering severe back pains. She returned to work looking pregnant but not announcing it, making it awkward for those of us working with her because we didn't know whether or not to offer congratulations.

Mickey Neiditch, the BBI staff executive in charge, noticed other strange occurrences at the museum and began building a dossier in order to dismiss her under union regulations. He asked me to report any suspicious activities that I saw. Before I did so, B'nai B'rith received a bill for expensive nursery furniture that was charged to the museum but delivered to her home, which gave him sufficient cause for dismissal.

This time, B'nai B'rith notified its search committee properly and everyone attended the meeting. However, by that time the museum's reputation had dropped so low that no qualified person applied and we were given several dreadful choices to consider. Among our search committee was Dr. Marcella Brenner, widow of Washington's internationally known artist Morris Louis and founding head of the Museum Studies department at George Washington University. Despite the push by B'nai B'rith leadership to resolve the matter quickly, Marcella and I refused to accept anyone until we found someone with qualifications for raising the museum to its full potential. I was then delegated to find that person and the meeting was adjourned.

I asked our first director, Anna Cohn, for suggestions. She recommended Ori Soltes, a lecturer for the Smithsonian, but doubted he'd be interested. He was increasingly sought by leading institutions as a lecturer as well as by the Smithsonian and other organizers of educational travel as a leader/lecturer on foreign tours. Unmarried at the time, he was free to consider any opportunity anywhere, so why would he limit them for an ill-paying job directing a museum for a social service organization with no understanding of what it meant to house a museum?

Surprisingly, he *was* interested in the position. He envisioned the blessing it could be for all Jews as well as for all Americans to have a major showcase for international Jewish culture in our nation's capital. He sent an astounding resume and when we interviewed him, he gave an in-depth presentation that left the four of us with no questions. Finally, someone noticed on his resume that he was fluent in fourteen languages, one of which being Luwian, and asked "What's that?"

Ori explained that it was a form of late Hittite, which didn't do much to clarify it for us. We smiled, nodded and let it go at that. He took the job and later told me why he accepted: "Because I looked at the museum and saw that it had nowhere to go but up."

It wasn't long before I attended one of Ori's lectures at the Library of Congress. The subject was micrography, an art form in which lines are formed by minuscule Hebrew letters quoting passages from Scripture.

Someone asked if that had been the subject of his PhD dissertation. No, he said, his dissertation was on Plato. Later, I asked him when he had studied micrography.

"Last night," he replied.

That was the beginning of an ongoing, cherished friendship. I knew I would enjoy working with him and learning from him.

Murray Shusterman, the BBI board member who chaired the museum committee, lived in Philadelphia and was relieved to have me as his surrogate. I succeeded him when his term ended. When I officially became chair of the museum committee, I was positioned to help Ori both publicly and as a "friend-at-court." I recalled how much it meant to me and Jack to have a few such friends during his early years at the Temple and was doubly pleased to be able to fill that role for Ori.

I invited potential donors to dinner parties so they could meet our talented director. One of his skills was playing piano. I remembered my mother's Sunday night soirees, which I always wanted to replicate, and bought a piano hoping that Ori could be persuaded to perform. Those guests didn't encourage it so it didn't work out, but I enjoyed having the piano for the pleasure of hearing him play at other times.

We joked about who was in charge. He introduced me as his boss, which was technically true since I represented his employer, but in every other sense I was like his intern because I knew very little about art and Judaica. My official status often served as a useful ploy for both of us when I wanted to attend one of his lectures and he needed a ride. One Sunday morning he called asking me to come to the museum to help host some special visitors, and I ended up going with him to an afternoon exhibit in suburban Washington, after which he missed his train to Baltimore for a lecture. We continued in my car until I took him home at midnight and finally went home myself.

Reflecting on it afterward, I realized that the incident highlighted a freedom I'd never contemplated. I'd never missed it because I was happily married. Now, although I would certainly have preferred coming home to David, this exemplified a positive aspect of living alone.

One of Ori's and my initial changes at the museum was to give it a more relevant name. Generally known either as the B'nai B'rith Museum or the Klutznick, both of which veiled its full purpose and contents, we began emphasizing its complete name, the B'nai B'rith Klutznick National Jewish Museum, in order to describe it more accurately as well as to raise its image.

For the same reasons, I began referring to my committee as the Museum Board. Its members had never been asked to contribute financially because they contributed to B'nai B'rith, which supposedly supported the museum. Those allocations gave only life support, however. The museum needed a paying membership to become a valuable asset. We began by requiring Board members to pay minimum annual dues of $250 and urging all who could afford it to give $1,000. We knew that would cause drop-outs, but there were only two and we soon replaced them.

Ori jump-started visitor attendance via art exhibits. Having a minuscule staff, untrained and underpaid, he slaved what seemed like 24/7, at times working through the night to complete the installation of an exhibit opening the next day. I assisted in whatever ways I could.

One day I was helping him dismantle an exhibit, prying linoleum from small platforms needed as partial walls for the next show, when an Israeli artist came looking for him at a moment that he wasn't there. Seeing me frantically tugging at a strip of flooring, she declared, "That's a man's work. He has no right to make you do that. You should report him to the union for making you do that."

Before I could answer, he appeared and introduced me as the chairwoman of his board. The look on her face made my day.

We used my car to pick up objects for exhibits on several occasions, and I once helped by bringing a painting from Israel. When Kitty and Harold Ruttenberg wanted to give the museum a painting in my honor, Ori and I drove to Pittsburgh, stayed with them overnight, chose one from the selection they offered, and brought it back to Washington. We also went to Philadelphia for him to meet Rabbi David Wice and see his remarkable collection of Judaica. Shortly afterwards, Rabbi Wice joined our museum board.

The most rewarding and lasting innovation of my time at the museum was Ori's introduction of a citywide public school contest citing the personal meaning today of George Washington's famous phrase in his letter to the Jews of Newport declaring that this new government would give "to bigotry no sanction." The letter had been on loan to B'nai B'rith for many years but never spotlighted. Ori began by having a showcase built for it simulating the entrance of the Newport Synagogue, then inaugurated the contest with a ceremonious presentation of awards. As our first presenter we invited Governor Zell Miller of Georgia, who was currently urging his legislature to remove the image of the confederate battle flag from the state flag. It was especially gratifying each year to see the winners coming from immigrant and racial minority families.

Through Ori's exhibits demonstrating intercultural exchange between Jewish communities and their host countries, we formed relationships with various embassies. As board chair, I was invited to their events and worked with several embassies co-sponsoring cultural programs. I lunched at the Swiss Embassy, once planning an exhibit on early Hebrew printing, and again honoring Arthur Cohn, a producer of *In the Garden of the Finzi-Continis*, a film about a wealthy, aristocratic Jewish family in late 1930s Italy. Our collection included a centuries-old wimple embroidered and signed by one of the Finzi-Continis.

After the opening of our Moroccan exhibit, the ambassador held a dinner in our honor. On another occasion, I represented the museum at the British Embassy reception honoring American heroes who saved British lives in WWII. We also had joint events with the French and the German embassies. I dined with President Václav Havel of the Czech Republic when B'nai B'rith hosted him and participated in many celebrations at the Embassy of Israel. After artist Yaacov Agam visited the museum, Ori and I took him for a drink and he drew a picture for me on the cocktail napkin.

Those rewards largely compensated for the problems and increasing frustration of dealing with B'nai B'rith. Ori had barely begun as director when Micky Neiditch, his immediate superior and de facto boss, turned against him. He'd even tried to force a wedge between the two of us (and almost succeeded). Ori caught it in time to read me the riot act. "You can't be loyal to both of us," he said. "Make up your mind. Quickly."

Eventually our nemesis left B'nai B'rith, but another soon emerged, one who wielded more authority with less veneer of civility. When Sidney Clearfield became executive vice president of BBI the atmosphere turned toxic, severely affecting Ori and testing his forbearance, sometimes causing him to explode in the presence of supporters who greatly admired him but blinked at foul language. They didn't tell him. Like our well-meaning friends in Atlanta too timid to criticize the rabbi directly, they told me. As Yogi Berra would have said, it was "deja vu all over again."

Granted that BBI was having a tough time. The Anti-Defamation League and B'nai B'rith Women, both organizations David had worked hard to keep happy, had left the fold and gone out on their own. Hillel, B'nai B'rith's presence on college campuses, soon left as well. B'nai B'rith was in a financial quagmire, deeply in debt and hemorrhaging memberships. One morning, after a well-received exhibit opening the night before, I entered the elevator with an upper echelon staffer who greeted me saying, "Congratulations. When are you leaving?"

I didn't understand. "Every other agency of B'nai B'rith leaves after getting successful," he explained. "So I figure the museum will be next."

He had a point. B'nai B'rith couldn't afford to support a *real* museum, and it still lacked the leadership required to understand its needs or make the effort to meet them. As chair of the museum committee I was nominally a member of the Board of Governors, but I was unrecognized and muted at its meetings. David's old friends greeted me warmly, but as David's wife, not as a colleague. Once they asked me to give the *d'var Torah* and, after five years, the president called on me to read my report. Despite a slow rise in the inclusion of women that David initiated, the Board was still an old boys' club. I used my time at those meetings to lobby for the museum, as everyone else did for his or her interests. When I asked several generous friends why they hadn't joined the museum as they said they would, each one, surprised, told me he had designated $1,000 of his BBI contribution for the museum. The books showed no sign of that. When Ori and I questioned the comptroller, he gave us a mollifying answer that I didn't understand, but nothing changed. We loped along as best we could financially, gaining recognition and gifts from outside B'nai B'rith but ever more frustrated within it.

Into the seventh month after losing David I began to realize that, in addition to missing *him*, I missed having a man in my life socially. Married friends had been wonderful about including me for dinner, both at home and at restaurants, and after I overcame the awkwardness of insisting on paying my own check I felt free to enjoy it. That wasn't the same as being part of a duo, however. I didn't want another husband, but I *did* want a playmate.

I had hardly returned from David's funeral when my downstairs neighbor, Irving Wallace, whose late wife Lillian was one of the first women who befriended me at the swimming pool, made the first condolence call. He ran for the condo board the same time that I did and was equally pleased to have lost. Walking together to the elevator after the meeting, he invited me to his apartment to celebrate our defeat. Thereafter I suspected I would no longer lack male companionship.

The second time he invited me to dinner he told me to make the reservation wherever I wanted to go. I chose the Old Mill because I'd never been there. David didn't balk at high prices but he didn't like driving out of town just to eat dinner. Since Irv was a stockbroker and mentioned several times that he was a millionaire, I assumed that anywhere I wanted to go would be okay without checking prices. The dinner was delicious, but he never let me forget how much it cost. That confirmed my prediction that our companionship would be temporary.

In the meantime, however, I enjoyed going with him, especially to the beach. Marge and Adelaide had warned me that I must learn bridge and tennis to be invited for weekends there, but with Irv that wasn't necessary. He didn't play bridge, he started me playing tennis on the court at our building, and he had a house at the beach.

I was too occupied with the museum to give much thought to what other people might deduce. One day at the pool a recently married senior couple asked us if we were going to get married. We set them straight but wondered what made them ask. I learned it was because they themselves had met and found romance at the pool.

At another neighbor's dinner party someone mentioned that we appeared to be a twosome. Soon thereafter, Irv said he felt sick and excused himself. We thought he might be having a heart attack so I offered to walk him back to his unit, but he insisted he could make it alone. When I checked on him later he assured me he was okay. It wasn't a heart attack but an anxiety attack brought on by the suggestion that we were becoming an "item." Did he flatter himself that I had designs on him? I assured him that wouldn't happen.

I met Irv's brother, Mike Wallace of CBS *60 Minutes* fame, once when he was visiting his son, Chris, for Christmas and we were invited to a family dinner. When Mike emceed the groundbreaking for the FDR memorial, he obtained invitations for Irv and me. It was at the luncheon afterward that I met my childhood imaginary friend, FDR's granddaughter Eleanor Seagraves, then known as Sistie.

I also had a nice visit with Mike Wallace at his home on Martha's Vineyard the following summer when Rabbi Harold White invited Roz Chayes and me to visit there. Irv wanted me to call Mike. I refused because I believe celebrities deserve not to be pursued when they're on vacation, but Irv insisted, giving me a message for his brother as I was leaving for the airport. I spoke to Mike's wife, Mary, who invited me to come for morning coffee along with Harold and Roz, and we had a lovely visit on their wrap-around veranda facing the bay. Mike was dressed for tennis, having just finished his daily set with columnist Art Buchwald. Legs are a dead giveaway for age, but not Mike's. His looked thirty years younger.

Irv and I had good times together, for which I reciprocated regularly by inviting him to home-cooked dinners. Although he showed generosity to me personally, I tired of overlooking his general stinginess and gladly accepted when friends began fixing me up with other men. On one occasion, my stepson Jimmy entered the apartment just as my "gentleman caller" put his arm around me. I felt like a teenager whose parent walked in.

When Marge learned that the husband of a recently deceased lifelong best friend was coming to Washington she invited him to dinner planning to introduce us, but not knowing if he was ready for a fix-up, she asked me to hold the evening open until she learned more. At the last minute, still in angst and ignorant about the gentleman's stage of post-bereavement, she told me to come anyway. I had a pleasant evening but wasn't smitten and apparently neither was he. After I left he told Marge that he was already engaged to marry a woman in Florida.

Florence Brody also made a valiant attempt on my behalf. She and her husband took me to dinner with a nice man who had just lost his wife and inherited her fortune. I enjoyed the evening but again did not yearn for more of the same, nor did he. Shortly after that he remarried with a woman who had a PhD, *chutzpah*, and great ideas for spending his inheritance, much of which, to her credit, she directed to Jewish and educational needs.

Other friends, Bob and Trude Edwards, had a bit more success when they invited me to dinner in their gorgeous new condo at Somerset House in Chevy Chase, along with a newly widowed attorney who also lived there. Admittedly I was impressed when he picked me up for dinner on our first date in a chauffeured limousine that took us to Lion d'Or, then the most expensive restaurant in town. The maître d' knew his order without asking. I overlooked his boasting as a temporary fault on a first date, thinking it might cease on further acquaintance, and opted to see where the connection would lead. He was to migrate south for the winter soon, which would give us a natural cut-off if either of us wanted it. When I visited Julie and Bud Weiss in Key Biscayne, he came from Palm Beach in his chauffeured limousine, visiting briefly with them before taking me to see the Vizcaya Museum and Gardens, then to dinner and back to the Weisses. Julie expressed her reaction to him so emphatically that I would have been ashamed to see him again even if he had asked, which he didn't.

So much for my life as an overaged debutante. I disliked that game when I was young and I still disliked it.

One day Marge and Nathan invited me to a chamber music concert at the Library of Congress but I couldn't go because I'd invited Irv for Shabbat dinner that night. Marge was furious.

"That's ridiculous," she fumed. "It's more than he'd do for you."

True, but no reason for me to be equally rude.

The next day Marge was further exasperated with me for not going to the concert. They made friends with a nice man sitting next to them who was alone, our age, widowed, and loved classical music.

"That's nice," I said. "Invite him to dinner. What's his name?"

She didn't remember, but he was a scientist retired from government service at the Naval Reserve Laboratory.

A few days later, Ruth St. John called to invite me to one of her fabulous dinner parties and asked me if I'd ever met Maury Shapiro. I hadn't, although each of us had been on her guest list for decades. She noted that he had been widowed for forty years, briefly remarried twice, and usually attached but not at the moment. He was a scientist, she said, "something to do with astronomy," retired after a long career at the Naval Reserve Laboratory. He traveled a lot to international conferences and loved classical music. Since he lived in Alexandria, approximately halfway between her home and mine, she suggested that she call him to say that I would pick him up on my way to her house for the dinner party. I agreed, he called to introduce himself, and we made plans. As the day of the dinner party approached, Washington received one of its rare but paralyzing snow storms, rendering impassable all roads other than the main arteries. Ruth called to postpone her party. Less than five minutes later Maury called to say, "Since you also have no plans for tomorrow night, why don't we have dinner together anyway? We can go to the Cosmos Club and stay afterward for a chamber concert of Mostly Mozart."

That was the beginning of our long, enduring friendship.

Fifteen

ADVENTURES WITH ORI AND MAURY

The weekend after Ruth's cancelled dinner party, I went to St. Louis for great-nephew David's wedding. His mother Geri, then happily remarried and Missouri's Democratic candidate for the Senate, was coming to Washington for a fundraiser that I planned to attend the next day. Maury Shapiro met me at the airport, took me home to change, and, while I dressed, entertained himself perusing my books of poetry shelved in the living room. I found him reading "The Rime of the Ancient Mariner."

Maury claimed that he couldn't believe in God because he was a scientist and that his aversion to pork and shellfish was atavistic, tastes established in childhood. Nevertheless, he asked to attend services with me on Pesach—to hear the music.

Afterward we had lunch at the Cosmos Club, a private social club founded in the late 19th century, with membership limited to those who had distinguished themselves in the arts, sciences, literature, or public service. It was now housed in a mansion on Massachusetts Avenue first built in 1873. Had Phineas Fogg been in Washington rather than

London when he bet his club members that he could go around the world in 80 days, they would have been there.

We relaxed at my apartment before going to dinner. That's when we realized our relationship indicated longevity.

I understood Maury's *mishugas* (craziness) in light of his background. Born in Jerusalem in 1915 to ultra-orthodox parents, his father was a scholar who died in the flu epidemic while walking home from a Turkish prison in Damascus after World War I. His mother, uneducated other than in Jewish ritual appropriate for women, then married an ultra-orthodox rabbi who brought them to Chicago when Maury was six. Shabbat restrictions precluded his participation in school sports as well as using the public library on weekends because both required public transportation, and neither operated on Sunday. At age ten he read Darwin's *Origin of the Species*, fell in love with science, and thwarted parental intentions that he become a rabbi by leaving Jewish Theological Seminary after six months to study physics at the University of Chicago. In WWII, he worked with J. Robert Oppenheimer testing the atom bomb.

In most ways he was the playmate I sought, a man who enjoyed classical music, theater, books, and travel. Although the only foreign language he knew was Yiddish, he *kibbitzed* with strangers everywhere and readily adapted to local customs. I recognized from the start that he had social characteristics I didn't like, but with no commitments either of us could leave whenever the negatives outweighed the positives. I told him that my first priority after family was the museum and that I wasn't interested in living together or getting married. Neither was he, he said. When I told our former museum director, Anna Cohn, about him, she responded, "Great! That's just what you need. An international egghead."

Other friends made no secret of their disapproval but accepted him after getting to know him better. His many long-time friends and colleagues loved him dearly and greatly admired his work.

When I told Irv that I wouldn't go out with him anymore, he predicted that Maury and I would split within two months. "I'll take my chances," I said, confident of surviving that possibility. Irv and I had accepted invitations to events celebrating a friend's adult bar mitzvah celebration the next weekend which would have been awkward to cancel. After that, I told him, we could remain friends and play tennis together, but no more socializing as a twosome.

Before Maury entered my life I'd signed up for a tour of Turkey led by Ori, emphasizing the country's Jewish heritage. On behalf of the museum, Ori and I went ahead of the group to stop in Geneva for Dr. Oscar Ghez, founder and director of The Petit Palais museum, to show us his École de Paris collection and hopefully lend us pieces from it for exhibition in Washington.

Our flight arrived too late for sleep before our appointment and I went through the day dazed. Dr. Ghez received us cordially, showed us through his museum, and then brought us to his palatial home for lunch with his wife Nicole and several friends. Afterward he took us to his vaults below the city where he stored most of his collection, including works by Mané-Katz, surprisingly brighter, both in color and subject, than I'd ever seen by that artist. Dr. Ghez not only agreed to lend us a selection but also gave us a generous check to start the process.

Unfortunately, atmospheric conditions in the B'nai B'rith building did not meet the safety standards for a long-term exhibit so we couldn't take them.

At lunch, where conversation was in French, I was too tired to think even in *English*, so after a few polite responses I left it to Ori. Dinner was more problematic. I'd welcomed going to Geneva, not only for the art but also to see Roger and Rosemary Aubert again after many years. Roger's stepmother Odette, my mother's special friend, was still alive and so eager to hear about the family that she sat next to me and questioned me throughout dinner. Odette didn't speak English. My French is bad enough when it's *good*, but that night I was so tired that it failed me completely.

In Istanbul, before the group arrived, Ori showed me sites that weren't on the itinerary. The imperial excesses of the Ottomans didn't thrill me but I was fascinated by the Islamic art we saw at a private mansion where Ori had arranged a visit. In Izmir he had friends who entertained our group for lunch in their lovely home on the beach, after which we continued by bus along the Anatolian coast.

Ephesus was a mind-opener for me. The vestiges of this ancient Jewish settlement were sufficient evidence, but finding Hebrew names on the best seats in the theater at Miletus gave specific proof of Jewish prosperity in the area during post-biblical times. When I noted to Ori that we met the same group of Christian tourists at every stop, their banner reading "In the Footsteps of St. Paul," he chided me, asking, "Who do you think St. Paul was preaching to?"

In Bodrum we spent the weekend in a hotel descending like steps from the top of a cliff, two guest rooms to a terrace with its own pool, overflowing with flowers and a breathtaking view of the bay. On Sunday we toured the bay on a small boat, mooring at a barren rock island where some of us went swimming before our picnic lunch on deck. Dinner that evening was at the fortress of the Knights Templar, "hosted" by an automated three-dimensional image of an ancient princess constructed from the skeleton of a woman who actually lived in that era. Authentic or not, her story was entertaining and the food was good.

In central Anatolia we viewed hidden churches, whirling dervishes, pornographic topography in the so-called Valley of the Phalli, and stayed overnight at a hotel carved into the side of a ravine. Formerly a Club Med, it maintained sybaritic French cuisine, including unlimited portions of halvah and chocolate mousse for breakfast.

At the national museum in Ankara, with little time for sightseeing and lunch before boarding our flight home, we exasperated our guide who tried to move us on as we remained just inside the main entrance listening to Ori translate the lengthy inscription on a stele there. The guides, though generally very good, were less knowledgeable than he about their own history and culture.

Very soon after I met Maury, he invited me to join him on an upcoming trip to Sicily and meet the Pope. Maury was a director of the

World Center for Scientific Studies in Erice, where Pope John Paul II was coming to celebrate its 30th anniversary.

I thought Maury was joking. He repeated the invitation each time we met, and eventually I realized he was serious.

"Are you crazy?" I asked myself as I began to consider the trip and the relationship that would ensue with Maury. It was surely a risk, but I was in my late 60s, had never taken a risk, and doubted I'd have a better chance to do so. When I called my children to tell them, without hearing the other's response, each reacted alike.

"I want you to know that the St. Johns introduced me to a very nice man who invited me to go to Sicily with him for the weekend to meet the Pope, and I'm going," I said to each of them.

Marcia and Bill both responded, "How old is he?"

Apparently, they weren't shocked.

Maury was 76, four years younger than David and Jack would have been, and with an eight-year gap was closer to my own age than any man I'd gone out with since I was 14. He walked with a sprint, swam every other day year-round, and played tennis regularly.

That weekend in Erice initiated many adventures for me. Our hour-and-a-half drive from the Palermo Airport began in bright sunlight with spectacular views of rugged cliffs on our left and intense blue sea on the right. As we turned up into the foothills and into the clouds, gray mist prevailed.

As a favored director, Maury was always given comfortable quarters and told me about the magnificent view we'd have from our window. We checked in at headquarters, received instructions, and, leaving our luggage to be delivered to our room, proceeded on foot to the address we were given. After going far beyond the area with which Maury was familiar, we found our room at the top of a narrow staircase with no railing and no upstairs toilet.

Maury, certain it was a mistake, suggested we go to lunch and then to the office when the top brass would be there. We were so far off the beaten track that he got lost trying to find the restaurant. When he finally found it, we joined a jovial group of his international friends for antipasto and couscous before returning to the office where, with profound apologies, we were sent to Erice's best hotel.

By the time His Holiness arrived the next morning, all spaces on his route, including windows and balconies, were jammed with onlookers. We had seats inside the 14th-century church of San Domenico, Maury in the front row with other dignitaries, me halfway back in the center aisle, affording a full view of proceedings as well as a warm handshake from Pope John Paul II as he exited. At the luncheon, Maury was seated at the head table, only one place away from His Holiness, and I in the best space for special guests, at a table centered in the entrance atop broad steps leading into the main hall.

We spent the rest of our time there with Maury's other guests, Franco and Leda Stanzani, then returned with them to Rome, where we spent a few days at their home in the elegant suburb of Ariccia. During our visit, Franco mentioned having been captured by the Americans during WWII in 1943 and interned at Fort Benning. I asked if he remembered girls flirting with him through the wire fence at lunchtime and admitted that I might have been one of them.

When we left the Stanzanis, I returned home and Maury went to Germany. After committing to give lectures there, he had been notified by the Navy that he was to be given an award at a ceremony in Washington during those days. He asked his son Joel, who lived in Chicago, to accept it for him and wanted me to go along. I invited Joel to stay overnight at my apartment and we bonded immediately.

I met Maury's second child, Elana, who also lived in suburban Chicago, the following Pesach when we visited Joel and his wife, Carol, for Seder. We had already spent the Thanksgiving holiday in San Marino, California with Maury's youngest, Raquel, her husband, Mark Kislinger, and their daughters, Lara and Marnie. It was then that I began to notice Maury's absentmindedness.

Maury mentioned that the Kislingers' house rules directed everyone to abandon shoes at the front door only as we pulled into their driveway

Janice Rothschild Blumberg

that brisk November night. As I navigated the cold stone floors of the Spanish-style home barefooted, I wistfully envisioned my drawer full of socks and footsies that I could have used.

I fell in love with the Kislingers despite my discomfort and Grandpa's absentmindedness, which surfaced again the next night. When we took nine-year-old Lara and seven-year-old Marnie to the movies, he locked his keys inside the car.

Back in Washington, I also noticed peculiarities in Maury's driving. He often braked as he approached a green light and accelerated when he saw a red one. I wondered about his being both mad scientist and absentminded professor but continued taking chances. I liked having him attend scientific lectures with me and escort me to exhibit openings, and I enjoyed socializing with his diverse assortment of friends. Closest to him were physicists Hongyi Chu, an effervescent Chinese genius, gourmet cook, and novice pianist whose after-dinner entertainment diametrically opposed his cooking; Rein Silberberg, a bland Estonian; and Al Arking, who was a strictly observant Jew along with his wife, Vivienne. They frequently invited us for holiday feasts and Shabbat, which I especially appreciated.

Our favorite entertainment was music, especially chamber concerts at the Library of Congress. Those evenings began at Radicchio, an Italian hole-in-the-wall on Independence Avenue, for all-you-can-eat spaghetti. Then, with most other early diners there, we walked to the Library of Congress, got good seats (free but unreserved) and *kibbitzed* with friends until the lights dimmed. For pre-concert dinners at Georgetown University, the Embassy of Israel, and other nearby embassies, I prepared dinner at home.

At the Cosmos Club, our most frequent destination, in addition to concerts we heard lectures by other notable members such as presidential advisor David Gergen, and while Maury served on the membership committee we attended festive dinners welcoming new members, some of whom were famous. At a club party one New Year's Eve our friend David Carliner brought *The Feminine Mystique* author Betty Friedan, who had lost weight, gone to a hairdresser, and looked so attractive wearing a long red velvet gown that I couldn't help telling her so—with an apology in deference to her denunciation of women's concern about looks.

One night, as we approached the club, we saw television trucks jamming the corner of Massachusetts Avenue and cameramen perched on the garden fence. "She's inside," confided the attendant who took our car. The doorman whispered advice to look carefully as we passed the bar, so we did.

There sat Monica Lewinsky, making an appearance during the brouhaha over her affair with President Bill Clinton. Upstairs in the grand salon where members gathered for champagne and hors d'oeuvres before special events, I joined an unfamiliar group of dignified looking ladies and almost choked on my fried oyster when I heard them discussing the President's genitalia.

Other events with Maury were less spectacular. One time we went to an event for Chicago University alumni at Dumbarton Oaks and ended up with former Senator Chuck Percy, Sharon Rockefeller's father. He was handsome, charming, slightly inebriated, and needed a ride home. One summer evening, in the lobby of Theater J at the Jewish Community Center, we encountered a mutual friend who began a conversation with Maury without introducing his companion, a tall man in a sport shirt whose face looked familiar. After a few increasingly awkward moments, the stranger extended his hand to me and said, "Hello. I'm Bill Rehnquist."

The Chief Justice of the Supreme Court! No wonder his face looked familiar.

I had one notable encounter at the supermarket. A woman stopped me in the produce aisle to remark on the pendant I was wearing. She recognized it as a replica of a pre-Columbian *huaca* from Panama, which led to conversation. She introduced herself as Marlene Stone and we realized we'd met years before, when David was president of BBI and her husband Richard was the fair-haired Democratic senator from Florida, deeply involved in the Panama Canal issue. The Stones had just returned from Denmark where Dick was ambassador.

In the years that followed, we spent memorable evenings together at their home and mine.

Maury and I also became friends with several Israeli ambassadors. I'd met Eliyahu Ben-Elissar and his wife Nitza in Toronto with David when Ben-Elissar was in Canada. When they arrived in Washington in 1996 I met them again, this time at the U.S. Postal Service ceremony dedicating a new stamp featuring a Hanukkah menorah. I saw them fairly often afterward because they were close friends of Ruth and Robert St. John. When Robert turned 90 in 1992, the Israel government began celebrating his birthday annually with a huge reception. The Ben-Elissars, as personal friends, threw a private party as well. When they departed for their post in Paris in 1998, Nitza told me to call her when I came there.

In 1999, Ambassador David Ivry arrived in DC and became Maury's friend. I never knew him or his wife very well, but they invited both of us to their family Seder. It was nothing like I expected it to be. Their only other guests, besides family, were the Slovakian ambassador and a new Jewish congresswoman from California with her husband. Instead of the long traditional service in Hebrew that I grimly anticipated, the ambassador used an English language IDF Haggadah and conducted the shortest Seder I ever attended.

The most lasting gift of life in Washington is touching history as it happens. Stuart and Fran Eizenstat, longtime friends from Atlanta, invited me to Stuart's swearing-in ceremony when he became ambassador to the European Union and again for his swearing-in as Undersecretary of State. They were probably the first couple in State Department history to use a Hebrew bible for the ceremony and were acknowledged to have established in Brussels the first kosher kitchen in any American embassy.

I was with Adelaide Eisenman and members of her family at the Embassy of Panama when she received that nation's highest award for the help that she and Richard gave in bringing down the Noriega regime. In 1990 she arranged for news commentator Marvin Kalb to interview their nephew Roberto (Bobby) Eisenman, publisher of *La Prensa*, Panama's only free press, who, while exiled, was studying at Harvard's JFK School of Journalism. Afterward, at my apartment for lunch, Adelaide and Bobby excitedly recounted Kalb's reaction. Bobby had convinced him to initiate the publicity that awakened our government to the need for intervention, toppling Noriega and leading to his arrest.

While enjoying that history-filled social life, I continued pursuing other interests. I entered photographs for Towers residents' art shows. I served on a jury finding the defendant guilty of manslaughter. I wrote articles for publication, including an essay about Jack for *Quiet Voices*, edited by Mark Bauman and Berkley Kalin. I also spoke at meetings, in Richmond for a Hadassah convention, in Memphis for a seminar on southern Jewish history, and in Orlando for an event at the JCC. At the Southern Jewish Historical Society conference in Norfolk, I introduced Bob Lipshutz for his keynote address after hearing two of the authors present new books that mentioned my husbands, David in a story about Knoxville Jews and Jack in Clive Webb's treatise on civil rights.

Most significantly, I began research on Great-Grandfather "Alphabet" Browne (1845-1929), which took me once to New York and twice to Cincinnati on a grant from Gary Zola to work at the American Jewish Archives. I especially enjoyed that, living on the Hebrew Union College campus in the former dormitory where Jack lived in the 1930s and meeting other researchers who were accomplished scholars. (I would finally publish his biography in 2012.)

Melissa Faye Greene, while writing *The Temple Bombing*, called to introduce herself and arrange interviews. We became friends and I liked the book, pleased by her references to me and Jack, although critical of her tendency to embellish facts with colorful imaginary detail. When she sent drafts of chapters about Jack for my approval, my return conversation usually began by asking, "Melissa, this is supposedly non-fiction, isn't it?"

On one occasion, Melissa had written a meticulously researched detailed description of the Atlanta Airport when Jack first arrived in

Georgia in 1946. After my opening question, an awkward pause, and her cue to continue, I told her Jack took the train.

Another author who interviewed me and became a good friend was Marcie Cohen Ferris. Marcie came to Washington with her husband, Bill Ferris, when President Clinton appointed him to head the National Endowment for Humanities. While researching her doctoral dissertation (which later became the southern Jewish history cookbook *Matzo Ball Gumbo*), she called to ask about my family's traditions in southern Jewish cooking. I refrained from saying, "*Oy vey!* Have you got a wrong number!" and simply told her we had no recognizable traditions in food, inviting her to visit if she wanted to have a purely social conversation minus recipes. She did and used one of my stories in the book—the one about Coretta King and the coquilles St. Jacques—but did not include the recipe because scallops are *treif.*

My passport did not gather dust in those years. Maury went with me on trips that Ori led for the museum. The first was to Morocco, where we visited cities I hadn't seen before, including Marrakesh, and I learned more about the country's Jewish heritage. While there, we were dinner guests in an urban mansion and lunched with a Jewish cave dweller at her home in the Atlas Mountains.

Visiting Prague, Krakow, and Budapest in the mid-1990s was an adventure of a different sort. The former Soviet bloc countries didn't appeal to me, although I returned to the Czech Republic and Hungary in later years, after their Soviet influence waned, and loved them. On that first trip we also visited both Terezín (better known as Theresienstadt) and Dachau, two concentration camps that surely added to the gloom. Terezín affected me most because of the contrast between its fictional life presented by the Nazis for the Red Cross and other inspectors and its reality.

Maury and I returned to Erice each year, where he conducted his own seminars and lectured at others'. True to his original claim, our home-away-from-home was indeed a room with a view. In a renaissance building originally a dormitory for monks, large and with a private bath, it overlooked the Mediterranean coastline all the way to Monte Cofano, the westernmost point of Sicily.

While Maury worked, I wandered the town's narrow streets and stepped alleyways with camera in hand as I did in Jerusalem, unable to resist changes of light on scenes I'd already shot on previous trips. One day I noticed a street sign reading "*Viale dei Giudecca,*" Street of the Jews. Erice once had a Jewish community! I wanted to see the cemetery but *Centro* authorities wouldn't take me there because it was outside the walls and unsafe. They introduced me to the city historian, however. He answered my questions, showed me a fallen fragment from one of the Jewish graves displayed on the wall of the city museum, and gave me copies of his transcripts from state archives in Palermo and Rome documenting that Erice once embraced a thriving Jewish community.

We encountered adventure on each trip. Before leaving home, Maury asked where else I wanted to go and arranged for it by notifying a colleague at its university that he would be in the area. The colleague then invited him to lecture and hosted us as guests of the university. After the first session I attended, we visited Catania. From there we took a day trip inland by bus to see Piazza Armerina, the restored palace of a Roman general with remarkable mosaic floors depicting history and mythology.

We then went by boat across the bay to see Syracuse and walked too far looking for Roman ruins that we never found. We realized we couldn't walk back to the dock in time to get the last boat of the day for Catania, and seeing no cabs, we hesitated to ask for help at the only building nearby, a stark warehouse-like structure that looked uninviting, because we were warned about violent crime in Sicily.

Thankfully, before we panicked we saw two nuns emerge from the building carrying packages. We followed them to their car, told them our problem, and they delivered us to the dock just as the boat's whistle blew for final boarding.

That summer Maury had two more conferences to attend, the

first on Volcano, a sister island to Stromboli, where Ingrid Bergman and Roberto Rossellini famously filmed the movie of the same name. Reached by air boat from Messina, it offered white clay mud packs, which I declined, but I delighted in dinners on the terrace with the magnificent seascapes and sunsets.

From there we went to Israel, going first to Maury's conference at Eilat. I found it much changed since my last visit, and not for the better. It had become a noisy resort city, a Red Sea Riviera with nondescript apartments climbing the cliffs. The conference hotel claimed international status by featuring everything from restaurants to music in the style of another country. The only acknowledgment of being in Israel was that the signs were in Hebrew.

From there we went to Jerusalem, where I had an adventure visiting Maury's bedridden aunt, the sole survivor of his parents' generation. She lived in the compound built by their ancestors and long vacated by more prosperous descendants. Maury's sister with whom we stayed occupied a comfortable apartment that was centrally located, but was also culturally foreign to me due to her lifestyle. The sharp contrast between her family dinner for Maury and our Shabbat dinners with Vivienne Arking's equally observant orthodox parents a few blocks away demonstrated a chasm between two cultures despite equal devotion to Judaism.

The Arkings went with us for one of Maury's sessions in Erice. On that trip, they showed me that it's possible to be strictly observant without making a show of it or distracting from the plans and pleasure of others. I loved being with them. The four of us went to Tunisia afterward to see the historic Djerba Synagogue and enjoy the beach as well as view Tunis and Carthage.

Our other travels from Erice were confined to Italy. In Bologna, at the world's oldest university, one of Maury's former lady friends, a professor there, hosted us. In Milan, after Maury's lecture, we met my friend Ada Calabrese, a retired singer with the Metropolitan Opera who helped us get tickets for *La Bohème* at La Scala.

On another trip we stopped to see Naples and the Amalfi coast on the way to a conference in Capri. Heeding warnings to dress inconspicuously and carry no valuables in the city, we walked for most of the day, then took a cab back downtown, intending to stop at a place we wanted to see and walk from there to a café on the waterfront to sip *apéritifs* while watching the sun set on Vesuvius. Rush hour traffic kept our driver in the center lane, preventing him from letting us off. Suddenly someone opened the door next to me and tried to grab my tote bag from my shoulder. I held on but so did he, causing my sleeve to slide up and expose my watch, which wasn't expensive but *was* gold plated, so he wanted it. When the traffic moved he fled, but not before tearing the bag off my arm and pulling so hard on the watch band that he ruined it, leaving me a bruise the length of a banana.

After we rolled a bit further and stopped again someone opened the front passenger door, threw my bag in, and disappeared. Our driver ignored our pleas to let us off when the traffic eased and raced to the edge of town where he met a waiting undercover agent who spoke a little English. Even though nothing was stolen, the agent begged us to go to the police station and report the crime. We agreed, I answered questions, and it was worth missing our sunset over Vesuvius to see the look on the interrogator's face when he asked for my date of birth. I was 72.

The following day, we contemplated the volcano while munching our picnic lunch on the sunlit doorstep of an ancient's home in Herculaneum.

Another pleasant adventure awaited us after taking the hair-raising Amalfi drive from Sorrento. At the top in Ravello we noticed posters advertising a concert that night by the Valencia Symphony with Mstislav Rostropovich as soloist and left our tour to remain for the music. It was all the more delightful for being performed outdoors against the breathtaking backdrop of sunset and sea.

Maury's mad scientist persona manifested itself in Capri. The conference scheduled a cruise around the island and into the Blue Grotto, which was canceled at the last minute due to high winds. Maury and some of his much younger colleagues decided to see the Grotto regardless by swimming into it. I had no intention of joining them in the foolhardy plan but went to the platform with Maury, gritting my teeth as I watched him descend the ladder and swim through the entrance. Others returned streaked with blood after navigating the sharp rocks and hot coral inside the Grotto. Maury, although an excellent swimmer, was 80 years old. I held my breath. Miraculously, he emerged unscathed.

After that and my experience in Naples I'd had enough adventure for one trip, but Maury almost involved us in another. Our airport shuttle was stranded by an accident on the Autostrade, causing us to miss our flight home. While waiting several hours for the next flight we were joined in the lounge by a group of noisy chain-smoking students. It would have done no good to bring out my pin saying, "Yes, I mind if you smoke." Maury decided to speak to them, which I begged him not to do because they appeared likely to become violent. He went anyway and talked to them for a surprisingly long time. After the discussion, two of them snuffed out their cigarettes. When I asked him what happened, he said, "I told them they seemed to be enjoying life so much that I wondered why they wanted to end it prematurely."

Maury's unsolicited advice to strangers worked then, but I never knew when it might get him in trouble. That possibility loomed again the year we stopped in Florence to see grandson Jacob, who was studying there during his junior year at Yale. After landing in Rome, Maury was behind me running to board the train for Florence and didn't make it in time. I waited at the station until late afternoon, expecting him to appear on each half-hourly arrival from Rome and becoming increasingly concerned when he didn't. After three hours he finally arrived, chipper as ever and surprised that I worried, introducing me to a charming man he'd met at the Rome station. They'd been too engrossed in conversation to take an earlier train.

The highlight of that visit for me took place when Jacob and I were crossing a piazza and a tourist stopped us to ask directions in English. Jacob replied in Hebrew, astonishing her as he did me. When I asked him how he knew that was her native language, he said her accent was too guttural for French or Spanish but not guttural enough for German.

Those trips with Maury made me fall in love with Rome. When he had a conference there, we stayed in a small hotel on a residential street across from the Villa Borghese gardens, and I spent days gobbling up its wonders. Nearby steps led into the gardens with paths through to the Spanish steps. To the right was the National Etruscan Museum, beyond it a left turn into the Piazza del Popolo, and then a cluster of antiquities, fountains, and twisting streets lined with boutiques. I visited the synagogue with its tiny yet exquisite museum, meandered through the forum to revisit the Arch of Titus where Jack had photographed heartwarming Hebrew graffiti saying *"Am Yisrael Chai"* ("The People of Israel Live"), and admired the Colosseum I'd toured with Jack from the bus stop across the piazza. While attending the session at which Maury presented his paper, I met a Jewish scientist from the Republic of Georgia who was surprised to learn that our museum was planning an exhibit about his country's Jewish heritage. Topping it all, the al fresco farewell banquet atop Capitoline Hill, with the lighted forum below and blossoming trees spreading fragrance and moonlit shadows, was so romantic that I regretted not being in love with Maury.

On one of our trips we again visited the Stanzanis, whose home in Ariccia was on the other side of the mountain from Castel Gandolfo, the pope's summer residence. The Stanzanis were devout Catholics and Franco a devotee of science, so Maury arranged for a friend, a physicist priest assigned to the Vatican Observatory, to give us a tour. While there, pointing to the pope's private quarters from a balcony above, our host told us that he was on guard there when Pope John XXIII died. Ordered to remain, preventing anyone from entering until the new pope was elected, he noticed the open ledger where His Holiness had been working. It listed archbishops next in line to become cardinals and our friend was happily surprised to see the name of his dear friend, Archbishop Paul Hallinan of Atlanta, first on the list. I couldn't suppress my own excitement hearing that and told him that the archbishop was also *my* friend and a close friend to my husband Jack as they led their congregations in Atlanta's struggle for civil rights.

I had other adventures with Maury via meetings unconnected with Erice. Our first trip to Germany was to Sonneberg, a place we couldn't find on a map. Neither could people at the German Embassy. Eventually we discovered it on the huge antique globe in the Cosmos Club library. It's a small town in the Thuringian mountains, near the Czech Republic, that had been in East Germany until the German reunification in 1990 and wasn't yet identified on western maps. It was picturesque but too cold for winter tourism, even with two sweaters and a leather jacket under my overcoat. I was further challenged by getting stuck in the Soviet-era hotel elevator, between floors and alone. Eventually someone pulled me up through the shaft.

From there we went to a conference in Munich by chartered bus, stopping for several hours in Nuremberg to see the Christmas market. Unable to stray from the crowded square, I was nonetheless pleased to be there, just imagining what it might have been like for my Oettinger and Weichselbaum ancestors who lived nearby in Fürth and worked in Munich. Here I had a wonderful time with Jacqui Domberger, my loquacious multilingual friend from B'nai B'rith, and her husband Joe. I also spent delightful days alone at the Neue Pinakothek viewing my favorite Van Goghs and Gauguins.

Another occasion for imagining the lives of ancestors was when Maury had a conference in Hamburg, where my father's maternal forebears lived many centuries ago. This time, unlike when Jack and I visited the city in 1972, I thought it was beautiful and enjoyed being there.

When Maury had a meeting in Madrid I had a great time trying to speak Spanish and visiting the Prado and Reina Sofía museums. We attended Friday night services at the synagogue, which was in such an obscure neighborhood that our taxi driver almost couldn't find it. The women's section was on a balcony too heavily curtained for me to see the action or hear very much of it. Afterward, Maury introduced me to a young American who wanted to take us to dinner at the home of the local Chabad *rebbe*. I wanted to decline, but Maury reminded me of my eagerness to experience foreign customs and accepted.

The *rebbe*'s emissary led us further into the depths of the district, finally turning into an apartment building and leading us up four flights of unlighted stairs where we met the *rebbe* himself, also a young American. Our guide then disappeared. Our host led us to a washroom for ritual hand-washing, then to the parlor where a table was set, and informed me that women were not permitted to join in the singing.

The only other woman present was his wife who, from what I could see in the dim light, was young and pretty. With one baby in her arms, another obviously on the way, she barely noticed the comings and goings of several more children popping in from the back hall or out from under the sofa.

After dinner, the *rebbe* gave us directions to the nearest street with public transportation and we carefully inched our way down the pitch-black stairwell. With the streets also dark, we lost our way and were truly frightened until a young Israeli approached us offering help. He led us to a lighted thoroughfare where we boarded the first streetcar that stopped without asking where it was going. Eventually we reached our hotel, thankful and ready for a restful Shabbat.

Upon leaving Madrid, we drove to Ávila and Segovia. Then we flew to Porto, Portugal, where a physicist friend met us and took us to his parents' home for dinner. While sightseeing the next day, he had someone open the synagogue for us, which I didn't expect. Our host wasn't Jewish and in Spain, Jews were still somewhat secretive about their institutions. When I asked him, he laughed and said, "Most of us here were Jewish once."

He drove us south to Lisbon, showing us breathtaking scenery, magnificent architecture, and the combination of both at the University of Coimbra, which was so beautiful that I thought the students must wear blinders to keep their eyes on their books.

At a conference at The Sorbonne in Paris during President Clinton's impeachment proceedings we had difficulty explaining to Maury's international colleagues why Americans were so concerned over extramarital conduct. The weather was cold but beautiful so I did much walking, one day going with a friend to the Rodin Museum, then to the Jeu de Paume to pay respects to Monet's Water Lilies, followed by a meander through the Tuileries Gardens to the Louvre, munching roasted chestnuts for lunch. We arrived too late for viewing so we continued walking across the Pont des Arts, past the currently upscale Hotel du Quai Voltaire where Jack and I had stayed in the 60s, loving it despite creaking floors and paper-thin towels. When we began to feel tired we were already near our hotel on Montparnasse.

Paris dressed for Christmas was a frosted fairyland. It also enhanced Hanukkah, which I celebrated with two adventures, one of them with Maury. After visiting the newly opened Jewish Museum, while warming up at a heated outdoor café on the Places des Vosges, we noticed a large neon *chanukiah* on a building across the square and went to investigate. It identified a synagogue where a children's holiday service was about to begin. We were invited to stay for it and we did, much to our delight.

My other celebration was with Nitza Ben-Elissar, who invited me to tea at her apartment, the embassy residence, after which she suggested I accompany her to a Hanukkah party for the staff families to see the embassy office. It was a work of art, formerly the home of a wealthy Jewish family who engaged artists to paint murals on the ceilings and sculpt intricate carvings on the woodwork. When the Nazis approached, the owners had the art plastered over to hide it, knowing that they would be deported and their home occupied by Nazis. The family died in the Holocaust. When the Israelis bought the building, it was relatively inexpensive. They discovered the art when they opened walls to install security wiring.

Among Maury's meetings that I attended in America was one in Atlanta, unforgettable because Stephen Hawking was the lecturer. Having lost his voice completely years earlier, he spoke through a sophisticated computer device that detected tiny hand movements.

I went to other conferences primarily for the side trips they suggested. After one in New Hampshire, we drove through New England visiting Bud and Julie Weiss in the Berkshires. From a conference in southern California we visited Maury's family in San Marino, then took an Elderhostel (now Road Scholar) weekend in the wine country. We toured Yellowstone before his meeting in Salt Lake City.

On that trip, Maury's absentmindedness may have saved our lives. When we checked in at Dulles he couldn't find his ticket. Still rummaging through his luggage when the flight was called, he told me to go ahead and wait at the airport hotel where we were staying overnight prior to early morning pick-up for the tour. Had he been with me, we would have spent the afternoon touring the city. While I waited at the hotel a tornado struck, only shaking the building but devastating a main sweep of Salt Lake City, where we had planned to be.

I enjoyed seeing Old Faithful and other phenomena at Yellowstone, but for me the highlight of the trip was the Mormon Library, where I researched the Dutch side of my ancestry (Grandma Rose Hamburger Oettinger). I learned that Great-Grandfather Jacob Hamburger emigrated twice, first as a single "merchant" (meaning peddler) and the next time as married clergy. That whetted my appetite for more research.

The Hellers and I had shelved *Deadly Truth* after our agent suddenly dropped it, but when Maury had a conference in South Africa I grasped the opportunity to update the story. Although apartheid was over, I planned to revise our plot as testimony to the Truth and Reconciliation Commission, but I needed to attend a trial to witness the procedure. Fortunately, there was still one ongoing in Durban, where Maury's conference was held. There I met the two widows of the victim, a prominent Zulu lawyer murdered by a surrogate of the former government. The older woman, who spoke English, explained that she was his city wife, her young companion his village wife, and then told me his story. She wrote to me afterward, enclosing a picture of him embracing their daughter as he left home for the last time.

Durban also yielded other memorable experiences. I saw a huge anti-Israel demonstration by the local Islamic community, a frightening forecast of future protests closer to home. And once again, Maury's daredevil absentmindedness caused me angst. I didn't plan to use the beautiful beach just outside our window because it was mid-winter in the southern hemisphere, but I did go under wraps with Maury and his polar bear friends when they went to swim. Others stayed close to shore and came in when the whistle blew warning of a strong undertow, but not Maury. He, alone and farther than the lifeguards considered safe, didn't hear their whistles.

We went sightseeing before and after Maury's meeting, enabling me to visit places I'd written about based on my co-authors' description but never seen. We visited the vineyard thanks to its current owner, a grandson of the one in our story. He invited us for lunch with his family in their home that I wrote about, enabling me to experience proof that not all Afrikaners fit a negative stereotype.

After the conference, Maury and I went to Kruger Park and had the very good luck-of-the-draw being housed in a simulated *kraal* (African village) where every room was a separate round hut called a *rondavel*. The establishment issued flashlights to guide us through the pitch-black jungle for dinner in an enclosure warmed by torches set into wall sconces. The meal was a typical *braaivlais* with traditional dishes I'd written about but never tasted. Our animal viewing on paved roads surprised me until I realized that, unlike the horses we ride, animals in the wild don't wear cumbersome iron shoes that click on the pavement. Our best sighting was in a traffic jam waiting for a pride of lions to cross.

We also went to Kimberley and the de Beers property with the enormous defunct diamond quarry known as the Big Hole. In Kimberley, a Jewish physician opened the synagogue for us. We asked him about post-apartheid conditions and he told us that many whites, including his own grown sons, were suffering.

Rather than stay overnight in Johannesburg before flying home we visited neighboring Pretoria, the co-capital, where Maury again shocked me with his *chutzpah*. Offered a private car and driver for the afternoon portion of our tour, we asked to see Pretoria's residential section where embassy residences are located. Maury, recalling that a friend suggested he call our ambassador James Joseph, then decided to do so—on a Sunday afternoon, from the embassy gate, hot and grungy from sightseeing! I was appalled.

The gracious ambassador and his wife invited us in and spent an hour entertaining us. As we passed their piano I noticed a photograph of them with Andrew Young and his new bride, and later remarked that I knew Andy and his late wife, Jean, in Atlanta. Mrs. Joseph told me the picture was taken at the Youngs' wedding in the Cape Town embassy. She and the ambassador were their attendants.

My only real downer on that trip was the granddaddy of all bad colds that hit me on our first day in Cape Town and hung on for weeks after we returned home. I was so sick from the long flight back that for first time ever I wished I had a husband to bring me home and put me to bed.

The Hellers and I self-published the revised *Deadly Truth* in 2000, with Izzy marketing and managing financial arrangements. I did a few talks, one in Atlanta and one in D.C., but mainly left that to him and Zelda, who were much better at it than me. Between researching Alphabet Browne in Cincinnati, New York, Atlanta, and Columbus as well as at the Library of Congress, the National Archives, and on the internet, I was too busy writing my next book to be interested in selling the last.

Because I was on its board as chairperson of the museum committee, B'nai B'rith itself occupied some of my time during these years. That included board meetings in Washington as well as conventions, and in 1993 events celebrating its 150th anniversary. President Clinton spoke at the Havdalah service, held outdoors on the Mall across from the Lincoln Memorial, commendable in spirit but distinctly uncomfortable for those of us awaiting the President on a brutally cold November night.

Sidney Clearfield, then the executive director of B'nai B'rith, exhibited toward me the rudeness and hostility he had long shown Ori, and our volunteers noticed. Despite the handicaps, Ori's genius and our generous friends enabled the museum to grow, raising ninety percent of our budget independently. However, the gifts had to go through BBI to be tax-deductible, and when our leading local supporters learned that their contributions were not being allocated to the museum as specified, they perceived the need for change.

Our two major Washington supporters invited a group of their generous friends to breakfast with Ori and me at the Four Seasons in Georgetown and drew unanimous consent to establish an expanded, independent, truly national Jewish museum. B'nai B'rith would have its name on a special gallery housing the current collection and a representative on the museum's board as it has with other independent institutions founded by it. Since B'nai B'rith was deeply in debt and hemorrhaging membership, I was hopeful that the offer would be welcomed.

Not so. It was vetoed, possibly because the proviso in Phil Klutznick's original million-dollar bequest to the museum specified that if it closed, the endowment would go to another Jewish organization. Not only did B'nai B'rith deny the museum's request to obtain independent, tax-deductible status, but its president couldn't even find time to discuss the matter with the philanthropists who proposed it.

A final point of contention arose when the museum scheduled a seminar about Jewish-owned art stolen by the Nazis. Because BBI management was less than cooperative about our use of its assembly space, as a last-minute emergency we had to hold the event at an outside venue, a boutique hotel near Dupont Circle. When it made the television news, we were blamed for not having B'nai B'rith's name visible on camera. Then, when the stolen art issue gained momentum continuing to make news and reporters interviewed Ori, we were scolded for not referring the press to BBI's president or executive director.

I may have hastened our ultimate clash with BBI by deciding to retire as I approached my 75th birthday. After seven years as chairperson, I wanted to concentrate on writing about Great-Grandfather "Alphabet" Browne. We persuaded Dobra Marshall, a long-time supporter and board member, to take my place. The museum honored my retirement with a benefit reception at the Israeli ambassador's residence. Marcia, Bill, and Jacob came to celebrate with me and it sold out to capacity.

Then the crash came. Weeks later, Ori returned from his first vacation since taking the job and found his dismissal notice, effective immediately and without the organization even giving him access to his personal belongings. I had to retrieve them for him. They cited sexism in the workplace as the reason, but none of us who worked with him as volunteers had ever seen any indication of it. Our financial stalwarts and most other museum board members resigned immediately. I stayed on with Dobra to protect the collection.

This occurred only weeks before BBI's 1998 biennial convention in Jerusalem, which I had promised to attend. I was miserable throughout, even more so after the election for president. As I'd suspected, Richard Heideman had mostly shown friendship for the museum and for me personally to garner my support in his campaign. Ignoring the fact that museum members elected Dobra to succeed me at the museum, he appointed his wife, Phyllis, as both board chairperson and director. That buried our last hope for the museum, and we resigned.

Before things turned sour, when I still believed we could make the museum all that it could and should be, I had planned my 70th birthday party there, hoping to start a trend that would provide a new source of revenue. I wanted to encourage the use of it for celebrations, also hoping that, when the invitation specified "No gifts, please," guests would choose to make contributions to the museum.

The night before my birthday an ice storm came, stranding many local friends in their homes. Despite the weather, all but two out-of-town relatives and friends made it. At dinner Bill did a masterful job as emcee and I enjoyed it to the fullest, except for the fact that it didn't produce a lasting benefit for the museum.

Bill and Brenda hosted great parties for me in Atlanta for my 75th birthday and again for my 80th. The first was best because most of my friends were still alive and because of the marvelous toast that Bill wrote, which included congratulatory letters from Mother and Jack. Since most of the guests knew them, they enjoyed Bill's humor as much as I did.

Maury was with me for that party and the one in Washington.

When he turned 80 we celebrated twice, once on his actual birthday when I surprised him by getting all of his children and mine to Washington for it, and again eight months later in Erice when the Centro held a huge event, notifying him in advance so his children could be there. It began at twilight with a public reception in the main piazza with musicians and a buffet and continued with a banquet featuring the chef's trademark swordfish with sword intact. For dessert, the chef served his signature "volcano" cake depicting the map of Sicily in colorful frosting with a chocolate Mt. Etna aflame.

For Thanksgiving 2001, with both Kislinger daughters at eastern universities, they and their parents joined us and my Rothschild family in Washington. I stashed an incredible amount of food. Raquel, Maury's daughter, brought even more, and we had a great celebration with all the kids plus two of their friends staying at my apartment. None of us suspected it was our last time together.

In December the cold, gloomy aspect of Erice foreboded sadness. I sensed that it would be my last trip there but I didn't know why. We spent a fascinating two days in Palermo as guests of its Rotary Club and took a beautiful Sunday drive so I could see Agrigento, with sunny, spring-like weather both times when we came down from the mountain. That day in Agrigento, with no incident to trigger it, I began to feel a crack in our relationship. Maury was beginning to unnerve me. Never had I been close to someone with so fragile an ego. The gentlest contradiction offended him. I knew that my growing impatience was hurtful and eventually would cause an acrimonious break. It would be better to separate before that happened, but I didn't know how to end things, so I did nothing.

For several years I'd attended conventions of NAORRR, the National Association of Retired Reform Rabbis. At times, Maury considered going with me to reconnect with rabbis he'd known at the *yeshiva*. In January 2002 he planned to go, but at the last minute changed his mind. I don't remember why, but I'm grateful he did. It was *beshert*.

Sixteen

LOVE STORY

Gunther and Elizabeth Plaut had been Jack's close friends since they first met at Hebrew Union College and later became mine when Jack and I married. When Jack spoke in Gunther's Toronto congregation we stayed at their home, as Gunther did with us when he spoke in Atlanta. He was the only one among Jack's contemporaries who treated me as if I had a brain, and we developed a warm, yet truly platonic, relationship. I never thought of the possibility that it might become anything else.

When Gunther visited us in the late 1950s he was writing a history of Jews in Minnesota and remained in his room working until mid-morning. Later, as we chatted over coffee, he asked me if I cared to read what he'd written. He then discussed it with me, which I deeply appreciated as it further indicated his recognition of my ability. I didn't realize it at the time, but he was fast becoming recognized by his colleagues as a leading scholar of their generation. To this day he is perhaps best known for the Torah commentary that he edited and mostly wrote, first published in the 1970s. It has long been the standard *Chumash* of the Reform Movement.

Jack and I spent time with Gunther and Elizabeth at conferences, some of them in Europe and Israel. After Jack died I saw them only twice, once when David had a meeting in Toronto and Elizabeth took me sightseeing, and another time when Gunther spoke in Washington and we took them to dinner.

I only learned of Elizabeth's stroke in 2001, when the Union of American Hebrew Congregations (which would change its name two years later to the Union for Reform Judaism) met in Washington and I happened to see Gunther at services. He looked terrible. She had been in a hopelessly vegetative condition for more than a year. After a quick hug and a few words, he went his way and I went mine.

It didn't occur to me that I would see him at the 2002 NAORRR meeting in Fort Lauderdale, but he was there and gave the sermon on Shabbat morning. He spoke of his determination to continue professional engagements throughout those two painful years, visiting Elizabeth every day that he was in town, looking into eyes that focused but gave no sign of recognition.

After the customary hug and "Shabbat shalom" following services at NAORRR, Gunther asked me to go for a walk, saying that exercise was the one thing he couldn't live without. That's when I learned he was more than just a good tennis player who easily beat Jack; he was an accomplished athlete. He had been an amateur soccer player in Europe before World War II and played on the German team at the 2nd Maccabiah Games, held in the British Mandate of Palestine in 1935. He was such a devout Zionist that his mother suspected he would remain there after the games ended. He returned home, but that same year he departed for the United States along with four other promising young scholars who were saved from the Holocaust by scholarships to Hebrew Union College in Cincinnati.

We spoke of many things on that Shabbat morning walk, but most memorable for me was his story about his parents being continually denied entry to America after the war. Following repeated refusals, he appealed in person to a Congressional committee that questioned him harshly and continued to deny his application without giving a reason. His friend Hubert Humphrey, upon going to Washington, obtained the visas for them as well as the reason why they had been denied: our State Department considered his parents a risk because Gunther belonged to a Zionist organization.

After our walk, we sat together at the Shabbat luncheon. Friends at the same table told me that even then they suspected something was happening between us. I didn't realize it. I went on a boat tour with some of the women while he spent the afternoon and evening with relatives in Palm Beach. We planned to get together for a drink after the meeting that night if it wasn't too late.

It was too late.

By the next morning I realized that something was going on inside my head that I couldn't turn off. I slept fitfully, and kept waking up thinking of Gunther. Only once before had that happened to me, also when I wasn't consciously seeking it and couldn't understand why it was happening. That was the night I met David.

Again I was mystified. I found Maury increasingly annoying and I found myself increasingly unable to conceal that annoyance. I wondered when his fragile ego would find that unacceptable but hadn't thought of proactively ending our relationship. I was so busy and content with the rest of my life that I had no problem ignoring my dissatisfaction with him.

Gunther and I sat together at breakfast the next morning and at the closing dinner. Another rabbi had invited me to lunch and I tried to concentrate on him for the moment, unsuccessfully. After dinner Gunther lacked the patience for sitting through the program and asked me to call him when it was over, which I did. He came to my room.

Neither of us spoke our hearts then, nor could we predict the future even inwardly to ourselves. He was about to begin a six-week intensive treatment for prostate cancer and was putting his life on hold until after that.

The next morning, as I sat in the lobby with friends awaiting the airport shuttle, he walked past me on his way out with only a slight pause and a smile to say goodbye. At the door, he turned to give me a hurried glance. Recalling it sustained me through the weeks that followed.

Meanwhile, what was I to do about Maury? I knew I had to break up with him, but how? Should I say that I was in love with someone else when the affair hadn't even really begun? As far as I knew, it was only in my head. I knew that Gunther wasn't like other rabbis whose passes I ignored, but circumstances might cause him to suppress any feelings he had for me. To pursue a relationship while Elizabeth lingered was, at the very least, questionable.

I had no contact with Gunther other than a brief note thanking me for sending him my latest book he had requested and a brief note he wrote in return on my letter responding to it.

As for my relationship with Maury, a woman in her late seventies can easily avoid sex with an understanding partner, but I was still at a loss as to how to tell him my true reason for refusing.

Our social life was as closely bound as if we were married. We had obligations with mutual friends, especially with Ruth and Robert St. John, who introduced us. They were still throwing wonderful dinner parties, which she prepared and he, at age 99, served. Our last time there we held our breath as we watched him fill each of our plates at the buffet and bring them to the table. As Robert's 100th birthday approached, Maury asked me to make arrangements to take them to dinner ahead of the official celebrations. Ruth suggested doing it on my birthday, a month before his, and I enjoyed that in spite of worrying about how to tell Maury goodbye. When we gathered for dinner at the Israeli ambassador's residence on Robert's actual birthday in mid-March I still hadn't told him.

I forget when I told my children. Both of them knew and liked Gunther. I began studying his book, *The Torah: A Modern Commentary*. When I mentioned that to Marcia, she said it was wrong to study Torah alone, which led me to begin attending Torah Study at Washington Hebrew each Saturday morning. I've continued that practice at the Temple in Atlanta, and it remains my primary means of observing Shabbat.

One night around 11:30 I was in bed reading the *Commentary* when the telephone rang. I heard a low, sexy male voice and my heart leapt to the ceiling. "I hope I didn't wake you," the voice said. "What are you doing up so late?"

"Reading Commentary," I replied, as if in a dream.

"Whose?" the voice asked.

"Why *yours*, of course," I purred.

There was a pause. Then I realized my mistake and was horrified. It wasn't Gunther.

Ori had always known he could call me at any hour but it had been a long time since he needed to do so. He knew both me and Gunther well enough to grasp the situation.

All I could do was stammer, "I don't know what's going to happen. Please don't say anything."

He reassured me and I knew I could trust him.

The following week I had appointments in Atlanta and a speaking engagement in Columbus. I worried the whole time. When I confided in my family, daughter-in-law Brenda advised me to break it to Maury as soon as possible, warning, "At his age it could bring on a heart attack."

When I returned, Maury and I were scheduled to go to a concert on Friday night and a dinner party on Saturday so he stayed overnight at my place. I told him over breakfast Saturday morning, saying that we could always be friends but no longer partners. He was hurt and angry, but as aware as I that we had family and friends to consider. I called his children who, along with his grandchildren, remain close to me even today.

Telling mutual friends at home was more difficult. We agreed to go to the dinner party we'd accepted for that night without saying anything, but were thoroughly miserable doing so.

Four nights later we were due at Vivienne and Al Arking's home in suburban Rockville for Seder. Knowing that the news would spoil the holiday for them, we waited until after Pesach to tell them. Being together with them for the Seder was much easier for both of us than the previous weekend's dinner party had been. As I later learned, the reason was not entirely due to time lapse or different company. Maury had renewed an old relationship who soon became his fiancée and, six months later, his wife. So much for any concern about causing a heart attack.

It felt like years, but it was only six weeks after leaving Ft. Lauderdale before Gunther and I connected by telephone and email. He taught me wonderful expressions in Hebrew that I would never have learned in synagogue. Some of them are in Scriptures (*Shir ha-Shirim*), but we're taught that those apply to God's love for mankind. Sadly, a recent bout of cyber virus erased these messages from my computer. But not from my heart.

When Gunther's treatments were over he received a good report and quickly called me to begin making plans. He was boxed in throughout April with speaking engagements, the last of them being in Brooklyn, after which he had two days free. He suggested that I meet him there, go with him to his lecture, and then go into Manhattan together for the remaining time.

I felt like a giddy 20-year-old. Beth Pierce, my shopping maven friend in Baltimore, lured me to an elegant lingerie shop there to outfit me for the event.

On the appointed weekend, I flew to New York on Saturday morning to spend the afternoon with Jacob, see his set-up as a newly established business consultant, and have dinner with him. He took me for a walk in Central Park, led us to a Japanese restaurant for excellent sushi, and then put me in a cab headed for Brooklyn. We had a great time together and if he had any misgivings about his grandmother's rash behavior he didn't voice them.

As for me, I wasn't too comfortable asking the hotel clerk for the key to a man's room, but Gunther had instructed me to do so and I complied, reminding myself that this was Greater New York in the 21st century and I was well past the age of innocence.

Gunther was flying in from the west coast so I knew he would be late checking in. I tried in vain to check my excitement, bathed and slithered into my slinky new aqua satin ensemble, and tried to get interested in whatever was on television. (Unsuccessfully, of course.)

The next morning, Rabbi Stanley and Marianne Dreyfus picked

us up to take us to the synagogue where Gunther was speaking and to lunch afterward. Then we took a cab to Manhattan and checked into the Roosevelt for the next two days. Jacob joined us there for dinner and we had a lovely evening with him.

Gunther and I did emerge from our hotel twice during our two days in New York. Neither of us had seen the then-new Museum of Jewish Heritage downtown on the Battery, and he especially wanted to go because his mother's ring of keys she possessed as housekeeper for the Jewish orphanage in Berlin that his father directed were there on display. She took them with her when they fled Nazi Germany.

On our second day we emerged in the late afternoon to meet Gunther's friends, Eugene and Emily Grant, for dinner. They were due at Christie's for an Israel-related fundraising event so they took us with them, which gave us little chance to visit. We made an early departure since neither Gunther nor I wanted to hear the speeches.

Gunther returned to Toronto the next morning. I had lunch with my dear, lifelong friend Blanche Ross and then returned to Washington. But not for long. I promised Gunther I'd come to Toronto in early June.

I gave serious thought to what I anticipated would be a secret relationship in Toronto. Elizabeth, although hopelessly unresponsive, was still alive. Remembering my closeted relationship with David while he awaited his divorce, I steeled myself for a similar situation. We'd be living in a cocoon, unable to risk being seen together in public, meeting only his closest friends.

Those thoughts were unwarranted. As we drove out of the airport, Gunther asked if I would like to stop by the country club for lunch. Between the door and our table, he introduced me to what seemed like half of Toronto's Jewish community.

I had never met either of his children although he had known mine for many years. His daughter Judith, like Marcia single and a special education teacher, came to visit when she returned from work that afternoon. I met his son Jonathan and his wife Carole on my next visit

Janice and Gunther Plaut

when they made their monthly trip from Detroit to Toronto to check on their parents. All three welcomed me warmly.

Gunther and I often reminded ourselves of how lucky we were. Imagine, at our age—he a few months short of 90 and I at 79—ecstatic like teenagers in the first throes of young love! Even better, we were free of its constrictions. We spoke often of our gratitude, most aware of it as we stood in his kitchen at midnight locked in each other's arms, looking out at the lights of the city. Amazed at our good fortune, we were thankful beyond words to be alive and well and together while there was still time.

Not much time, we knew. But we never perceived how very little.

Our days began late. Most mornings we stayed in bed for hours, just talking. Or singing. Sometimes we awakened each other with a song, each of us off-key but close enough to the real melody for the other to recognize it. Our favorite, "La Marseillaise," remained a rallying cry for us, stirring us as it does the French in good times and in bad. Often he awakened me with Hebrew songs not set to music, poetry attributed to King Solomon.

One of the things I most enjoyed was our banter in a mixture of languages. He was completely fluent in German, French and Hebrew. The only one that I could manage to any useful degree was French, but I so yearned to be multilingual that I reveled in having the opportunity to use it and to learn as much as I could of Hebrew and German. He taught me nursery rhymes in German, some of which I wrote down, hoping to remember. What he taught me in Hebrew was love.

Gunther often spoke of Jack when we were alone reminiscing. He suspected, as David did, that my marriage to Jack had been less than perfect, but although both men knew him and admired him, Gunther knew him on a more personal level. He often reminded me of Jack's greatness, which made me appreciate and love both of them even more.

Except on Shabbat, when we went to services, we began each day's activity with a drive out Bathurst Street to the hospital to see Elizabeth. I went upstairs with him my first day there and thought I detected a slight change of expression on her face when she saw me. He said it only denoted that she saw something different. She hadn't recognized him or anyone else in over two years.

After that first time, Gunther asked me to stay in the car for his few minutes with her in order to save him the long walk from a parking space. On our way home he stopped at Holy Blossom Temple to pick up mail and messages, always greeting members of the office staff with an exuberant, "How are you? And why not?" On most days he would then usher me into the staff break room, partake of coffee and whatever goodies were being passed around, and stay a while to *kibbitz* with any of the staff free to stay.

On one of those visits he showed me through the building, all the way to the remote space on the top floor that he had chosen as a retirement office. In the far corner, dominating the small cluttered room, was a life-size bronze sculpture of an old man blessing a young boy, a masterfully detailed piece that he himself had made. I was amazed. Even those of his colleagues who knew him well, who visited in his home as we had done, did not know that he was a sculptor. I then realized that he had also made the several small pieces that I admired in his apartment, human figures in action. I especially loved one of a runner in flight that he kept on the ledge between his kitchen and the breakfast table. He wrote my name on its base, intending for me to have it someday.

We often spent summer afternoons at the country club. On Shabbat his daughter Judith would meet us there for lunch on the terrace overlooking the golf course and play a few rounds with him afterward. On other days, he began taking me with him in the cart and I helped him retrieve balls. I loved it, unaware that club rules prohibited a non-player being on the course. When the law caught up with him I began bringing a book to read while he shot a few holes alone. The weather was beautiful, not too warm, and breezy enough to appreciate without having it ruffle the pages. When cold weather set in, he played tennis indoors with the pro at a city club and I watched from a comfortable observer's perch above. Some days we walked around the top of a bluff near his apartment for exercise.

I stayed in Toronto a week on my first visit, after which Gunther came back to Washington to spend the next week. The first day there, as we were about to pass Washington Hebrew Congregation on our way home from the grocery store, he asked to stop in briefly to say hello to his colleague, WHC's senior rabbi, Bruce Lustig. We told Bruce that we'd see him the next morning at Torah study. He apparently announced it at services that night because when we arrived the next morning, there were so many people that they could hardly make room at the table for us. As might have been expected, Bruce asked *rabbeinu*—"our teacher"—to lead the class.

When the session ended, one of the group invited us to her home for a Havdalah service and supper that evening. It was a moving experience for me. Ending Shabbat with friends, arms linked and swaying as we sang "Eliyahu haNavi" and wished each other "*Shavua tov*," gave me a visceral appreciation of the Sabbath that I'd never had. Being unfamiliar with most Jewish traditions I tended to dislike them, but this one suddenly grabbed me. Gunther found it meaningful, too, so we began observing it regularly. On weekends that we were separated we did it by telephone, each holding our candle, he in Toronto and I in Washington, reciting the blessings in unison and wishing each other a week of peace, a week of joy, which it continued to be. One day in Washington I took him to the

Hirshhorn Museum on the National Mall to see the towering outdoor steel sculpture that was used pictured on the cover of his book, *The Magen David*, published by B'nai B'rith as a memorial to my husband David. Seen from the inside looking straight up at the sky, its beams form a six-pointed star. As I lay on the ground trying to photograph Gunther in front of that star image, a couple of Japanese tourists awaiting their turn to enter eyed us quizzically. When we explained, they offered to photograph both of us looking up at the star.

On yet another memorable afternoon we visited Ruth and Robert St. John. Robert's health was beginning to fail, but he seemed eager to meet Gunther and the feeling was mutual. Gunther's special reason for wanting to meet Robert was to thank him for keeping Elizabeth aware of his whereabouts in the final weeks of WWII. Gunther was a chaplain with the 104th Division in the vanguard of the American forces, and Robert's newscasts on NBC gave some indication of their location as they fought their way towards Germany.

Sadly, that was the last time I saw Robert. He died the following winter while we were in California.

After our first weeks together, both Gunther and I had commitments that kept us apart for a while. Mine were deadlines, a speaking engagement, Marcia arriving the day after Gunther left, Jacob visiting for a few days, then Marcia and I reserving a few days at the beach before meeting our entire Rothschild-Levinson family in Philadelphia for David's sister Jean's and her husband Cal's 50th anniversary celebration. I planned a few days alone in Washington to catch my breath before returning to Toronto. Gunther couldn't wait that long. When Marcia and I returned to Washington I found a message saying he would be there the next afternoon.

After that visit, we flew to Toronto together. I stayed a week, then came home. Ten days later, I joined him and his family in Detroit for the birth of his first great-grandchild. This was yet another incredibly beautiful day for me. I can't describe the joy I felt as I held the baby and shared those precious moments with Gunther.

After Detroit, I went home to prepare for Gunther's arrival in Washington a few days later. I made tennis dates for him, set up plans for us to go to dinner with friends, and called others to invite them for Shabbat dinners at home. After ten days we parted for five before I returned to Canada for the High Holy Days.

It was wonderful to be in Toronto then, going to services at Holy Blossom Congregation with Gunther preceded by dinners at the homes of his friends, a decades-long tradition for him and his family. We attended services on the early shift which meant an extra-long fast on Yom Kippur, but for the first time ever I felt no pangs of hunger beginning at three o'clock and no headache at four. The cantor dragged out closing prayers until long after dark, so it was eight o'clock before we reached our destination for the breakfast, but I still felt no rush to eat. That benefit of newfound romance has remained intact.

Since his retirement, it had become a tradition for Gunther to give a brief sermon on Yom Kippur morning, and hearing it was the highlight of the day for me. A few days later, we stopped to pet a dog while walking on the bluff and the young woman holding his leash introduced herself, saying that as an adult she always asked her father to bring her to the morning service to hear Gunther's sermon. For me, that awakened long-dormant memories of gratifying moments as a rabbi's wife.

I'd never thought to ask Gunther about the small ribbon he wore in his lapel, similar to the French Legion of Honor. One night a stranger in the elevator with us noticed and asked, "Is that what I think it is?"

"Yes, it is," Gunther replied with a modest smile as the elevator stopped at our floor. When we got off, I asked what it was. It was Canada's national honor, the Order of Canada, second in prestige only to the Order of Merit and comparable to the U.S. Presidential Medal of Freedom. Gunther was named a "Companion," highest of the three ranks within the Order of Canada itself.

Gunther had told me that his congregation was planning a celebration for his 90th birthday on November 1, 2002, and I prayed that I could be there to share it with him. I was, but my joy was slightly clouded by a first hint of what the future had in store for us. That morning, brought on perhaps by the excitement, he had a frightening episode where he lost his temper. He made me promise not to report it to his children.

His children, grandchildren, and their spouses arrived in the afternoon, as did Rabbi Stephen Franklin, a former assistant who had been closer to Gunther than any other. The congregation poured out its love at the evening service and reception afterward. Knowing that my turn would come later, I didn't attempt to stay close as the well-wishers crowded around the family. The following night his children hosted a dinner party at the country club, inviting his closest friends, and we sat together all evening with his arm around me, exuding happiness.

I stayed in Toronto for two and a half weeks, then came home alone for a few days before he joined me for Thanksgiving and Hanukkah. Jacob came for Thanksgiving. In those three weeks Gunther and I began to settle into something of a routine, each of us continuing to write and discuss our work with each other. He wrote his weekly column for the *Canadian Jewish News* and asked my opinion before sending it in, while I drew heavily on his scholarship for *Prophet in a Time of Priests*. He laboriously deciphered my copies of Browne's letters to Herzl, written in German, providing me with an authentic translation after seeing and despairing over the translation originally given me by a German-speaking friend unfamiliar with 19th-century scholarly discourse.

We parted briefly, with plans for me to come to Toronto on Christmas ten days later. It was then that we suffered a first, mutually terrifying experience.

Gunther was not at the airport to meet me. It was snowing heavily, so at first I suspected he'd been delayed by having to drive slowly. After a while, with no call from him on my cell phone, I became worried and called his apartment. No one answered. Judith was away for the holidays and I didn't know who else to call. After waiting two hours with no word, I called the number he had given me for his driver service and went to his apartment. He had just arrived, frantic both from his own experience and from worrying about mine. He'd missed a turn in the road and, blinded by the snow, couldn't read the signs and lost his way.

I understood then why his children begged me not to let him drive. I thought they were being overly cautious because his reflexes were perfect and his judgment on speed and traffic better than that of any man I'd driven with since Jack died. Now I detected something else. I suspected it was a decline in his memory of routes and perhaps in his ability to read directional signs while driving that gave his children concern. He must have realized it too, because from that day on, without discussing it, he let me take the wheel and he no longer went to the airport without a driver.

Meanwhile, we enjoyed our winter holiday week and I learned something of British culture. Gunther told me that Boxing Day was an extension of Christmas reserved for repackaging and returning unwanted gifts, not, as I had naively assumed, a commemoration of the Boxer Rebellion or something having to do with prizefighting.

I went home on New Year's Day to prepare for a six-week stay with Gunther in southern California. Jonathan had called during the summer to ask if I was willing to do it and said he would make the arrangements. He had been urging his parents to escape winter in Toronto for years, but Elizabeth never wanted to go. I welcomed it, and we planned to attend the NAORRR conference in San Diego in January, so we asked Jonathan to make reservations for us in Palm Springs.

At some point during the fall Gunther and I learned that Jonathan had not given the travel agent confirmation for the hotel she suggested, and by then it was too late to get reservations there. Rabbi Erv Herman and his wife Aggie, who lived near San Diego, highly recommended Paradise Point, so we went there for a week following the conference. We couldn't stay longer because the hotel was filled for the 2003 Super Bowl, to be played in San Diego.

At the conference, colleagues treated us as if we were honeymooners. Rabbi Irv Bloom and his wife Pat, then the managing secretaries for NAORRR, saved us a room on the VIP floor, and other friends arranged a tennis foursome for Gunther. We attended only the sessions that intrigued us, mostly spending our time socializing. When it was over, we rented a car and checked into Paradise Point.

Paradise Point was a beautiful resort with at least one very good restaurant on the property, but it was much more conducive to weekends away than for longer stays. I took a few tennis lessons; Gunther watched and supervised my practice. When the pro had free time after my lesson, he hit balls with Gunther. We rarely used the car there but needed it for excursions elsewhere, like to nearby La Jolla, and into San Diego for services and dinner with Rabbi Martin and Anita Lawson. At the resort we either walked or hopped onto one of the carts that shuttled guests within the property.

We enjoyed Paradise Point but were not sorry to leave after ten days. I gladly took the wheel for our drive north into the desert, as unimpressed with the bland scenery as I had been with our resort experience.

The company of friends wintering in the Palm Springs area improved our outlook, but only a little. Our accommodations, while adequate, were far from the developments where our friends had homes or rented condos for the season. We drove long and far to be with them, and did not encourage them to visit us. Josh Shubin, a friend from Atlanta, came once or twice to play tennis with Gunther. Others, mostly Gunther's friends from Toronto or his earlier pulpit in St. Paul, invited us for lunch and an afternoon of golf for the men. Lynn Selig Zimmerman, whom I hadn't seen in the thirty years since she married and left Atlanta, reconnected with me and was wonderful, offering guest privileges for Gunther to play tennis at her club and getting us tickets for a sold-out symphony concert. When we went to services one Shabbat, the rabbi entreated Gunther to preach for him the following week and invited us to his home for dinner. It was so far away that Gunther had another anxiety attack and wanted me to turn around and go back before we ever arrived. I didn't, but it furthered my fear of his oncoming dementia.

Both of us brought laptops with which we attempted to continue our usual work. Gunther managed to produce whatever columns were due for the *Canadian Jewish News,* and occasionally I tried to work on my book but with little progress. We sometimes took walks, but only around our complex because it was on a major highway that wasn't safe to cross on foot. Once we indulged in the outdoor hot tub but weren't inspired by it or the swimming pool, which did not lend itself to serious swimming. Once my nephew David Levinson came over from L.A. with his family. His daughter Michelle, about four at the time, gave Gunther some fun and exercise playing hide-and-seek with her. We spent part of one day sightseeing at a lovely park with a memorial to victims of the Holocaust. There, stopping at a panel describing General Eisenhower's horrifying visit to a concentration camp, Gunther reminisced about his own experience as the Jewish Chaplain attached to the group that liberated another camp, Mittelbau-Dora. It had a profound and lasting impact on him.

I had a pleasant three weeks in California but realized fully why Elizabeth didn't want to make a habit of spending winters there. She was a serious, accomplished genealogist who enjoyed her work as I enjoy mine, and like me had no athletic inclinations to whet her enthusiasm for diversions that Gunther relished, such as tennis and golf. I began thinking of a better way to avoid the snow in future years.

We returned to our respective homes via a stop in Atlanta over my birthday. I'd set Gunther up with Harry Popkin for a day of golf at the club, and while they played I inquired about guest membership for the following winter. I reasoned that this, along with a three-month rental apartment in Atlanta, would be both cheaper and more enjoyable for both of us than another season in vacationland. It never occurred to me that we wouldn't have another year together.

Jonathan had called me earlier to ask if I was willing to go with his father to two speaking engagements, weekends in residence in Greensboro, North Carolina and St. Paul, Minnesota. He wouldn't confirm them otherwise because he realized that his father could no longer go alone.

After two weeks apart in our homes, Gunther came to Washington and I drove us to Greensboro, thinking he would enjoy the beautiful road trip. I was wrong and regretted my mistake the whole weekend. Gunther became agitated during the drive and remained so throughout the trip. In St. Paul with his former congregation, surrounded by old friends in a familiar setting, he suffered no anxiety and the visit was pure pleasure for both of us.

Between the two rabbi-in-resident trips, we attended a few sessions of the 2003 CCAR convention, in Washington that year, and delighted in greeting old friends. I invited some of his younger colleagues along with several close contemporaries for Shabbat dinner. We heard Eli Weisel and former Secretary of State Madeleine Albright speak, both Gunther's friends, and visited with them afterward.

Not having attended a CCAR convention in the thirty years since Jack died, I was unprepared for the sea change that time had wrought. Crossing the Shoreham Hotel's lobby was sometimes hazardous due to crawling toddlers tended by their dads. Another insight to progress was seeing a rabbi leave a session to nurse her baby.

The conference, however, was not without a darker side for us. Gunther had another episode of impatience one afternoon as I was taking him and the Blooms to see the cherry blossoms. His condition had worsened.

When I went with him for his annual checkup in Toronto, his doctor told me to stop thinking of the future. He told Gunther, "We have your physical condition well in hand. You're in good shape there. I think it's time for you to get an evaluation of the *other* part of your well-being. I'll make the appointment for you."

That took longer than we expected. The SARS epidemic had just hit Toronto. The diagnostic office to which his internist sent him was in the same hospital where Elizabeth was, and although Gunther could visit her, he couldn't see a doctor because all the offices were closed. In order to contain the epidemic only essential personnel and patients' next of kin could enter hospitals.

Meanwhile, we continued to enjoy our life together. We celebrated Passover with Seder at the home of Elizabeth's best friend, as the Plauts were accustomed to do. I brought the haroset, which I would never have offered to make had I realized that Elizabeth hadn't equipped her kitchen with a food processor. We attended a symphony concert we might not have attempted had we realized that, due to the epidemic, we couldn't hold onto bannister and escalator railings as usual, even wearing gloves, because they too might touch our face. We clutched the rail through the sleeves of our coats. Attending public gatherings, even worship services, challenged everyone. As the service ended, the rabbi regularly reminded everyone not to greet each other with embraces or handshakes, but only with a smile and "Shabbat shalom."

Our spirits soared one day when Gunther received a call from HUC/JIR in Cincinnati, inviting him to its forthcoming graduation ceremonies to be awarded an honorary doctoral degree. Despite having already received ten or more honorary doctorates from other prestigious schools, this meant more than all the others because it was his beloved alma mater. Why had this not occurred sooner? His answer was to remind me that the seminary's still-powerful professor emeritus Rabbi Eugene Mihaly, with whom he had publicly disputed for many years, had just died.

That weekend in Cincinnati was our last trip together. Gunther's dementia clearly revealed itself. Pride, anguish, love, joy, and sorrow engulfed me throughout. His children served as life support for both of us.

In mid-June Judith and I took Gunther for his examination, grimly expecting the diagnosis he received. Apparently, so did he. Outwardly, he accepted it as if he had been told he had the flu.

His equanimity held until bedtime. Alone with me in the darkness, anguish engulfed him. He couldn't sleep. I tried to comfort him but he knew better than to be fooled by words. I could only hold him closer and assure him that I would always be there for him—which I naively believed I could be. I knew nothing of how Alzheimer's progressed.

Gunther was still able to take care of himself personally but needed live-in companionship for the periods when I couldn't be with him.

We didn't anticipate early need for professional caregivers but thanks to Rabbi John Moscowitz, then the senior rabbi at Holy Blossom, we learned of two excellent ones: a married couple from the Philippines who were newly available due to the death of their long-time patient. It seemed prudent to meet them while the opportunity prevailed. Judith joined us for the interview and was as favorably impressed as we were. Gunther related to them instantly. I stayed for the next few weeks until they were ready to begin.

I went home in mid-August, planning to return to Toronto for the Holidays some four weeks later. On September 13, Judith called to tell me that her mother had died. The family did not want me to be there for the funeral, during the week-long *shiva,* or for the upcoming Holy Days.

After catching my breath and expressing condolences, I said that I would honor their wishes but would still visit between the *shiva* and the Holidays because Gunther expected to see me. After the excitement died down, he would remember and wonder why I wasn't there. I came the day after their *shiva* ended, stayed four days, flew to Atlanta in time for dinner with Bill and Brenda on *erev* Rosh Hashanah, and returned to Washington for Yom Kippur. Home and alone, I appreciated as never before the benefit of spending that day of meditation in the synagogue.

It soon became apparent that I had to stop going to Toronto. Because I didn't live there and couldn't see him continuously, Gunther had periods of severe agitation before I arrived and after I left. I understood that it would be in his best interest to let me fade from his memory. When I discussed the situation with Jonathan he agreed that I should exit gradually by shortening my visits and lengthening the time between them. The caregivers, Ray and Arline, removed my pictures from his tables and my telephone number from beside his bed, but that didn't prevent him from calling me daily. He dialed directory assistance.

I still don't fully understand why Jonathan and Judith immediately began treating me as if I were the enemy. It compounded my sense of loss to be cut off from familial communication with them. My only contacts other than Gunther himself were Ray and Arline, who were friendly, open, and honest with me.

Except for the period immediately after Elizabeth died, Gunther called me every day as usual. Visits were less joyful than before. I returned for a week over his birthday, and for a few days in mid-December following a speaking engagement in Detroit. There Jonathan and Carole took me to lunch and he was again friendly—possibly due to three martinis, but I was too grateful to need a reason. It provided a happy memory.

In January 2004 I flew to Atlanta and, with Marcia, drove the rest of the way to Ft. Lauderdale for the NAORRR conference. Our rabbinic friends were all-embracing, even electing me to the NAORRR board for the coming term.

Bill scheduled a big party for my 80th birthday that year, a week ahead of the actual day because he and Brenda planned to be away on February 13. Since Gunther still called me daily and was aware of what he was missing, I spent my actual birthday in Toronto with him. We celebrated at home with Judith and the Shiers, Gunther's closest friends, and enjoyed a traditional Philippine dinner prepared by Ray and Arline.

When Ray drove us to the airport for my departure I tried not to let Gunther know that this was the last, but he must have sensed it. We stood together by the car, holding each other in a tight embrace as we had done in his kitchen on glowing nights less than two years before. We looked in each other's eyes, loving, searching, reading what we could not say. Then we kissed, long and hard, and I walked into the terminal.

Throughout the next few months Gunther continued to call at least once each day, still getting my number from directory assistance. By late spring he had declined so much that he forgot we'd spoken the moment we finished and called again, repeatedly, until I forced myself not to answer. That ended in June.

I never stopped wondering how he was getting along, yearning to speak with someone who could tell me. But no one called me. My relationship with Judith had ended. I tried calling Jonathan twice, actually hoping that Carole would answer so I could talk with her, but both times Jonathan answered. He said nothing about Gunther and left me with the clear impression that he would rather not hear from me again.

After that, my only word came from an occasional call or visit with friends who had seen Gunther, and what they told me was worse than not knowing. His towering mind had died. It would be eight more years before his body followed.

Seventeen
STRETCHING THE SUNSET

I didn't fold when Jack and David passed away, and I was determined not to fold now. My mind told me I could handle it.

My body ruled otherwise. I didn't think of the different circumstance; this time no one knew I was bereaved and needed help. Nor did I remember our disbelief when David's sleep problem was diagnosed as geriatric depression, probably stemming from his having assumed that deep angsts had been dissolved when in fact they were still there, suppressed and manifesting themselves internally.

My symptoms, vague but recurring body aches, had begun almost a year earlier, in 2003 in Toronto, assuaged by a therapist who practiced Eastern medicine, moving her hands above me without touching me. Relief was temporary. Now a pain in my breast became so bothersome it interfered with my writing. Two mammograms assured me it wasn't cancer, which relieved my mind but not my body. Eventually my doctor, unable to identify the cause of the pain, heeded my request to authorize therapeutic massage, which did relieve it.

Recognizing the need for company, I invited friends for Shabbat dinner each week and urged them not only to consider the invitation a standing one but also for them to bring others. "Just notify me by Wednesday night so I'll know how much food to buy," I told them.

Having no special man in my life gave me more time for other friends and more appreciation of their relationships with me. Carole Ashkinaze, a prize-winning journalist currently freelancing, subscribed to the Shakespeare Theater with me and advised me about my own writing. Cecily Abram became a close friend, sharing common interests and support for each other's projects. I now realize that these women fulfilled the age-old admonition to seek friends of a younger generation, but I didn't think of it at the time. They gradually moved into spaces in my life formerly filled by near-contemporaries like Adelaide and Marge, who were now restrained by age-induced disabilities.

The friend who generated most new vistas for me was Georgetown University professor Rabbi Harold White—considerably younger than I and surely not a candidate for romance, but a friend since I joined his interfaith study group in 1990. Now we bonded as confidantes and frequent companions. He seemed to understand my loneliness, as I believe I understood his, having many friends but no partner. He became my mentor and I his sounding board.

Harold was a zestful companion for appreciating life's blessings, whether it be an impromptu invitation to spend the day in the mountains viewing fall foliage, a night at the opera, or an early spring excursion to Chincoteague to walk on the windy beach. He spent summers at Martha's Vineyard in a small cottage with acreage on which to indulge his passion for gardening and invited me to visit him there, which I did regularly for several years. A week at the Vineyard each summer restored my sense of serenity.

Harold was one of the few friends who took me at my word about bringing others to my Friday night dinners, which friends began calling "Janice's Shabbat Salons." Once he brought a visiting professor from Israel, Michael Oren, who returned to Washington a few years later as Israel's ambassador to the United States. Another time Harold brought Max Kampelman, the distinguished American diplomat who led international denuclearization missions for presidents Carter, Reagan and Bush. We became friends and occasionally went out to dinner together.

My own experience during the civil rights period drew invitations to speak to history classes at American University and NCU in Chapel Hill. Harold invited me to do the same for Shabbat services at his Eastern Shore congregation in Maryland and his Hillel congregation at Georgetown, the latter a special annual event known as Hallelujah Shabbat. Various African American churches participated. He wanted me to talk about my friendship with Martin and Coretta King, which terrified me lest I seem disrespectful by referring to them informally, as I knew them. My fears were unwarranted. The church members encouraged me throughout with choruses of "Amen!"

Representatives of two of the congregations invited me to speak at Sunday night services. One of them especially pleased Harold, who happily noted, "That's where the recovering drug addicts and former convicts go."

I didn't share his enthusiasm, but he assured me he'd be with me for support (and protection, if necessary).

The experience was an eye-opener for me. Focusing on personal show-and-tell, one of the speakers described her life as a tenant farmer's child who had to stay home from school during harvest season to pick cotton and demonstrated the back-breaking process of doing it.

My basic solace derived from writing. Expecting to return home to Atlanta when I grew old, I valued the opportunity to stay in touch there, one means being to submit a regular column for the bi-monthly *Jewish Georgian*. I called it "The Jewish Georgian in Washington" and began by reporting on other Georgia natives living there.

The imminent project on my work agenda then was to complete my research and write about Great-Grandfather "Alphabet" Browne. Days scouring microfilms of newspapers at the Library of Congress proved not only fruitful but also delightfully pleasant, especially in good weather when I brown-bagged lunch outside overlooking the back of the Capitol. Interesting encounters happened often. One day, on the escalator down to the subway station on my way home, I passed a man wearing the yellow robe of a Buddhist priest. He looked familiar. Someone standing alongside him on the escalator asked, "Are you who I think you are?" He nodded and posed for pictures when they reached the landing. He was the Dalai Lama.

Another day the surprise was less pleasant. I arrived to find the Library of Congress suddenly closed due to a threat of anthrax.

My research elsewhere led to surprising discoveries. It reconnected me with distant relatives and old friends in Atlanta and Columbus. At New York's Public Library, it developed like a scavenger hunt. The department head I contacted found nothing, but her colleague in Special Collections noticed her listing on the library internet and produced boxes of relevant documents in the collection of an attorney who handled Browne's litigation. His depositions revealed his childhood in Europe.

Another treasure chest opened when Harold met Tweed Roosevelt at Martha's Vineyard. Roosevelt said he was researching his great-grandfather, President Teddy, regarding his relationship with the Jews, whereupon Harold mentioned me, saying I was researching *my* great-grandfather, the rabbi who corresponded with his great-grandfather. Tweed wanted copies of my four letters from Teddy to Alphabet and called to thank me upon receiving them. In the course of our conversation he said, "I assume you've seen all of the other letters between them in the Library of Congress."

I had not. I forget what I told him, but the next morning I went to the Library and learned that presidential correspondence since the mid-nineteenth century had been microfilmed as a Works Progress Administration project in the Great Depression. I possessed all I needed from Roosevelt, but found reams of Great-Grandpa's correspondence with Benjamin Harrison, Howard Taft, and Woodrow Wilson, whom Browne encouraged to enter politics while Wilson was still president of Princeton. The letters provided a much-needed lesson in political history.

The project itself drew me into a final stage of recovery from the hovering twilight. The clouds parted, opening another era of sunshine.

Ori's and my 1990s dream of an international museum of Jewish culture in our nation's capital was still alive, but barely. We occasionally met with Jay Kaplan, the attorney who set up our 1993 meeting with Dr. Ghez in Geneva, and used his influence to get Congress to pass a bill on which the establishment of a National Jewish Museum had been placed as a rider. It reached the Senate floor, but died there. Jay also connected us to a major hotel chain vying to buy the old Post Office building and needing a non-profit cultural element to satisfy the zoning code. We met for lunch with its representatives several times, once even touring the property with its chief architect, but our good fortune tanked when Donald Trump outbid his competitor.

When B'nai B'rith had to sell its building at 17th and New Hampshire and move into cramped headquarters on an upper floor of a K Street office building, the museum collection went on life support. The ongoing Klutznick bequest, which specified an alternative recipient for its annual earnings should the museum be closed, provided salary for the part-time director. She became disenchanted, suspicious of BBI and its executive director, Dr. Sidney Clearfield, and began documenting what she observed. After resigning her position, she discussed her findings with Ori and me. We agreed that she had convincing evidence for a winning case in court, but that it would be inappropriate to air the dispute in public.

My chief concern was less for the museum's art than for the historical records it possessed. As America's oldest service organization by half a century, B'nai B'rith was endangering a primary source of American Jewry's collective heritage by permitting the rapid disintegration of its physical records in the damp, moldy basement of its building on Rhode Island Avenue. Rabbi Gary Zola, director of American Jewish Archives, authorized me to offer his services to have the records microfilmed immediately so as to save their substance, but B'nai B'rith officials ignored it.

Decades later, with BBI offices still cramped upstairs on K Street, I tipped an enterprising reporter from *The Forward* on sources for tracing the whereabouts of the museum's art and archives. He pursued it, forcing officials to reveal their storage location in Maryland. The publicity ultimately led to the museum's artifacts being placed in responsible institutions, properly maintained and accessible to the public. Most of the art went to the Skirball Museum at HUC/JIR in Cincinnati and the documents to the Jacob Rader Marcus Center for the American Jewish Archives on the same campus.

My wanderlust resurfaced in 2005 when Rabbi Joshua Haberman announced that he and Maxine were leading a cruise in the Adriatic and eastern Mediterranean. I'd already visited most of the ports on their itinerary and wasn't especially fond of cruising, but I joined anyway. With them leading the trip and Professor Marc Saperstein lecturing, I knew it would be interesting. Josh and Maxine arranged for me to share a cabin with the mother-in-law of one of their children. She provided delightful company, as did others in the group, but I hated the ship and realized unquestionably that luxuriating on a monstrous floating resort is not my idea of travel.

Soon afterward I learned that the Atlanta Temple's rabbi, Jeff Salkin, was leading a tour to Cuba. I joined it and was able to meet members of Havana's Jewish community and gain insights into their culture. I enjoyed every minute of it.

Since Marcia was no longer working, we began taking extended trips together. First we drove through New England, visiting Harold at Martha's Vineyard, attending a Union for Reform Judaism *Kallah* in New Hampshire, and wandering through the Berkshires where we viewed the remains of the Watts' home, Himmel on the Hill, the former headquarters of the Experiment in International Living in Putney, Vermont where I had lived and worked in 1946.

One day Marcia mentioned that a friend of hers was planning a joint bat mitzvah with her thirteen-year-old daughter, which gave me the idea of *us* having a joint bat mitzvah. Marcia agreed, and we set the date to coincide with my 83rd birthday, the traditional age for men to celebrate their second bar mitzvah. Our *parsha* was *B'shalach* (Exodus 17), which Marcia studied in Atlanta and I in Washington, first with Bruce Lustig, the senior rabbi of Washington Hebrew. When I realized he was treating me with kid gloves, wasting his own valuable time as well as mine, I managed a tactful transition to his young associate, Sue Shankman, whose grandfather, Rabbi Jacob Shankman, was Jack's close friend. Young as she was—it was only her first year on the job—Rabbi Sue related to me on a collegial level, encouraging me to learn the Hebrew my own way rather than that developed for twelve-year-olds.

After two sessions—six months ahead of the scheduled event—she declared me ready to read directly from the Torah. We entered the empty sanctuary, she turned on a light over the *bema*, rolled the Torah to *B'shalach*, and I read "Miriam's Song of the Sea" with only one mistake, which I instantly self-corrected. When I finished, Rabbi Sue looked at me with moist eyes and said, "I think it's time for a Shehecheyanu." Together, we recited the prayer of thankfulness for having lived to enjoy that moment.

My time with Rabbi Sue in the empty sanctuary was so meaningful that I considered it, rather than the subsequent public ceremony in Atlanta, as my true bat mitzvah.

As the date approached, Marcia and I realized we'd committed to a social event as well as a religious one, much as we tried to avoid the former, normally the responsibility of parents. We only notified family and close friends via Rosh Hashanah greetings six months before, telling them they were welcome to attend the ceremony but should not send gifts or expect parties. When we learned that more than a dozen of our nearest and dearest were flying to Atlanta for the event, some from as far as the west coast, we had to plan something beyond Shabbat dinner at the Temple and the traditional synagogue lunch after services that Bill and Brenda offered to host. Naomi Popkin rescued us by organizing five more friends to host a Saturday night dinner for the out-of-towners.

The main event went well, as did all else. Marcia chanted her part, which came first, and I read mine—partly because I can't sing, but more significantly for me because I dislike hearing it chanted. Jack always read the Hebrew with understanding as if he were reading English, which engaged many of us and encouraged us to learn Hebrew. The beautiful poetry of my portion, when read with meaning and cadence, can be sensed even without knowing the words. My adamance against chanting shocked Rabbi Salkin but not my old friends in Atlanta. They were already fully shocked by my wanting to celebrate the bat mitzvah at all. They viewed it as a throwback to Orthodoxy.

While no longer serving on boards, I remained minimally active in all three historical societies. SJHS gave me annual assignments and, as a past president, I attended board meetings. I didn't expect to do more, but the Jewish Historical Society of Greater Washington asked me to chair its host committee for the 2007 SJHS conference in D.C. Because I had enjoyed co-chairing the Washington conference of the American Jewish Historical Society in 1992, I accepted. Had I known that I was also expected to raise funds, I never would have done so.

That misunderstanding wasn't even the worst of my difficulties. I could still organize work and workers easily, but I didn't realize I'd lost the patience to deal with higher-ups who remained aloof and unreachable. I vowed never again to chair anything, an unnecessary pledge considering that at age 83 I was unlikely to be asked to do so.

Nevertheless, when representatives of Emory University approached me to raise funds for a chair in Jack's name, I conceded. My initial protestations that I couldn't make a major gift and lacked experience in getting others to give fell on deaf ears. "But you have well-to-do friends who were the rabbi's great admirers," they responded, ignoring the likelihood that our friends found other worthy recipients for their largesse in the 35 years since Jack died.

They persisted and I took the bait, thus embarking on another stressful, though ultimately very gratifying, project. Eventually Emory realized that the cost of an endowed chair was an unrealistic goal and reduced their expectations. They settled on an annual lecture which, after several years of struggle and considerable help from Bill and Brenda, we achieved. Although disappointing at the time, the effort paid off in ways I didn't anticipate, reconnecting me with Emory as part of its donor community and giving me access to its world of learning.

In 2008 my Washington friends were leaving, either retiring or moving to assisted living facilities to be near their children. I promised mine that I'd come back to Atlanta when I got "old."

After visiting there twice in the spring of 2008 for Dorothy Hamburger's and Cecil Alexander's 90th birthday parties, I returned in June for the wedding of Brenda's daughter Stephanie. The next day, someone told Marvin Sugarman, my longtime dentist and family friend, that I was there. He called, took me to dinner the night before I returned to D.C., and thereafter called each night. On subsequent trips he met me at the airport, occupied every waking moment that wasn't previously filled, and drove me to the airport for departure. Eventually he insisted that I stay in his guest room instead of with my children in order to save him the long drives to and from their homes. That undoubtedly pleased them, sparing them airport runs and staying up late to let Mom in after nights out. When Marvin's daughter Brenda Goldberg visited from Cleveland, she thought the guest room wasn't adequately cheerful and ordered it freshly painted to receive me.

My visits to Georgia were fun but tiring. I came in September for the Emory project, in October to commemorate the 50th anniversary of the Temple bombing, and in November for the SJHS conference at Emory. One night when Marvin called I admitted having a few pains and he scolded, "You should live here so you'd have somebody to take care of you."

That triggered my move. Marvin would help me make new friends and reconnect with old ones. I wouldn't be starting over; I'd be coming home.

During my next trip in Atlanta that December I looked at condos. I'd visited friends at Park Place on Peachtree and was 99 percent sure it was what

I wanted, but I checked other possibilities anyway. Nowhere else even came close. I found my perfect unit and hurried back to Washington to prepare my condo for sale. Zelda Heller, my former writing partner and a phenomenally successful real estate agent, gave me great advice: she told me to spend a few thousand dollars buying a refrigerator to match the other kitchen appliances and replacing the carpet in one room. She insisted I'd get the money back many times over and save myself the aggravation of having the condo on the market for a long time. I followed her advice and the condo sold two days after she put it on the market. Two days later, on my 85th birthday, I signed both contracts and moved out four weeks after that, ending 25 years at The Towers and 35 years away from Atlanta.

When Thomas Wolfe wrote *You Can't Go Home Again,* he wasn't thinking of me. He referenced homecoming in the light of expecting to find everything as it once was, or as we nostalgically believe it was. I knew it wasn't and came prepared.

Marcia, Bill, Brenda, and Marvin all contributed immeasurably to making my transition an easy one. Marvin more than filled my social life taking me to dinner five nights a week. He played bridge on Mondays so I had one night a week to reconnect with women friends, and I continued hosting Shabbat dinners except when his children, Ed and Beth or Richard and Helaine, invited us. I enjoyed his company and that of his friends who were our frequent dinner companions, but noted that the conversational menu contained more carbs than protein.

Less than a year after I moved to Atlanta, Marvin suffered a stroke from which he never recovered. With his mind as alert as ever, he lingered physically impaired for nine months. I visited almost every day. He rallied sufficiently to enjoy his long-planned 95th birthday party, celebrating at his home with three generations of his progeny, and died three months later.

From the outset I realized that I had to build a new life, and I thank him for convincing me to begin while I still had the good health and energy to enjoy doing it.

I had two visitors that first winter in Atlanta. Marge Goldman came, and I subsequently visited her in her assisted living facility in New York. Then Harold came to visit, bringing with him his young friend Ross, whom he later adopted. He and Ross planned to go to Brazil in March and invited me to join them, an offer I couldn't refuse.

We met at the São Paulo airport, flew directly to Rio for two days and then to Salvador, where Harold and I were absolutely enthralled by Afro/Brazilian culture. The exuberance of its art, the dexterity and subtlety implicit in kick dancing, and a voodoo-like ritual in which a woman sitting next to us fell into a trance topped our many reasons for wanting to return. In Recife, Ross went surfing while Harold and I explored Jewish history. Then we rented a car and Ross drove us further up the coast to Natal, where we stayed at an ecologically sensitive jungle-like resort far outside the city, on a bluff high above a beautiful, seemingly endless beach. On one beach walk we watched that year's crop of newborn turtles break out of their shells and inch toward the sea.

I was eager to finish my book about Great-Grandfather "Alphabet" Browne and wasn't ready to get involved in volunteer work, but I realized I must do so to reconnect with the community so I trained as a docent for local history at The Breman Museum. I was rarely called to serve until 2013, when the museum mounted a very popular exhibit on Rich's Department Store. I thoroughly enjoyed doing it, but by then age had caught up with me and I had to sit down at intervals during the tour. As I entered my nineties I realized it was too tiring and had to forego guiding tours.

When I received a "save the date" notice in late 2013 for a wedding in Jerusalem the following May, I ignored it. I'd barely met the bride, Meredith, I didn't know the groom, retired U.S. Marine Corps General Robert Magnus, and I couldn't understand why they'd want me at their wedding. I also wondered why two previously married middle-aged Americans would stage an elaborate destination ceremony in Israel.

By the time the actual invitation arrived, I realized I hadn't been to Israel in sixteen years. I wanted to go back one more time and this presented a good opportunity. Since my only connection with the couple was having met the bride at Cecily Abram's home, I called Cecily to say I'd go if she did. She'd never been to Israel or had any desirer to go, but the invitation was intriguing and I convinced her to accept.

It was a mitzvah for both of us. I delighted in introducing Cecily to the Israel I loved. We had only a week, two days of which the bride and groom scheduled ecological tours for their overseas guests, led by Israel's top authority on birds and their usefulness in agriculture. Arriving three days earlier, I arranged for a special guide to walk us through the Old City on our first day and a car with a driver for a trip to Haifa the next, stopping for lunch on the beach at Caesarea and a drive-through of Tel Aviv/Jaffa before returning to Jerusalem. We spent Shabbat, our third day, browsing through the Israel Museum, and in the late afternoon visited Rabbi Josh and Maxine Haberman at their apartment overlooking the Old City, thus introducing Cecily to the typical Israeli social practice that I loved.

The wedding was held on a terrace overlooking the Valley of Hinnom with the Mount of Olives as backdrop, under a sky so clear that we could see the Dead Sea on the horizon. Attendants were heroes of Israel's War of Independence as well as Bob's fellow Marines, including some currently stationed nearby who made the ceremonial crossed-swords arcade for the bride and groom as they left the *bimah*. We mingled with VIPs at the reception, some of whom (unidentified to maintain security) were Jordanian and Palestinian.

The next day, at the invitation of my longtime friend Marcia Lewison, I gave a book talk at the Association of Americans and Canadians in Israel, lunched with friends I met when they were stationed at the embassy in Washington, and prepared for departure at midnight. I was deeply grateful for having made the journey and pleased on behlaf of Israel to see such progress. Exclusive shops of Paris, London, and Rodeo Drive now replaced the crumbling housing between King David Street and the Jaffa Gate. However, I was saddened to sense the loss of Old

World ambience. I missed the likes of Teddy Kollek and Abba Eban, the Yallons, the Astars, and others of their generation. I'm glad I went, but I have no wish to return.

That journey recalled so much of my past that it might be appropriate to end with it, but I can't. Life kept happening.

I came to realize most of all how much I appreciated Marvin Sugarman's persuading me to come home when he did because that gave me valuable time with Marcia. Our interest in Judaic studies brought us together for learning opportunities at Temple, usually including dinner before Monday night classes, before theater, and before events at Emory that she also attended with me.

The Hellers and I had engaged Marcia professionally to edit *Deadly Truth* and she did a remarkable job. Now she helped me prepare my own book, *Prophet in a Time of Priests*, for publication, which included digitalizing antique family pictures for illustration. In 2012, when Apprentice House honored authors of books published that year, she drove me to Baltimore for the event and later to southern venues on my self-arranged mini book tours.

Whenever possible we added a day or two to those trips for sightseeing and visiting friends, as we also did when she accompanied me to family gatherings and National Association of Retired Reform Rabbis meetings in California. There we also visited San Diego and, on another occasion, Death Valley and Sequoia National Park. She joined the Southern Jewish Historical Society and began attending its annual conferences with me, immediately connecting as she did at NAORRR.

Together Marcia and I planned and executed my 90th birthday celebration, an informal open house at my apartment. She designed and emailed notices in lieu of invitations, helped me with baking and preparing hors d'oeuvres, and worked in the kitchen all afternoon because an ice storm came and prevented the hired help from getting there.

On the rainy Sunday afternoon of April 19, 2015, I returned home to find Bill and Peter Berg, the Temple's senior rabbi, waiting for me with downcast faces. That morning, as Marcia drove alone to Knoxville for the funeral of a friend's husband, her car hydroplaned off the highway in a driving rain and crashed into a tree near Sweetwater, Tennessee.

Since returning home I'd lost many dear friends. But I never imagined I'd lose a child. I was too stunned to think clearly. Once again Bill shouldered the burden, as he had done throughout.

We expected only a few friends and family to attend the simple graveside ceremony. Some 200 people came. Afterward, for the *shiva*, so many arrived at my apartment that the crowd extended all the way out to the elevators. I had no idea how many friends Marcia had, and how many of Bill's and my friends would come out to support us. Condolences exceeded even those when Jack died, so many including charitable contributions that those designated for the Rabbi's Discretionary Fund alone enabled Peter to buy a Torah scroll that he needed for the Temple's bar and bat mitzvah students. He dedicated it to Marcia, had her name inscribed on it, and mentions her name whenever it is used.

Marcia's passing overwhelmed us. Bill handled the legal business and the greater chore of cleaning out her house in Smyrna.

It was a terrible summer for both of us, yet even from tragedy something very good arose. Marcia and I had regularly attended Torah study on Shabbat mornings at the Temple. On the Shabbat morning six days after her death, Bill took me, and we've been going together ever since. We developed a rapport that I had sorely missed, and Bill developed a camaraderie with the study group that I suspect he had missed as well. A few months after Bill joined, he was asked to lead the study session when the Temple's rabbis were not there and was so well received that he's now asked to fill in regularly.

In the middle of August I visited Jacob, who had just bought his own home, a tiny condo in uptown Manhattan. The plan was for Harold to pick me up there on Monday morning, visit Marge in her Westchester assisted living facility, then take me to his newly acquired 1799 house in Connecticut for two days before driving me to visit Julie Weiss for a week in the Berkshires. I had a great time with Jacob, met his new love, Charlie Duncan, and saw my dear friend Blanche Ross, incapacitated by Parkinson's disease. Harold called me Sunday night to confirm, saying he would call as he was leaving the next morning so I'd know approximately when he'd arrive in Manhattan.

The call came at 7:30, but it wasn't from Harold. It was Ross, in Washington, telling me that the driver had just called to tell him he found Harold on the floor, unconscious. They took him to a hospital in Hartford, his birthplace and home of his closest relatives. Ross was driving there and asked if I wanted him to pick me up on the way. I declined. There was nothing I could do to help and I'd be in the way. I called Julie, told her I was coming two days early, and took a bus to the Berkshires.

Harold never regained consciousness. After a few days, they moved him to a hospice, and a week later he died. The family buried him privately in Hartford. Georgetown University planned a public memorial for him on a Sunday morning several weeks later, and the Interfaith Family Project that he founded scheduled theirs the same afternoon. I couldn't wait that long. For the first time in my life I felt the need for a *shiva*, and I needed it *then*, not three weeks later. The night I returned home from my stay with Julie, Cecily learned that a few of Harold's close friends were gathering the following evening at someone's home. I flew to Washington to join them, desperate for the immediate, intimate memorial.

The last time I saw Harold was on his 83rd birthday that May, at his uniquely untraditional celebration of a traditional second bar mitzvah. It was a Jewish ritual conducted in a synagogue by the Protestant female pastor of his Interfaith Family's congregation, with music provided by an African American gospel choir. His wide assortment of friends packed the large sanctuary, showering him with love and admiration. That's how I wanted to remember him.

Without realizing it at the time, my return to Atlanta coincided with the 50th anniversary of many turning points in the civil rights movement. I didn't anticipate the series of commemorations in addition to that of the Temple bombing in 2008 that involved me as a surviving participant. Even before returning I had received an invitation from Morehouse College to participate in a convocation honoring Martin Luther King Jr. and Yitzhak Rabin, the two martyred Nobel Peace laureates. Then calls came for television interviews and panel discussions commemorating 50th anniversaries of civil rights legislation. In 2014, on the 50th anniversary of King receiving the Nobel Peace Prize, I was a panelist with his sister, Christine King Farris, and former Atlanta mayor Sam Massell Jr. at the Carter Center. Two months later, on the anniversary of the groundbreaking city dinner honoring King, I was again a dinner guest and panelist at the Atlanta History Center honoring survivors of those who sponsored the 1965 event.

In May 2015, *Moment Magazine* sponsored a program at Washington's Newseum commemorating the 50th anniversary of the Voting Rights Act and invited me to be a panelist along with former Massachusetts congressman Barney Frank, D.C. Representative Eleanor Holmes Norton, civil rights leader Julian Bond, and my own heroic congressman, John Lewis. Commentator Steve Roberts moderated. I was enormously honored to be among them.

I soon started getting requests for filmed interviews, several for television, one of which with a live audience. Before it began, a woman approached me and introduced herself as the daughter of the family whose home Jack and I considered buying in 1947. When the neighbors heard that a Jewish family might move in, they pressured the woman's mother not to sell it. Shocked and offended, she wrote a letter of apology to Jack. She also charged her daughter with ensuring that all of the children would know and remember that incident. By now her letter had made its way to the Rothschild collection at Emory, and, true to her mission, the daughter had taken her siblings to see it and take home a copy. Hearing that I would be on television, she had come to the station to hand me a copy as well—and to demonstrate that, almost seven decades later, she fulfilled her mother's assignment.

I can't remember how many times I was interviewed on camera, the first being for the documentary *Shared Legacies*, sponsored in Atlanta by the African-American Jewish Civil Rights Alliance. It premiered as the opening for Atlanta's Jewish Film Festival in 2020, giving me the pleasure of being a featured participant. The next filming was for a mini-documentary on Atlanta Jewish history for public television commemorating the congregation's 150th anniversary (now permanently installed at the Temple). Then came a brief interview for the Jewish Studies program at Emory, a much longer one in a major production for Atlanta's Civil Rights Museum, and one even longer than *that* for the archives of the National Museum of African American History and Culture in Washington.

Undeniably flattering as these were, my greatest joy derived from the many students who interviewed me, from independent scholars and graduate students to undergraduates, high schoolers, and even one extraordinary sixth-grader who turned out to be the great-grandson of dear friends from the 1950s and 1960s. Another, a high school senior with an audio recorder but no camera, after turning in her work, was asked by her teacher to arrange a live repeat of the interview open to all schoolmates and their parents. Another student, for a different project at the same school, chose me as her elderly female inspiration (her beloved grandmother having been preempted by a cousin in the same class). I could never have imagined honors such as these.

Even more astounding, the Southern Jewish Historical Society gave me its Samuel Proctor Award in 2013 for outstanding career scholarship in southern Jewish history, and in 2017 the New Israel Fund chose me to receive its first Atlanta Tzedek Award. These seemed all the more amazing because I was a comparative late-comer to Zionism and very much a late-comer to serious scholarship.

In 2016, almost as a joke at age 92 and lacking academic credentials, I answered a call for papers for an international scholars' conference on transnational influences in American Jewish history at the University of Potsdam, and it was accepted. Based on a chapter of *Prophet in a Time of*

Priests wherein Browne advised Herzl on American Jews' attitude toward Zionism, it didn't read as an academic paper, but the other presenters appeared to appreciate it and responded graciously. I loved meeting them, hearing their papers, and especially learning that keen interest in American Jewish history is shared by scholars who are neither American nor Jewish.

I'd hoped that Cecily would join me in Europe then for a river cruise but she couldn't go. I went alone and instead of taking the cruise, I spent a few days each in Budapest and Berlin. I had a friend in each city who made arrangements, met me at the airport, and took me sightseeing.

My ego boost soared highest during the congregation's 150th anniversary celebration with the Alliance Theater's production of *The Temple Bombing*. The documentary portrayed me as both lead character and narrator, using my own words from books and transcripts. Developed and co-produced by the Tectonic Theater Project of New York, the leading roles—Jack and me—were cast in New York. Playwright and director Jimmy Maize invited me to rehearsals, consulted me as he developed the script, and asked me to help the leading actors, Todd Weeks and Caitlin O'Connell, understand their roles. For me, a one-time aspiring actor/ playwright, it was the apex of an impossible dream.

This would surely be the place to end my memoir, but there's more. Honesty demands that the bad be remembered along with the good, even though I've managed to find some glistening silver linings in much of the bad. The year 2017, in addition to the aftermath of the presidential election, had a sobering impact on both me and Bill. That August, he had a triple bypass surgery. Pleased as I was that Bill inherited his father's intellect and sense of humor, I would have preferred a much different inheritance regarding his heart. Fortunately, medicine had advanced enough in three decades to save him from his father's fate.

On September 1, two weeks after Bill's surgery, I awoke unable to see other than dark shadows and silhouettes of furniture and doors, as if I were looking through heavily frosted glass. I'd been having problems with a fold in the retina of my right eye, which the specialist had been treating successfully with injections. Just the day before, he found a similar fold developing in the left eye and injected both. He didn't know what went wrong but assured me that it would clear in time. How much time? He wasn't sure. The condition was rare and there were no statistics.

I suppose you could say that "old age" found me that day in September. I'm grateful that it took so long.

I still hesitate to conclude. My life did not end on that day, only my freedom to drive a car. That was, however, my first loss of independence, of radically diminished lifestyle, of bending to old age.

My vision began clearing immediately, but slowly. By the next day I could feed myself without help as long as I put my finger in the cup so as not to spill and didn't risk using a sharp knife. Brenda and Bill brought chicken soup and finger snacks the first day, then friends shopped for me and brought frozen entrees that only required pin-pricking before heating in the microwave.

And good things kept happening. In December 2017, the Temple inaugurated the "Jacob M. Rothschild Institute for Social Justice," which Arthur Blank had graciously endowed and, at Rabbi Berg's request, had even more graciously agreed to name after Jack, the Rothschild Social Justice Institute. It perpetuates Jack's legacy through the efforts of at least 100 congregants at any one time working on ten areas of need.

In January 2018 our beloved grandson, Jack's namesake, announced his engagement to Charlie Duncan. Jacob and Charlie were married in New York on July 20 of that year amid loving families and devoted friends of all races, backgrounds and lifestyles.

Several months later, Bill told me that he, Brenda, and Jacob were throwing me a party for my 95th birthday in February 2019 and asked what manner of celebration I wanted. I chose a cocktail hour blowout, inviting everyone I knew and a few I didn't, friendly neighbors at Park Place, some whose names I couldn't remember. Friends and family came to town for it, seven from Washington, nephews from Texas and California, and Blumberg grandchildren from Illinois, including first great-grandchild, Jolie, about to graduate college. It can't get better than that.

Still life goes on. Thankfully, the good continues to out-distance the bad and I retain dominance over my attitude. I'm hopeful, which is essential in this time of constant change and seemingly endless crises.

I remain hopeful, but realistic. Whatever is ahead, I want to know about it. My curiosity prevails, eagerly asking, "What will I encounter as I turn the next corner?"

I embrace life, whatever it brings.